1965

Ernest L. Norman
Author, philosopher, poet, scientist, director,
moderator of Unarius Science of Life

UNARIUS
UNiversal ARticulate Interdimensional

Understanding of Science

TEMPUS PROCEDIUM

OTHER BOOKS BY ERNEST L. NORMAN

TEMPUS PROCEDIUM

By

Ernest L. Norman

Published By
UNARIUS, SCIENCE OF LIFE
P.O. Box 1042
El Cajon, Calif. 92020

Table of Contents

(cont'd)

Table of Contents (cont'd)

Note

"The various articles comprising this book were given at different intervals, sometimes in reply to some student's letter or questions; other times, when some article of interest appeared in the news, TV, etc., that attracted the Elder Brother's attention to the point where he would voice his reply and objectification of the topic in question; a few were given in a class lecture. On other occasions he would simply be contemplating and come up with one or more of these dissertations.

They were given without any thought in mind of becoming a book but were simply individual and separate articles that our Moderator voiced, and form a great and important addition to the various other texts of Unarius.

These dissertations have been used, in mimeograph form, to send to students who contribute to the 'Cause' as a sort of thank you or appreciation gesture. Some articles were given at the very beginning of the work, in 1955—'56, others, as recently as 1967. Many students who have received some of them acclaim them to be of greater importance than all other Unarius texts, and I quite agree."

Ruth Norman.

FOREWORD

In any scale of human equivalence and comparative evaluations, man has, throughout the many ages of history, attempted, in numerous ways and in countless instances, to perpetuate what he believed to be a segment of human immortality. Whether it was through the classical arts, building a pyramid or an empire, always the human motivation for immortality was apparent; to become immortal in the eyes of all men or to become immortal in some heavenly abode—as it was so constantly promised in the precepts of religious systems.

Unique among the histories of the world, is an entirely new concept of life—evolution, and an infallible immortality, which is now being made available, and for the first time, to those persons who have long sought the correct approach to this age-old question of immortality. A new and totally complete Science of Life, which at once cuts through the age-old Gordian knot of rhetorical dogma, false creeds and credos, slays the fiery dragons of superstitious religions and lays bare, for the first time, the golden future, where, upon the rung of the ladder of evolution, an aspiring man can climb into one of those heavenly mansions—a Science of Life, which, for the eyes and ears of mankind, is called Unarius.

It should be noted at this point, and again differing in its origins and dispensations, Unarius is not a singular effort, such as that which has started many religious creeds, political factions, induced great conquests and crusades or festooned the walls and galleries of castles and museums with paintings and statuary. Unarius is, in its embodiment, a host of millions of Advanced Beings; persons from many worlds and many ages of time who have climbed the evolutionary ladder to their heavenly abode;

and who have, in the vast matrix of their own individual personalities, combined their power and wisdom in a great humanitarian effort; and through all processes and channels known by them, aid any dedicated aspirant in his particular evolutionary climb. And one of these ways is, that the aspirant prepares and conditions himself, to also aid and assist any or all other neophytes. As of today there are many thousands who have, through this aid and assistance, attained their own personal miracles; all a part of the way of preparation and inspiration which is part of the Unariun curriculum.

Finally, to take advantage of a most propitious time—a time of science and expansion—one of these Unariun Hosts came to earth, assumed the mantle of flesh, so He could best lead the vanguards of aspirants and to combine, through himself and through certain polarizing agencies which were so incarnated at this time, to gather about him and in their combined efforts, spread the Power and the Light of the mission to many thousands who had also gathered on the earth at this time.

There is more—much more, which could be added to this chronology; but the strongest proof of all is in the individual testimonials. And especially to those who have, through their efforts through the books, tapes, and lessons, made the Message of Unarius, its transforming power immediately available to all those so dedicated. And so, in tribute, and as their own individual testimonial is so contained in their works, is the name of Helen Moore; and as you read the pages of these last two books, it is her untiring efforts, her skill, which imprinted the words across the page. And there are others; Viola Tennant devotedly scanning the first printed pages for possible human errors and discrepancies; to Dorothy Ellerman, who also contributed a large share in this work as well as numerous other clerical-like tasks and kept the machinery running more smoothly.

*And of course there is Ruth, the shining angel, who al-
ways stands beside Him, to make—what would otherwise
be to Him, an earth-life almost too difficult to compensate
—possible. And there are many others too, in their own
individual way, who bear their own testimonial, how they
too, through their own individual evolutions, their many
past lives, and especially in the lives in between earth lives,
have prepared themselves for this advent. For as it is, and
rarely so, do the Shining Angels of the Unariun Brotherhood come to these earth worlds; as it is in the cycles of
cosmic interplay, seldom do these little earth worlds so
come into the time and place where certain of those inhabitants of these earth worlds can, through their dedicated efforts, be delivered up from the hellish purgatory
which is the lot of those who live only in the animal-like
lusts and passions of these worlds.*

*And so the last days have come. The long-promised
return of the Messiah is fulfilled! But He has not come to
the countless millions who have not prepared themselves;
and they see Him not, through the mists of their own illusions. Immortality is not a promised resurrection. It is not
and cannot be a fulfillment of some religious creed; for all
these promises and assertions are made by common men,
caught up in some fancied promise, some false statement
of divinity. Neither will those who carve or paint or try to
hew a temple or a pyramid be caught up in a tide of
immortality. But only to those who have recognized within
themselves, a small spark of sublime Wisdom; a spark
which, when fed the fuel of human endeavor, fanned with
the breath of undying dedication, will grow into a lambent
flame, which will, forever, warm this man's soul, and light
the pathway that leads to the doorway of heaven.*

Prelude

The pages of history have portrayed for us a great pageantry of man. Through its pages are emblazoned in the passing epochs of time, the rise and fall of many civilizations. Egypt, India, China, Greece, Carthage and Rome have risen from the soil of earth; like some passing meteor or sun have streaked across the earthly skies and left behind in rubble, heaps of stone, the testimonies which bear mute witness to the untold millions who have come and gone among these places, who have sung their song of life, who have carved and sung and built, and yet with the passing of time, as the leaves which grow and die in the seasons, as the tides which rise and fall, yes, even the millenniums of time which see the changes of the patterns of stars in our skies.

So, too, that while man in one time builds up into new greatness, new power, new glory, he must know that he is also building into the time and place of his passing, for one generation belongs only to the next; and from the womb of time are born many generations, many civilizations whose parenthood cannot be determined in the color of his skin, the strength of the walls which surround his cities or the number of soldiers in his legions, but comes only as a victim of time and circumstance, betrayed by the weakness of his own emotions—the Judas-like longings of earthly desires which bring him time and again in the trial of flesh and in the courtrooms of many civilizations.

Nor can it be said he is not forewarned of all these things, for his very existence becomes the kaleidoscope of life and death. The regular and rhythmic succession of cycles of birth, death and rebirth should place within his mouth the taste of things to come. Neither can it be said that any emperor, king or dictator has unto himself the power to forestall this unending procession, nor can he build against it. The sarcophagus of the Egyptian king, desecrated and barren in the desert sun, becomes the shroud of any newborn hopes or aspirations of those who would build in such earthly dominions either temples, castles, pyramids or any bastions made from stone wherein he can tread in fancied security, for surely every stone he so erects will become his epitaph and writes with unfailing hand the weakness of his thinking.

And if a man so seeks an answer from all this, must he not also be forewarned of the impending doom which leads him to search the unanswered question to life in the shambles of some bygone age and that the characters written in stone may lead him to the trap door which will plunge him into the abyss of self-delusion.

The quest for life, its origin and ultimately the answer to all things lies not within the circumference of any man's life or any earthly plane, in any epoch or civilization, for the earth itself is but a vast and complex mirror upon whose complex surface there ever plays this pageantry of life and death, portrayed not as the earth as giver and taker of all things, but one of the many facets of shining imagery which are reflected from the all-creative substance from within.

And internally there shines about each man in his age-old processions through time, the countless and innumerable reflections of this procession. His footsteps leave behind the haloed dust of his creations, which shines in its reflected glory his pathway which leads each man ever onward into the infinite vistas, into the shining cosmos of creation.

How then can it best be said or brought about, that man can build for himself a place of security, for if it is that all of his earthly creations have come to naught and have given him no form or substance for his long hoped-for security and peace of mind and that even as he created all things from each time and place, these were only, in themselves, a mute testimony for that which he inwardly strove; each life he lived a strong emancipation for his spiritual freedom.

CHAPTER I

What Is Unarius?

Throughout the Bible, in both New and Old Testaments, there are references and prophecies made about the 'Last Days' . . . 'The Return of Christ' . . . 'The Battle of Armageddon' . . . and other such prophecies pertinent and relevant to our present time. Several of these prophecies describe 'Jesus' or the 'Lord' returning to earth on a 'Golden Throne' or as a 'Thief in the Night'—the earth is burned and cleansed by fire, the wicked destroyed, etc. While these prophecies do contain a modicum of truth, there is, however, quite apparent, a great and unintelligent emotionalism which betrays the underlying psychotic nature of the prophet who uttered them. It is quite unintelligent for Jesus or God to burn the earth. To punish or destroy sinners defeats the promise of Immortal Life which is the birthright of every man. The destruction of the world denies the entire facade of an intelligent progressive evolution.

No, Jesus and other Intelligent Beings in the Higher Worlds would not use such violent reactionary materialistic actions. Instead, they could quite obviously be expected to use a much more intelligent re-entry into the earth world. They would not come as a great Heavenly Host, with beating wings and fiery breath; instead they would, through scientific Principles, establish communication and directive action through the intuitive faculty of the earth man.

Moreover, these Heavenly Hosts would establish and maintain such communication and direction only with those who had been preconditioned through many lifetimes and Spiritual lives for this personal advent

1

which would, in all effect and purpose, be the 'Second Coming' to that particular person.

These Heavenly Beings, however, are not interested in this most directive effort with the unconditioned average earth man. They know how useless their appeal would be to any man who is still thoroughly steeped and saturated in the earth life. Therefore, to make their plan feasible, communication possible—along with all their accrued benefits—one of these Intelligent Higher Beings must become the Messenger.

He will come to the earth, don the mantle of flesh and, appearing as an ordinary earth man, He will, in various subtle ways, reach out and contact these numbered earth people who have been preconditioned. After contact is made, he presents to them the entire procedium of creation. Unknown mysteries and principles of life are lucidly explained; and while these fortunate, (comparatively) few persons are studying and learning, their efforts are further aided by expurgencies of creative energy, psychokinetically projected by these Higher Beings. Also, they are given sleep teachings in the classrooms of Celestial Mansions.

All this great work, the actual 'Second Coming' has already begun. It started in the beginning of the early 1900's, at a certain birth; at which time a great Spiritual Being established contact with this newly born infant. This Being is, incidentally, the same Intellect who worked through the man known as Jesus. Throughout the early lifetime of this child earth man, this Spiritual Being remained comparatively passive and quiescent, awaiting the proper time when He could more actively project His Intellect and great Spiritual Powers through the earth man. This proper time began at the beginning of World War II, in which might best be described as the formative period and which lasted

2

about eleven years.

During that period this ordinary looking earth man did, on thousands of occasions, display the highest and most advanced demonstrations of extrasensory perception, attendant healings, guidance, adjustment, etc., to many thousands of people.

In many aspects, this formative or development stage was much more remarkable, much more miraculous than was the mission of Jesus—all done, of course, by the High Spiritual Intellect; much more advantageously displayed and demonstrated in a scientific atmosphere; for these great Beings are also great scientists and Their work is pure creative science. During this formative demonstration period, however, this earth man's body and psychic anatomy—constantly in the presence of this great Spiritual Intellect—became more and more refined, so to speak, to a point where earth life, as a physical being became increasingly difficult.

Finally the second and final stage was entered into when this earth man was brought together with a certain polarity who became his wife. It was extremely important at this stage that this earth man could have such a polarity. Through preconditioning in the Higher Spiritual Worlds, it was only a short time before she mastered the basic fundamental concepts of Creation. She could, and did, also give great physical aid and assistance to this earth man who had, by now, advanced in the refinement process to a point where the physical life was hardly possible.

With her strong polarity she was able to stabilize the earth man's life to the extent that he was able to bring forth into the world the great Wisdom of the Higher Spiritual Worlds; a Wisdom which was all creative, all scientific, all truthful and all explanatory, devoid of mysticism, stripped of rhetoricism and which demanded subjugation, making a personal demand of moral integrity and responsibility to every person who studied this great Wisdom. And as the student studied, he came under the benign influence of the Heavenly Hosts who were awaiting this opportune moment.

Thus it is, each student is so lifted up; miracles happen to him, but the greatest miracle is in the transformation of self. The wicked sinner of the past is, in essence, destroyed; and like the phoenix bird, from its ashes rises the new man—imbued with the Creative Wisdom of Infinity.

And so it is, as of today, and at this hour, a great Spiritual Being speaks into the world, through the vocal cords of a humble earth man, giving to those who are prepared, the Message of Immortal Creativity—a realization of Immortality. And while it is this earth man calls this Message 'Unarius', it is scarcely known to the multitudes of the world, for their awakening is in another time.

Yes, this great Being does, in a sense, walk the pathways of the world, wearing the clothing of the time and presenting only ordinary differences. He is almost unknown. He came, not heralded by trumpets or a fanfare of drums. He cares not for accolades or applause. He lives beyond the strife and turmoil of the world in the security of a Heavenly Mansion, built from the Creative Substance of Infinity.

To meet him on the street you would not know him save that, in some future time, you would find a great strength and Intelligence that had been given unobserved in this chance meeting.

Soon, however, the great Mission will be accomplished. The great 'Advent' and the 'Second Coming' will have transpired and become a reality to those who had ordained themselves for it. They, too, will pass on to higher worlds, leaving the earth men to their wars and strife.

Yes, like the pages of a book, this great earth man Messiah is turning to the last chapter; in its remaining paragraphs will be written the immortal glory of those who have triumphed over the barbaric savagery of their past.

To those who have dedicated their future to bring the effigy of creation to those who are still struggling to escape, Eternity is like the waves which beat ceaselessly upon the shore, each wave bringing its own effluences, its own civilizations, its own great emancipations. And as it dies upon the sands, it becomes a decadent memory in history.

So is the Way of the Infinite—not savagely, nor with the noise of the trumpets, neither are there war-like sounds of destruction, but the passive Message of Peace, so eloquently expressed in even the humblest form of creation.

Let this be the Unariun Message—live It in posterity, not as a symbol to be worshipped, but as expressive continuity of life; and as the Message is spoken, Its Voice never ceases and brings Immortality to those who have the ear to listen, the eyes to discern and the heart to beat in unison.

The Unariun Brotherhood.

CHAPTER II
The ABC's of Immortality
Part 1

To any person the subject of healing or to be healed is all important, and particularly to those who have religious affiliations and to those who are suffering from any of the infinite variety of mental and physical conditions. The Unariun student is, of course greatly concerned with healing, in fact his whole future evolution depends upon whether or not he is healed from any and all aberrations as well as a countless host of physical experiences called karma, through which he has passed in his many lifetimes. Quite frequently Unariun students have wonderful miraculous demonstrations, and, also, quite frequently their friends or relatives; yes, and unknowingly, strangers may also be miraculously healed of some condition after the Unariun student has made some kind of contact with them. These miraculous transitions may give the Unariun student a sense of power or a belief that he (or she) is now a 'healer'. This false assumption is very dangerous and should be watched for and instantly suppressed when the student finds himself incurring such a belief.

No student, or for that matter, no earth man is a healer, nor can he consciously heal by thought projection. The reasons are many and scientific and have been explained many times in the lessons and books of Unarius. When any person develops the capacity to heal an earth person, he will no longer be an earth man. He will be a being, perhaps best described as a Super Angel or God, and as such a being he would be sufficiently intelligent to restrain from healing any earth person for the simple reason that it would defeat the master plan of evolution, that through experience and the gradual developed knowledge and ability to conquer each experience is the principle of progressive evolution; and through countless eons of time in this evolutionary development, any person can become wise enough to heal himself and to avoid further recurrences. So, if you feel tempted with a false feeling of power, remember that Jesus said, "Of myself I do nothing, but it is the Father within that doeth the work."

The Father, of course, is the Infinite Intelligence, the sum and total of all things, including the evolutionary principle of creation. This Father is not emotionally disposed or inclined. So far as It (the Father) is concerned, every person must suffer his respective inclemental karmic burden until he becomes wise enough and has developed beyond its constant inception. In all cases, however, as the fight is very long and prolonged, each individual must have countless demonstrations which reaffirm his resolution to overcome in his quest for a better life. Personal demonstrations of healing are hard to come by and he must be frequently given aid and assistance by certain Advanced Spiritual Agencies. In all cases, however, where these agents and agencies assist and help the individual in obtaining a healing or miracle, they do not basically change this individual person in the process. The healing then, can and should be considered a temporary lift and an incentive whereby the person can be further inspired to learn to overcome and thus change himself which is the inviolate prerogative of every individual.

The reason for all of this is very scientific. Any disease or condition has its specific oscillation or vibrating point, and the person so suffering is therefore tuned in to it. He cannot consciously tune himself out for two reasons: first, he lacks the knowledge, secondly, this oscillating frequency is actually a part of his psychic anatomy. If a Spiritual Being or Agency heals this person, then this oscillating frequency must somehow be prevented from reflecting its image into the physical body or the conscious mind. By temporarily changing this frequency or by changing the basic plane rate vibration of the psychic anatomy, except the diseased condition or aberration, will accomplish the miracle. The scientifically Advanced Scientists and Doctors working as part of the Unariun Agency know how to do this, and they are working around the clock on numerous Unariun students. They accomplish these healings by incorporating certain types of apparatus described in the books, together with the Mind Power which They have and which is developed through their understanding.

When a person joins Unarius as a student, he automatically becomes a charge of this Advanced Spiritual Organization, and from that moment on he is actually enveloped in a huge nimbus of power—a radiant energy envelope which does not know the barriers of time or space and which is actually composed of Super Infinite Intelligence. The student, however, cannot direct this power through his conscious mind. The frequencies of energy which he develops in his thinking are too low in frequency to have any effect on this Super Intelligence with which he is surrounded. Moreover, this Super Intelligent Energy knows far better what is good or not good for this individual. It knows all about this person, his past, present and future. It waits, as it were, until any propitious time when this student can tune into It, and even a partial attunement always incurs miracles. Yet this Super Intelligent

Energy cannot and does not change this person permanently until the person begins to learn about this Super Intelligent Energy, the Infinite Intelligence, etc., which is the Father; and as the person learns, he changes the different oscillating or vibrating frequency planes of his psychic anatomy. And as he is so changed, so he becomes more and more a part of this Higher Intelligence and he gets further and further away from the old earth world dimension where he incurred all his troubles.

The above paragraph was given and included with certain misgivings, and with certain reservations lest the student inadvertently or consciously use this information as a new escape mechanism and plunge himself into a state of euphoria—a practice similar to that indulged in by certain miscalled mind science or metaphysical groups. While it is true the Unariun student is surrounded by a highly intelligent aura, the protection will always be derived in proportion to how well he can tune himself into it. For, in tuning in, even to a small degree will, as long as this attunement lasts, mentally place him in a position which is not so emotionally susceptible to the indispositions of his material world. It does not prevent things from happening to him, but gives him greater protection in the sense that he is not mentally affected by them. Yes, and it is usually the case, the more he becomes attuned to this Infinite Power the more the material world will come to him and try to upset him, and the stronger will the temptations be to give in to these material happenings. There is a scientific law which governs this: the stronger and more positive polarity he becomes to Infinite Consciousness the more negative materialism he will attract to him, and as posed in two opposite polarities, the differences will be, mentally speaking, much greater than they would have been had he remained back on the material plane.

At this point in your introspection, however, and at times of temptation and stress, you should immediately ask yourself this question: do I wish Immortal life enough to overcome or should I give up and go back to the hell-hole? And if you honestly ask yourself this question, you will always find the courage to overcome. So don't use the knowledge of the fact that as Infinite Intelligence is, in a form, temporarily projected to you as a personal protective energy shield, that It should be used as another escape hatch. If you do, you will quickly find It has dissipated because you have removed yourself from It. You can only keep in touch with It by being conscious of It—what It is, how It works and other attendant factors—and in whatever attunement you are able to achieve, you will have a proportionate levitation above the material worlds in a mental capacity which gives you greater realization, adequate compensation, the reason for and the knowing of.

Success then, in your Unariun contact, will be achieved differently than any other affiliation you have ever made, because results will be proportionate only to your endeavor and to your understanding. The purpose of Unarius is simply to develop your mentality as a human to a point where you no longer need the material physical life. Unariun science can give you all the ways and means, all knowledge and wisdom, the how to. And it can and does give you a lot of initial boosting, but eventually your future will depend much more entirely upon your efforts than it does now. The more you learn and progress, the wiser you become, the greater the demands will be made upon you; and you will be tried to the limits of your capacity and endurance. That is the only way you can develop the mental capacity, the strength of character, the unflinching faith, the personal integrity necessary to insure your evolution into a higher way of life where again, and in proportion, the demands upon you and your services will be greater. You may wonder about all this, a more ultimate answer to this mysterious riddle of life; why are there vegetable and animal kingdoms—why is there life, why races of people, what is the necessity of life and why does it exist? Yes, and even to the more ultimate question, what is Infinite Intelligence, and where did It come from? These are good questions to keep in mind and the solutions or answers as more ultimate objectivisms, we may attain in our evolution.

At the same time, however, it is not wise to try to solve such questions until we have mastered the more primary and elemental of the creative concepts. To know of and believe in Infinity makes it inconceivable, yes, impossible, ever to arrive at the most ultimate of all questions or to its answers. For, in doing so, Infinity would cease and we, as humans, would at that point also cease to be. For the present then, be patient; learn to familiarize your daily life with thoughts and association patterns which give you the truer inside reasons or what you are—what life is in the present. Your future, if it is progressive, must be lived in an equally progressive state of consciousness. Each millennium that you live will be only a fleeting moment of consciousness, realized in attaining some of these answers. Space and time are valuable to man only in his first elemental stages and in overcoming space and

time he finds one of the long-sought-after answers—
Immortal life.

Therefore, dear student, in the future, go forth in
your material world with confidence and with faith in
the knowledge that you are surrounded and protected
by a Supremely Intelligent Energy shield, that It will
not only protect you, but It will supply you with all the
essentials of your existence. It will heal you temporarily, at least, until you learn more about It and
become a part of It. It will heal others around you as
you walk your pathway of life. This It will do, and many
other things, so long as you are conscious of It—not as
an emotional god or deity to be placated with prayers
and inveigled with false promises—but as a conscious
reality, as the sum and substance of Intelligent Creation. And you, as a humble participant make of yourself and your life a mirror to reflect some small part of
the vast magnitude of this Creation and should not
attempt to usurp power over this Infinite Intelligence
by believing you are Its directorate, or that you possess
sufficient intelligence to make It subservient to your
will. For indeed It created you and your life, and made
of Infinity a vast storehouse from which you have
drawn—lo these many ages and lifetimes.

Small indeed and like dregs are the particles of life
from this Infinity which you have grasped and clutched
in trembling fear; you have groveled and scrounged
like all other creatures of the earth, hardly daring to
glance above into the bright Light of Infinity. And when
you did, you shielded your eyes with the shadows of
false gods. How then can it be that, as of now and for
the first time in your life, as you have begun to glimpse
the true Light without images; and you are witnessing
the transforming miracles of Its warmth in your life

that you could believe you could direct It into the lives of others; and that while It was intelligent enough to create all things, It was stupid enough to bend Itself to some emotional whim coming from out the carnal cesspool of a physical mind?

Be thankful that It is not an emotional Power, for if It were, It would have long ago in anger destroyed you and all mankind for having constantly violated the constructive Creative Principles of progressive evolution by constantly refusing to recognize and to become cognizant of this Infinite Intelligence and making of yourself an agent and instrumentality to It. The memory of the past is very strong—in fact, it is you. In the matrix of the psychic anatomy are impounded the countless experiences from previous lives. To the future in a higher world, this past is a sinful purgatory and if you live in the future in a higher world you must be healed of all these things. In other words you will no longer oscillate or vibrate to them as the sustaining power agency of your life. You will remember them but only in wisdom from having gone through them, for this is evolution—the Progressive Creative Principle.

To the future then and to the greatest of all miracles —the miracle of Understanding—for understanding is wisdom and Infinite Wisdom is Infinite Realization. Life, as you live it now, from one moment to the next, is only a reflected facet. The image of your past can dull its surface and make it nonresponsive to the glorious vision of Immortality, not as a reward but as an achievement in which we have justified and vindicated Infinite Intelligence.

The ABC's of Immortality
Part Two

In the world today, just as in the past, there are many references to the term 'power', power in a multitude of forms and uses. Some forms of power are real, others imaginary; some exert their effect in a reactionary way, some autosuggestively. In all cases, however, where reference is made to power—and if power exists in any suggested or supposed manner or that it is felt or realized in any manner or form—all such power forms must be, like anything else, a scientific extension of principle and must be scientifically understood. Power then, is simply a motion of energy and whether a quanta of power is large or small, it must be a scientific proposition wherein a certain principle of Infinite Intelligence is expressed for this is indeed the true origin of all things. The expression of power in the physical world is therefore a determinant of motion. Electrical power through wires is a great motivating force in our civilization. The electrical impulses in the nervous system are also energy in motion —power—and one of the agencies which make life possible on this planet.

It is well known that water turns the dynamo; this is an energy conversion process. The human brain regenerates electricity—also a conversion process. The source of this energy is not known to the present-day scientist or doctor and which, however, has a very simple answer. The 'water' which turns the brain generator is the psychic anatomy which, in turn, receives its supply from the Infinite, just as the stream which turns the dynamo receives an infinite supply of rain. The differences, however, are fourth dimensional. While rainfall and water turning the turbines is a compound of third dimensional reactions, such as evaporation, condensation, gravity, etc., fourth dimensional transpositions depend and function entirely upon the principle of frequency compatibility. The brain, therefore, is an energy converter which converts energy from the psychic anatomy into physical motion and consciousness, and as these processes depend upon the frequency principle, they are, of course, extremely complex. On the basis of understanding therefore, you will be able to much more adequately understand a certain branch of science called psychokinetics.

Briefly, psychokinetics is the conversion of mind energy into physical motion or reaction. Under this definition, then, every person is unknowingly practicing psychokinetics. He is converting the mind impulse energies into his daily life, the reactions of which again, through the physical brain, restimulate the psychic anatomy and biases the return or counter-reactive energies into the brain, etc., ad infinitum. Bear in mind all this is possible only on the basis of frequency relationship. If your psychic anatomy does not oscillate or contain compatible frequencies to that which you see, feel, hear, touch, taste or smell, then it won't register and you won't understand it. Simple logic will, therefore, quickly prove in this understanding, that psychokinetically speaking, you cannot psychokinetically and voluntarily project some kind of healing power which could be used in a forceful way beyond the normal domain of interaction which would heal some condition.

Healing is not a magical hocus-pocus-abracadabra situation. It's not a gift, specially conferred. Healing is an exact science, practiced by the more Advanced Intellects, all of whom have passed through many thousands of years of intensive training. They know how to wisely use the developed Power of Their Minds in conjunction with Infinite Intelligence. This Mind Power is the combination of great and Infinite Understanding—how to oscillate with the Creative Intelligence—how to project by attunement and many other scientific factors and apparatus, all a part of the healing process which goes something like this: first, the power or energy would have to be a 'charge' contained in your psychic anatomy. This 'charge' would have to contain millions of frequencies of energy all compatibly tuned according to the frequency of that which you were going to project the power into. In other words, if you were to heal a person of cancer, you would first have to gather together, so to speak, in your psychic anatomy, a complete and scientific knowledge of what cancer is—what caused this particular cancer, past lifetime psychic shocks, etc. You would have to know about and put into this 'charge' such knowledge as basic differences in wave length frequencies of cancerous atoms and molecules as compared to non-cancerous, and you would have to put into that 'charge' certain knowledge so energies would change the cancerous atoms, molecules and cells back to their original frequencies.

Then you would have to know how to take this tremendously complex 'charge' of energy and hurl it, so to speak, like a thunderbolt into the psychic anatomy of the individual who had the cancer. If this were done correctly, and done so that you did not in any way change anything else in that psychic anatomy except the malformed vortex which caused the cancer and if your 'charge' was powerful enough and intelligent enough in all respects, it would therefore change this malformed vortex back into its original healthy psychic anatomy energy, and the person would be instantly healed from cancer. The cancer would disappear in a flash because now the psychic anatomy would reflect only the picture of healthy tissue.

The human body, like everything else material, is only a mass of energy atoms temporarily held in a certain form or condition by its psychic anatomy. It is an atom picture. An artist daubs paint on a canvas; the psychic anatomy uses atoms to create an image of what created it and this psychic anatomy was created from past life experiences which were gathered together in the evolutionary process again on the frequency relationship principle. Now you can begin to see how utterly impossible it is for you or any person to be a healer. You would have to possess and be able to use psychokinetically, all of the Infinite knowledge of the Infinite Creative Intelligence. That is what Jesus meant when He said, "The Father Within doeth all things". And the same conditions and principles, the same usages, etc., apply in every moment of your daily life. It is only through your compatibility developed through evolution that you are now able to live in the physical world; and as was stated, you are psychokinetically projecting in understanding, the necessary power into your life to make it possible for you and the reaction thereof regenerates through your mind this constant never-ending process.

Now here is a very important concept: in this constant, never-ending regenerative process of life, there is always the tendency—especially for humans—to be selective; humans are much more selective than animals and in this selective tendency, humans often incur their greatest errors and difficulties. People, like animals, are inherently lazy. An animal with a full stomach is a lazy animal. People are therefore, always trying to get something for nothing. They are always giving way to their baser and more compulsive instincts. On the other hand, there are other motivating

17

forces in man's life which make him struggle for a better way. The competitive aspects of life make him labor furiously to build a better home, a better temple, or a better civilization, etc., than his neighbors, or the rest of the world. These drives are all part of the various equilibriums which every person must sustain in his life or suffer serious consequences. Yet these equilibriums, powerful as they are, sometimes become too intangible when other pressures are incurred. That is the reason why man has found the necessity to be governed by different systems of laws and governmental agencies, and he has attempted to be spiritually governed by different religious beliefs based on unknown but ever-apparent creative and natural forces and phenomena.

It is the misunderstanding of, and the lack of knowledge of all these aspects of life, the true governing and motivating forces, the true origin and understanding of evolution etc., which still relegate the earth man into his vegetative earth life. The rapidly increasing perspectives of his civilization proportionately increase his misunderstanding and each new truth contradicts what he believes. Today mankind is living in the greatest contradiction of all times, and particularly the contradiction between his religious beliefs as is posed in Christianity and the sciences of this time. While science has just begun to give man a new and greater understanding of Infinite Creation, yet this understanding is being even more vehemently opposed by the Christian dogma. Science is atheistic when compared to this Christian dogma, yet a paradox, if you please, for it is the Christian who is the atheist.

Every scientist believes in God, but not the emotional vindictive pagan god, the Christian scapegoat, who is blamed in his mysterious ways for every mis-understood happening—the Christian God who will, in the days of resurrection, collect his subjects like trading stamps and redeem them. The scientist knows something about a new kind of God—the All-Intell-igent God who moves immutably in the creation of atoms and universes—a God whose Mind is larger and more incomprehensible than the vastness of the star-filled space around us—a God who is not influenced by the temperaments of people or the vileness of their ways, but lives as a vast storehouse wherein any hu-man can reconstruct himself into a creative entity—a God who supplies the answers to all questions if they are sought in the cause of wisdom—a God who knows no want or insecurity, does not determine good or evil, but leaves all these things to those who would take from Him the substance of their lives and create for themselves their own differences; yet knowing as they did so, the very purveyance of their evil ways would drive them to goodness.

So suffering becomes the necessary force to create in each man the desire to seek liberation, and in seeking he will find many doorways through the labyr-inth of his material world. Yet always the silken goss-amer thread of Infinite understanding will lead him through the maze IF he does not let his feet become tired, and IF his faith remains strong, and IF he can become humble enough to accept, then, he has hope of Immortal Life—hope which will be realized if it is not abandoned in the mad fantasy of materialism.

You as a human living the human life, must there-fore, always be subjective to it as long as it is lived and as this life is a carnal struggle of survival based on the more primitive emotional phases and values of life, so will all these things never be adequately met or compromised within your jurisprudence. Your personal evaluations or ego consciousness will be constantly violated and deflated, and you will require equally constant re-inflation, self-inflation, if you please, quite often indulged in, even in values and concepts beyond the realm of possibility or comprehension.

Every person values his own opinion beyond all others. This he will do despite overwhelming evidence to the contrary. He even condemns that which he knows nothing of, or what it is, and all in the cause of saving face. So each person is his own Judas Iscariot and not for thirty pieces of silver, but for the pauper's fraud of self-respect, he betrays himself in every act, in every hour of physical consciousness. For in sustaining his physical life, he does so by virtue of his belief and abandons all else, even the Immortality of his life to a vague and indefinite future—a future which only the pressure of death will force him to seek a way to circumvent. For is not death the greatest of ego deflations? Yes, strange are the ways of those who will not face themselves realistically, who blame any and all things for their own discrepancies and faults, who attempt to evade the ever-attendant and never-ending parable of their own existence or its end, yet clutching at straws to every whim or fantasy which presents the false superiority of the personal ego.

Thus healers are born, and with them are heard the first wailing cries of the crusaders—those who would save others in some mad fancied frenzy to avoid the subconscious guilt which pronounces their own doom, signed on the wrinkled parchment of ignorance. To those who evaluate life for others in the false promises of equalities and Eternal Life and as they are led further down the vale of ignorance and despair, so it is that those who lead them are the first to fall into the quicksands of their own false promises.

Salvation or Eternal Life is sought by all in the frenzy to avoid death, yet the way to Immortality is always impeded by the sacrificial altar upon which every person sacrifices himself to the false god ego. Yet if ego is all bad, then man has no future; for ego is the first cell of self which fertilizes the ovum of the future personality; one which will, when incubated in the warmth and Light of Infinite Wisdom, give birth to the Super Being—a person devoid of self, yet being part of every self, and again recreating the infinite metamorphosis, the facsimile and function of Infinity and Everlasting Consciousness.

ABC's of Immortality
Part Three

In our previous discussions on healing, it was em-phatically stated that no earth man is a healer. This is true not only with any Unariun student, but with any and all individuals who may practice spiritual healing in different churches or religious groups throughout the world. Some of these people state they are 'gifted healers', a completely false claim. How could they be more powerful than was Jesus who openly admitted He did not heal? In all fairness, however, to these peo-ple and to the Unariun student, there are countless numbers of cases of spiritual healing where it seemed some miraculous healing or adjustment took place in circumstances involving a so-called healer.

The Moderator grew up as a member of one such church which practiced spiritual or (divine) healing by the laying on of hands by specially ordained ministers, and he saw miracles happen when these rites were performed. However, here again these ministers were not the healers. They, like any other so-called healer, as well as the Unariun student, are what might be sci-entifically called healing polarities. No earth person—with possibly a single exception (and who is factually, not indigenous to the earth, but came from a higher spiritual planet for the sole purpose of bringing Unar-ius Science to earth man) has sufficient knowledge and training to bring about a healing by himself. He can, however, make of himself a sort of a channel wherein that extremely complex electrical energy charge can be projected into the body and psychic anatomy of the person to be healed. Here again the reasons are very scientific in nature.

Every person has an aura. An aura is a field of energy which radiates outwardly from the person for a distance of several feet. These energy radiations contain millions of different oscillating frequencies. All of these are grouped according to frequency into seven different plane rate classifications. There are three karmic or physical planes, three prana or mental planes, and one spiritual or Superconscious Radiation. Now most earth people have auras which vibrate very closely together even though they are all slightly different. There is not much of an effect when any number of these auras come together. However, if an Advanced Personality, like Jesus, walks among them, the situation is quite different. That is because the aura of this Advanced Person is radiating in frequencies on much higher planes than do the auras of the people around Him. This highly vibrating aura is also highly charged with Infinite Wisdom. It, therefore, can be considered positive in respect to the other auras as it is the Creative Law or Principle that positive must flow into the negative and the negative into the positive. This Advanced Person would be immediately aware that great energies were passing from Him and the negative energies or conditions of those around Him were flowing back into His aura.

This was exactly the situation when the woman with the issue touched Jesus on the hem of His robe and He said, "Who touched me, for I felt virtue leave me?" Virtue, of course, is the highly charged Intelligent Energies of His aura; and so it is only a matter of a short period of time before the Advanced Person or Jesus must leave the presence of other people and He must retreat to a spot, such as his home which has been previously surcharged, so that He may rest and recharge His aura. That is why the Moderator and Ruth cannot and do not have but very little intercourse with the outside world, and it is especially true with any student who may come here to the Center and draw upon them so heavily; they (the Channels), would become incapacitated for several days until the recharging took place.

Under the most favorable conditions, the material world is a very difficult place for any person like the Moderator or his wife to live in; even though they do not physically associate with the students, there is a constant and never-ending draw on their energies and which is especially heavy during the meeting periods (student groups). The reasons again are very scientific. When any kind of intelligent corrective healing energy is used to heal a person, much of this energy is of too high a frequency to affect the condition, or the psychic anatomy of the recipient. It must be mixed, as it were, harmonically speaking, with vibrations of a more physical nature which are more closely related to the person or condition. This is the point where the 'so-called' healer comes in. The Unariun Doctors and Scientists use the auric radiations of the healer as a channel to convey the healing energies to the sick person, and as these energies flow from the intermediary or polarity, the higher healing energies projected from the Advanced Minds and from especially developed apparatus or machines, are interjected or mixed into this flow where they enter into the body or psychic anatomy of the recipient—this is conscious polarization.

Among all people there is a small interchange or flow of auric energies, usually of little consequence. A person who calls himself a healer is a person who has, in some way, become a polarity or intermediary; he may have prepared himself or been prepared, which is usually the case, before he incarnated into his present life; that is, a certain amount of preparatory training in which certain base plane rates of his psychic anatomy were slightly stepped up or were made to vibrate in a slightly higher frequency by this training.

As an earth man, however, he does not remember, consciously, anything about this training. He may somehow accidentally find out that people feel better when he has come in contact with them. This type of healing is usually called 'magnetic' as it occurs in the interchange process from the karmic or physical portion of the aura. Some of the energies which flow from this auric emanation can and do make others feel better when they become charged with it. However, bear in mind the conscious mind of the healer did not project these energies. This was merely the positive flow of energy on a slightly larger scale than is normally the case among all humans. A person cannot be considered to be a healer until he can voluntarily and consciously project healing energies into another person, and as previously stated, no earth man possesses this knowledge or ability.

Now we have discovered what 'magnetic' healing is and how certain people have capitalized upon finding out they can, to some extent, discharge a little auric energy into another person. So they make a 'big deal' out of it. They advertise in magazines, call themselves 'gifted healers' etc.; yet, what they work with and what they do is about as valuable as many of the other false promises and concepts people indulge themselves in under the rosy aura of mysticism. However, this magnetic healing or positive to negative flow condition is always very valuable to the Advanced Intellects who have the earth world as their charge. They may, unknowingly to this earth man, when conditions warrant and are propitious, interject a healing bolt of energy when the so-called healer is practicing his art, or when his hands are placed on the head, or when he comes in contact with a sick or negative person. This healing bolt of energy which was especially compounded for this case, would be mixed with the energies of the magnetic aura and under those conditions, that sick person would have a miraculous healing. Then, as it is in all cases, this magnetic healer takes all the glory, although he does not really know what happened; so he puffs up his chest and struts; he boasts saying he is gifted by god, etc.

Again it is indeed fortunate that Infinite Intelligence and the Higher Intellects do not consider these things in an emotional or personal way; the Advanced Intellects have a rather difficult time anyway trying to do as much good as They do for the earth people; and many times They are forced to use any ways or means possible to correct some condition for an earth person so that his life cycle can be sustained to enable him to finish what he came to do. You, as a Unariun student, can consider yourself a polarity or an intermediary and any moment when conditions are right and you come in contact with other people, energies will begin to flow from your aura, and at which time the Advanced Intellects may add some of the Infinite Intelligence with which They oscillate.

Infinite Intelligence is not personal; It does not vibrate with you except on the very lowest physical plane and through the world with which you are familiar. These vibrations, therefore, are earth world vibrations. They are your life; but again, as Infinity is impersonal, you take Infinity as your earth world and use it to suit your purpose or you accept it in a reactionary emotional manner. You even divide It and call It good or evil. Under these circumstances, then, as Infinity is impersonal, It cannot heal you or help you. The Advanced Intellects, however, can oscillate with this Creative Infinity at a much higher and more creative level. In these oscillating processes they make It personal. Just as bees eat pollen and digest it in their stomachs to make honey, so the Advanced Intelligences take this impersonal Infinite Intelligence and by digesting It in Their Minds, They reshape It and reform It into personal elements which can be projected into you and your psychic anatomy or through you into some other person.

So you see, dear student, there is no magic, no hocus-pocus, nor abracadabra. There are no gifts or special endowments. A progressive evolution is lots of hard work in learning and application. It's sweat and tears; and unfortunately, sometimes many misguided people shed their blood in an attempt to gain what you have at your fingertips. Becoming an Advanced Intellect and living an Immortal Life is a serious proposition. It means thousands of years of highly specialized training in the science of creation.

In this scale of evolution, the material worlds such as the earth are, to many souls, the starting place. They are, to many others, the pits of hell. There are countless millions of planets like the earth—some dead and desolate, others teeming with hordes of humanity much like your own world. They too, have reached and passed the apex of their cycle and their civilizations are now on the descendency just as it is with this world. The future history of this world has been written many times in the skies above you. You cannot depend on these things or the world for your future; nor can you depend upon the promises of the hypocrites who have set themselves up in high places. Again and again you will have to make your choice; you will either have to pursue the pathway into the Inner Kingdom or you will have to follow the multitudes into oblivion.

The impersonal Infinite Creative Intelligence is not emotionally concerned with those who tread this downward trail. Sooner or later It will absorb them back into Its embryonic consciousness, there to start a new cycle of regeneration. The Infinite does not destroy Itself, nor does the death and destruction of one person destroy even the smallest part of Infinity. Yes, and the Infinite is even more than indestructible; It is constantly regenerating into new forms of consciousness and it is in this way that you can attain Immortal Life, for in attaining an Immortal Life, you have regenerated a new form of Infinite Consciousness.

The ABC's of Immortality
Part Four

During our previous discussions on healing, you have been presented with certain scientific facts and aspects, together with a number of other very important elements relative to this vital subject. The sum and total of this analysis and introspection may lead you, the student, to a rather hopeless impasse so far as your own future is concerned. You may say to yourself, how am I or any other person, for that matter, going to be healed from certain incurable conditions, and in general, think the whole situation as tinged with a gloomy hue. Actually, however, this is far from the truth.

Infinite Intelligence is, in many ways including the evolutionary cycle, reconstructing and healing the material earth man from the many diseases and aberrations incurred in his daily life. These healing discussions were presented primarily to accomplish several purposes: first, to more fully acquaint you with common practices, subterfuges, delusions, and illusions under which the earth man labors in attempting to gain relief from his many ailments. And there is a direct warning carried in this information and in these facts, that you, the student, will cease to be tempted by these common and quite useless practices and beliefs. Second, to more fully open up the avenue upon which you will travel in your quest to seek healing from the earth world purgatory and to gain for yourself a higher and better way of life. The temptations and ruses which you will find along this pathway will be numerous; many will be well disguised and you should not for a single moment cease to be alert, but be constantly aware of these many dangers.

Now at this point we have reached a very precarious point in our introspections, for what is about to be said may seem to completely refute the entire consensus of healing evaluations; yet again, in a fair warning: consider all factors and elements as they are presented, and do not unconsciously accept or reject what you wish according to your own situation. For if this is done, you will be defeated in any attempt to gain a progressive evolution or to be healed. What is about to be said is this: yes, there is instantaneous spiritual healing, just like the kind which was described in the New Testament as performed by Jesus, even though there was much coloring, distortion and lack of accurate descriptive fact. As of today the cause of evolutionary progression and healing, as it was preached and administered by Jesus is much more fully, much more comprehensively being carried on through the Unariun Administration. The same great Spiritual Brotherhood is working with the same great Master Mind and Super Intellect which worked through Jesus two thousand years ago. This Super Intellect, aided and abetted by the vast Unariun Brotherhood, works through the Moderator and his polarity, Ruth, to bring to all earth people, and especially those who have preconditioned themselves, all the necessary and correctly administered healing, the pertinent and scientific knowledge, personal demonstrations, etc., which will enable any of these persons to carry his cause of emancipation into a higher way of life.

This statement is an incontestable fact proven not only in the many thousands of testimonials written by students in terms of undying gratitude—nor did it start at the beginning of the Unariun Administration in

1954; there was, previous to this, a preparatory period of about fourteen years wherein the Moderator lived the most incredible life ever lived by any man, far surpassing, in many ways, the life of Jesus, and there are many people still living who could bear testimony as to the truth of that statement.

Beginning in 1941, before World War II, the Moderator began to actively carry on a campaign (if it can be called that) into almost every nook and cranny, to every type and kind of people, men, women, and children found wherever they lived, on street corners, busses, in cafes and taverns, defense plants, churches and dance halls; the Moderator sought out and found the sick and maladjusted, and guided by this Super Intellect, they were instantly healed of their conditions. Diseases that ran the gamut of medical nomenclature: Cancer of the cervix, breast and lip, headaches, crossed eyes, streptococcic throat, back-aches of many years standing, a deep coma of two years' duration was instantly healed more than two thousand miles away. Mild forms of insanity and mental aberrations, impetigo, high blood pressure, ulcers, blindness, obesity, alcoholism, colds, virus, tuberculosis, asthma, the lame and the halt walked again, marital and financial problems and many other conditions too numerous to mention at this time, all were instantly healed and corrected and just as miraculously without preconditioning, very subtly too, and practically unknown to any others; for these healed people accepted their blessings, sometimes almost as a matter of fact, sometimes tearfully, but hardly ever did they advertise their blessing.

Along with this, these people were given personal facts about their past about which only they knew.

They were given information on events yet to happen even several years into the future and they often came back to tell Him how exacting they worked out, and sometimes too, a great Power came over them and they perspired copiously, felt extremely hot, gasped for breath until He turned the Power off.

And so as the great war progressed, the Moderator —as He walked among these people—became a living legend, never openly discussed or talked about, yet recognized and sought after by other thousands; yet quietly He worked. There were no multitudes who followed Him, no pandemonium, no wide acclaim which is, in itself, incontestable proof that this Super Intellect would never again permit a situation to develop as it did two thousand years ago; never again would the conniving minds of men be permitted to use this great Science of Life as material from which they could contrive a great religious blasphemy. Then quietly and without palm branches or fanfare, without mobs crying "Crucify Him", the Moderator disappeared; yet with the meeting of Ruth to again resurrect the great 'Unariun Cause', and with the Brotherhood, bring back together all those who had been implicated in the crime upon the Hill of Calvary.

Yes, here again a great testimonial, a great proof for among the closest and most devoted students are found those who pressed the crown of thorns upon His head, those who fashioned the cross and drove the nails; yes, even Pilate, Judas, and the priests are numbered among these students; for each one unto himself and with the help of the Unariun Brotherhood has seen his past projected into his present consciousness as a vivid moving picture. And when the pernicious effect was washed away in floods of tears, then this person, for the first time in the many elapsed centuries, found a great relief in this remission of sin. These people are, as of today, living testimonials of their past; and even though He has claimed nothing, they know the Super Intellect as one and the same as it was two thousand years ago. Indeed, He even bears physical scars of that crucifixion.

All this and much more will, in the future years, be written in a biography, a book more incredible than any which has yet been written, for it will span not only the two thousand years to the time of the Nazarene, but it will go back into Ancient Egypt and Akhnaton to Osiris and to Atlantis and the time of Ernos Ra, sixteen thousand years ago, even to the time of Ancient Lemuria and its beginnings. For thusly as the Super Intellect of the Unariun Brotherhood resurrected the cause and purpose of man's existence in these different epochs, the evolutionary progressive cycle which constantly reinstates and perpetuates Infinite Intelligence into all forms and all motions, culminates its highest expression in mankind, just as it begins with all men upon earth-like planets.

To you who read these words do not doubt them for they are your history and your future, written in the cause and purpose of all these things. Do not use them as diversions or escape devices. Your own end is from moment to moment, tailored by your thoughts and actions. You cannot escape the price you will pay if you doubt. Only in the fullest and most sincere dedication to the cause of your personal development will you find the answer to the riddle of your life, to your own Immortality. To doubt and to dawdle, to use subterfuges and devices, to attempt to circumvent or to change the immutable truth to your own way will bring disaster; and you will find untold millions living in the pits of hell to keep you company.

Conversely, if you find truth in your heart, truth in the Unariun Brotherhood, and truth in your own effort, your path will be well marked to the Higher Worlds and you will find all aid and assistance which can be intelligently used for your own benefit. This is not coercion or a threat. As with all presentations made by Unarius, these are cold hard facts presented to you over and over in different ways, in many forms and which always resolve into one important fact: you and you alone can choose your future, your destiny; and may it be that you will not find the bitter tears of recrimination—drink the bitter dregs of despair which you will do if you do not take advantage of this, the greatest opportunity of your life.

The ABC's of Immortality
Part Five

During the past many centuries and up to the present time, many religionists, evangelists and other
religious groups have preyed upon and exploited the
physically and mentally ill; in fact, every religion of the
world, including the greatest of all Christian churches,
are exploiting the masses of humanity with coercive
tactics which are based upon the fears, insecurities
and superstitions of these people who are ignorant of
the facts of life. They preach the false hypocrisy of
intercession, the remission of sin, forgiveness by confessional, washing away the sins by blood, etc. They
have literally and figuratively, partially or wholly hypnotized entire populations and nations into a semi-
subjugated state of control through these coercive tactics. They use the false and assumed depictions from
their so-called 'holy' books, and they have set themselves up in their priesthoods as the dispensators and
the intermediaries of their false gods. There is no other
human iniquity so depraved as that which capitalizes
and exploits the human weaknesses of ignorance,
disease and superstition. Yes, they have even clothed
themselves in the so-called 'divine vestments' of a
murderous and adulterous god, holding up the cruci-
fied image of this god's son as one who was conceived
in adultery, attempting to clothe this iniquity in immaculate conception, a pagan ritual still believed in
and practiced by the savages in the jungles; all this
great iniquity is superimposed in our present-day
society as the highest sustaining moral virtue which
is demanded of all people in allegiance to the conformities of this society.

Strangely and paradoxically, the children of this great Christian church are told and taught they are born in sin—a direct reflection that sex is a sin—entirely contradicted in the necessity of human procreation; yet all of this, vile as it is, recedes and becomes insignificant when one considers the destructive and demoralizing effect on any human who allows himself by allegiance to this or any other church, to be robbed of his birthright of progressive evolution, for by making the priest or minister the conveyance of his spiritual and moral values, he has automatically ceased in any forward progressive evolution. He has relinquished the most cherished of his possessions—his birthright—to choose for himself the values of life and the exercise of his franchise as a human being to make of himself and his life what is predicated in the values of his evolution.

Every human has the inalienable right to express his own quotient of life according to his position on his scale of evolution. This individual human expression is always a part of the total infinite expression. To usurp, to thwart, or change or adulterate any part of any human expression by any other human is to usurp, to thwart and misuse the net sum and total of infinite expression. Again, the classical sparrow that falls by the wayside: if a sparrow's fall can be noted in Infinite Consciousness, then is not every other motion so noted? And if these expressions are changed in their most ultimate values as they concern individual human consciousness, then Infinite Intelligence is also changed so far as any and all elements and factors which are connected with this human; yet Infinite Intelligence remains absolute. The net sum and total of all human expressions remain in Infinite Consciousness as absolutes, not subjective to change. The change of values then which occurs in any human consciousness is his perspectus of values when they are reflected into his life as the motivating impulses and determinants of his life. So far as Infinite Intelligence is concerned, any human has a more ultimate capability of expressing an infinite number and variety of lives. He could at the present moment be any one of a hundred billion people. Conversely, his past evolution could have also assumed any one of innumerable identities.

At this point you may think this is pandemonium. Nothing could be further from the truth. As it has been presented many times, Infinite Intelligence is highly ordered and organized. The principles of Infinite regeneration automatically convey this total infinity of expression to any form or substance including man, which is an evolutional form in a dimensional perspectus. Any and all forms and creatures, including man, are automatically selective in their expressions and life concourses according to these well-defined scientific principles. This selective process is never intelligently conducted or made use of until knowledge of these creative principles become not only individual knowledge but actually a way of life, automatically lived with these creative principles ever in effect. Such a person, however, would be a Super Being and not a materialist, an earth-bound man subjective to the vicissitudes of emotional values constantly superimposed in every life transmission. In this material phase he is selective only on an emotional basis, not one principled in more ultimate creative values expressed by Infinite Intelligence.

Any person, therefore, be he a government official, an executive officer, a priest or a minister, does, to some extent in his particular capacity, usurp moral values as they concern individual expression. There is, however, some justification to this system, especially in our present societies; as every human is subjected to emotional values, so every human likewise reacts and determines these values differently. The difference in any human disposition is the net sum and total of his many past lives and the differences of the experiences so compounded in these past lives. Again this is Infinite Intelligence expressing itself infinitely in some small part in each individual human consciousness.

There is at this present time an attempt being made in this country to equalize all forms of human consciousness into a singular level, an attempt to vindicate a false religious assumption that all men are created equal. Up to this present time the net result of this attempt to perpetuate this false doctrine has been racial riots, mass demonstrations, even bloodshed and death. How much better it would be if all peoples could see the individual and racial position of human consciousness on the scale of evolution, to respect these various and different positions as expressionary elements and attributes to Infinite Intelligence and to see this Infinite Intelligence in action in every human; yes and even in every other form of life. For if the sparrow that so falls is noted, so indeed are all other human forms of expression. To deprecate one such expression on any assumed material reactionary values is to deprecate Infinite Intelligence.

Any attempt to philosophize our past and present civilizations, their values as being either redundant or decadent in the prime motivating necessities of human existence, whether or not they are moral or amoral, should not be done without a more fully comprehensive perspective of Infinite Intelligence, of its many kingdoms and mansions, its infinite number and variety of forms, human and otherwise. Such values as are now in existence as expressionary forms of human conduct can be rationalized as born from out the necessity of this form in evolutionary transitions.

Religion, as it is now currently expressed in the higher echelons of our society, is still basically and essentially the same barbaric spirit worship practiced by jungle savages. The priest is only an evolutionary form of the witch doctor separated only by a few hundred or a few thousand years time. The priest is still using the same coercive tactics as does the witch doctor; he is still capitalizing upon the fears and superstitions of an ignorant people. He does this not because he is more learned than his victims or that he is 'divinely' commissioned, for his god is as false as the god of Babylon. He is simply astute enough to become an executive part of a system which has, in one form or another, victimized man since the beginning. So long as there is a planet earth and it is peopled by humans, so will there be religions and political systems. They will assume many forms and be called by different names, but basically they remain the same.

The intellectual level of any race of humans who so inhabit this earth remains comparatively stationary; the plus or minus of this level of intelligence amounts to only a few thousand years in his evolution, and only many countless thousands of readapted forms of consciousness which he began learning in the early stages of his earth world evolution. Do not look for any great changes in the future; the intellectual capacity of any human always relegates him into the environment which is best understood by his particular intelligence.

When that time comes, when he is more or less intelligent, he passes from that particular environment into that which is again the most suitable. This is a built-in and inviolate law of evolution and as the earth man is still ignorant of the greater capacities of this law, he is still ignorant of Infinite Intelligence, so does he so contain the perspectus of his knowledge as the incumbency of his earth world life, and from this limited horizon he attempts to span the limitless reaches of Infinity with an intellect capable of living only in an earth world.

Today he is busily engaged in fashioning rockets which he hopes will hurl him to the moon or some nearby planet. He thinks once he has escaped his terrestrial boundaries he will be able to solve the riddle of the physical universe or even life itself. How senseless and foolish, for this is but a new contrivance in which he will attempt to circumscribe Infinite Intelligence within his limited earth world. Even more senseless if we remember the words of an Emissary from a higher world who said, "Seek ye first the Kingdom which is Within".

You as a Unariun student have at your fingertips the means and the whereby, the pertinent knowledge, yes, and even well-regulated help from higher Advanced Spiritual Organizations to achieve and attain your own personal miracle. The greatest of all miracles which could happen to any human is the metamorphosis of an animal-like earthbound material consciousness into the expanded consciousness of a Superintelligent Being who lives and functions in the Celestial reaches of the higher worlds.

CHAPTER III

Man Versus Television

In different places in the works of Unarius—and especially in the first lesson course—comparisons have been made whereby a human being was compared to a TV set; and how science had drawn exact parallels in various electronic devices which were, basically, exactly similar to the life processes of every human—that is, the human was, in reality, an electronic instrument, stimulated from different third dimensional sensations, through the five senses, where they reactively stimulated the psychic anatomy. Once again I will make a comparative analysis of a very familiar electronic device, known as an audio-amplifier, whereby we can study and gain a comprehensive concept, which will relate us in our present moments, to the many past lifetimes and their dispensations.

An audio-amplifier is an electronic device usually consisting of two or three amplifier type vacuum tubes, together with associated resistors and capacitors, properly connected and powered by a suitable power supply, and terminating with a loud speaker. There is an audio-amplifier in every radio and TV set, as well as the more advanced and specifically designed types used in Hi-Fi.

The function of the amplifier is to take relatively small electronic signals and amplify them sufficiently to activate the loud speaker. Now, an audio-amplifier has, like everything else, certain imperfections; there is a certain amount of hum which is amplified. Tubes and parts are self-resonant and produce harmonic distortion. Different kinds of electronic signals also produce intermodulation distortion when they are amplified together. These different distortions may be so high as to render the amplifier almost useless.

However, here is a curious phenomenon: if we take a part of all these amplified signals and return them to the front end or input of the amplifier and introduce them out of phase, with the incoming signals, then lo, all the distortion and hum vanishes. Returning part of the signal in this manner is called feed-back, and makes possible the high quality of modern musical reproduction. However, if we return part of the amplified signal, inphase with the incoming signal, then the amplifier will oscillate and the speaker will howl, like a stuck auto horn. The inphase and out of phase condition is obtained from selecting the proper terminating polarity where the loud speaker is connected.

Now, let us compare this amplifier process to you or any human. The loud speaker is the surface of your life, the motions you go through, what you say, etc. These things all started in the dim distant past, at the input. Through many lifetimes these experience quotients, which you call life, were constantly amplified as they were relived and gave greater power and strength to the psychic anatomy, so that at the present time you are actually reliving, as certain basic patterns, the entire past amplified into the present.

Now, if you know about the past—reincarnation, living from life to life, and all the principles which are taught in Unarius—you will, by this positive introspection of this conscious knowledge, be returning a part of the net sum and total of your negative present, back into the past, and to your very beginning—and therefore, out of phase, which will, automatically, cancel out all of the distortions, etc. which you have incurred in these past lifetimes.

The average person who knows nothing about the

principles which are taught in Unarius goes on day after day, amplifying all the distortions and faults from his previous lifetimes; then, sooner or later, these distortions will pile up to the point whereby he becomes physically or mentally incapacitated—he is sick. Then he makes himself even worse, as, unknowingly—through frequency relationship—he links his present back into the beginning of his past or inphase way. This will consequently double and triple the intensity of his present condition; he will, in effect, be oscillating with his past.

It can now be seen how important it is to thoroughly understand the concept of phase relationships and of the basic oscillating principles carried on with the present exterior world and the psychic anatomy. This science is most important and vital to you; for a full and complete understanding will enable you to consciously and automatically cancel out the constantly occurring and recurring negations of your present life. This knowledge will also prepare you for the future; for, indeed it is, that as you use this knowledge day by day, you will be very busily tearing down your old past, as it is oscillating in your psychic anatomy and replacing this old past with new and constructive material which will enable you to reincarnate—in the distant future—into one of those Heavenly cities which have been described in our books.

Each day, each hour, each moment of consciousness should, therefore, be lived with our feed-back connected; that is, the always present knowledge of our lives as resurgent life patterns, learned and lived in other lives and their attendant experiences, psychic shocks, etc., all of which must be, and will be relived time and time again, until we cancel them out, by applying the scientific knowledge of Unarius. Our feed-

43

back should always be 'out of phase' with this past, which means that as we view the vast breadth and depth of Infinity, as we are correctly placed in our personal position in evolution, we are, therefore, positive; and we can then positively objectify the negative facsimile of the present into its proper place in the past, and thus cancellation takes place and we are freed forever from this karma.

In viewing our past lives, let us leave any greatness or goodness untouched and unsmirched by our present ego. Let us be concerned only with our past evils, for they will overwhelm us in apathy or ignorance; our past goodness and greatness will take care of itself.

CHAPTER IV

Flashbacks, Workouts, Reliving

During the past several weeks certain circumstantial evidence has indicated specific conclusions in regard to the development of various Unariun students and in particular to those who are attending the Glendale group meetings. In view of this evidence, I would like to present a few of the many thoughts which have been coursing through my mind in this respect.

Presenting these thoughts is done with certain reservations—a point of constructive criticism, if you please; but certainly, criticism which you can all profit by and most certainly I am doing this for your own benefit. As you know, I believe implicitly in the principle of personal development which is best achieved when any individual is called upon to use the highest quotient of his mental faculties.

The inception of the group meetings was an introductory phase in personal development as it was recombined in associated factors present during these meetings which were particularly auspicious for the projection of certain intelligent energies for healing, correction, and adjustment, etc.

Although I, personally, have not attended any of these sessions in the physical, I have participated in them, nevertheless, and have carefully noted their conduct. In the beginning there were many apparent adjustments and healings and some subsequent psychic discharges or 'workouts'. As you all know, I asked for and received many wonderful written testimonials to this effect, for which I am most grateful.

It should be noted that a genuine 'workout' always takes place on a different mental plane than is normally in effect; it is quite important to polarize this experience on the normal physical mental level. This is best and most safely done in writing. A written testimonial is also incontestable evidence to anyone who is hoping for help but has strong 'sales resistance', and needs this evidence to help him muster up the necessary faith. Also, the written testimonials will be most valuable in the days of inquisition when Unarius will be challenged by the rhetorical materialists of the world.

As time went on, however, it became increasingly evident that the most important part of Unarius was being missed or not fully realized. It is quite important to have psychic discharges or 'workouts'; however, these should come about quite normally and in combination with other factors and elements. In other words, as a 'workout' eliminates a malformed part of the psychic anatomy, it should have been replaced beforehand with energy structures derived from the constant usage of the Unariun Science.

To paraphrase an old quotation, "new lamps for old", the 'workout' phase of the Unariun Concept should not be used as a new diversionary device. There should be no attempt to consciously instigate 'workouts', nor should there be any rivalry between students which would be, in all effect, simply a new diversion.

In the common psychology of life, the material world is merely a vast multitude of symbols which you have learned to recognize through usage. Your life is a combination of conscious or autosuggestive symbolic forms recombined in any particular circumstance. It is impossible for you to think independently without these symbolic forms. To do so, you would have to have a completely paranormal consciousness or have the mentality of one of the Advanced Personalities; that is the development which you are now working toward.

Therefore, if you attempt to 'read' for yourself or for any other person or, in other words, tell some person that you 'see' him as a certain person in some specific circumstance in some past lifetime; you should first question the validity of this picture. Until you more thoroughly and completely understand Infinity as it is presented in the Unariun Concept, you cannot hope to have valid pictures unless they are projected to you by the Higher Intelligences; and you must remember there are many other forces who can project invalid pictures just to confuse you.

Yes, you can even dream them up yourself as a way in which you are subconsciously getting even with someone or you are inflating your ego with a false sense of power. So you see, the dangers of the psychic world are ever about you just as are the beneficent blessings.

These blessings can come about only if you conscientiously and thoroughly apply yourself to understanding Infinity. It is well and good to constantly realize that your daily life is a recombination of the past. A broom handle may become a spear, or any other artifact or combination as its own autosuggestive connotation; but we should always bear in mind and remember the scientific principle which sustains these forms of consciousness. We should continuously try to visualize the whirling energy forms within the psychic anatomy; how they link and relink to form and reform our physical life and make it possible to make all apparent forms justifiable.

We should also keep constantly in mind other dominant and ever apparent creative factors within our mental vision which run the gamut from the atom to the Universe and the vastness of Infinity itself. The business of acquiring immortality is a serious one. Your life depends upon it. Don't play games with it like the proverbial Russian roulette.

One of the more final stages of my earth mission will be the development of certain individuals who can carry on this work when I have left the physical. To be able to do this, however, means that any such person should be able to carry on and demonstrate the highest form of conduct in the Unariun Concept.

Briefly, this means the ability to clairvoyantly attune mental consciousness in any way, manner or form which it may be called upon to do. To manifest and demonstrate the inner plane of consciousness which materializes as the answer and supply to all demands; to be able to meet any and all scientists, doctors, college professors, literates, etc., on their own ground; to be conversant with them and to give them answers to undefined problems. Anything less than this would sell Unarius short because Unarius is demonstrating the evolutionary continuity of life into that Kingdom Within.

Perhaps this may sound like an impossible goal and it may be, for some of you, at least in this lifetime. The future, however, always presents its own challenge. What you do today can well determine whether or not you will appear in some future lifetime and demonstrate Infinity just as I am doing with you today.

Yes, I have traveled the same road as you are now traveling and, for that matter, I am still doing so. That again is the challenge of Infinity; the wondrous promise of Immortal life which never ceases to yield new horizons for those who aspire; for those who can give up the 'seemingly', safe and solid past and devote themselves to unfolding Infinity through evolution.

History yields many grim facts which have happened to the doctrine of life preached by other Avatars. The lofty idealisms of Immortality are always squeezed into the limited dimension of the earth life where this malformed remnant of truth is further embroidered with false artificiality of orthodox conventionalities and other banalities which make it acceptable in common conformities.

No, I would not like to see Unarius decay into some decadent ritual, an expressionary form devoid of leadership, for indulging in spiritualistic activities in an attempt to vindicate its existence, we, the Unariun Brotherhood, would feel a great loss for we would know that again, in death, your faces would all turn toward the earth.

We would know we had not accomplished the most valuable part of this Mission which was to acquaint you with the true intellectual science of Creation. No, it would not be because we have not used any and all efforts and devices. In the books and lesson courses, we have impounded this Immortal Wisdom in simple easily understood form. *We cannot make you think;* neither can we, with some magic wand hocus-pocus, make you into Super Beings. That would defeat the purpose of your creative evolution.

We can only present this Immortal Wisdom to you and we can only help you demonstrate what it will do for you and what you can do for yourselves, if you use it. But that is your determinant, your prerogative. And how well you do or do not use this Wisdom will determine your survival, your Immortality. You cannot achieve Immortal Life without it. Just as you find yourself in rather straitened psychic circumstances, remember that these circumstances have piled up from the past. The situation will grow worse unless you correct it. That is retrogression.

Also bear in mind in 'workouts' that this eliminates a certain portion of the psychic anatomy. Too many 'workouts', no psychic anatomy; like cutting off small parts of your body. The logical thing to do is to build up that psychic body to replace the anticipated discharges, and build it good while you are at it, from out the Immortal stuff from which Creation is made.

Later on, in the hundreds of thousands of years and lifetimes to come, you will polarize this Wisdom in your daily life just as you are now repolarizing the evil circumstances of the past in your present life. And you should know by now that for people who have accumulated too much, the earth world is purgatory. In fact, in contrast to the Higher Worlds, the average earth man is still an animal living in an earth world purgatory with his mental faculties developed to a great proportion in hellish activities.

And so dear friends, always remember the success of this Mission will depend upon you, and how well you achieve its purpose will depend your immortality and the immortality of those who follow after. For there will be others, many of them, who will need Unarius and they will need messengers to bring it to them.

Principally, my Mission at this time is to rectify the great tragedy of Jesus' Mission and to reinstitute its purpose in the scientific idiom of the Twentieth Century. However, this Mission also achieves many other purposes. At the time of the crucifixion, the close followers of Jesus numbered only about one hundred fifty persons. These people, as well as certain others embroiled in the crucifixion, are presently the strongest advocates and students of Unarius and they are working out karma inherited from that episode.

Other purposes will be aiding and assisting the Twentieth Century scientific element in re-establishing the science of Atlantis and Lemuria. Also, Unarius represents a great stabilizing polarity in an explosive world and has already been successful in helping to avert a world catastrophe. The millions of Advanced Personalities who are the Unariun Brotherhood are vitally concerned with this and many other earth worlds as part of their expressionary effort in recreating a portion of Infinity.

I am presenting these facts to you hoping thereby to achieve, in your mentality, the enormousness of a functional Unarius; your responsibility to it, not merely as a person who will be personally benefited but rather, in a long term proposition of development whereby you, too, will become one of these expressionary agents in the Unariun Brotherhood.

The proposition of Infinity transcends the boundaries of mortal mind; it cannot be comprehended by such a mind. Evolution is predicated upon a more ultimate expansion of consciousness which can more fully appreciate Infinity. For only then, can the pagan gods of numerous religions be so displaced in consciousness.

You, as Unariun students, and so gathered together as you are, do so by virtue of great planning and hard work by the Unariun Brotherhood to give you all the opportunity—which you requested—to free yourselves of the hellish nightmare of the past, to again re-establish yourselves upon a healthy pathway of evolution. My time with you will be short; nor can I do more than I have already done. For the days of my earth life are given with each Word I give to you, for these words are my Mission. They carry the Power of Infinite Wisdom projected by the Brotherhood. Yet, I feel great confidence with each one of you. I know that everyone will somehow, more than justify and vindicate all that has gone into this Mission.

It is not easy for one who understands the Higher Way to maintain a physical body in this dimension. How this is done requires great forethought and planning; yet it is limited in its endurance. Just as the carnal world destroyed Jesus and His Mission, so will it destroy my body. Yet, somehow, I know that the Mission and Its purpose will endure; and endure it must if any person hopes to achieve immortal life.

To each earth man, his life is extremely valuable. This is a personal emotional evolvement based on what each person believes is the necessity for his survival in a hostile environment. Infinite Intelligence, however, is not so emotionally involved. It knows that each person is part of a re-creative cosmogony and part of Infinite Intelligence and through evolution all mankind can survive according to the function of re-creative Principle.

Yes, even one death or many deaths is the concept of evolution. For as each man dies, so is he born again in a new world. It is not the task of mortal mind to quibble with Infinite Intelligence. For within the Inner Kingdom, the Many Mansions, the vast Interdimensional Cosmogony is the sum and substance of Infinite Creation—a great, resurgent, ever creative and re-creative, expressionary sea of energy which manifests any earth man's life as an Infinite mote in Its Consciousness.

Yes, even a hundred thousand earth lives lived by any man is still smaller than the smallest atom. How craven is each man then, who lives life from the dawn of birth to the twilight of death in a nightmare of insecurity despite the great and ever apparent effulgence of Creation everywhere about him. He feasts his eyes and saturates his body in its essences, then defiles his existence with his offal. And thus, he makes of his earth a dung heap, heaped high with his iniquities. Yet, even here, the Infinite Creator is at work, and *from such dung heaps, the fairest lilies grow*, just as each man learns, within himself, to refine the experience of his earth world into subliminal consciousness, even as does the lily.

Give, then, the fairest virtue of your being; let the rising sun of tomorrow find your face as the whitened lily blooms, turned to the sky. Let the greenness of your leaves be the understanding of your earth world, stretched out to hide its ugliness. And let your stamens hold the golden pollen of immortality to be seeded in fresh, clean soil of a Higher World, nurtured in a higher concept and understanding of life which ever falls into consciousness as the rains of heaven.

Let your stalk be firm and hold your head erect against all adversaries; but always yielding to the softest zephyr breeze of Wisdom. For these blow only that ye may be refreshed; and never say, now wasted am I, even as you have fallen back and again become part of the mire.

And if I have come to you as such a breeze and you have been refreshed, gather also the courage from me to hold your stalk high. For surely, if I am such a breeze, then tomorrow brings the sun and the time to hold your whitened face aloft; a time to cast your seed into the sky. The promise of tomorrow, far greater than ever lived by man in earthly worlds, or all the worlds, and all the men, for these, too are but the smallest part.

CHAPTER V

The Symbolic World

It has been observed that man is a creature of many and diverse proclivities. In this respect he is somewhat different than other forms of life abounding on the earth plane whose life expressions are more closely confined within specific dimensions.

While the earth man is quite capable of expressing and re-expressing an infinite number and variety of expressions in his earth life, he would no doubt be nonplussed and horrified to be suddenly confronted with the realization that all these expressionary forms, even the most grandiose of intellectual efforts were almost entirely a system of idolatries constantly reasserted into consciousness in symbolic forms.

For indeed it is that in all forms and manners of life, mankind universally worships the idolatrous forms of life which; existing as symbolic forms linked to past expressions, become the basic instigating power behind his life.

There are many forms of idolatry whether it is in the worship of sex, cars, homes, fur coats, etc., or such common public adulations which center about movie 'stars', politicians and other public figures. In fact, mankind does universally worship all forms and artifacts of life with which he is familiar, nor are the religious systems exempt. The Mohammedan points his finger at the Christian and cries 'Infidel', the Christian points back and cries 'pagan', while the Jew is looking down his nose at both of them as the Hindu stands by in complacency knowing full well Buddha is the 'true Prophet'.

To all these religions, the effigy and the symbol are immediately apparent. The savage headhunter in Borneo hangs the empty skull of his adversary on a pole in front of his hut believing he has incarcerated his adversary's spirit in this skull forever. The basilica in St. Peter's is adorned within and without with effigies of eulogized saints. Even the supposed likeness of God, Himself, is painted in the dome with the direct connotation that somehow there is a spiritual connection between these figureheads and the place where their effigies reside, thus making the supposed Christian morality possible. Yet, is it any different in basic principle than the headhunter and his skull?

Nor are the forms of idolatry and idolatrous worship confined to the artifacts of life or in religious expressions. Even the word on the printed page is an autosuggestive effigy which, through past associations which have been learned, brings about the desired mental reaction to help sustain the oscillating process called thought. So it is that in the most complete and broadest abstraction, the material world is, just as it has always been, a place of idolatry and worship; a place lived as a continuity of autosuggestive forms worshipped as the most complete and absolute reality of life itself, hardly daring to venture into the realm of the unknown.

For, even as the would-be swimmer tries the water with his toe, so is the man of today—through science and through the fancied security of his earthly perch, attempting to try the waters of Infinite space.

The morality of our discussion is not an attempt to condone or condemn idolatry and the effigy. The broad perspectus of evolution demands a beginning point which mandates any expressionary form as an embryo, successively regenerating into higher expressionary forms through association and usage. There is, however, a point of diminishing returns wherein the earth life or embryonic evolution will cease to satisfy the evolutionary demand.

It is at this point the embryonic consciousness begins to expand and reach the higher dimensions of expression. From then on, deistic configurations, the recognition of extraterrestrial power and intelligence are acknowledged. Thus, religious forms and religions are developed; always, however, rigidly confined within the precinct of the reactive effigy of symbolic form.

The final phase of our analysis now enters into a critical point for here we must determine that, as the symbolic form is an effigy, and as its true origin, meaning and purpose is unknown, and as it is combined and recombined in the grand scale of evolution, those who believe in these symbolic forms, use them and pursue them are, therefore, idolatrous.

These statements may be challenged by those who claim to be well versed in the rhetorical or pedantic phases of intellectual culture. They may point to great universities, libraries, laboratories, etc., where an infinite number and variety of classical expressionary forms seemingly present a solid cultural background, a facade of knowledge which apparently might answer all facets and phases of earth life. A close scrutiny and a pursuance to the ultimate ends of these diverse expressionary cultures always leads into blind alleys. The ultimate disillusion of the illusion of the sophisticated cultural expression can only sum up reactive expressions as they are posed in the third dimensional earth life and at no point do any of these expressionary cultures go beyond the line of demarcation bounded by the physical world and repeated from a conclave of historical elements.

Nor has history revealed any such extension of cultural synthesis beyond the rigorous confines of the third dimensional world save one, which is best defined as the Unariun Concept. In several instances, written and unwritten, in different anthropologies, there have been attempts to educate the earth man in the basic elements of Infinite Creation. The life and mission of Jesus was one of these other instances which relate to civilizations not known or recognized.

At the present time, and in the scientific atmosphere of our twentieth century, the greatest of all efforts is now being made to acclimate the earth man into a mental atmosphere more suitable for the growth and propagation of this interdimensional science. This effort is especially intended for those already quickened for the possibility of enlarged mental and spiritual perspectives.

But for the present, however, and for some time to come, the masses of the world will still continue to live largely under the shadow of rhetorical despotism. Society demands rigorous conformity. It violently suppresses creative spontaneity yet gives immortal eulogy to those who have died for the cause of independent creative thinking.

Virtue is not subject to quantitative measurement, but resides purely as an expressionary abstraction which can be constructively used in proportion to understanding. The virtue of any man's life is therefore not measurable in terms of reactive or reactionary values, but rather in esoterical values which challenge man's thinking beyond the need of his reactive life.

In conclusion, if evil and good can be summed up, if a classical definition can be arrived at beyond the normal frame of reference, it would be well said to say the greatest evil in the world could be found in the symbolic form: the symbol without logic, reason, or knowledge to explain its existence and to confirm its continuity in constructive universal expression.

For to believe in and to reside in the influence of a symbolic society only terminates all consciousness at the point of physical death. Even the reason for life and the necessity for its expression is defeated in the symbolic form and those who live completely in the symbolic world face a death in all values which are based on symbolic forms, and which live in consciousness without reason, logic, or the conscious knowledge of their continuity in the interdimensional cosmos.

Perhaps it was more simply summed up by Jesus who said that the camel could pass through the eye of a needle more quickly than a man who loved the world could get to Heaven.

The difference in the material world, the world of reactive form, the false illusion of the transparent solid is quite different than other worlds or planes of life found in the more upper reaches of the spiritual cosmos. Swedenborg tried to describe them in the "Seven Celestial Kingdoms", and most religious liturgies have some sort of a descriptive chronology of the future lives lived beyond death; none, however, present the cold hard scientific facts, nor do they present the entire scope of Infinity.

These factors and all attendant elements can only be learned through progressive evolution. No human can understand them beyond the circumference of his present understanding which is based entirely on the past. And the future, the Infinite breadth and depth of Infinity becomes to him a nebulous theorem if so presented.

To those who are interested in their future, the greatest single accomplishment in personal evolution will be attained at that moment of emancipation, when their mental horizon can be extended beyond the dimensions of the symbolic world.

CHAPTER VI

The Last Supper

One of the daily tasks performed here at the Center is the reading and answering the numerous letters which come to us from those who would aspire to a better way; yet, hardly a task, for it is more often that we joyously read of wondrous happenings.

With all this, however, there is reflected in these letters, the rising and receding tides of emotionalism and desire, defeat and victory in personal conflicts; and in seeing all of these things, I am often reminded of an incident which took place nearly two thousand years ago, a scene depicted as the Last Supper, a time when the Nazarene sat with His twelve disciples and shared with them the symbolic bread and wine. And as this was done, He spoke of one among them who was a traitor and who would soon betray Him to the high priests.

So it is, as I read your letters and watch the conduct of your lives, I know also there is a traitor. For in Unarius we are indeed sharing together the last earthly supper. We are breaking the bread which destroys the symbolic earth life. We are drinking the cup of Immortality; and as we do this, history may well again be repeating itself, for as I look into your faces, I again see the traitor.

No, he is not called Judas Iscariot, but is called the 'Old Self' and he is not one among you—but is a part of each and every one. He will not betray me, or Unarius, or the Infinite, but it is you he betrays. He does this not once but hundreds of times each day; countless thousands of times in the years of your life.

And each time he betrays you, he will deliver you up to the high priests of the underworld.

"And how does he betray me?" you may ask. Through the countless thousands of incidents of daily life, their importance to you, their ability to mandate paramount importance, the way they constantly knead you in emotional reactions. These are all betrayals sponsored and fostered by the 'old self', the person you once were years ago, or in any lifetime and in hundreds of lives. You would not know this betrayer if you saw him, for he is the sum and substance of what you call life—the material life you live from day to day.

Yes, even in death he will betray you, for this death, too, must be relived to justify and compromise the betrayer; and even as you utter your first wail as a newborn infant in some future life, you have again surrendered to the betrayer. Yes, you will continue to live and to be constantly betrayed until you learn to recognize the betrayer.

You must cast upon him the Light of Immortal Wisdom which will bring his countenance into your vision, in all its stark ugly reality; for this Wisdom Light will also show you many other things, a background of Immortal Life lived without the ever present betrayer, lived in constructive reality which harmonizes and unifies all thought and action, without the emotional drive which now makes your earth life possible.

How well you will learn of this betrayer is your personal problem. Do not sleep as did Peter in the dawn of a Gethsemane, for the cock has crowed thrice. The betrayer may well be 'delivering you up' in your last crucifixion, one in which you cannot hope—as you are hoping—that an Angel will roll away the stone from your tomb. For surely has this stone been rolled away many times, yet with each rolling you are all the

61

weaker for not having participated.

As it is with all things, Angels, too, have their limitations, not that they are limited as Angels, but in the limitations they find in helping others who would like to become Angels, yet have neither the strength nor fortitude to extricate themselves from their earthly mire. For indeed this mire can be as quicksand, sucking the poor unfortunate into its depths with each struggle. How best then, can this emancipation be achieved? How can one extricate himself from the quicksands of the material life? Only as it has been so often said: freeing one's self from such mire is cleansing the mind and psychic anatomy from the importance of the material life; for so long as it supersedes in its importance, over other desires and aspirations, so will it cling and grasp and hold.

And in each struggle against it, do not relinquish, even for a brief moment, for you will surely be sucked deeper into it with each surrender. For the material life as it is lived by you or any earth man is, in itself and in its quantitative expression, the supersedence of power which every earthly act of living intensifies as it is so lived in its primary importance.

Only in Infinite Wisdom, the knowledge and desire of a higher life and all things pertaining to this Wisdom, will you find a way to free yourself from your betrayer, and the quicksand of your material life. For Infinite Wisdom will reach out through this blackness to the place of your struggling, and you will be able to grasp it; and when so grasped in complete dedication, your faith will then lend to it its mighty strength to lift you from your earthly mire and you will leave the shadow of your betrayer enmeshed therein forever.

CHAPTER VII

The Kingdom Within

Throughout the many ages of man's written and unwritten history he has, universally, in his daily conduct of life, expressed one great universal fault or error. This fault is that he has always constantly striven to change the outside or exterior surface of his life, in an attempt to make it conform in all factors and elements, in ways, manners and means which seem to best suit his personal interests.

The fallacy of this common psychology is at once apparent to anyone who makes even a cursory analysis of human welfare. All the wars, strifes, human emotionalisms, crimes, perversions, etc., which are expressed by humanity are the direct result of this senseless life psychology. It is in direct opposition to the doctrine of self-development taught by Jesus who said, "Seek the Kingdom Within." The direct interpretation and the solution to all ills and evils suffered by mankind would at once be soluble and eventually disappear, should each person, constructively and objectively, apply himself to this seeking which would, in effect, change this person for the better; thus changing his perspective and position to the reactive world, and so eliminating the strife and turmoil in which he was formerly embroiled, in an attempt to make the world conform to him.

The pages of history reveal the many individual and collective attempts which have been made to re-conform the world. Knights in shining armor made their own individual conquests; the crusades were another collective attempt. Yes, even religion is either directly or indirectly an attempt to conform 'deistic' forces for purposes best suited to individual and collective conduct.

Throughout the Eastern world, and for thousands of years, countless multitudes have rung temple bells and burned incense in the same attempt to use these unknown and vaguely envisioned 'deistic' forces to their own advantage. Perhaps mankind has vaguely and subconsciously, or even consciously to some degree, realized this universal error and has, in his social societies, set up certain rigorous systems of conformities which he may hope will, even partially, invert this error so universally expressed.

The proposition of social conformities at once challenges other agencies of law and order in human conduct; for these conformities, in themselves, should be generally sufficient to define all human conduct. It is quite apparent, however, such is not the case; hence governments which consist of legislative and judicial law enforcement agencies and which again leaves us at the starting place of our analysis. Specifically, it is an individual proposition for every person to begin to constructively analyze his life; to indoctrinate a new system and a new approach to his, and mankind's, reason for existence. And above all else he must realize that all world deficiencies are not subject to reconformity according to his dictum.

Therefore, such a person who is so seeking the Kingdom, who is earnestly seeking the answers to these human enigmas, must objectively apply himself to a constructive analysis of all the apparencies of life. He must seek the real and basic reasons for their expressions and existence, and he must do this without becoming emotionally involved. Unfortunately, as of today, neither religion, science, nor governmental systems, etc., have any answers to these basic reasons of existence. Why man lives on the planet earth . . . why all such things are in apparent necessity, and even the necessity of existence.

It is at this point all analysis ceases and introspection has ended in a blind alley, unless the analysis escapes the third dimension and is carried into the many adjacent planes of existence. Jesus called these the 'many mansions', which obviously comprise the 'Kingdom'. Logically also, it must be assumed in these higher planes and dimensions, that life is quite different in all forms, manners and ways of existence. To learn of this life and these other worlds or planes would be indeed a hopeless and futile undertaking, if the seeker depends upon third dimensional information to yield him this vital knowledge; and which must, obviously, come from other sources.

Fortunately, for mankind, all necessary factors, informative sources, etc., have been built in. In a universal constructive process, Infinite Intelligence has anticipated all needs and provides for them, and on such preface it becomes an individual proposition to discover, through these informative sources and agencies, the new worlds and the new life which fulfills the promise made: that all things are 'added' to anyone who finds this 'Kingdom'.

As an informative source and agency, Unarius is by far, the greatest and most easily accessible source; and anyone who completely devotes and dedicates himself to the pursuance of this 'Inner Kingdom'—through self-development—becomes a wiser person, etc., and has at once defeated the age-old human error of conformity; and he has begun to fully justify the esoterical teachings of Jesus.

Science, too, is equally guilty of this same universal conformity proposition, and as of today, one which still expresses the false doctrine of spontaneous regeneration, despite wide acclaim that it long ago abandoned such a ridiculous assumption as it was postulated in the eighteenth century. Today science tells the story of the first proteide molecule synthesis, generated billions of years ago when the right elements of heat, chemical reaction, etc., were brought together in some primitive ooze. This first proteide molecule then subsequently, synthesized into one-cell protozoa or vegetable chloroplasts. Darwinism, as a whole, does indirectly attempt to vindicate this false doctrine; for here again the real reason for life and what life actually is, has somehow escaped—even the regeneration of new life in a cell is still as great a mystery to science, as it was to the first primitive savage in some predawn age of man's existence.

Nor will the answer to life or what life is—its reason for existence, ever be found in this or similar earth life environments. It will be found only where life more properly begins, in the higher dimensions or the 'Kingdom Within.' And when this true origin is understood, the earth world dimension then becomes, as it properly should be, merely a reflective surface wherein this great Creative, Infinite expression again regenerates a facsimile scale of evolution, bounded by the third dimensional reactive plane factors.

All this information and knowledge is contained in the expressive liturgies of Unarius as they are currently being circulated among those wise enough, and with sufficient conditioning, dedication, etc., to pursue the quest of immortal life, through the channel of knowledgeable self-development. And so long as they so pursue and remain dedicated, so will the promise of the immortal future be gradually unfolded unto them. They will indeed be finding the 'Kingdom Within'.

And so, man is as he has always been an avid conformist. All acts, ways and means of his daily life are always an individual challenge to him to conform them to his own personal mental scale of equivalents and values; so necessary to allay the fears and insecurities of his earth world existence.

He invents systems of social structures, religious orders, governmental systems, etc.; he makes of his world a great and preponderant edifice of false artifacts and idols, and even in the idolatrous worship of his symbolic world, he is again, only attempting to reflect what he believes, the virtues of these things into his well-being. This he will continue to do so long as he is an earth man ascribed to its systems of conformities and protocols and refuses to believe or to conceive that life can be lived any other way.

Even as he probes the Heavens, as he is doing today, he still relegates his judgment of life on other planets from the basic plane reference of his own earth world and condemns life to nonexistence, save by what he is himself. This he does in great opposition, of his knowledge of the atom and of the convertible factor of mass versus energy, as is posed in Einstein's proven theory. He is constantly defeating any promise of logic or reason by proving himself always wrong and that he does not know the answers to his science.

Yet, we must give him some credit; we must reserve judgment and resolve our answers into a philosophical consensus based upon, and predicated by our knowledge of the interdimensional cosmos. As to the future, prophecies and prognostications are for fools who are insecure and lack knowledge, for the future is always immediately apparent to any person who can see beyond the reactive veil of materialisms expressed by the earth world. And in viewing the future, this earth world and millions of others like it, will remain basically much the same.

Like all other things in the cosmic scale of evolution, the earth world occupies its position which is necessary in the first environmental stages of man's development; the reactive stage of his existence where he takes his first step from out the animal kingdom.

CHAPTER VIII

To DNA Or Not to DNA

During the past several years, there have been a number of news articles appearing, which have hinted vaguely, that science was on the edge of a great 'breakthrough'—a discovery which would finally give them the secret of life and the reasons why there were different species of plant and animal life. More recently several articles have appeared in national publications which have exposed this new discovery as centering around the newly found DNA molecule. DNA, incidentally, is the initialed abbreviation for deoxyribonucleic acid.

On December 16, 1962, the National Broadcasting Company exposed a nationwide TV show sponsored by the Bell Telephone Company which was moderated by Dr. Frank Baxter who gave a complete rundown of the DNA molecule. As usual, and as could be expected, this show was done in the customary ostentatious manner which has characterized Dr. Baxter's presentations. Aside from this, however, it was a rather lucid explanation and anyone watching would have gained considerable information.

Briefly, the show first presented Gregory Mendel, the Austrian Monk, who is credited with being the 'Father' of modern genetics. The Mendelian theory of genetical character units was then further developed into the organic bits of substance known as chromosomes, and how science has photographed, through time-lapse photography, the actual reproduction process of cell fission. All cells in any plant and animal life, contain chromosomes. The number varies widely with the species, and apparently science has not discovered the reason for this numerical difference.

A shrimp may have two thousand chromosomes in each cell, a human only forty-six. Also the male and female sex cells, the ovum and sperm, contain only twenty-three each. When a body cell splits or divides, the chromosomes begin to do what could best be described as a country dance, or a Virginia reel; finally dividing and going to their respective half of the cell which then splits.

When a male and female germ cell mate the reverse process goes into effect, after which normal fission begins to take place to develop the embryo. However, science has long known that the chromosomes are not responsible for the different character traits and which vary widely, especially in man. These character traits were supposedly contained in submicroscopic bodies, known as genes. These genes form pearl-like strings around the outside of the chromosomes.

In the early 1950's, research work done on these genes revealed that they, too, were not responsible for character traits, and science began probing deeper for the answer. By 1953, the gene was found to be largely composed of thread-like molecules which have been called DNA molecules, and it is estimated that there are several hundred million miles—if they were connected end to end—of these DNA molecules in every human.

These DNA molecules are remarkable and quite different than any other chemical molecules. They resemble, somewhat, a spiral staircase or, more correctly, two spiral staircases coiled around each other and with a number of steps connecting them laterally along the entire length. These staircase-like molecules are actually composed of atoms such as carbon, oxygen, nitrogen, phosphorus, etc. Also, they are extremely small and must be magnified 100,000 times by means of the electronic microscope before they can be seen. (They are about one ten millionth of an inch in diameter.)

Now, one peculiarity of this DNA molecule is that apparently, as nearly as it can be ascertained, it is the same in goldfish, dogs, and humans and looks exactly alike. Science knows, however, that there must be a difference, otherwise there would be no difference in species. It is believed that the kind of atoms and their arrangement in the step formations inside the spirals determine the species, and also the numerous traits of that species.

Right at this point, however, science has arrived at the end of the usual blind alley. While they know something about the molecule, they have yet to learn why the atoms of different chemicals and in different combinations become so arranged. In other words, they do not know about the evolutionary factors of these atoms, from life to life, and which are controlled from the psychic anatomy. And perhaps the greatest of all enigmas is that while they know atoms are energy solar systems, they cannot seem to determine their behavior as electronic elements or constituents, which in reality they are.

Science does not know that every atom has a psychic anatomy which is the true source of power and contains the idiom of intelligence which characterizes any particular atom. This atomic psychic anatomy is fourth dimensional and is nonreactive and cannot as yet, be measured or discerned in the third dimensional world; it does, however, reflect the idiom and intelligence and the life stream of power into its respective atom. In other words, the atom is an exterior reflective surface. This atom also, in turn, reflects into its surrounding third dimensional world, a certain vibrating energy called a force field or electromagnetic field; and it is compatible or noncompatible with any other or all atoms on the basis of frequency relationship in these respective electromagnetic fields.

Even if science does succeed in relocating the atom in its proper perspective as an expressionary electronic element, science would still have to find its psychic anatomy. From there, the search would have to proceed into the fourth dimension where the idiom of intelligence quotient could be found as an evolutionary factor, cyclically re-expressed and rejoined in all other cyclic movements with the Infinite Cosmos, or the inner planes—the Kingdom, the fourth, fifth, sixth, etc., dimensions. The third dimensional world is, as has been stated, an expressive reactive plane and is part of this cyclic evolution. And whether it is in singular atoms or in the development of new species, the process is always the same and analogous.

These facts have been thoroughly presented and discussed in other Unariun liturgies—particularly the second lesson course; and all recent developments, including Dr. Baxter's exposé, only point up the complete scientific validity of these Unariun presentations. Even further proof is contained in other discoveries, pertaining to this character-conveying DNA molecule.

Through experiments with fruit flies, mice, etc., intense radiation by X-ray machines produced mutations or deformities. The situation here is the same as if you had blocked off the antenna of your TV set with a wire screen. You would get a wobbly distorted picture as long as the screen shielded the antenna from the transmitter. When the DNA molecule is radiated with X-rays, these rays in effect, partially or wholly block out—temporarily at least—the natural, pulsating energy life stream from its psychic anatomy. The molecule then loses its intelligence quotient, and it cannot reproduce its character traits as it would have normally done; hence a mutation or deformity.

This fact should be quite obvious to science, but as long as atoms are sacredly held in the realm of chemical synthesis, they will not get the answers. The same situation holds true in medicine or in any other field of human interpolation. When this barrier is broken down and these false chemical syntheses disappear, science will have by that time arrived at some of the answers which are now being presented to you.

How far into the future this will take place cannot be accurately predicted, as it will be a very slow process. The bastions and citadels of these different scientific dispensations are indeed difficult to broach; even more difficult to overturn the pedestals used as perches by the pedantic overlords of these various sciences. So far as your own personal position is concerned as a Unariun student, if you can, somehow understand what has been presented to you in the liturgies—and even vaguely—you will still be wiser than all the combined scientists of the world today.

The highlight of the show, and a very humorous one, was in Dr. Baxter's explanation of sex determination, which he said was, and I quote, "a fifty-fifty proposition". This was dramatically demonstrated by him, by taking forty-six numbered poker chips—23 white and 23 red—and placing them in a gambling device known as a chuck-a-luck, a cage-like affair which can be rotated, and after several turns the chips were spilled out upon the table. This 50-50 chance proposition was startling.

When I went to school, it was thoroughly drilled

into me—and to my fellow students—that science had to be very exact or it was not science. Apparently, however, when it comes to the sex of a child, natural scientific laws are tossed out of the window. However, what this really amounts to is an evasion, because science lacks the answers.

Dr. Baxter went on to explain the "X" and "Y" factors; it seems the female sperm cell has 23 complete full fledged chromosomes—the male cell only 22 complete, plus 1 (one) which has lost some of its genes and when the mating occurs, if this incomplete chromosome gets the upper hand in the scuffle with the female chromosome, the child will be a male or vice versa. Now this knowledge could be dangerous if it got around; the so-called 'weaker sex' could really crow and say they were complete and superior. It might also be said that so far as the adult male was concerned, in his affiliations with the adult female, that he had 'lost some of his genes' (or marbles). All of these assumptions are quite evidently incomplete and slightly ridiculous. The scientist does not know the many other important controlling factors involved which can more correctly determine the sex of a child.

In the original Mendelian concept of genetics, a mathematical formula of sex and characteristics was developed. This formula apparently has been dropped with the discovery of DNA. The scientist does not know however, that the psychic anatomy of a spiritual being attaches itself, harmonically speaking, to the embryo and actually becomes the new human being. This spirit being then reflects its own characteristic personality, a process previously described in our liturgies.

While it is possible and most likely true, DNA does, however, convey many or even all physical characteristics of parents or ancestors, DNA cannot and does

not, however, convey the individual human characteristics which are so evident in all people. If there are
similarities in human characteristics between parents
and children, they have not been instituted by DNA.
They have been developed as polarity through former lifetime associations. Also, in any conveyance, DNA
serves only as a carrier; the determining intelligence
comes from the respective psychic anatomies. (DNA is
not the life nor the intelligence, but only reflects or
conveys certain life intelligence.)

These facts, too, have all been adequately described throughout Unarius' teachings. To sum it all up,
therefore, these latest scientific discoveries only reveal
the great and obvious disparities and enigmas which
exist in various scientific dispensations. It is also
a revelation in comparative values as to how low in
the scale of evolution mankind still is; worse, new
discoveries in the same third dimensional vein, only
intensify this position and make it increasingly difficult
to break down the barrier between this and the adjacent dimensions.

A thought could be introduced at this point: it
could be that our present-day scientists are largely
comprised of reincarnated aboriginal tribes-people who
formerly lived in the Atlantean or Lemurian ages
at which time, the Master Scientists of those eras
attempted to teach these same concepts to these elemental minds. The failure to learn produced a mental
blockage in the development of these people; hence
their striving for an evolutionary outlet wherein they
can attempt to learn, conform, and re-express this
higher science as was taught by the Master Scientists
from other worlds. If this is so, it is quite apparent
that they are still laboring against the jumping off
place. They can learn and express third dimensional

quotients and equivalents, but cannot carry their science into the Infinite Cosmogony.

Note—the author does not assume responsibility as to the accuracy of any figures or statements quoted from the aforementioned TV show or for any such figures or statements from any existing science; such existing concepts are constantly changing as these respective sciences uncover new information. Only the Unariun facts, concepts and principles will forever remain valid and irrefutable.

CHAPTER IX

Miracles?

In a number of places in the Unariun literature we have mentioned miracles. We have used this subject in frequent discussions in our books and, in most cases, a distinct attempt has been made to play down the miracle and its importance, and for reasons which we shall discuss. We have even used references and claims of miracles in our advertising media; so in all fairness to you and to us, we will 'lay it on the line' so to speak and be perfectly frank and honest.

No, we are not attempting to back down from claims we have made regarding miracles that have happened to people who have become Unariuns. In almost all cases, miracles have happened to those who have joined Unarius. There is, however, an occasional, and fortunately quite rare case wherein some individual becomes disturbed, who thinks he has been cheated because he claims no miracle has happened to him despite the obvious fact that even without a miracle he has become a much more intelligent human by simply reading the Unarius works which would make this small investment mere trivia.

We here at the Center, including the Moderator, do not deny miracles and we are constantly at work with the Unariun Brotherhood to achieve at least one miracle in each Unariun's life. However, we do this with certain reservations: that every Unariun must thoroughly understand the nature of a miracle and the reason it was worked for him.

Unless it is so thoroughly understood, a miracle is more dangerous than a stick of dynamite in the hands of a child. Instead of doing great good, it can actually become a deadly opiate. It can make a person dependent on future miracles for the dissolution of all future problems and crises. Thus, it will destroy his moral integrity, the will to learn, the reason to live, etc.

Finally, to clarify the subject of miracles, we should describe what a miracle is. Of course you have read about the miracles of Jesus and you may have had your own miracle. All of this however, may be a lot of magic, hocus-pocus-abracadabra, etc., until all elements and processes are clearly understood. There is no magic in a miracle. It is a lot of preparation and hard work using the highest scientific principles and knowledge available to personalities who have advanced beyond the earth life.

A miracle therefore, should be received as a personal beneficent blessing; one to help us overcome some great problem but above all, it should convey to us a personal message which portrays to us the undreamed of, unlimited potential of human consciousness. It should suggest to us the possibility that you, or any person can develop this potential to the point where and when the miraculous way is a way of life and, in this realization, the great desire is born to achieve this development and thus acquire this great human potential as a realistic life expression.

Therefore, as a Unariun, if you had, or that you may have a miracle happen to you, then accept it as a challenge to develop your own potentials. Do not let it become a moral opiate whereby you will become dependent and mentally flaccid or unable to solve your own problems. And if you work at it hard enough and long enough, you will be able to acquire miracles by your own efforts.

Until such time, however, the Unariun Brotherhood

stands ready to assist in and deliver miracles to those deserving students who have met and fulfilled the necessary requisites which are most necessary in the initial stages of their development.

A miracle happening in anyone's life took, quite possibly, hundreds of years in preparation and preconditioning. Finally, at the right moment and at certain junctions of cycles, etc., certain great energy Powers come from the Minds of the Higher Beings, psychokinetically projected. Other Powers come from certain kinds of scientific apparatus which have been described in the books. The combination of these intelligent energy Powers changes, alters, cancels and reconstitutes psychic anatomy malformations with subsequent rehabilitation of the physical anatomy and the expressionary phase of life.

So, if you look forward to the time when you can perform miracles, just remember it is hard work; harder work than you have ever done before. (And perhaps it is fortunate that the Advanced Personalities do not perspire, otherwise the earth might well be drenched and drowned by Their efforts to keep the world in some semblance of harmony and make evolution possible for the earth man).

CHAPTER X

Reflections

In our pattern of evolution there are many Gardens of Eden when we are tempted by a serpent and which is, of course, a symbol or material representation of values which seem the most pertinent to our existence. Perhaps this might be a good point to clarify my position in general with Unarius. We are not teaching a new system, a new rote, or a new form of symbologies; we are teaching personal emancipation from all symbolic forms. This can best be visualized when we realize that, up until the present time, this past and present life, to you or any human, has been lived in a dimension of symbology. Everything about you or in this world, and to every other human, is a pattern of symbologies. Even writing and speech are visual and audible symbols.

Every human, therefore, who has ever lived or is living, has extracted his values of life by comparing one symbolic form against another. The house he lives in is a dimension of symbologies which he is constantly comparing with his neighbor's house. His political and religious affiliations are also symbolic. Even the priest in his church is a symbolic representation to a symbolic god; and so this human, whoever he is, has not yet learned to live within the pure dimension of understanding the Infinite as an integrated, recreative function.

Therefore, in his present comparative system of symbologies, all things, in these comparisons, become reactive against each other. It is in this reaction that we find the destructive or constructive content which people call evil and good; whereas, within the pure dimension of understanding the Infinite, evil and good attain a functional integration which is independent of any reactive comparisons.

The Infinite resides in consciousness as a complete wholeness in everything. It cannot be understood on the basis of old symbologies which have existed in the past, nor can It be understood in present symbologies. Even science is still a symbolic form as it resides in mathematical calculus, yet science does contain third dimensional elements which, while pertinent to this world, exist solely by virtue of the fact that these third dimensional scientific elements are possible only as an adjunctive expression of the Infinite.

Therefore, any human who is still, in essence, a third dimensional creature, who wishes to aspire to a higher way of life, must begin to understand the Infinite in the most logical manner which will enable him to do so. This he does by beginning to understand third dimensional forms as they exist as part of the Infinite, not as symbolic forms, but as constructive entities of expression which are part of the whole.

Mass, therefore, must be resolved into tiny solar systems of energy called atoms. These, in turn, are re-linked, through their respective vortexes, harmonically interplaying with certain forces of cosmic hysteresis into a great, expanded consciousness of the Infinite. Thought, too, becomes an adjunctive principle of function; for, here again, within the interplay of dynamic wave forms, we are constantly functioning with our respective psychic anatomies which are, in turn, inter-linked in a like manner to the Infinite.

This interdimensional concept does not require symbols for proper understanding, for when such understanding is acquired by any human, he will not, by that time, be living in a third or reactive dimension. Instead, as an entity of consciousness, he will be living in the interplay of Infinite Creative Function which is vastly different than the third dimensional reactionary systems. Such an interdimensional understanding, however, is far beyond the understanding of any human presently living.

Most people, however, have a vague sense of an underlying consciousness of this great Infinite. It is the problem of Unarius to approach the more advanced and preconditioned element of humanity and begin to explain to them the first principles of creative harmony. This is done through the doorway of presently existing sciences. In this way future evolutions and lifetimes can be presupposed to be relatively larger expansions of consciousness which will gradually emancipate this human from his old world of symbols.

Unarius must, by necessity, therefore exist in its first stages as a symbology. It must to a certain degree or extent, represent form as it exists in present consciousness, for it is understandable that any person would instinctively rebel against any unknown elements with which he may be confronted.

However, it must be ultimately resolved by the aspirant who is studying the works of Unarius, that all symbologies must be dissolved in his consciousness as reactive elements of life; and instead a much more expanded degree of consciousness will subsequently reunite these various reactive elements into functional harmony with the Infinite.

Unarius, too, will reoccupy a new position, not symbolically, but as an amalgamated representation of this same participating consciousness with Infinity wherein, individually speaking, each person assumes an integrated function with the Infinite and can, in this position, live within the pure dimension of consciousness. So far as I, individually or personally, am so concerned, I do not wish to become a symbol as did Jesus, Buddha, Mohammed, or any others who have given something to the posterity of mankind; granted of course, that the teachings of Unarius would reach some world-wide proportion; nor have I any wish to be eulogized either in the present or the future. My position with the Infinite is such that I do not depend upon the platitudes of great multitudes. Applause is only food and drink to a psychopath.

In fact, I do not even claim to be a teacher, for in expressing the concepts and principles with which I am familiar, they, in themselves, as forms of consciousness with the Infinite, will transform any person who succeeds in integrating them into his consciousness. For who can say he is a teacher when even as he teaches he is being taught and which, when it is all summed up, merely means that I, as a human being, would like to be subtracted as an ego form or element from these works. For only in this subtraction can any aspirant hope to wean himself from dependency in such personal representation which I might assume to him.

In other words, the cause of Unarius would be lost to any person who transfers his quest and pursuit of Infinite knowledge from the dimension of pure absolute impersonal consciousness and focuses his attention upon what I might represent to him. This subtraction of self from what I represent and express becomes, in turn, a way in which I am personally expressing unison with the Infinite as a creative entity of consciousness, and which in re-transferring it into expressive third dimensional forms becomes substance of my physical life and as I so reside within the dimension of pure consciousness, so will the Infinite re-express Itself in constructive evolution wherever I might be. So my physical body is nourished and housed, for it, too, has become a transitory element of expression.

This then, dear ones, is the way of life, such as any human will learn if he succeeds in attaining evolutionary continuity into Infinity; conversely he will destroy himself. This is not a problem of personal relationships which may exist between us, but rather it is a personal problem where, individually speaking, we attain a more correlative existence with the Infinite.

It is my wish, therefore, in the future that any whispering or doubt which may come to you shall not subtract from your purpose which might occur if you personify Unarius through me. Rather, Unarius should represent to you—the Infinite and a way and means in which you will achieve immortality and a Higher Way.

Personally, our relationship should assume a brothership wherein we become united in Principle, but not into such personal elements which may arouse personal conflict. For, as kindred souls in expressing Principle, we are indeed true brothers—not as two reactionary elements or dimensions of consciousness so poised that we are either destructive or constructive to each other on the basis of emotional comparisons. In this way I can always look at you as a perfect expression of the Infinite, just as we should all ultimately resolve all third dimensional aspects into this harmonious continuity of expression with the Infinite.

May you never again be subtracted from a higher destiny; may your sincere dedication always reside upon the highest niche of your altar of life and out of reach of the dirty fingers of the underworld.

CHAPTER XI
Long-Cherished Science Theory Proved False

Chemists Learn That So-Called Inert Gases Do Combine With Other Elements

Chemistry has received an embarrassing nudge because at least a million scientists during the last half century failed to be skeptical about a simple gas experiment.

Essentially, chemistry students the world over have been taught and have accepted the idea that chemical elements called inert gases would not combine with other chemical elements to form compounds.

This now has been proved to be wrong. Inert gases can and do form compounds with other elements. And, as a result of this discovery; most chemistry textbooks, including those published this year, must be revised.

The Noble Gases

A theory of bonding to explain what holds elements together must be looked at in a new light.

A host of new chemical compounds has been made possible.

The inert gases are argon, neon, helium, krypton, xenon and radon. They are also called the "noble" gases because it was thought that they would not mix with anything else.

The inert gases are natural constituents of the atmosphere. Three of the gases—neon, argon and helium—have found wide and varied use. But the others, largely because they are expensive, have few important commercial uses today.

Most textbooks describe the inert gases along the lines of the following excerpt from a college chemistry text published last year: "The inert gases are distinguished by the fact that they already have complete outer electron levels and do not gain, share or lose electrons. Having no bonding energy, they form no compounds and thus exhibit no chemical reactions."

Concept Invalidated

This is what students last spring, like their fathers and grandfathers before them, had been taught and had failed to question. But this summer a series of simple experiments, requiring nothing that was not available to chemists a half century ago, invalidated this long-held concept.

The table-turning discoveries began last summer when Prof. Neil Bartlett of the University of British Columbia mixed colorless xenon gas with a brownish platinum hexafluoride gas and produced a yellowish powder which identified as xenon-platinum hexafluoride.

Bartlett conducted his experiment because he was curious about the results of his own earlier investigations with platinum compounds that easily combined with molecular oxygen.

Complex Chemical

Bartlett's xenon compound—the first ever reported —was a complex chemical. It was for this reason that three scientists at the Atomic Energy Commission's Argonne National Laboratory decided to try a simpler approach. After first repeating Bartlett's work, John G. Malm, Henry H. Selig and Howard H. Claassen decided to explore the possibility of a direct relation between xenon and fluorine, which is the most reactive of all elements.

The Argonne research team placed one part of xenon and about five parts of fluorine together in a sealed nickel container. The mixture was then heated to 400 degrees centigrade for one hour, then rapidly cooled to room temperature.

What the scientists found as a result of this simple process were colorless crystals of a new compound—xenon tetrafluoride.

Since that time, the Argonne chemists have succeeded in forming other xenon compounds, as well as radon compounds, and they are now looking for ways to produce krypton compounds. Six other laboratories have now confirmed the fact that inert gases form compounds. And more recently, scientists at Princeton University have developed theories to explain what holds these particular compounds together.

The discovery has its theoretical and practical consequences. On the one hand, the new knowledge that inert gases form stable compounds opens the door, as the Argonne scientists reported, "to investigations which should more closely integrate this group of chemical elements with the rest of the periodic table."

On the other hand, compounds formed with inert gases will find use in space science, reactor technology and other research fields. One possibility, for example, is that they will provide a means for taming volatile fluorine gas to make it easily transportable and usable.

In a recent issue of Science, an editorial by the distinguished American scientist Philip Abelson had this to note about the discovery: "There is a sobering lesson here, as well as an exciting prospect . . . all that was required to overthrow a respectable and entrenched dogma was a few hours of effort and a germ of skepticism—the great shortage in science now—is more of that healthy skepticism which generates the key idea—the liberating concept."

HERE IT IS

A frank admission in bigotry—only partially mitigated in confession. Indeed! Could it be that in retrospection, all world sciences, religions and philosophies could, by comparison to infinity, be likewise bigoted and apocryphal?

On December 19, 1962, a certain article appeared in the Los Angeles Times which exposed a scientific discovery of great importance. So much so, that it has been reproduced for you in its entirety in the foregoing. This article first appeared in the Washington Post and was exclusively reprinted in the Los Angeles Times; and while it reveals a scientific discovery of considerable importance, it is also, as you have read, a situation of great embarrassment to a million or more scientists, as well as teachers and professors who are involved in this situation.

Briefly, the article deals with a time honored and 'hallowed' concept taught by science, that the so-called 'free' or noble gases as listed in the article could not be combined with other elements. For more than half a century, this false and erroneous assumption was taught in schools, colleges and universities to hundreds of millions of students. Only quite recently, simple experiments which were available at the time that this assumption was postulated, have proven this assumption false.

The article, however, deals more specifically with all factors involved and does not need repeating. The point in toto, which is again being emphatically, stressed by Unarius, is that this article and exposé so dramatically point up the unintelligent attitude science and the scientists take—a sort of rhetorical pedantic despotism which attempts to crush all opposition, suppress all new enterprise, except those enterprises and endeavors which must come from within the 'sacred' halls of science itself, despite the very obvious fact that progress in science is predicated upon new revelations, irrespective of origins or personalities involved in such revelations.

Science or scientists, however, can take some small measure of consolation in their embarrassment in this exposé; there have been hundreds, yes, many thousands of incidents of a similar nature when 'hallowed' scientific concepts have been exploded as myths. Even the 'sacred' and revered Newton has been, in some areas, proven false and incomplete in the face of new quantum mathematics, postulated by Einstein and others who followed.

As a matter of fact, science, in its pursuance and quest for new knowledge, is constantly either directly or indirectly, proving itself wrong and insufficient. Now the reason for this situation is quite apparent; it is trying to validate a material science based upon a third dimensional hypothesis, rather than develop an interdimensional science, which would prove valid in all extensions and in all dimensions. This interdimensional science has been constantly reinstated in the Unariun Concept.

However, for the present at least, as this is a material, third dimensional world, scientists therefore are quite human and it is quite logical to assume that they will go right on making mistakes and suffering embarrassment; needlessly perhaps, for mistakes are justifiable in progress. They are not justifiable, however, when perpetuated as a false dogma, such as has been revealed in this article.

This article does also, once again prove, that as of this time, mankind is—even in his highest expression and form of life—still on a comparatively low plane of existence in his evolution. He is still practicing a crude and barbaric life based on the emotional plane and has only faintly begun to discern or recognize the tremendous possibilities of Infinity—an understandable Infinity which has been compounded for you, dear student, in the Unariun books and lesson courses.

CHAPTER XII

People Do The Dog-gondest Things

In making observations in the daily conduct of human affairs throughout the world and sometimes with certain Unariun students, I am often reminded of one of those classical stories and bits of philosophy left to posterity by Aesop.

This story concerns a certain dog who, after the manner of dogs, spent much of his time foraging among the dump heaps of the neighborhood. Now it happened one day that this dog found a particularly choice morsel, a large bone with succulent bits of meat still adhering to it. Eagerly grasping his prize in his jaws, he started to trot back home where he could better enjoy his repast and, on the way, chanced to pass over a footbridge under which was a pool of water; and as he was passing over, he chanced to look over the edge and saw his reflection. As a dog, he knew nothing of the laws of optics and so, thinking this was another dog approaching him to rob him of his prize, he opened his mouth to growl and in doing so, lost his grasp on his bone, which fell into the water.

How often it is we see the emotional interplay of peoples, of communities and nations, growling at each other and, in their emotion, losing the many and obvious blessings of everyday living which could be theirs with a less emotional conduct. The arms race between this country and Russia is a typical example of growling at imaginary dogs.

However, we can, to some extent, partially philosophize the conduct of nations and people. They, like the dog, do not really know the scientific reasons behind life, what life is, proper conduct, etc., even though they may profess, in their religion, a higher and less reactionary way of life, they will, at any given opportunity, growl at the next imaginary dog.

To the Unariun student, however, there is a double indemnity if he still persists in his old imaginary reactive way. In joining such an organization as Unarius, he has, automatically, confessed and acknowledged to himself and to countless billions of advanced Personalities living in higher worlds, that he has been in effect, living a dog's life; he has been growling at shadows from the past for lo his many lifetimes! And each time he opened his mouth to growl, he lost—temporarily at least—all of the goodness and virtue in his life, always followed by a period of self-recrimination, sometimes self-flagellation, new avows, new resolutions to do better, etc.

Up until the time that he became a Unariun, however, we could say he was just another earth man and didn't know any better; nor did he have the necessary strength for reform—until he had certain definite knowledge of life—and the answers to many heretofore unanswered things. After joining Unarius, however, he was given all this pertinent and vital information. He was also given personal demonstrations that there was a higher way of life which had been achieved by others who were now in a position to help him.

Sometimes he saw these people as bright pin points of Light—others have smelled Their effulgences . . . . . . felt the power of Their presence, etc., but in whatever way it was that he received his demonstrations and inward convictions, he now had a great power in his hands—a power which could be constructively used to mold him into a better human being.

This molding process, taking place through evolution, would gradually bring him to that time when he would not open his mouth to growl at imaginary dogs. However, as time is—interdimensionally speaking—nonexistent, there is always confronting the Unariun the proposition that, if he is mentally capable, he can in a moment's time, so to speak, grasp the entirety of this evolution and to a certain extent, eliminate much of that backbreaking ground work called karma.

In other words he will see at this particular moment that his emotional reaction to the world about him is only his old dog growling, brought up to the present; and if he has an ounce of brains, he will stop it right at that point. Unfortunately, however, these resolutions may be frequently made and just as frequently broken; it requires considerably more than spurts of self-determination and resolutions to stop growling. It requires the personal accumulation of a vast knowledge of the Infinite, plus the requirement of never-ending objective self-analysis, universal retrospection and real and genuine attempts to use this knowledge, as well as to see it in action.

Such a determined course of evolution to become a better person will definitely achieve results. The results are always proportionate to the effort; and it should be well to note to these self-determined Unariuns that the shadowy dogs of the past will appear in many forms—not just as dogs, but in practically any particular aspect or way of life—even your daily living habits are these dog images; and so long as you react to them, you are growling at them and each time you respond to their influence you are, in effect, losing temporarily at least, some of that determination, and hard fought for progress.

Therefore, do not attempt to placate yourself by saying, "I'm still in the world or a human being" or "I have to do as others do", etc. Put this world and your life in it where it most properly belongs—in your past, even though you may live it hundreds of lifetimes in the future, you will have to constantly remember that this physical material life at any present moment is your past; and in your response to it as a primary consideration is a dog growling at reflections.

The effort then, which must be constantly made, is in this realization: these scientific laws of regeneration are constantly at work and they are inviolate; your present physical material life is made possible only from this past. Like the water under the bridge, the psychic anatomy is at all times reflecting this past into your present; and if you do like the dog on the bridge did —believe it is the real thing—you will be constantly reacting emotionally toward it. It will have primary importance in your life and you will constantly be losing your strength, your purpose and a better future.

So let us take a new and firmer resolution—not merely to quit reacting emotionally, but to always carry foremost in our minds this most important equation in life: to understand the material life in the present as merely new and readapted forms of the past and to keep it more properly where it belongs, in the past, and of secondary importance. We must always carry in our minds the supreme wisdom of Infinite Intelligence and how this Intelligence conceived the only possible way that any form of life could evolve, could readapt itself and become a better expression of life, is through evolution.

Evolution is possible only through the doorway of personal experience. To become infinitely wise means going through an infinite number of experiences and to have mastered them in a way which gives positive impetus to future evolutions. The net product of each experience can thus be maintained infinitely as part of the personal intelligence, thus making wisdom infinitely possible.

How this is done is most adequately explained in the books and lessons. May it be that you will return again and again to them; and each time you do so, you will be able to glean more from them and they will in effect, not only be your lifeline in the present circumstances of life, but they will plainly mark your course into the future.

CHAPTER XIII

The Incredible Laser Beam
(Light Amplification by Stimulated
Emission of Radiation)

One of the most difficult propositions for the Unariun student to acquire is what might be called the speed differential, or all known third dimensional speeds versus the fourth dimensional concept which eliminates such a point-to-point speed differential, and automatically eliminates space. How this is done has been simply explained in cyclic phenomena; for any fourth dimensional entity of expression being cyclic in motion is self-contained, thus eliminating time and space. Even this simple explanation, however, is difficult and must constantly be worked with; and life on a higher world will be largely dependent upon how well you master this concept.

For instance, the faculty of communication between people in higher worlds is not done through speech or any other forms as you know them. It is a process best described as mental telepathy, quite similar in some respects to 'ordinary' mental telepathy, even as it is used consciously or unconsciously by earth people, is not, however, a third dimensional proposition. The vibrations or oscillations which radiate from the psychic anatomy in this process of communication are fourth dimensional in nature. They oscillate within themselves at incomprehensible speeds where, in such motions they regenerate a system of harmonics which links and relinks them, individually speaking, to the innermost reaches of the Infinite Cosmogony.

You can picture this better if you see these little circles of vibration already in existence throughout the

Infinite in all sizes, and vibrating at slightly different speeds. Your thought then, automatically attunes itself in a somewhat chain-like fashion throughout the Infinite. This thought and any given thought, which you may be thinking, is at all times, so attuned to the Infinite where it constantly regenerates itself forever. And right here is the moral lesson: not to cast off into the Infinite, destructive or degenerative thoughts, for as they are attuned to you, so they will remain a part of you forever and you can only prevent their destructiveness from recurring through scientific knowledge and application.

As of today scientists have a machine known as an electroencephalograph, which they believe, measures brain waves; however, while it is true they do measure a certain subharmonic, which has been regenerated as a carrier in the thought process, these wave forms are not thought waves. These mysterious electrical impulses which activate the nerves are such that science cannot measure and knows nothing about save that they create muscular action.

In recent years scientists have bounced radar or radio waves off the surface of the moon where they returned to the earth. The round trip takes about two and one-half seconds (2½) and although these waves travel at the speed of light (186,000 miles per second), they are slower than a snail compared to thought waves. However, man, and particularly scientists of today, have been and are still confused about speed. Our present day science still tries to measure speed between two given points. Such concepts are not adequate when measuring fourth dimensional speeds.

For instance, scientists today, throughout the world, are madly and enthusiastically working on a new discovery; it is called a laser beam, which is simply a coherent beam of light. Now when light comes from any given source, it tends to fan out in a wide area because there are many frequencies of light, which tend to bounce upon each other, thus the spreading effect, and quick dissipation. A laser or coherent light beam is, however, different. It is a single beam of dark red light which has been accelerated in its vibration to a tremendous speed—about 750 trillion times per second. That is much faster than anything else known to science; and it is estimated that such a simple single beam of light can carry simultaneously, at least 2000 or more TV programs.

Now this is a great mystery to the scientist. In ordinary TV transmission a single wave vibrating roughly at 100 million times per second can carry only one TV program; however, when this vibration is speeded up some 750 million times, a single beam of light the size of a pencil, can now carry several thousand TV programs. The reason for this phenomena is not known to the scientists; he does not yet comprehend that it is the speed of the vibration which determines the ability to carry one or more programs. In other words, at 750 trillion times per second, the light beam can pick up and deliver 2000 TV programs so quickly that the scientist cannot measure the differences in individual pickup and delivery in terms of any known speed.

The light beam does not really carry 2000 programs at the same time; what it does, is to pick up and carry each one individually at any given point, so rapidly that as many as 2000 can be picked up and carried individually without any measurable difference in time. Thus the scientist believes it is simultaneous. However, even 750 trillion times per second is still slow compared to thought waves.

The astronomer speaks of millions of light years

between universes. Light traveling at its 186,000 miles per second speed has been believed to be measured at more than two billion years in the length of its transmission; yet thought waves could span this same distance in less time than you could wink your eye. As has been stated, this may be quite incomprehensible to you or to our scientists; it is a concept, however, which will have to be mastered before you can communicate and live satisfactorily in a higher world. However, do not despair if this seems too enormous a proposition. To be perfectly fair with you, it should be stated that as a human, you already began this process, although in a very vague way; and further along your evolution as a Unariun you have recognized the obvious necessity and have begun to work more comprehensively to master this most necessary science.

As a small child you learned the guttural sounds called speech which you now use to communicate; this same speech which you now use, might have been incomprehensible in a former lifetime; likewise, mental telepathy or voluntary thought transmission, as used in the higher worlds, will, in some future time, be just as comprehensible as is your present speech. And when you acquire reasonable mastery in mental communication, you can and will be in simultaneous communication consciously and in a usable form with the entire Infinite Cosmogony.

Because of its great importance, the subject of the laser beam should be explored to its fullest extent, for it may well be, that this new development will actually be the doorway through which science will, in the future, lead the people of the world into that era of life which is being lived so redundantly, by more advanced peoples on other planets; and it will, at the same time, make the interdimensional science contained in your

Unarius books and lessons a reality to all people, and an integrated and useful part of that future era of life.

Perhaps scientists of the present have, intuitively to some extent, realized the important and prophetic possibility. That is why the U.S. government, along with large and small private corporations, such as Hughes Aircraft, Douglas, etc., are spending hundreds of millions of dollars developing the laser beam, and its possibilities.

Let us first find how this beam is generated. First there is a synthetic or manufactured ruby rod, about five inches long and one-half inch in diameter. The ends of this rod are made optically flat, then silvered; one end being more lightly coated than the other. Around this rod there is coiled a small glass tube; several turns are made in the coil and it is filled with an inert gas. The ends of this tube are then connected to an oscillator which is a coil and capacitor arrangement capable of vibrating electricity. This vibrating electricity then, in turn, vibrates the molecules in the gas tube, very similar to a neon sign. As these molecules vibrate, they induce a vibration in the molecules of the ruby rod. These vibrations then, begin bouncing back and forth between the silvered ends; as they do so they are jostled or pushed into higher speed by the bouncing gas molecules. Finally when this bouncing back and forth has created an enormous speed, something like 700 or more trillion times per second, then this wildly oscillating energy bursts forth in a thin pencil-like beam from the end which had the thinnest silver coat.*

At present laser beams last only a fraction of a second; but scientists are working on devices to give a continuous uninterrupted beam. The possibilities of this beam are enormous. It has already been used to 'weld' the retina on a human eye and no doubt it will find, in the future, many uses in medicine and surgery. The laser beam is extremely powerful; it has burned holes through the hard steel of a razor blade and has destroyed diamonds. In this area it is a potential death ray weapon which might be used by the armies of the future. A laser does not spread or disintegrate as does ordinary light. Recently a laser beam was bounced off the moon and when it returned to earth, it was only two miles in diameter. An ordinary light beam would have been lost in the first few miles.

Scientists believe the laser beam will be the way in which man can communicate across the vast distances of space, should he ever succeed in developing inter-planetary travel. These beams may also be used in future radio, TV, and telephone transmission systems; a single laser beam can carry 2000 or more transmissions simultaneously. In short, the laser beam has already suggested numerous uses of electrical energy; some have already been in use for eons of time by more highly developed people living on other planets in our galaxy or universe. There are also other great possibilities not yet envisioned by our scientists. For instance replacing archaic and primitive power generating and distributing systems now in use throughout the civilized world.

In the subterranean cities of Mars, laser-like power beams connect the houses to the generator, replacing the unsightly and dangerous wires, poles, transformers, towers, etc. which are now in use in our cities. Inside the house tiny motors the size of ping pong balls would replace the huge heavy and inefficient motors such as are used on your vacuum cleaner, washing machine, etc. These tiny motors would produce more power at a small fraction of consumed energy as the conventional ones now in use. The walls and ceilings of the house would be luminescent, replacing our present old fashioned lighting systems, which are only a step removed from the candle. Heating would also be done in a different way; the house and the people inside would be warmed by a certain kind of high-frequency radiation done with oscillators, replacing heaters and furnaces now in use. The housewife would find no dust in this home; the house would be hermetically sealed against the outside; and the air taken in through an electronic purifier would be thoroughly cleansed. The science of high-frequency electronics ushered in by Tesla in the early 1900's could also be developed, not only with the above suggested usages, but there would be thousands of other uses in industry and agriculture. High-frequency generators situated on tall towers could remove all the smog from the polluted air of a large city.

Sewage could also be reconverted into pure fresh water to be used for irrigation purposes; solid substances extracted from sewage would become fertilizer and other by-products, all made perfectly safe and practical through high-frequency radiation, thus eliminating a great present day problem of sewage disposal, contamination of oceans and beaches, etc. Household trash and garbage as well as sewage could be quickly and easily disposed of, without smoke or odor by disintegrating this waste with high-frequency radiation. Offensive smoke from cigarettes and other sources would be instantly banished. Cooking a meal would be a heatless, odorless proposition, food being cooked without heat or odor in a few minutes' time, from the inside out, by high-frequency radiation a process now already in use.

By controlling positive-negative ionization in the upper atmosphere and ionosphere, the weather could be controlled to suit the needs of mankind. Fresh water in abundance could be easily procured by de-salting sea-water, at a few cents per thousand gallons, making our present water distribution systems from dams, lakes, and reservoirs obsolete and old fashioned.

Super-heated steam traveling through small pipes at enormous speed would connect up different cities where this steam would be condensed into water and distributed. Vast underground reservoirs could be made with nuclear explosions where water could be stored for thousands of years; yes, even the production of atomic energy would become old fashioned and obsolete a cumbersome, unwieldy and dangerous process of producing energy, which would be laughed at by citizens in that future time. All this and much more will be made possible when science hurdles the now invisible barrier which separates this third dimensional world from the Infinite Cosmos—a false barrier erected by the ignorant and bigotrous masses of people who have refused to admit the abundance of Infinite Creation, a barrier which will become a monument to those hypocrites who are now still trying to confine this Infinite Creation in their mathematics, their test tube, or their Bible.

Yet, even so, all of these uses of ultra high-frequency energies which man may find in his future, as they have been suggested, in the preceding paragraphs, are but a small part of a tremendous potential storehouse which is the Infinite. The scientists of the future may indeed find a way to tap this vast invisible sea of pulsating energy which is everywhere about us, and while though invisible to man, fills—so-called—space; and when he does so, he can build his flying saucer which being propelled by these vast invisible forces, can easily escape the gravitational field of this small planet and at tremendous speeds many times faster than light, he can journey from planet to planet, solar system to solar system, galaxy to galaxy. Yes, he will find planets much like our own and there will be others who have been using this higher science for thousands of years.

He may even find lost and dead civilizations, people who have had a way of life—yes, they have even developed much of this science, but in doing so they have gone beyond the normal course of their evolution. They have been mentally incapable of keeping up with the rapid rate of mental expansion which that science thrust upon them, and being mentally unable to compensate and adapt themselves, perished by the science of their own making. And here could be the moral lesson for the earth man; even at this time there are strongly marked signs that mankind in general, has exceeded the normal progress of his evolution. The peoples of the world are becoming frustrated and decadent in the fast moving pace of their scientific society. They have been unable to compensate for the many synthetic factors of life which have been thrust upon them; for there is nothing in their former evolution which they can use to compensate in this vast melange of scientific society. The handwriting is already on the wall—it has written its dire prophecy of doom to those who cannot compensate, who cannot adjust, and who will not prepare themselves for the future. Nor will any present day religious system offer any hope, for they are only the primitive remnants of a deistic witchcraft, which has somehow survived as part of man's evolution.

What will your course of action be? Will you perish by either of these systems, a false synthetic society devoid of life-giving progressive evolution? Will it be death through dependency for salvation and future life, through intercession by some false god? Or will you prepare yourself logically and sanely by learning of the Infinite; how to progressively reinstate the entity of your own personal intelligence in successive and progressive stages of development into the Infinite, thus automatically insuring immortal life. This will be a choice you will have to make—not once, but constantly as you wander through the chaos of your everyday life; for you will see everything about you, temptations of an infinite variety which seem to shout some false message of security. They will be church steeples and temple bells; they will be doctors' offices, clinics and hospitals. There may be flying saucer sightings, and a rash of movements and cults all vainly promising your immortality; how well will you survive these temptations? How well can you remain dedicated to the one true course through evolution in your seeking and finding the Kingdom Within?

* This reoscillating or jostling process, while of academic interest could be more scientifically described as the ability of different atoms, such as chromium, etc., compounded in the ruby rod, to absorb energy in sponge-like fashion and under right conditions release this absorbed or stored energy in harmonically attuned bursts. The process, however, is difficult to understand, hence the more easily comprehended bouncing or jostling presentation.

CHAPTER XIV

My Time Is Your Time

Ordinarily, in my presentation of universal concepts, I have shunned the word 'law', as one which smacks too much of dogmatic material usage. The coercive mandatory effect of too much law can and does lead to less exemplary human conduct, and makes people flaccid in problems of self-determination, proper perspectives and in moral values, etc. Perhaps, however, the usage of this term can be justified in denominators of common understanding, especially when it concerns visualizing the invisible and pondering the imponderable—Infinity.

I have frequently restated the dynamic principle, or law, if you please, of Infinite regeneration, the proposition of the ever-expanding, ever-contracting cosmogony, the interdimensional macrocosm and microcosm. To the average earth man who seems to have established within the dimension of his own life, a certain set of values which he believes to be stable, he is traveling across the desert of materialism, chasing the mirage of security. There is nothing stable in this Infinite; that is in such values as have been set up in social systems among the races of mankind. While Infinity Itself is the only real and tangible element in the proposition of living, yet understanding and living in Infinity demands the highest flexibility. It also mandates that Infinity be understood, not as a tangible solid, but as an ever-changing ever-regenerating sea of energy wave forms, wherein life is sustained only on the basis of understanding at least a small part of this Infinity.

This small part, and whatever part it is, is the facsimile of life which is, at that moment being so beheld; and again beholding some such small fraction of Infinity does more than present the personal intro- spection of life, as it is so lived by any individual. This beholding also creates this life in the beholder, even though all thought or action, individually or universally expressed by the beholders and recipients, are seem- ingly contradictory in most general aspects as to what this great Infinity is. While man, in his earth life, is so busily engaged in the contrivance of new ways, man- ners and forms of life that he believes them to be essentially his own discoveries, his own creations—not realizing that the expressive fabrication of this life is merely another one of those multitudinous forms of regeneration constantly being expressed by the Infinite.

And so each man develops his personal ego, the nuclei of self-consciousness; he nourishes it and keeps it carefully enclosed within the dimension of his earth life, not realizing that all of his expressionary forms and attitudes of life are only a small compound of that constantly regenerating Infinity. Infinity, in Itself, is in- comprehensible. It can be said that It is at once com- pletely tangible and intangible; It is not solid, liquid or gaseous. It is not seen or felt by the five physical senses, but resolves Itself, at least in some small part, into consciousness as a seemingly solid world in which man lives. While the Infinite is constantly regenerating Itself in never-ending sequences of new forms, It there- fore never presents Itself even in a small facsimile part to any beholder in that life proposition as the same solid.

This seemingly solid world is merely a purveyance sustained in consciousness from one moment to the next; and while the Infinite has regenerated the old form into newer and more relative adaptations to the present, the individual man is not conscious of this change. Man has only recently discovered that energy cannot be destroyed; and as matter is energy, immortality is also sustained in all things, even though there may be an apparent destruction. It is, in reality, a change of expression and form of that ever-changing Infinity.

Man lives in constant fear of death and is always contriving new ways to extend his life span—not realizing that every moment of his life, he is, in all ways, manners and forms, dying; and as this death occurs, so is he again reborn. He goes to bed at night only to arise again in the morning believing he has taken up the thread of life where he left it the night before, not realizing that during the night, he has, in effect, passed through eons of time; and upon awakening merely reconstitutes his new day from the memory or purveyance of his past. Thus it is, in this consciousness, each man travels his own personal trajectory, while the Infinite is ever-moving and changing at an incomprehensible speed. Man does, through this common faculty of memory consciousness, succeed in traveling through this same timeless, spaceless, Infinity, and at the same incomprehensible speed. He does then, in effect, keep up with the facsimile of the world about him. The infinitely solid, infinitely invisible, Infinity then does in this small facsimile become the reality of his life.

As he is traveling with these regenerative cycles, and at the same speed, so they become solid to him even though at any time, as in death, they become immediately invisible. If he should at any time, succeed in grasping his situation and voluntarily change this speed, or to stop, his seemingly solid world would immediately vanish. Clairvoyance, or any of the other 'so-called' mystical gifts is merely a consciously developed human attribute of consciousness, acquired by any individual who understands to some extent—Infinity. He can, at any time, place his consciousness at any given point in the past or in the future. This, however, is not a faculty which can be acquired by the material conscious mind. It is the natural mental faculty of a highly developed Superconscious Mind, whose natural habitat is in the next dimension or more directly connected to Infinity.

And so the great illusion of life persists. The seemingly solid world which is the all—the only tangible reality in most peoples' lives—is, as such a solid reality, only an illusion—a hallucination perpetuated from one tick of the clock to the next, from day to day, year to year. And so man lives in the ever-changing ever-regenerating Infinite, concerned only with that life and death struggle with himself. To constantly reconstruct this Infinity into the fabric of his life, he must mold it, reshape it, and reform it into what he believes is solid and real, even though these self-constructed images are horribly malformed and distorted, and he will writhe in the pain which they will inflict upon him; for as he so molds them, so must he conform with them. How great the tragedy of this life is then, that while Infinity maintains within Itself a perfect continuity, It has no good or evil, but is equalized in all creative effort. It has no emotion, yet lives in perfect concept as It is everything. Only man has, in his evolution, extended the premise of his mental faculties beyond the immediate needs of survival; and in this extension he has made his first attempt at creativeness; yet not knowing of what he does, aborts this creation with endless evils in his daily life. No, the other creatures of the earth are not so foolish; they live only for the need of survival, and from the substance of their lives there again is formed and reformed the countless nuclei of future lives and evolutions.

So while we muse upon the ever-apparent disparities of human conduct in contrast to the Creative Infinity, we can, at least partially, justify and equalize these disparities. We must know that within the intricate workings of Infinity, all this and much more has been conceived and equalized. It is part of Infinite expression. While man seems to be a profligate, wasting himself endlessly in destructive efforts, re-creating these destructive effigies only to again destroy them; he may be, in some blind, unconscious effort, only making his first attempt to become a constructive entity of expression in the Universal Infinite.

*If you believe your world to be solid, substantial and immovable, try to remember it is traveling through space in five known, different directions simultaneously, possibly two more unknown motions or movements, several of which exceed many thousands of miles per hour. The earth travels around the sun in an eliptical orbit some six hundred million miles at a velocity of about 18.5 miles per second or 66,000 miles per hour. The earth rotates at a speed of 1,044 miles per hour 17.4 miles per minute. The polar axis of inclination of 23 degrees also rotates as it points into the sky, making a complete counterclockwise rotation every 26,862 years. This is called the precession of the Equinox, or the point in which the sun crosses the equator at the vernal and autumnal equinoxes. The sun and the solar system planets are also moving through the galaxy in the swiftest of all motions—a velocity of 140 miles per second or, 500,000 miles per hour. Also, it is known that the galaxy is moving through the universe, but at what velocity and in what direction are yet unknown. There is a 2% wobble in the precessional orbit as it counter-rotates in its 26,000 year cycle. Finally, our universe itself is moving at a tremendous rate of speed around the central axis of a super universe. This, latter fact is, as yet, unknown to present day astronomers.

You are, in effect, merely an electrostatically charged dust particle, adhering to the surface of the earth by virtue of that charge, called gravity.

*These facts and figures have been compiled from present day, 1967 science sources such as "The Reader's Digest Almanac", Encyclopedia Britannica, etc.

CHAPTER XV

False Gods and Graven Images

Throughout the works of Unarius, there are many admonitions against certain religious practices, chiefly that of the common subterfuge called prayer. Like Jesus, who said, "Do not pray as does the heathen on street corners and in synagogues, or temples", etc., the Moderator (of Unarius) does not believe in prayer, and there are many important facts and considerations which point out the falseness of this practice (or for that matter, in religion itself). First, any person who prays to some god, lord, Jehovah, or any other (so-called) saint or intercessor, etc., is praying to a false image. There are no such gods, and any person who prays to one or more of them is deluding himself with a common image constructed under the pressure of an escape mechanism. It is true, there are spiritual agencies and Beings who are sufficiently powerful or developed to be able to bring about certain changes in peoples' lives when prayed for; however these agencies and Beings are far too intelligent to grant such prayers as they are asked for, and under their specified conditions.

The wholesale granting of prayers would quickly turn the world into wild chaos, far worse than can be imagined; for, if you think a moment, granting all such prayers would be impossible without dire results. All people who pray do so selfishly motivated, even though they may think they are praying for other people or objectives. They are, in reality, only trying to achieve their own ends, to exercise power, and to differentiate right and wrong for other people and conditions of life. Two armies going into battle pray for victory over each other; that would be difficult for any god to solve, but not nearly as difficult as answering the hundreds of millions of people all praying for, not only themselves but that their god should change the world to suit their personal needs, or what they believe to be a better world. They could not recognize the obvious fact that in changing either themselves or other people through prayer, they would be changing the normal course of evolution for all involved, thus cheating themselves and others out of the beneficial advantages of a normal course of evolution.

Prayerful people do not see other obvious facts: that Infinite Intelligence has, in creation, an inflexible law or principle which equalizes all things, good or evil, and makes progressive evolution possible to a more intelligent way of life. For every evil, small or large, there is an equal amount of good, plus a 10% bias which insures progression. People who pray do not recognize certain psychological implications which are involved. The granting of prayer, individually or collectively, would tend to morally weaken any individual and make it more difficult for him to determine his own course of life. Collectively, it could develop into a great hypocrisy, for the granting of prayer on a mass scale would induce even the most vile and iniquitous people to pray for their own ends and would result in great moral prostitution.

Therefore, any spiritual agencies or Beings who would have power to grant prayer, do so only on very rare occasions when circumstances are such that it justifies such changes and when such a prayer can be granted under conditions which do not generally appeal to the masses of people or that they cannot capitalize upon it, or that it cannot be tangibly proven to all, etc. Under such conditions then, prayer and any benefits from it still remain too intangible to be an effective threat against a normal course of evolution. Individually or collectively, the average prayerful supplicant does not know that in prayer, he is actually confessing his sins to himself, even though he is directing his conversation to some supposed god or deity. This confession does have some beneficial effect; it temporarily diverts the straight thought line of certain negations from the repetitious oscillating process which tends to increase itself with each counter negative reversal. There is also a slim chance that sooner or later, the supplicant will recognize the fact that he is in self-confessional; and in a more expanded concept of life, he will realize that all his trials, troubles and tribulations are really those of his own making. He committed them in ignorance and perpetrated them in increasing numbers and forms in the same ignorance of life. In this way then, through self-confessional, any person can by such objectivism, develop a strong personal moral responsibility, one which is free from false gods and deistic intercessions, for such personal moral integrity must be built upon a firm foundation of self-realization, one's own personal position in the scale of evolution—what creation is—and the determinant which makes life possible at any point in this evolution.

The most difficult task any person encounters in his personal evolution is in obtaining for himself an honest objective self-confession or analysis; and before that point is reached, all people fight like madmen, commit heinous crimes, invent endless subterfuges, suffer endless tortures before they finally corner themselves—so to speak—and begin to admit that they individually, are morally responsible for their thoughts and actions, their conditions in life, and by the same admission, their future.

Today's chaotic state of the world is, in a very broad sense, the ultimate result of such endless fighting against self-realization; and as of today, there is an even greater variety, a more endless chain of circumstantial evidence which every human now presently living is using to avoid the inevitable ultimatum which he must some day arrive at, or face gradual and eventual self-destruction.

Today's religious and political systems are all part of this self-invented machination which man has contrived to avoid the inevitable. Just as a prayerful supplicant attempts to justify his ignorance, his wrongful conduct, his poverty, his pain, etc., before some fancied deity, so the world, too, indulges itself in mass hallucination that there will be peace and good will among nations; for how can there be such when each person is a veritable volcano of suppressed desires and emotions. They live in an atmosphere of carnal lusts and desires; and they are literally mired to their very chins in the cesspool-like mud and slime of insecurity which has been cast as offal into the material world by those who live it and all its temporal materialism.

Perhaps you personally might attempt to validate prayer, that it is a relief valve or that it temporarily deviates destructive oscillating processes. If you do, remember such excuses or vindications, such as prayer, are only moral opiates, they are habit forming because you acquire a dependency upon them; and like opium, or other narcotics so continuously indulged in, moral opiates will destroy you just as quickly and much more thoroughly than do any of the chemical opiates.

If you wish to become a better person, to live a better life, then you must do so by first learning how such a life is lived; that such a life is possible in one of the many mansions. This is your personal task; but more than a task—for only in its accomplishment will you find immortal life. And so the next time that you rail against your circumstances or that you bemoan the evils in your life, your sickness, poverty, the indispositions of others toward you, don't get down on your knees to some false god and pray to be relieved of these conditions, or to change other people; but instead, get yourself off in the quiet corner and have an honest objective face to face talk with yourself. Try to analyze and realize that any circumstances in which you find yourself, are there because you realized and conceived them in your own mind; you believed in them to the extent that you became subjective to them; and, conversely, realize that when you have instituted new circumstances, new conditions, etc., and believe in them, just as completely as you have done with your past circumstances, then these new circumstances will form your life.

It is almost needless to point out that these new circumstances should be more desirable and less fraught with evil indispositions than are your now present circumstances. These simple elemental metaphysics have been repeatedly stressed throughout the works of Unarius. They are a fundamental logical approach to self-realization and a better life. These same concepts were taught by the Nazarene; they have been taught in a similar form many times by other Avatars and this concept of self-realization will form the cornerstone in whatever you achieve in the future.

> *I will not bend my knee to seek the truth of life*
> *But from within it is, I'll find*
> *And then I'll cease my endless strife*

CHAPTER XVI

The Sad, Searching, Seeking, Saga Of Sex

Occasionally a student, or some person will mention the terms, 'soul mate', or 'marriages in heaven', 'biune' etc., and although all necessary information on this subject—more rightfully called polarity—is contained in the books and lessons, it might serve a good purpose to again point up and reinstate the concept of polarity, which has been so sadly misconstrued and malformed by people ignorant of this subject.

The term, 'soul mate' or 'marriages in heaven', is sometimes used as a gimmick—usually brought out, mistaught and generally misused by sundry religionists, cultists and spiritualists. To properly understand this subject, we must refer back to the entire concept of the psychic anatomy, and how it develops through the earth world dimensions by experiences. No, marriage rites are not performed in heaven; even though there is a strong development of polarity between two or more Advanced Beings. This, however, is a scientific interplay of intelligence, and cannot be degraded into common earth-world derivatives associated with sex and procreation.

To understand polarity better, let us take two primitive people, a man and wife, living as naked savages in the jungle; for convenience we will call them Flora and Fauna. Like other women in the village, Flora has borne her husband Fauna several children, and she grinds the corn, digs up the roots, builds the huts, and does all the other hard work women do in that village. Now this may cause her a little resentment at times; she may envy her husband who has nothing to do but hunt wild animals for food and battle the warriors of other tribes. Fauna too, may envy his wife; she doesn't have to go out and risk her life, to hunt and fight. But whatever it is they do, or think, they are building up the energy wave form facsimiles in their psychic anatomies.

Each one is impounding his opposite male and female association counterparts. When Flora and Fauna have gone into spirit and they are about to make a connection to again be reborn, they will not have a personal prerogative to say, I want to be male or vice-versa; but the millions of wave forms which compose their psychic anatomies will have a definite effect on determining the sex of the child at the moment of conception and when the respective psychic anatomies make contact or union. Also, the common and well-known principles of genetics may combine to help determine rebirth in the opposite gender.

So, while Flora was a woman in the previous life, she may now be born a male because all the wave forms which she impounded about males were, at least at the time, reflecting more strongly than were the female counterparts; and the same process in reverse could have held true for Fauna. So now they were again reborn into the world but were in bodies of the opposite sex. They could conceivably grow up, remarry, and repeat the whole process many times. Also, through delays, when one or the other was not born at the same time, they could become brother and sister, even father and daughter, or son and mother, and son or daughter. Or they might, in the hundreds of following years, find themselves as relatives, such as uncle or aunt; or they may go together through several lifetimes as very close friends two males or two females. And in a percentage of such close male and male or female and female relationships, one of them may assume the role of the opposite sex, and believe she is the husband or he is the wife, so strong is this sex polarity development incurred.

Homosexuals are people who belong in this category; they may be living either in male or female bodies, but so strongly and predominately is the sex potential developed, that they will remain true to this most strongly developed sex—either male or female—even though they are living in bodies of the opposite gender.

However, disregarding for the time, these more off-shoot developments, let us go back to Flora and Fauna and the most normal development of their polarity. We will find them, after many thousands of years, and hundreds of lifetimes, emerging in our present time. They could be Mamie and Ike, or Dick and Pat, or in any other of the numerous polarities which we might chance to see or know about. In the case of Pat and Dick, it is quite evident that Pat—even though she is the female, still maintains her more strongly developed polarity which is masculine, and which is conversely true with Dick. Of course Pat does have a female body and Dick a male, but so far as their psychic anatomies are concerned, they are respectively, as has been stated, predominantly of the opposite sex.

This same situation can be true with any other developed polarity type, but most usually it is held more closely within the limits of its own sex; but in understanding this polarity development, you can easily see how it is that every man or woman is a combination of both male and female, and a percentagewise evaluation could range from ten to forty percent of the opposite sex.

One more point on these polarity developments: in

the case of Pat and Dick, or Mamie and Ike, this polarity which they have developed, gives them much greater strength than is normally possessed by people who are living together, but with a comparatively underdeveloped polarity. That's the reason why these strong polarity developments usually emerge as some sort of public figures. They may not even be married, as was the case with Tschaikovsky and with Beethoven; Schubert had his polarity helping him from the spirit side of life. Other specific examples by the thousands could be enumerated.

A developed polarity then does give great strength between two people, because they are oscillating together on certain planes, and thus psychokinetically projecting greater unified energy, which has the effect of making them more powerful in whatever they do. Also, in the polarity development of two people, they will, through frequency relationship constantly seek each other out; like homing pigeons, they may travel thousands of miles to find their polarity or some polarity they have been closely associated with in previous lifetimes.

Karma, or the working out of evil (and good) circumstances also by the same means, causes two or more people to seek each other out from among the multitudes of the earth; and in some way, try to reconstruct the circumstance—whatever it was—to try and work it out; or that they must simply relive it in some way, because it is a strongly oscillating focal point or polarity. Thus, you will find, and wherever you look, people seeking each other out, finding each other in numerous ways and walks of life, trying to re-establish a continuity between them, and continuing their former lifetime associations.

Races of people are thus perpetuated because each

race, its manner of living is a polarity, and intermixing races of people promiscuously, without knowledge, often does, individually and collectively, destroy the positive drive of polarity, leaving those affected helpless and confused in unfamiliar circumstances, unsupported by previous lifetime polarity associations. If these facts were known in this present day, there would be much less of a segregation problem. All races would function together more harmoniously and with understanding and with the retained ability to function in a more progressive evolution. This brings us to the subject of twins.

In a previous discussion (in the book, "Infinite Perspectus", chapter 29) twins were described as two persons being born from the same placenta, and these two persons shared a common psychic anatomy. This is not a polarity development, but means that two bodies were developed at the time of conception and that these two people will go through life sharing the same psychic anatomy, even though they may be living hundreds or thousands of miles apart.

This may be difficult to conceive; remember, however, the psychic anatomy lives through the physical body by means of oscillation like the radio. The psychic anatomy lives in the next dimension; a radio wave can travel around the earth eight times a second; it is easy for a psychic anatomy to thus radiate into two bodies at the same time. Also remember, the subconscious part, which is most active with the conscious mind, is always developed afresh, starting at the moment of conception. Therefore, identical twins function from one psychic anatomy with two subconscious minds instead of one, as is the case with all other people including non-identical twins, triplets, etc. Yes, it is quite conceivably possible for even quintuplets to thus function from one psychic anatomy and five subconscious portions.

In the summer of 1961, at a kidney transplant, doctors had, at that time, found that kidney or skin could only be transplanted between identical twins, and an article explaining this was written by the Moderator. Since that time, doctors have found and performed a kidney transplant between two very good friends. This has been apparently bewildering, but it does again vindicate the concept of polarity (as taught by Unarius) for as has been stated in the previous paragraphs, two very close friends are, (or can be) polarities, and as such, their two respective psychic anatomies reflect this compatibility into their physical bodies and make this transplant possible.

In other words, here again the same concept is emphatically reinstated, that all life is lived from its respective psychic anatomy. Yes, this includes all atomic forms, called mass; and as no present-day doctor or scientist knows about the fourth dimension, psychic anatomies, and other concepts presented to you in Unarius, they are therefore still abysmally ignorant of life and the purposes they serve. When you understand, to some extent, Unarius, you will be wiser than all the scientists, doctors, religionists, philosophers, etc., presently living or combined with those who have passed on save possibly a few exceptions such as Jesus, the Nazarene.

And when you understand somewhat, you will not be confused and misled by such 'gimmicks' as 'soul mate', 'marriages in heaven', 'biune', etc., used by certain practitioners; and you will not be misled in your daily life, vainly seeking some fancied soul mate to whom you may believe to have been married 'in heaven', or that 'God cast you together in the same mold', etc. Instead, learn to look for, and seek out those with whom you can associate your ideals and principles of life; always try to visualize the oscillating processes which constantly go on with you or any person in the common artifacts of life.

People who live the earth life have developed a polarity to the earth life, and in a sense they are 'married' to it, until they divorce themselves from it, and which will enable them to find higher and more finely developed relationships. The same is true in your own life; whatever it is you conceive, you are in the bonds of, not matrimony, but frequency relationship to it; and so long as you believe in it, you are in the same sense, 'married' to it.

More literally speaking, marriage itself, as it is practiced by the earth man, is only a legalized or religionized excuse or attempted escape from the obvious guilt of sex and procreation. Unlike all other creatures of the earth, man indulges in sex for pleasure; and as such, it is a vice, despite attempts by psychologists, doctors, philosophers, etc., to unionize sex with conjugal love; and in direct line with these legal or religious subterfuges is the nonsensical 'heavenly union', 'soul mate', etc., ideosophy.

When people become Spiritual Beings in Higher worlds, they are not married; they never marry, and there is no sex. Instead, they use a much higher and more fully developed expression of polarity, either with one or countless millions of other Spiritual Beings. And, in their knowledge of the Infinite, they thus become a positive constructive polarity with It, and with all of the countless millions of inhabited worlds, their people, their atomic masses and numerous forms of life. They also oscillate positively and creatively with all expressive agencies of the Infinite. This could well be your destiny—a goal which you may partially or more totally achieve in the many distant eons of time, countless millions of years earth time; yet surely if you do achieve and develop into such a polarity with the Infinite, you will again find you are just starting out.

No, God did not join this man and woman together in holy matrimony. For the Christian God, like all other gods, are false image gods in what might be broadly included as the psychology of life. Modern medical psychology is a very complex organization of association factors which have been superficially organized into its present form. True human psychology, however, is relatively simple and can be defined in a few sentences. Man is, basically, still an animal, an animal which has developed his mental faculties beyond the circumference of his vegetative needs. This development, however, is still third dimensional and does not include all fundamental knowledge of creation so abundantly displayed.

Man, therefore, still lives by the carnal jungle law: survival of the fittest. Despite a great affluence of a so-called 'civilized' society, humanitarian efforts, and oft repeated human eulogies, every human lives primarily for himself, and everything which he does, regardless of what it is called, must have, or must cast some self-beneficence. It must have an element of personal reward, and all other efforts and objectives in which he may participate, he does so unwillingly and for conformity. Yet, even in conformity he will indulge himself in such platitudes as, "I'm a good guy, doing the right thing, loving my neighbor", etc. Man scorns and tramples upon inferiorities. He fears the unknown, and will always attempt to destroy it; he may temporarily try to ignore it, or deny it. If he can neither destroy nor deny, he will take this unknown and mold it into a god and make a religion of it. Such has been done in Christianity; and in this god image, he will include all of his own emotion and vicissitudes multiplied a thousand times. Then he can say, in any future events, which include him or the human race in general which are unexplainable, evil, murderous, or unjustifiable, that it was one of god's mysterious ways.

Through prayer he can bargain with his god and further reduce him to his own level. He tries to dupe his god, makes false promises, offers personal concessions, etc., in this effort. For reducing god thusly he, (the man) is always satisfying and rewarding himself personally. So far as his own community life is concerned, all such life is lived by each individual as a personal challenge to constantly vindicate his personal sense of superiority or ego. Every human realizes, secretly and otherwise, his own faults and deficiencies, but he will fight to the death before he will admit them, or that his evil circumstances are the result of his own making. This is the eto. The id always remains the great unknown, and conquering it is the daily problem of the religionist. It is also in another way, the problem of our modern twentieth century scientists. Anything unknown, unconquerable and unjustified represents the id, a challenge to every person to either scorn it, trample on it and make it a part of the eto, or put it high up on the shelf and worship it in an attempt to justify himself in his community life and all its aspects as he believes himself to be a kind, lovable person.

No human really knows what love is; and what people believe to be love, is only a thinly or heavily veiled self-rewarding motivation. Man has developed and idolized the sensations of sex in an attempt to hide animal-like implications. In procreation he is idolizing himself; dad says, "a chip off the old block", mother takes secret or open pride in daughter's attributes similarly feminine to hers. And finally, love always somehow becomes self-eulogy. Man believes he is loving and kind and god-like, etc. Not until he has sought and begun to find the Inner kingdom will he begin to do away with the carnal self-motivations of the material world. They are justifiable in that dimension as the selective agencies, the motivating drives, etc., which propagate and develop species; and as man is the most highly developed mentally prehensile species, spawned by earth, the carnal law is therefore greatly multiplied, intensified and diversified.

If you are one of these 'lonely' people who have not found their 'soul mate', there is at least a psychological reason you are lonely; because you want it that way. Chronic loneliness is a symptom of mental illness, classified in more advanced cases as paranoia or a persecution complex. By being lonely, you can indulge yourself in self-pity and you can blame other people and conditions for your loneliness. This is a diversion commonly called an escape mechanism; and in escaping from your own perditions, everyone and everything is to blame but yourself.

Also, do not chase that mirage of supposed heavenly bliss which you think will be yours if you find what is commonly referred to as a 'soul mate'. Such unions are sometimes much more fraught with internal oppositions than are the cases when two ordinary people marry who do not have such a strongly developed polarity between them. In all ordinary marriages, there is a constant struggle for survival between these respective males and females. The survival effort, of course, is in proving individual superiority. To people who have a more strongly developed polarity, these equations are intensified; and contrary to general belief, such more

126

strongly developed polarities only increase the differences. This is because a more strongly developed polarity situation may, in certain aspects and areas, seem to submerge strong individual characteristics and tends to blend physical appearances, mental levels and concepts; it is this blending which gives rise to the strongest individual oppositions which are instigated and supported by the personal ego.

This may be puzzling until you examine the scientific dynamics of energy in motion. All intelligence, all information, etc., is energy. The sine wave represents all transmissions of life and all forms—sine waves oscillating between the psychic anatomy and the conscious mind. In other words, any information or intelligence is carried in a sine wave as two polarities. To interpret the information, the sine wave must present this information first from one polarity and then in a 180 degree arc present the same information in an exactly opposite fashion which makes the conveyance complete. In the fourth dimension the arc becomes a 360 degree circle. Two people, as developed polarities, must then present all the information of their lives, first from one polarity, then in reverse fashion from the other. Such unified presentation does develop these two people into many apparent similarities. They may even look like twins; and as could be expected they apparently, and in general, share the same likes and dislikes.

To arrive at that point, however, involved hundreds of lifetimes of enormous and titanic struggles against themselves, as well as survival in a material world; and as might be expected much negative karma was impounded to be worked out in subsequent lives. And at their present stage of development as two earth people, they are still in the elemental phases of this polarity

127

development, and they cannot be in any sense expected to live in a heavenly state of connubial bliss until their polarity has developed into ramifications which are not involved in reinstating the ego, indulging the destructive ego, or placating the id.

Therefore, look elsewhere for the solution for your loneliness, as suggested; ferret out the secret hidden subconscious motivations which brought about this condition. It is much better and more sensible to learn of the Infinite and of yourself than to pursue some blind or endless pilgrimage in a vain attempt to assuage the carnal drive which sponsors these more primitive phases of your existence.

CHAPTER XVII

Survival and Procreation

The foibles of human dispositions and indispositions are often quite incomprehensible, either to the average observer or to some student or philosopher of human nature; and it is quite often and obviously portrayed in converse actions and policies which actually prohibit long-sought-after achievements. The reasons behind such perverse and unintelligent actions are derivatives of complex psychic pressures induced in many areas of human conduct and living. The carnal law of survival is constantly superimposed in dogmatic theological assumptions as to the sacredness of man's creation and the ability to procreate. Such sublimation is not always justified and often leads into many complex and diverse expressions of human conduct which have neither logic nor reason, and which is as the subject of this discussion—survival and procreation.

For some years now, economists, humanitarians, politicians, statisticians, philosophers and scientists have begun to openly express great alarm in the recent population explosions. At present it is estimated that of the three billion people who swarm upon the earth's surface, four-fifths of them or two and a half billion do not have sufficient food, and are constantly hungry. Asian and African countries in particular have had such great increases in population that untold millions are now living in abject poverty, without shelter and with insufficient food to survive. It is estimated, if present population continues to increase, that in a hundred years from now the capacity of the planet earth to feed and house these people will have been greatly exceeded. There will simply be not enough food to feed the hordes of people and that particular problem presents certain peculiarities which will not be discussed at this time. One reason for these population explosions first grew in the hearts and minds of people which might be called compassionate understanding, or that certain individuals became more acutely aware of human misery and death.

About one hundred or so years ago, a great renaissance of science began. Men like Pasteur, Lister, and others found disease germs and viruses, with consequent ways of controlling and eliminating plagues caused by these unseen organisms. Malaria, yellow fever, and bubonic plague began to be largely controlled through methods of sanitation.

Then in World War Two, the scientist carried his weapons against the invisible killers into the far Eastern countries. The occupation of allied troops in these countries instituted some of the primary measures of curtailment from insects, pests, and other disease carriers, with the inevitable result; and with the continuance of some control, the lives of hundreds of millions of people were prolonged; hundreds of millions more babies grew up into adulthood who would have normally perished, without some modern sanitation and medical control over death-causing conditions. Now, it is well to idealize human life, the right to live, etc., but the right to be well born is a much greater importance. It is a much greater sin to bring a child into the world in poverty and sickness, seeing him go through life in abject circumstances, than it would have been to have prevented his conception or to have aborted that conception in its early stages. And it is right here at this point in our discussion that we must enter into genetical factors and all other important factors to obtain a more comprehensive evaluation of this problem.

Through the several thousands of years of man's written history, certain natural factors were always incumbent to some extent, and which exerted some control over both the quality and quantity of human reproduction—survival of the fittest, being the most important and a most logical law, which could always function for people not intelligent enough to determine their own lives. Survival of the fittest largely determined the best babies which would grow up to be adults and could reproduce the largest families. However, in modern science man, to some extent, by partially or wholly eliminating some diseases by foreign aid and food supplies through relief agencies, etc., has eliminated some effect of the law of survival.

However, such foreign aid is very inadequate and does not, in any way—even temporarily—relieve hundreds of millions of persons, not reached by such relief agencies. Then, too, the total cultivatable area of the world which is only 10% of the 25% area, not covered by water, is rapidly being depleted; the soil is constantly being eroded, minerals and vitamins washed away or absorbed by over cultivation. Now again the same question. Does the premise of life mean that life must be lived without logic and reason and without even common necessities? Do we sacrifice sanity in the face of this overwhelming human compassion that human life must be propagated and preserved regardless of circumstances or conditions?

The science of genetics has given mankind a very valuable way to increase the abundance of his food supply; genetics has produced superior meat producing animals; fruits, grains, and vegetables have also been developed in quality and quantity and to resist natural diseases and enemies. However, while man has found genetics extremely useful and productive, even lifesaving in his agronomy, he has not yet applied the same genetics to himself. He still breeds promiscuously. He intermixes races, he permits mental and physical misfits of all kinds and varieties to marry and propagate their ills into their society; even worse, he spends vast resources in dollars and medical institutions, sanitariums, hospitals, asylums, and prisons to extend the life of the more physically handicapped, the mental incorrigibles and hopelessly insane. And when one stops to ponder this enormous and incomprehensible situation, we must indeed wonder if mankind possesses any true sanity or intelligence. Upon the preface that it can be called a human being, a fanatical desire and effort is always put forth to sustain its life, irrespective of the suffering it must endure, or that it reinflicts suffering and sacrifice to others, that it degrades the general tone of the society in which it lives. While it is well to respect and revere human life, it is much more important to respect and revere the franchise which every child should have, which is a chance to have a healthy, happy, normal life, a life in which he can be normally expected to work out part of his evolution.

It is indeed a crime of the first magnitude to bring a child into the world in disease, poverty, and ignorance even though we might say to some extent—in a broad reference—that here again evolution and karma placed this or any child in these conditions. And as of today this great problem remains among the nations of the world, whether to institute controlled birth through contraceptives, drugs, or abortion, or face a possible ultimate extinction of mankind on the planet earth, through starvation. The decadency and destructive decay is now rapidly rising, or even a possible reversal of evolution could come when mankind could possibly cause—through over-population, mass production of constantly degenerating peoples, famine and disease, further deleterious effects from radiation caused from nuclear explosions and other unnatural conditions— the last remnants of mankind to emerge as grotesque mutants, horrible monstrosities, living in caves, in conditions even more primitive than did their stone-age ancestors more than two million years ago. Only time will tell, even though an affirmative prediction could be made.

In the galaxy and universe there are thousands of earth-like planets which have seen the rise and fall of many civilizations of mankind, planets which now hold in their ancient and decayed ruins, the same history of life, the same rise and fall, the same evolution ending in obliteration because these races of men failed in the most important essentials in their development—to find through their science the true creation, the true cause and purpose of life, and the progressive principles of evolution which sustain life through Infinity.

In all fairness, however, it must be stated at this point, the situation is not entirely hopeless; several countries of the world have recognized the obvious necessity or the extreme urgency of a logical population balance. Japan, in particular, has instituted legal abortion and contraceptive methods. There are ninety million or so Japanese living in a cultivatable area less than the total area of the state of California. As of today, more than one third of all conceptions are aborted, and the Japanese people have succeeded in more closely equalizing the birth and death rate of their nation. India too, is attempting to institute a birth control program; however, they have not as yet been nearly as successful. A much larger country with three or four hundred million people, ninety percent illiterate and with almost no communication systems, the task of instituting birth control is almost hopeless.

In India, millions of people sleep in the streets and subsist on small scraps of food, their clothing a few rags. In Africa, populations are exploding in the hundred or more newly formed independent nations—and it might be well to note here that study of the reproduction ratios between the white skinned races and the dark skinned (particularly the Negro) reveals that these dark skinned people reproduce ten or more to one as compared to the white skinned races. Also, the Caucasians or whites have the same inverse ratio between classes which might be called the wealthy or intellectuals and the more elemental, ignorant and uneducated peoples. Here again these lower classes are reproducing ten to one or more. These are prophetic indications.

Could it be that in the future a thousand or more years from now, the intellectual, artistic, creative white people, the wealthy class of empire builders will have totally disappeared, and only decadent remnants of the Caucasian race, living in the out-of-way places, and away from vast hordes of black skinned people who would, at that time, be living on the land and in the cities which had been built by the extinct Caucasians? This question is posed, not as racialism but as one of the probables to be pondered upon. The inferiority or superiority of one race as compared to another is not one to be satisfied in pragmatic comparisons. It can only be satisfied and justified in the broad abstractions of evolution. For every human, regardless of his color, finds the same equal opportunity to progress and to obtain Immortality in a higher world.

The present position of any human in his evolution is unimportant to Infinite Intelligence. Likewise is the color of his skin; for Infinite Intelligence is not emotional, and is not disposed to pragmatic comparisons. As humans, however, it is up to us to properly determine for ourselves a progressive evolution and an understanding of what gives us the proper perspectives, the proper placements and an insight into human relations without the stigma of pragmatic racialism.

And so, whether it is the preservation of humanity through birth control and other very necessary objectives, the survival of any race, the evolution of the planet earth is, in itself, only an infinitesimally small fraction of universally expressed evolution by Infinite Intelligence.

CHAPTER XVIII

How Now — Brown Cow?

In the month of December 1962, and in the week just preceding Christmas of that year, a very important event took place. This was the 'contact' of the satellite Mariner II with the planet Venus, at a distance of about 21,000 miles. This satellite had been launched in the latter part of the month of September, crossing the intervening space of many millions of miles at a speed of some five or six thousand miles per hour, during which time it kept in constant contact with tracking stations here in the U.S. This satellite was designed to radio many different kinds of information about the planet Venus back to earth, when it passed in closest proximity to the planet. This information would be the magnetic and gravitational fields, infrared, radiation, and other types of spectral analyses which our scientists hoped would give them the first real pertinent information about this planet.

As you know, Venus has been kept hidden by the thick vapor cover. As of to date, little or no information—save one fact—has been revealed by scientists who say that this information, radioed back as weird sounds, requires extensive decoding and study. This one important fact, and which was apparent right from the first signals, was that Venus has no magnetic field; at least not one like that of the earth. If you remember, Venus is only slightly smaller than the earth and if it was a planet similar to the earth, it would, quite logically, have a similar magnetic field. This apparent lack of the magnetic field has, no doubt, posed a rather mysterious problem to the scientists, and along with other information which they are struggling to decode, the mystery will only deepen; for the scientists do not possess any information relative to planets which exist in a dimension somewhat different than our own.

If you have a copy of the book, "The Voice of Venus", you will have much of this information; and you will find within its covers a rather accurate description of life lived in beautiful Venusean cities and under conditions which do not depend upon magnetic or gravitational fields or relative temperature, humidity factors, etc., such as are found on earth, and necessary to support the type of life with which we are familiar.

In short, the findings of this space probe on the one factor of the magnetic field alone has, almost completely, vindicated all information and facts as they are set forth in our book, "The Voice of Venus". If and when a space man ever penetrates the 'misty' shield of Venus in his space capsule, he will only find more and greater mysteries; as an earth man untrained in his paranormal faculties, he will not be able to see this planet, land on its surface, see those beautiful cities or the glowing energy bodies of the people who inhabit them. In fact, his space capsule might pass right through the planet and the space man would be unaware of this happening, and our earth scientists would then call the planet some sort of mysterious ball of gas. However, here again is the challenge to your intelligence. You know that radio and TV waves can bring music and pictures through the walls of your room.

The great Infinite invisible macrocosm, as it has been described to you, is the only tangible reality which you are trying to acquire through your evolution through the primitive reactive stages—which is the earth life. There is a vast amount of irrefutable evidence to this fact, evidence which ranges from the quantum mathematics of Einstein to psychic phenomena and spiritualism, as it is now known and has been known for thousands of years. Even Jesus preached this imponderable fact, the "Kingdom Within", the "Many Mansions", etc.

Dimensionally speaking, as it is described in the book, Venus occupies a position which, so far as any and all elements are concerned, are not measurable or reactive in the earth man's scale of atomic weights; neither are there any other similarities in quantum reactions so far as spectral energies are concerned, when compared to such factors as are found here on earth.

In the more distant future, a probe is planned to the planet Mars; in fact, Russia already has such a satellite spinning on its way toward that planet. However, any analysis from information radioed back to the earth from that planet will be, in most respects, quite similar or identical to the earth as Mars is a terrestrial planet, similar to ours. Again some description of this planet can be found in our book, "The Truth About Mars".

In the future, the Moderator plans to reveal accurate information on several other of our major planets, particularly Jupiter. However, for the time being you can safely read your books called the "Pulse of Creation" series and know that the information contained in them is quite accurate, in a more understandable way; descriptions, while very scientific, can be grasped by the nonscientific mind. All this information which is being given to you from time to time, in comparison to scientific findings is done purposely to refortify your position with Unarius, to make you think beyond the vegetative need of your earth life; in short, to help prepare you in your first steps in that ever-progressive spiraling plan of evolution, and which will, in the distant future, make you one of the denizens of these

Heavenly cities, described to you in the Unariun books.

And so tonight as you retire, and as your head sinks back upon your pillow, do so with the consciousness that in a few moments when sleep has come, you will leave your physical body and in a split fraction of a second, span the many millions of miles to one of the lustrous cities of Venus where in the halls and class-rooms you will meet many other of your fellow Un-ariuns, some from your earth—others from other planets, all brought together in a common cause—to educate these earth people, to help make it possible for them to evolve into the higher worlds.

No, you most likely will not remember this nightly event, but let that cause you no concern; in fact; it is much better that way, then your reactive subconscious mind won't intimidate and destroy what you have learn-ed. This has been purposely conceived in that plan of development through the psychic or inner worlds, and what you have learned you will retain as polarized constituents in your psychic anatomy, where they will exert a certain beneficent, though unseen, active force to make your present life better and your future attain-ments possible.

No, the ordinary earth man will never discover the Venus you know about, unless of course, he too, passes through his evolution to that point you now occupy, and when he does, he, like you, will know of the great mystery he was unable to solve in the bygone lifetime; for surely as untold millions of planets exist, there are the proper life forms to occupy them, all most properly conceived and dedicated in their evolutionary purpos-es by the Infinite Intelligence.

Since compiling the above article, some additional information on this 'Venus probe' has been released; the most important item is the statement that the temperature of Venus is about 800 degrees Fahrenheit, or hot enough to melt lead, which would prohibit life to exist, as we know it, on this planet. However, the most startling revelation was that both the light and dark sides of Venus have the same temperature, and as Venus always presents the same side to the sun, the enigma is even more strange, and completely refutes all known physical laws of heat radiation.

The very slow rotation of Venus always presents the same face to the sun, just as does the moon to the earth; therefore, according to physics, the side of Venus which does face the sun, should be very hot (800 degrees); the dark side, however, should be close to absolute zero (—273 degrees C). This great enigma, together with the absence of a known magnetic field, is a situation which could puzzle scientists for hundreds of years, or at least until that time when they can include the fourth dimensional science as it is contained in Unarius.

Then it will be known that a planet does not get heat in a direct straight line radiation heat-wave situation. All spectral energies known as light, heat, etc., are produced by hysteresis, in various kinds of energy fields called gravity, magnetic, etc. Also, the future scientist will find dozens of different energy fields around each planet and through space; fields of force or energy which he does not, at this time, even remotely suspect as existing. He will also find thousands of atom forms, now not even suspected—atoms with properties not third dimensional.

And so once again Unarius has, through this space probe, been vindicated; and science has increased its knowledge, also its incomprehension. The probe also indicated other puzzling factors; the atmosphere is supposed to be largely carbon dioxide, similar to a condition on earth hundreds of millions of years ago, and which produced the great affluent vegetation of that era. The temperature of the atmosphere ranged from 60 degrees at high altitudes to 30 degrees plus at mid level, also contradicting the high surface temperature in several factors.

Venus then, as of today, is an even greater mystery than it formerly was before Mariner II was launched; and it could well remain so, at least until paranormal faculties of mind are developed which will give the earth man a way to communicate with the Advanced Peoples living there, people living in a manner and way which is unaffected by earth-world factors.

CHAPTER XIX

Water Need in Energy Conversion

The last several group meetings and particularly the most recent (Feb. 27th), have been according to reports, very wonderful and with outstanding examples of psychic phenomena which have been in different ways, felt or witnessed by all group members. This has given Ruth and I, and the Unariun Brothers great joy, for now we know that all your faces are turned toward the mecca of Eternal Life; and it is not likely, or possible that you will ever renege on your course of evolution—providing, of course, you always make a determined constructive effort.

One point of particular interest, and one which deserves explanation is that all of you felt very thirsty at the end of the meeting, and you attributed this thirst to previous lifetime desert experiences; and while it is true, all of you have had such experiences, your thirst, however, was from another cause. In the third or earth world dimensions, water is a universal reagent composed as it is, of two gases—hydrogen and oxygen— and which are, together with carbon, the basic building blocks of the atomic world, and as part of your evolution is still vitally concerned with such atomic forms, we must analyze this situation.

Your body is composed of such atoms, about 16 different kinds; each atom has its own basic rate of vibration which can be compared somewhat to the tone of a bell when it is struck by the clapper. While the tone may sound as a single note, it is actually composed of many tones or notes which, as harmonics, combine or oscillate together in such a manner, that to the ear, a single tone is heard. Like bells, atoms, too, have their own tones or vibrations too high to be heard or measured. The tone of each atom is, in some respects, different than any other tones of any other atoms, even though they may be of the same element. But as such an element, they all do, harmonically speaking, regenerate the same tone which gives them their basic atomic characteristics.

Your body has, in a sense, been your home for many lifetimes and like all other things of the earth world it is made up of atoms. Atoms in turn recombine to make molecules and cells. Your body is made up from about 16 different kinds of atoms or elements. In this way it is compatible to the earth world, and enables you to live in this world. However, in order to live in a higher spiritual world, this body home of atoms must also evolve or change, just as does your psychic anatomy. The present atomic forms could not exist in these higher Spiritual planes, therefore the necessity for physical evolution as well as mental, and both evolutions should occur in an equal fashion. And as the whole process of evolution is predicated upon learning through experience, it should therefore not be assumed that evolution should take place quickly in the matter of days or even a lifetime.

Rather, you must constructively learn of Infinity and with infinite time. To equalize physical evolution with mental or psychic means that the tone or frequency of each atom now existing in your body must be stepped up to a higher rate of vibration, as your body is constantly dying and being rebuilt (one and one half million cells per minute), all new cell forms composed of such atoms will also have this higher vibrating rate because the controlling factor of this vibrating rate is stemming from the psychic anatomy which has also adjusted itself to a higher rate. Eventually, through eons of time, these atom forms now comprising the physical body, will metamorphose into a higher spiritual energy body such as has been described in the "Voice of Venus".

It is a physical law that wherever there is a change or transmutation of such molecular and atomic forms, an amount of energy equal to the change must be used to cause the change. Water as the universal fluid substance of the earth world is used by the Unariun Scientists and by the Infinite Intelligence in making the change of vibrating rate of the atoms in your body. When this is done suddenly and in large quantity, as was in your last meeting, a larger quantity of water is consequently used. As your body is 80% water, some of this body water was transformed into the energy necessary to step up the vibrating rate of all your body atoms. As you did not drink water during the meeting, you were therefore partially dehydrated and hence the thirst.

In our daily work here at the Center, Ruth and I consume three or four times the normal water intake, most of which is used in this energy conversion process, and this energy, in turn, is used or projected into all our Unariun activities, and as catalytic energy it helps make all the miracles which are happening to Unariun students possible. In the future, it is suggested that you all make a more conscious effort to drink more water, particularly at group meetings and when studying. Also, try to use, if possible, the bottled spring water which is free from chlorine and much of the heavy mineral concentration found in tap water.

And now that you all have had real tangible psychic phenomena, we know that in the future you will all make an even greater effort in your daily lives toward

144

your progressive evolution. We and the Unariun Brotherhood will always be with you in these efforts.

It should also be borne in mind, your own energy conversion and stepping up process does also benefit all other students, peoples of the world, of other worlds and dimensions and re-creates more positive plus for the Infinite Intelligence, a part of the regenerative principle. Conceivably in some distant future, you will learn how to instigate and project various psychic phenomena, help in healing and other creative activities now being done by the Unariun Brotherhood; and when you do, your present position will be reversed, you will be one of those beautiful Beings which are now sometimes seen by you or other students in all their resplendent glory, and your intellect will reflect its own ethereal fragrance to those who are attuned.

CHAPTER XX

It's The "Little Things" That Count

From time to time through various sources of information, such as TV, newspapers, etc., bits of information are presented to the public which graphically portray the constant, never-ending struggle and search for the answer to life which is being made by sundry branches of science; and with every so-called discovery which they make, there are often wildly exuberant claims made that now, at last, science has the answer to life, etc!

One of these scientific exposés revealed the DNA molecule, which supposedly masterminded the creation of living cells in chemical biology; directly connected to studying cells, new discoveries and their consequent mysteries have been recently uncovered. Working with living cells from animal tissue, the scientist knows how to keep these cells alive and growing in a liquid food plasma. Normal cells will continue to grow and multiply until they reach the edge of the dish which contains the plasma; then they stop growing and remain inert. Cancer cells continue to grow upon reaching the edge of the dish; also normal healthy cells, when infected with virus, will also continue to grow just as do the cancerous cells. Now this poses a great mystery to the scientists, and especially to those who have segregated their particular branch of science; for such segregation is quite strongly marked and practiced in various sciences.

The answer to mysterious cell behavior, DNA molecules and any and all other mysteries of life will never be solved until such segregation is banished and all sciences recombine themselves as they should properly do, basically—as an electronic science. The books and lessons of Unarius contain all the answers, including the mystery of the cell, scientifically explained. But to further the general cause of knowledge, let's clear away this mysterious haze.

Reverting to fundamental concepts, all mass forms of the planet earth—including cells—are reducible to atoms; and atoms are tiny solar systems of energy, each atom, the nuclei of its respective vortex, revolving in the next dimension. All atoms have electromagnetic fields and are either compatible or incompatible on the basis of frequency relationship. When normal cells, growing in the food plasma reached the edge of the dish, they were repelled from the dish atoms because their respective atomic structures were incompatible on the basis of the same frequency relationship principle. A secondary result was also incurred. The EMF's of the dish atoms superimposed a subharmonic into the cell atoms, which, in a sense, paralyzed them or suspended—in an out-of-phase condition—the normal atom oscillating activity within each molecule and cell.

On the other hand, with cancerous cells or virus infected cells, this certain subharmonic had already been injected into them and in one of the many ways which did not shock the molecules and cells into a suspended condition. Subharmonics of many different kinds or frequencies can be, in many different ways injected into, or oscillated into atomic molecule mass compositions without any immediate apparent deleterious effects; yet through subsequent phase relationships—involving unlimited time periods—such subharmonic injections can re-create certain specific mass malformations.

For example, a woman who died from a sword

thrust in her breast several hundred years ago, can develop a carcinoma, or breast cancer in this lifetime; or the husband of this woman who witnessed this act could vicariously incur cancer in the same spot, hundreds of years later. However, there is an almost infinite variety of ways in which inferior, negative subharmonics can be injected into atomic structures and perpetuated through respective psychic anatomies, including the individual human psychic anatomy. The ardent quest of the virus pathologist who believes virus causes cancer may eventually have to resolve any cancer causing incidence from virus as an inclemental factor of frequency relationship, negative subharmonics, etc., or as a proposition to be more clearly defined in an electronic science.

The scientist who studies viruses is also becoming increasingly mystified as he discovers more about these submicroscopic particles. Viruses literally are germs which infest germs, so small are they that they actually infect bacteria, causing them to die from a virus disease, just as bacteria cause people to die. Through the electron microscope, many thousands of photographs of viruses have been taken, and the more pictures, the more mystery; for viruses follow no clear cut and dried lines as do bacteria and other organisms. The electron microscope uses the wave length of the electron, instead of light frequencies, and photographs on the order of 100,000 (or better) times magnification have been obtained with this instrument.

It should be pointed out at this time, however, that by using the electron wave length, a pseudo image may be obtained, that is, through certain kinds of distortions and aberrations, due to the compatibility or incompatibility of EMF's which are involved, including that of the microscope. However, to better understand this situation, let us discuss viruses and how they come into existence.

Photographs of viruses reveal an infinite number and variety of shapes: spiney, rod, hexagon, round, square, oval, etc. These shapes, as so seen, are molecular, that is, they are atom compounds. These atoms were thus compounded together in what might be called the process of living life. People who are amassed together in communities and cities are constantly in action; thought waves and other kinds of energy waves so generated are being radiated. Some of these radiations such as thought are more closely fourth dimensional. Other kinds of actions regenerate harmonics into this fourth dimension. Thus over each town and city, there is an intense smog-like radiation of fourth dimensional energy forms, which at their particular moment of generation, do not have psychic anatomies.

In the Infinite Intelligence, all forms and substances are successively re-created through their respective psychic anatomies from the higher dimensions into the lower. The aforementioned smog-of-life living generation is, in a sense, an opposition to Infinite Creation. These great masses of energy forms therefore, according to Infinite law, begin to create for themselves, psychic anatomies; thus all compatible frequencies begin to oscillate about each other, and their first form of a psychic anatomy culminates in the center of its vortex as a virus, (something like children playing ring-around-a-rosy with a child in the center).

Viruses then, can and do, manifest their infinite variety of shapes; their never-ending characteristics, according to the information which has been impounded in their psychic anatomies and as supersonic harmonic regenerations from an infinite variety of wave forms from life experiences from billions of people.

149

The reason for this peculiar virus situation now becomes quite clear; also on the same basis of frequency relationships, all viruses, irrespective of their shape, are attuned to people, animals and plants, but particularly to people, who are the greatest source of this negative virus material. That is why certain nontoxic virus can quickly become toxic. Colds and other virus conditions manifest in an infinite variety. The human system cannot build up a permanent resistance against cold viruses for the simple reason that there is a sympathetic vibrating condition with these viruses from the mind and body of the person it is infecting, and which may have in the past, partially been responsible for the creation of this virus which now infects the body as a cold.

Here again is the overwhelming proof of an inphase, out-of-phase condition. All people are literally saturated with virus, but usually suffer no ill effects from these multiple virus forms until certain inphase, out-of-phase conditions are imposed. A few hundred thousand viruses which, through the harmonic principle have been changed into cold viruses, can quickly trigger all the viruses in a healthy body into becoming cold viruses when they are injected into this healthy body, as through the respiratory tract. Certain wave lengths of energy such as thought radiations can also trigger these viruses in a healthy body into becoming cold viruses when this healthy person merely looks at the cold sufferer. He does not have to breathe the cold viruses; the autosuggestive processes through thought transmission are often sufficient. That is why colds are so contagious, also why they have such a degrading effect upon the human system, and through a negative discharge condition, the physical aura is depleted causing great discomfort and inability.

The concept of the virus is indeed complex; and it cannot be properly understood until all the laws which govern interdimensional energy transmissions and their functions are thoroughly understood. A third dimensional hypothesis based upon surface reactions, facsimile, photography, etc., is totally insufficient. Whether man will or will not solve this facet of his planetary life may be one of the keys which will or will not unlock a better future; and if this door is not unlocked, man may well bring about his own undoing and eventual doom, not through nuclear war, but through the very processes of living in the countless, never-ending generation of negative energy wave forms. He will constantly construct and reconstruct new killers and invent new names for them—yet even here the most insidious of all life process generations is that negative energy acid which is now currently eating away at the vitals of his very being. The bastions of his civilization and his very civilization is now in dire danger of falling into the dust of decadent morality.

Just as Daniel transcribed the handwriting on the wall to the Babylonian king, Nebuchadnezzar, so does the Moderator transcribe and translate the numerous signs and portents, the obvious derelictions, the decadent expressions into what should be a fair warning to all those who wish to survive. The question of immortality, life beyond death, will be resolved by any person who heeds this warning, or for that matter, any nation or the world itself. The Moderator does not stand alone in this position; there are many others who are well aware of this down-hill toboggan slide to oblivion; yet there are none among those who have the true answers, the absolute solution. For here again is the reason for Unarius, and of the great Message of life it contains for anyone who will dedicate himself to the problem of personal emancipation from the earth world life and to establish a progressive evolution. This he can do only for himself and each person must, likewise, at some time make this selection—this determination, or he will surely perish.

Jesus implied the same selection; and since His time, the hell-holes have been filled to overflowing by those who refused to choose this course. As one of the interplanetary Messengers, the Moderator is, at the present time, maintaining contact and consciousness through the physical form into one of these hellhole purgatories (earth). In this missionary work, He has devoted Himself, for lo—almost countless thousands of years; and He is not alone. There are others too, from the higher worlds who journey into the astral under-worlds to carry the Message of Immortal Life; Their purpose, Their dedication and Their knowledge is far beyond the earth man's comprehension. This is the Unariun Brotherhood. Heed Their Message well—if you would live—for it is your future.

And so the search for the answer to the riddle of life continues—a never-ending, ceaseless, quest; for man has an insatiable appetite to know the ultimate answer, the reason for being, the why of all things, the whence from where he came, and the whereto of his going. And like the building of the tower of Babel, his quest has become the clamor of many strange tongues, all claiming their own victory; yet even as they cry their exultation for having discovered some new bit of infor-mation, so are their voices lost in the frenzied clamor of other voices. Thus, it is from halls and laboratories of the world of science, men on pedestals and perches look down upon the crawling world of common things, and preach their dogma that life began as a cell. And in other places other men have built great linear betatrons and cyclotrons, believing that the atom holds the secret. And overhead in the far-off blue skies, a satellite swings in its orbit around the planet; one of many, each one trying to dig or pry the secret from its heavenly course.

Yes, even man himself has ridden in one of these 'fiery chariots'; but unlike the prophet of old, he returned to his earthly hell—unlearned; and the chemist, the biologist, and the nuclear physicist labor so assiduously, each believing in his own right, unashamedly admitting his ignorance, yet quick to use the scourging lash of censorship upon any individual who dares to broach the citadel with something new which he does not understand.

Yes, there are other men who ply their trade beneath the shadow of a steepled church; those who don the robes and set themselves up on altars to be worshipped as purveyors of the great secret; yet from their mouths fall the words of a false blasphemy: that man can be salvaged from the dregs and slime of an earth-world cesspool by a false god who ruled the pagan hordes of Babylon. This is man's civilization, his modern 'Tower of Babel'; and while he labors in his many ways amid the clamor, the clanging, grinding, knocking, screaming, hate-filled world of lust, vengeance and vice, a Tall Man stands upon a nearby hill—watches for a while—then turns away; for He had walked among them once before, and tried to give them that great thing for which they sought. Yet, even as he told them of the way and place, they stilled his Voice upon the Hill of Calvary.

And as He turns away, He knows how well it is that, buried deep within each man's heart, the secret lies, and answers not the dinning world outside, but waits until the time and place when all the clamor of the world is stilled. And then from out this silence, bursts a mighty strength that lends the secret to its cause; and like a flower bursting forth from out the dark brown earth, the new man borne from out the long-held secret of his past, becomes the fairy bloom, to live his newborn life resplendent in the glory of all things made whole.

CHAPTER XXI

Man — The Electronic Computer

Everyone who walks the pathway of life presents a certain quanta of psychic affiliations, not only from the present lifetime, but from a comparatively large number of past lives. You, like all people, retain in various parts of your psychic anatomy, certain vortices of energy wave forms which, in the overall oscillation patterns, reflect into the mental and physical life determining just what you are, how you function, etc., it therefore remains germane, that if various insoluble enigmas or incurable conditions exist, that all such corrective therapies entail a basic understanding of this complex process, also that the student be indoctrinated into a daily practice wherein these principles are seen as active and dominant forces which determine success or failure in this therapy.

Understanding, therefore, entails not only knowledge of principles of function, but also analysis into past lives to determine which psychic shock or shocks was responsible for the aberration.

This same analysis can be used in any and all cases where true cause and the correct determinants are entered into. Realizing that as yet, almost all people, with hardly an exception, are not specifically equipped to perform this necessary function (of past life reading), we therefore present to the student a basic analytical platform upon which we can enter into such analysis and on the basis of long term usage, begin to acquire the permanent benefit always incumbent when such analysis is entered into.

First, let us present some general information which is pertinent to all those who can be classed as "old souls" or to those who have reached a certain threshold in their evolution in which they have indicated in many ways, primarily a desire to relinquish the old reactionary way, acknowledgment or realization of a higher way, various complaints which can be largely listed as karmic or more accurately, psychic. To these old souls and to any others who might so benefit, let us start to construct a new basic understanding of life.

For convenience sake, we start around the time of Atlantis some 12,000 years ago and come down through the many civilizations to the present day. You, like everyone of us, first incepted as a basic formative pattern of psychic structure, such elemental fears as fire, water, earthquakes, storms, etc., which in turn were given such personifications as ogres, demons, spirits, or gods, as part of the first formative pantheologies of your religious life. These lives, of course, were lived many thousands of years ago in the more primitive stages of your development. Later on, coming down through successive incarnations, you began associating yourself just as did others with such existing pantheologies as were surrounding you at the time.

By thinking along these lines of introspection, you can very easily understand just how it was that we first obtained some of the fears which are psychosomatic in nature. Think about these things and visualize yourself as coming down through these ages of time from Atlantis, or even Lemuria, and that as a seeker of truth, you are naturally one of those persons who will again reincarnate into the future age of time which is called the Aquarian Age, that you along with countless thousands of others, are to become members of the Spiritual Brotherhood of this future age, and must have this age-old karma removed and thoroughly cleansed from the psychic self.

The earth plane is a place of working out of great transitions and the last remaining vestiges of karma, so you will be enabled to reincarnate into this future age as a spiritually minded person and live in close harmony with the races of peoples on the earth under the common denominator of the Golden Rule, or the expression of Infinite Intelligence from the inner self.

Every truth seeker knows of, or has heard of Atlantis, that ancient lost civilization which was predated by the Lemurian civilization many, many thousands of years ago. Atlantis was a very wonderful and beautiful civilization which flourished on a continent somewhere in the mid-Atlantic Ocean. This civilization was directed by spiritual leadership from a great temple, and stemming out from Atlantis into the four corners of the earth, there flourished numerous colonies largely directed by the same priesthood. Several thousand years later, a race of dark-skinned people succeeded in stealing certain secrets and machinery which were atomic in nature and which had been handed down from the Lemurian Masters. With these secrets, they actually succeeded in blowing Atlantis out of the ocean and into non-existence. As is depicted in the parable of the Garden of Eden, these people actually succeeded in deviating man from a true spiritual course, and thus, figuratively, destroying the Garden of Eden.

Naturally with this terrible destruction, there was a tremendous loss of life, but many thousands of people on being forewarned, migrated to various countries such as Egypt, India, Persia, Central and South America. From these remnants sprang other civilizations. Through the countless eras of time, the countless millions of people who had resided in Atlantis, knowing of this great spiritual leadership and wonderful way of life, began seeking to find themselves in some new age and time wherein these same spiritual concepts were further expressed, that they might gain more wisdom and advance themselves in their own personal evolution.

Every human being has a strong and motivating desire for spiritual wisdom and to advance himself in his own evolution. And so, the countless multitudes from these past ages, began coming and going into the various recent civilizations, such as the Hellenic Age, about 500 B.C., down through the dark Middle Ages to the present time.

The psychosomatic, sometimes referred to as divine intercession, means that in oscillating from a high sense of consciousness from the Superconsciousness, certain wave forms of energy can be projected into these negative vortexes which cancel them out and render them harmless to further influence your life. Remember, however, that you do retain the idiom of experience in different higher relationships of life which ultimately resolve themselves into part of that spiritual body or matrix of developed spiritual energy which you will occupy for many thousands of eons to come.

You, like everyone else, have come and gone through numerous lifetimes as either male or female, developing certain definite propensities and characteristics of either one or the other. This concept is a sure way of solving the present psychological enigma that everyone is ten to forty percent of the opposite gender, and can only be truly solved when we understand reincarnation and the development of polarity patterns. This principle holds true wherever man may live and these patterns also exist in the development of various other members of the family and close associations with friends.

Remember that the intelligence of every experience, idea, form, or consciousness is carried in that oscillation between the positive and negative poles, and in understanding this dynamic movement of energy as it portrays consciousness, you will understand the true secret and meaning of the constant resurgence of life in an infinite number of patterns and forms.

You must realize and to consciously conceive within your mind that whatever it is in your circumstances at the present time which relates to any unsolved blocks or physical conditions, they have their origin back hundreds or thousands of years in one of the many lifetimes you lived since Atlantis. Your future will depend a great deal upon your course of action in this present lifetime; how much of this remaining negative karma can be removed, and just how far you will go in accepting the dynamic principles which have been compounded together in the lesson courses.

Therefore, my most sincere advice to you would be to devote the remaining years in contemplative introspection. Look forward into the future with positiveness and assuredness of your immortality, and as being a part of the Infinite Intelligence. Each lifetime will draw you closer to the position of infinite introspection which is called Nirvana by Buddha. The magic elixir of life is simply the contemplative peace of mind one acquires when he has placed himself consciously in some positive position of unity with the Universal and Infinite Consciousness. There are many ways in which this Infinite Consciousness and peace of mind can be expressed outwardly or externalized to your fellow man.

There are also other valuable bits of personal philosophy one can adapt in gaining this peace of mind, one which primarily revolves around the concept of losing consciousness with one's own present material difficulties, physical encumbrances and mental handicaps. This can be done quite easily when you become vitally interested in other people's lives. This is not in the sense that you must bring them some valuable bit of philosophy or spiritual uplifting which you do not as yet possess, but one in which you can view mankind introspectively in seeing the numerous ways the Infinite Intelligence is working through all things about us. This is very valuable in obtaining this peace of mind, because here again is a factual portrayal of the immortality of life itself. The most mundane objects of the world about us assume luster and personality as infinite creations in our consciousness, and these can well be the focusing points which we adapt into our conscious way of life. Break these seemingly insoluble thought patterns of fixed circumstances or physical encumbrances; they are not only poisonous in nature, but actually lead to eventual destruction of the very psychic consciousness of the individual if prolonged into thousands of years.

Become serene, complacent; objectify your creation as being immortal and the life cycle of all things progressing into Infinity. You are one of these conscious participles of progress, and you possess this same immortality; the very elements of life which are manifested in your physical body, will actually be the sum and total of yourself in the coming spiritual dimensions of time. Jesus said to Nicodemus, "We must all be born of spirit before coming into the Kingdom of Heaven." We are thus born and reborn again and again, with the various incarnations and evolutions which we traverse through the eons of time.

In the near future, you may also look forward to

your own spiritual transcendency when you, just as others who have contacted Unarius, have gone through this transcendency and come into a new day and life where the world has become a rainbow-hued corridor wherein is portrayed renewed interest and contacts, spiritual manifestations and Infinite guidance which could not previously be envisioned until such transcendency occurred. Do not be too concerned with what has gone into the limbo of past lives. Many times students and truth seekers are deviated from the true course by having their consciousness warped and distorted by knowing of such past evolutions. Be concerned with the valuable condiment contained in every experience and the wisdom derived from mastering such experiences. Self-mastery is the ultimate goal of every individual before he can attain such spiritual consciousness which will enable him to live in higher elevations and plateaus of spiritual consciousness.

CHAPTER XXII

To Be or Not To Be?

One of the never-ending, herculean tasks performed here at the Center is in the constant urging for various students to remain sincere and dedicated in their Unariun studies, to realize the tremendous importance of Unarius not only to themselves personally, but to millions of others—yes, even to Infinite Intelligence Itself! In this respect, Ruth has served most auspiciously, and through her letters, has very greatly aided and abetted this cause, and sometimes, I might add, she is often at her 'wit's end', so to speak, to try and represent the great importance of Unarius and all that it implies.

Since the beginning or dawn of history or since man began his evolution on this planet, he has in this evolution, proportionately increased his fear of death with his knowledge of his physical life. Different deistic beliefs or religions became the placebos or opiates with which he attempted to assuage this fear. As of today, the situation is much more complex and proportionately increased.

Modern science, in any of its branches, does not officially recognize personal survival after death, even though it is at this moment, spending vast sums of money to further explore or extend different avenues in the material world to find the riddle of life, which could only ultimately and inevitably lead into different dimensions or the mansions, as Jesus called them.

Now everyone is very vitally concerned with death—his greatest fear; even though he may think he has it well hidden under his material life, it is there nevertheless. Every news report on some calamity or disast-

162

er, the first question asked is, "How many were killed?" and is of primary importance; and "How many were injured?" is of secondary importance, and every person who hears these reports gets a certain sense of satisfaction in knowing he is not among the killed or injured. You, as a student, may not believe you have this fear, that your studies or knowledge of these other dimensions, life after death, etc., may have dissipated the fear of death. And while it is granted that your fear may have been somewhat mitigated, you should nevertheless ask yourself, and honestly, these questions: Do I really possess sufficient knowledge to live in another world minus my physical body and my material world? Do I possess understanding and knowledge which will not only enable me to live in a spiritual world, but to determine what kind of a world it will be?

For there are many mansions or worlds, a few of which are even worse than the one you are now in, and unless you possess this all-important knowledge, and you know how to use it, you will only become another creature of circumstances, after you loose your physical body. You will float like a blob in a meaningless unearthly void, peopled only by the vivid nightmares from your subconscious, until you find a newly forming fetus to which to attach yourself, to again emerge into a material world! Conversely, if you possess certain knowledge and understanding—and granted that this knowledge is you or at least a part of you—this means that you, as the knowledge, are actually a functioning entity in a vastly expanded state of consciousness. You will therefore attune yourself too, to become a part of and to live in, one of the more advanced worlds or dimensions.

The proposition here is basically one of attunement. The more you understand, the more you oscillate with the higher reaches of Infinity, the more selective you will become in your place of abode in this future—after death—and the less desire you will have to return to the physical world. This is just plain simple logic and reason.

Picture for yourself a moment—would you feel at home in the wilds of an Australian wilderness, living with the primitive, naked, stone-age aborigines who are still living in that part of the world? Of course you wouldn't; you'd miss all of the accouterments and impedimenta of your material world. The reason is simple: like a radio you oscillate with what you now have and in this respect you have, in a sense, chosen all the conditions and other things which you now have, even though you may not like some of them or that they are painful. They are yours by 'choice' nevertheless, and through evolution you experienced these things at different times and in different forms believing in them to the extent that they became part of your psychic anatomy. Again, logic and reason demand that if you wish better circumstances and conditions, if you desire to survive after death, and logically to live in a better world, you will have to begin now and at this present instant, to make it a 24-hour-a-day proposition, to learn as much as you can about survival after death and how to live in a better world.

And remember you are very much in the same position as the man who is spending his last few hours in the death row of a federal prison, knowing that he will be executed at dawn. Even if you could live another hundred years, and you spent every moment of it studying, learning and practicing the interdimensional life-giving science of Unarius, you would still find that all you had accomplished in that hundred years would be even less than the pocketful of white pebbles used by Hansel to lead his sister out of the forest.

In other words, dear friend, to paraphrase, "It's later than you think." The handwriting is clear and black upon the wall. Even as you were born and uttered your first infant wail, you were condemned to die. The almost never-ending repetitious cycles, birth and death are the heritage of all creatures in elemental phases of their evolution and with every birth and death, there goes the promise of everlasting life, bestowed by Infinite Intelligence upon all these creatures and by whatever way they manifest and remanifest their own immortality, it remains for man alone to achieve a more ultimate destiny wherein he portrays individually, the collective intelligence of this great Infinity.

Will you meet this challenge; will you achieve this more ultimate destiny? How important is this achievement to you and how important it is to your fellowman? And finally, can you begin to fulfill this more ultimate promise of immortality given to you by Creative Intelligence—or will you break yourself upon the wheel of karma and break this immortal pledge defiling the complete entirety of Infinity and defeating Its purpose or Its being; or will you constructively lend yourself to this Creative Infinite Intelligence? Will you lend yourself to the cause of logic and reason, to the necessity of being and to the most ultimate of all creative achievements—Constructive Immortality?

The answer lies with you, my friend. I can only give you the first elemental curriculum to the proposition of Infinity. I can only temporarily demonstrate Its efficaciousness in transforming you from mortal flesh into Immortal Beings. Yet, with all I can bring or demonstrate, the answer to your own destiny lies within your own heart and mind; and only the future will reveal your answer—whether you will die a slow and everlasting death in a purgatory of your own making or whether you will ascend the golden spiral staircase of evolution into the Higher Worlds and live an Immortal Life as a Celestial Being.

CHAPTER XXIII

Man — His Own Worst Enemy!

I have often said and will repeat, every person is his own worst enemy; that is because every new truth, every new aspect or condition of life, every and any thing which could do him good, and from which he could derive benefit, must be warped and distorted into the narrow confines and configurations of his own opinions and beliefs, based upon the past. In most instances this practice is quite useless and impedes the progressive evolution of the individual; and if the new truth cannot be warped or distorted, then it must be destroyed. Today this is basic Freudian psychology, but it is also basic human psychology and has existed as long as man, for man lives by it. It was this psychology which caused the crucifixion.

Let's clear up a few delusions about healing. First, no one can heal by directing the 'so-called' magnetic aura, simply because you don't have one. True, you do have an aura but in true scientific classification, it is not magnetic. Irrespective of what it is called, the human aura does not and cannot heal. The aura is an outward radiation or field of energy which results from the net energy radiations from billions of electrical energy fields of billions of atoms which comprise the human body. The human mind or consciousness also radiates, to some extent, its own energy field, but this energy field is developed through the oscillating process as with the psychic anatomy. You cannot direct this energy field or any other energy field with your conscious human mind, simply because you do not know how to attune yourself consciously to these respective energy fields; and even if you could, you still could not heal any portion of the human body by directing auric energies into this defective part. If your body is defective in any way, it must always be healed through the psychic anatomy, which means simply the aberrations and effects in the psychic anatomy must be cancelled out and replaced with healthy configurations which, in turn, will reflect a healthy picture and a controlling force into the defective physical part and it will rebuild itself accordingly.

Remember that your aura is only reflecting the net sum and total of your physical anatomy; to try to use this auric radiation to heal you would only be reflecting it backward—or in reverse into the body and in a sense only increasing or doubling the sickness which was already there. Wave forms carry information; the out-going auric vibrations carry information of your physical condition. If you reverse this energy, you will only increase the total negative picture of what is already there.

Moreover, just because energy is energy does not mean that it will heal. Scientists, doctors, etc., have been working for many years to try and develop different forms and types of electrical energy therapies; pseudo quacks have a multi-million dollar a year business going, treating gullible people with all kinds of gimmicks and contraptions; and the daily newspapers quite frequently carry accounts of raids and crackdowns on these nefarious practitioners. The U.S. Food and Drug Administration is a public agency which exposes thousands of these quacks each year—a type of criminal potentially more dangerous than a gangster, because they often prevent sick people from getting better and more correct treatment from legitimate medical practice.

If you are one of these people who has been or is

presently being duped by some false practitioner, or that you are indulging yourself in some self-contrived treatments—of either real or imaginary ailments—it would be advisable to take a close look at what you are doing. If there is some really serious physical condition in your body, then you should seek out competent medical assistance, until the future time when you can become wise enough to cancel out the true cause of your illness. The legitimate medical profession can and does give great aid and assistance in many physical conditions. The treatment of mental conditions, however, is much less effective. In all cases mental or physical, medical science—as it exists today—is third dimensional and believes only in apparent causes, whereas the true cause is always psychic aberrations. This fact is already partially verified by psychosomatic medicine which recognizes some types of physical illnesses as having their cause rooted in the psychic or subconscious—a halfway measure to be sure, but a step in the right direction.

As of today, there are no legitimate electrical energy or mechanical devices which can heal; science does not know how to build electrical generators which could generate electrical impulses which could cancel out a malformed vortex in the psychic anatomy, for science does not even know of the psychic anatomy.

You cannot be healed by putting your finger into a light socket; in fact, you might be killed. All forms of moving or dynamic energy known as of today can, at best, only stimulate, such as heat rays from an infrared lamp. Ultra-violet or X-rays burn and destroy, and do not heal tissue. The rays from radioactive material also burn and destroy. High frequency radiations of any and all other types known to science can also be considered dangerous and possibly destructive. Powerful radar beams have been known to cause serious physical damage. The reason here again is in the problem of frequency; and until science can generate energy rays to correct psychic aberrations, there will be no progress in this field, because no energy ray can be projected into the physical anatomy and instructed how to heal a damaged organ, remove a tumor, etc. All such building and rebuilding information must come from the psychic anatomy. The cells in your body respond only to the impulses which flow into it from the psychic anatomy.

Therefore, again the same proposition is quite evident. You must learn how to destroy defective portions of your psychic anatomy and rebuild it with intelligent wisdom. A legitimate doctor can set a broken leg; he can remove a small cancer before it becomes dangerous; he can give you insulin to help maintain the correct sugar balance in your blood stream and he can do many other things of great value to your physical body, but in no instance will he ever correct the true cause. For these malfunctions, you and you alone must seek out and find them from out the shambles of your many past lives; and with the knowledge you acquire from Unarius plus an added measure of help from the Brotherhood, the disease-causing slums of your past can be cleared away and your tears of joy, when you are delivered from this past will wash away the last foul stains and traces.

It should be noted that when reference is made to legitimate doctors, a distinction must be made, and I am referring only to doctors who have had the required medical training in accredited universities and hospitals. There are several fraudulent types of practice which are permitted in different states in this country. Such types are easily distinguished, such as the belief that spinal adjustments will cure a disease. The spine cannot be adjusted by manipulation; it is held together by flexible muscles, the respective segments cushioned by flexible discs of cartilaginous material. By exercise, the spinal posture can be changed, but little or no good is ever done by manipulation, no more than a good rubdown. The same is quite true with different kinds of diets or 'so-called' natural methods. Sometimes a nature diet prescribed by some pseudo doctor, can do much more harm than good. In fact, some of these practitioners actually believe cancer can be cured by a diet or by an herbal compound!

The recent Hoxsey cancer investigation reached national prominence, and as of today, many people firmly believe their cancer was healed by taking a few simple herb extracts, even though it is well known that many cancers disappear by themselves without treatment. In fact, it is believed the majority of people who die normal deaths every year have had a cancer at one time in their lives. Millions of people have had tuberculosis and recovered, and some have never known. Others have discovered, through X-rays, that they have had this disease at one time. Every year hundreds of thousands of people visit doctors and go to hospitals needlessly, for conditions which would disappear by themselves. Hundreds of thousands or more correctly, millions of others carry imaginary illnesses through life and spend vast sums of money treating these imaginary illnesses.

And so the pattern goes. Man is the victim of his past, and even as he lives his present he is victimizing himself in his future. It should also be borne in mind that the legitimate medical profession is not entirely legitimate; the rank and file of this medical profession is shot through with charlatans and frauds. There are many legitimate doctors who have a genuine and compassionate interest in helping mankind. They believe sincerely in their profession and their ability to help. There are others who use their profession to subconsciously relive a gory past. In surgery, they are once again butchers on a battlefield, or executioners in a torture dungeon, and there are others who openly acknowledge to themselves that they use their profession to gain wealth and influence in their community. And so, once again the evident proposition. All healing must ultimately be done from the psychic anatomy, and you as a Unariun student still enmeshed as you are in the material world, must use the most expedient means to relive your physical and material conditions, not as an escape mechanism, but rather to help you learn of the only true evolutionary pathway of self-development.

Physical illness is a challenge to your intelligence. Learn to conquer it and eliminate it, not in a false assumption that some doctor, pseudo or legitimate, can heal this condition for you; you can be helped and temporarily relieved, but the true cause and its permanent cure remains with you. At its best, medical science is still comparatively ineffective and elemental. Cemeteries are growing in size and numbers, peopled by the countless thousands of bodies placed there by the ignorance of medical science, which openly professes it does not know the true cause of most of man's fatal diseases or even a really effective treatment. Medical science openly acknowledges that it knows very little of the human anatomy. The human body, to be sure, has been thoroughly dissected in the past several hundred years and all its parts classified; yet the reason for, and the true cause of any organic malfunction of this anatomy is still to be discovered and classified by medical science. Even the riddle of that mysterious life force which energizes all living things is still the imponderable mystery, just as it has been through the many centuries.

Science repeatedly makes new discoveries and heralds each one as the answer; as in chromosomes, they, in turn, took second place to the rediscovered genes which comprise chromosomes; now the mighty gene has fallen to the DNA molecule as the key to life, and you may see in some near future, a new discovery which will obscure the DNA molecule. Again the pattern, every day new discoveries—in space, the macrocosm and in molecules and atoms, the microcosm; and with each new, long awaited discovery, science only confirms its ignorance in past suppositions. The man of science adds to his confusion in comparative values and he reinstates this pattern of discovery and rediscovery, reaffirmation, in some future revelation, oblivion for what he now just discovered. How long will it be before he will push the probing tentacles of his mind beyond this third dimensional world? How long will it be before he recognizes the completely obvious mystery of life? Mystics and clairvoyants, yes even religionists, have attempted to partially verify the existence of other worlds and dimensions; yet these have remained pseudo to science which still positively affirms spontaneous life, generated from ooze or slime; his own world is a proposition which exists without cause or reason in a cosmic void in which he has just faintly envisioned the possibility of life on other planets in other solar systems.

How asinine is the complete portrayal of planetary life lived by the earth man isolated in space, his intellect refrigerated in rhetoricism, yet parenthetically all extensions, all discoveries always supporting interdimensional evolution, which he is attempting to deny in the rigorous atmosphere of third dimensional reactions. Yes, in the latter days there are many false prophets and teachers; and all mankind may indeed be as wolves in sheep's clothing, for in the reactionary stances of his material life, he attempts to destroy the idiom of Infinite Intelligence superimposed in the abundant life of the earth.

Trying to heal the physical body by any conscious effort, such as believing you can direct magnetic energies, is even a worse fallacy than trying to heal a broken leg with a hot water bottle. All such beliefs as they currently exist today—whatever they are called, metaphysics, mental science, mental physics, etcetera, are all pseudo developments in the evolutionary scale of man's history. Today these same beliefs also exist with witch doctors in the jungles of Africa and they exist anywhere with every person who is ignorant of the facts of life, and still tries to correct the defects of his everyday life, his physical body, through some form of witchcraft or sorcery.

There is only one way to have a healthy physical body—that is to have a healthy psychic anatomy; but it also has to be a psychic anatomy which believes completely in the physical world and lives through the physical body. Conversely, the more intelligent you become in respect to the higher or more advanced dimensions and the more you can conceive and believe in them, the more etheric your physical body becomes. The basic plane vibrating rate of all atoms and energy wave forms involved, change and become much higher in frequency. When this happens karma or the past life experiences have an increasingly heavy toll, because they remain unchanged in their frequency. This is all understood much better when you understand the psychic anatomy, its different parts, etc., as well as energy itself. Eventually, the physical disappears because it is no longer useful to that developed psychic anatomy, and that person will then continuously live in the higher worlds.

You, as a student of Unarius have just taken your first important step in changing all vibrating rates concerned with your daily living. To continue changing them to the point where you no longer need a physical body will quite logically mean you will have to avidly pursue your Unariun studies, and just as avidly practice and use this knowledge. It's not a short term proposition, but one in which you will be engaged for countless thousands of years—that is evolution.

For the present, however, one of the first and most important steps you must take to change yourself is—and as quickly as possible—to divest and strip yourself of all concepts and practices which relate to religion, such as prayer, etc., the belief in an emotional god, or gods, mind practices which are only a small step removed from the jungle—such as trying to heal by thought concentration, etc. You cannot possibly begin to understand Infinity, the perfect concept of Interdimensional Intelligence which relates Itself as an integral Creative Function with a vast and an infinite number and variety of interdimensional forms until you realize in complete humility, how infinitely small you are at this present moment; how completely ignorant you are, in comparison, to even a small part of this vast Infinity; and you must realize that progressive evolution is the cornerstone of life.

You must constantly and at every opportune time, abandon old, outworn and outmoded things of yesterday and replace them with the fresh new life of tomorrow. You cannot do this if you cling to the past. The past is death, literally and figuratively. Only in the future will you find life. For the moment, do not overly concern yourself to the exclusion of all else with trying to heal your physical body or change your earthly conditions. Instead, try to change yourself from within. That is, start to rebuild your psychic anatomy, and build it out of Infinite Wisdom. When you begin to constructively reconstruct your psychic anatomy, your physical body and world will change and for the better. As you progress it will have less and less importance to you, and in some future time you will no longer need these vehicular accouterments which carried you through the first stages of your evolution.

Start at once to discard your ancient placebos, the old practices of black magic, witchcraft, etc., the superstitions of religion. Seek to gain an Infinite understanding and in this you will find the Kingdom of Heaven within.

Part Two

Lest there be some confusion as to our attitude or relationship to the medical profession perhaps some clarification is in order. The fact that we sometimes, and under strongly indicated circumstances, recommend that a person seek out a competent doctor to treat his condition, may seem in opposition and hypocritical to our doctrine of spiritual healing as it is sometimes called—the process and modes thereof having been thoroughly presented by us. There are several important considerations; certain instances demand an immediate solution which could not be accomplished by the inner method or spiritual means; the individual himself is the greatest single obstruction in his own healing. He may believe the Higher and more Intelligent Entities or Forces can heal him, and as indeed They could, he may apparently possess all necessary requisites to some such miraculous or inner spiritual healing which would remove a physical condition, yet he may not have had the very necessary indoctrination and preparation from the Higher Worlds when he was in the life in between worlds.

The advent of any miraculous healing and the true corrective therapy which removes the malformed aberration from the psychic anatomy is a culmination of many lifetimes of preparation, and until such a preparation is made, any person is too basically materialistic, despite his attitudes or apparent beliefs to have such a healing. There is occasionally, a Unariun student who to some degree, presents the same obstructions and lack of full preparation for a healing. He may have been only partially acclimated to the whole proposition. Moreover, on the material plane, any spiritual or inner healing is necessarily limited in its effectiveness for life on earth demands repetitious circumstances which could re-instigate the physical malfunction after it has been corrected. The earth doctor or physician can and does, fill a very great need to his society; he can remove defective kidneys—even transplant these organs under the right conditions; he can transplant a cornea and restore sight, remove ruptured appendix, or even a stomach which has become cancerous; yet these and any and all other physical conditions are only superficial apparencies.

The belief in the cause of such conditions by the doctor as he sees them in his atomical science is only coincidental. The true cause is always psychic; for instance: 46,000 people die yearly in this country from lung cancer, and by far the greatest percentage of these people are heavy smokers; yet it is known that millions of heavy smokers live to a ripe old age without lung cancer. While it is clearly indicated that heavy smoking does cause lung cancer, yet it is also autosuggestive and the smoker, constantly flooding his lungs with smoke is, in each instance, tuning himself, psychically speaking, back into other lifetimes where he was associated with death in smoke-filled rooms, war-torn battlefields, etc. Smoke and its association with his past, carry the double indemnity of death into his present life in the form of cancer which, in its true configuration, is a malformed vortex in the psychic anatomy, and by a specific attunement reflecting the same wildly gyrating configurations into cell structures of the lungs wherein they cease their normal function and also become wild.

Incidentally, the battle of lung cancer versus the cigarettes and other deadly killers is being hotly contested at this time. Smoking is not condoned; it is an asinine, health-robbing practice, but doubly so when it links any person up with past-life associations involving fire, smoke, and death. The doctor, therefore, when he signs the death certificate of a lung cancer victim does not know of these past lifetime associations which, when combined with the smoke and coal tar deposits from countless cigarettes, caused the cancer; and in death, neither is the minister who speaks the eulogy conscious of these facts. And so it is with the gamut of human diseases which beset mankind and which are the incidental by-products of his carnal earth life, and the situation will remain very much the same until mankind and medical science universally recognize and practice the Unariun Science of Life which the Unariun student has at his fingertips. Therefore, if we recommend medical assistance to any person, it is not because we believe the doctor can heal him. Almost all doctors acknowledge that they do not heal; and we, like the doctors, must ultimately resolve correction and healing as a personal effort and accomplishment. But unlike the doctors, we believe and know that this can only be accomplished when a fuller and more comprehensive understanding of the Unariun Concept and curriculum is conceived and practiced. Any circumstance created in ignorance is always evil, inasmuch as it is not constructively related to an intelligent motion of expression and it always carries a double or triple indemnity, for with each successive life, each year of each life, and each day of each year, all such ignorant circumstances are constantly repeated and, with each repetition multiply their strength seven times seven.

Thought and action are always synonymous for there can be no action without first the thought. The action, therefore, remains the reactionary element even though it may be self—contained within the thought and not re-expressed in physical motion. There are many other incidental aspects which make it necessary for us to compromise our relationship to the medical profession, one of which is the avoidance of unnecessary controversy which might arise in the minds of those who did not understand the Unariun Concept. This world is the heritage of those who believe in it, and to the almost total exclusion of all else, and as these beliefs are only evolutionary adaptations of the jungle law—survival of the fittest—we therefore, wisely refrain from arousing any antagonisms which would psychically revert any and all who were so involved, back into the more primitive phases of their existence.

If we are to serve a humanitarian purpose among those who have been preconditioned for this advent in their lives, then we will also judiciously discriminate these from among the others who cannot be alerted and served. As to his future, any earth person is curious and he is also always fearful and with the mixed emotions he has about his future—doubt, fear, insecurity, and inevitable death—he will become as a raging lion if he is suddenly confronted with the obvious proof of an intelligent survival after death and the method and manner of its accomplishment. For such is man's nature, gladly accepting in an infinite number of disguises, the multitudes and hosts of apparitions from his past. Yes, even sinful, evil and painful, yet each day he walks with them and they are his bedfellows at night; and in all this he lives a great hypocrisy of his life and refuses the obvious necessity of progressive evolution, and instead indulges himself with the opiate of a religious intercession, the belief he is forgiven of his sins and other religious falderal.

It is not strange, then, that we, the Unariuns, the Brotherhood of Infinite Love and Understanding must always maintain this Brotherhood in all circumstances. It is the equilibrium in which we find the wisdom in all things. Yes, this is a material world and as such, together with those who believe in it, we leave strictly alone; we know there are other ways and means, other agencies which will bring these materialistic people to the threshold of a higher understanding and in the way in which they understand. And as we come into these worlds to alert the ready ones, we are, indeed, as was "Daniel in the Lion's Den" of Nebuchadnezzar, protected, yet not by divine intercession but by logic, reason and Infinite Understanding.

CHAPTER XXIV

Man, the Grave Digger

In quite a number of instances, I have presented to the Unariun student the obvious necessity of progressive evolution, or conversely, the retrogressive evolution which leads back into oblivion. The thought has occurred to me on many occasions that I could very well be accused of using the same coercive tactics used by the religionist in his heaven or hell doctrine. If this is so, then may I paraphrase Daniel Webster who said, "If this be treason, make the most of it," so, if I am using coercive tactics, then you, the student, should make the most out of it. However, no defense is needed, nor am I using coercive tactics; for how else could I present to you the simple alternative, the progressive life or the retrogressive death principle, until the time when your mental evolution has carried you beyond the point where I need to use the reactionary elements of your third-dimensional world. I will have to, by necessity, use these elements in helping you attain the first perspectives of Immortal Life.

Every day that you live you are, figuratively speaking, taking out one more shovel-full of earth from that grave you are digging for yourself in which you will some day lay down your physical body. How much of you will there be left that will survive above and beyond this grave? Will you wiggle your way senselessly through a hellish nightmare to the next convenient hole and again re-emerge into some earthly world to repeat the mistakes and transgressions of the past, to relive in increased intensity the heavy accumulation of painful karma? For indeed, as your psychic anatomy is composed of these energy configurations, to live and relive, so they must be restimulated and refortified with similar energy configurations; or instead, would you not prefer to find yourself on that day of departure standing upright in the next world, to be able to see, feel, and hear telepathically which is the manner of these worlds, as there are no physical bodies?

And so if it is coercion, or by any other term or by any other method, it would be justified in usage if it would be the means of saving your life; if I can somehow jolt you out of the complete circumference of your personal ego where you can be confronted with the necessity of survival through constructive evolution, or death, which already has begun to manifest itself in your body and in your consciousness. As a progressive plane of evolution, the earth world can support and progressively incline, plant and animal life up to certain terminating points. All species are constantly changing to meet the demand of progressive evolution, for the world is indeed moving through the cyclic fields of force through the cosmic universe, and these fields as part of Infinity, supply at least in part, both the life sustaining and governing power which make earth life possible.

In your earth life you, therefore, are like a man who climbs a mountain; when he reaches the top, he must come down again unless he can find a higher mountain immediately in front of him. Unlike mountain climbing, however, in real life the downward trail leads to oblivion. Infinity always presents a higher mountain—more correctly, a higher, more expanded cycle of consciousness; and when this cycle is completed, you must have already begun to travel upon another even higher, more expanded cycle.

It is not simple to present, in the reactionary elemental vernacular of the earth world, a fundamental curriculum of Infinity or the elements to perpetuate your survival unless this presentation is done in the vernacular familiar to you. Within myself I have this curriculum minus the reactionary elements. Instead of reaction there is integration. Repercussion has been replaced with coordination and so on ad infinitum.

An intelligent hypothesis of life is achieved only when the human intellect can be developed beyond the point of necessity for such elemental reactionary elements of his earth life philosophy, and even though the earth man does, as of today, still live completely by them, he, individually and collectively, will always come to that jumping off place in his evolution where they can no longer sustain him. Life, itself, as is lived by the earth man, is coercive and all reactionary stances of any person's life are, in themselves, coercive elements. They demand that every person completely abscond to the conformities of his society. Fear is the negative or minus potential in every aspect of life, yet inversely in cyclic motion, becomes the positive dominant force of his life. So live on then, fellow student, not inducing reactionary elements from whatever I may present to you mingled in the package of Infinite Truth which I give you, for it is in this way I have made them presentable to you. But learn to live beyond the presentation and garner this Infinite Wisdom to help reconstruct your psychic anatomy, to build and rebuild your intellect to a capacity which will enable you to survive upright beyond the grave.

CHAPTER XXV

Coals To Newcastle

The following is a letter written by the Moderator to a student in reply to a question regarding a book pertaining to old religions—(old and present)—and which could serve many others with similar questions.

Dear Student: Regarding your letter, it always makes us very happy to receive testimonials—"The Joining" tape in particular is something new and evidently quite 'special' and we are especially joyous of the manifestation as Power which it carries which you and many other students have so strongly felt.

So far as the book is concerned, may I quote an old cliché, "like carrying coal to Newcastle". Yes, Ruth and I are quite familiar with most of the books of this sort and, in toto, they are the representative form of what Unarius is attempting to destroy.

Two thousand years ago Jesus tried to tear 'Jehovah' from the minds and hearts of his people and suffered death for his pains. Since then, history has repeated itself many times to those who have in some small way attempted to prove the heresy of the Jehovah concept. There are many books of this sort—the Oahspe, The Book of Mormon, Revelations in the Bible, as well as much of the entire contents of the Bible are of the same nature. Psychologically speaking, they have been produced by people undergoing a strong traumatic psychism; when in this trance-like state, they somehow saw into the fourth dimensions or the Inner Kingdom and attempted in writing to justify these visions in some symbolic form. The Unariun books, "Pulse of Creation Series", more factually describes

184

some of these places, the psychological reasons for their existence, and the science in their creation. Actually, they are bridging the gap in evolution between the material world and the higher worlds, and as dwelling places and teaching Centers, they are the gateway and way stations for countless billions of souls who are traveling back and forth in their incarnations.

Jehovah is an age-old deistic configuration which has existed in many forms and under many names and over the entire face of the globe. Jehovah represents some sort of a central configuration of creation which primitive and elemental minds have personalized; given it, not only great magical powers but also all the emotional vicissitudes of human nature. The earth man's primitive elemental mind has no reason or logic, no science or other information which would give him a tangible explanation for Infinite Intelligence and Creation. Even our modern twentieth century science only very partially explains an elemental form of creation.

In viewing all this, you should therefore doubly appreciate Unarius which gives you all the missing information scientifically proven and further substantiated by the many thousands of miracles happening to those who are beginning to understand life through Unarius.

May I add a word of caution; unless you can read books such as you have sent us very objectively and for their historical interest only, it would be wise to abstain from such reading. Unarius is complete in every respect and if you will pursue this study to the exclusion of all else, you will find that it not only will supply all the philosophy and science, all the answers in your present life, but it will open up the Inner Kingdom to you in the future. For the Inner Kingdom is the logical, philosophical, and scientific explanation and reason for Infinite Creation; and any person who aspires and evolves into the Inner Kingdom must do so by virtue of all knowledge pertaining to it and the correct usage of this knowledge as his own life.

All religions and their deifications are only symbologies; they only represent the emotional physical form of this very evident creation and as long as this creation is represented by such deistic beliefs, it will never be understood; for, any deity always usurps logic, reason, and moral responsibility, etc., from the individual. Religion, therefore, is immoral; and any religious person has, in his religion, relegated the transmissions of the highest virtues of his life to a fancied deity; he has abandoned logic and reason by placing all unexplained, all so-called mysterious happenings to emotionalism, to these false gods. But I believe I have stated these things many times before (in the teachings) and I would suggest, for your own sake and your own safety, that such reading material as you have sent us be left alone. There is greater danger that you may inadvertently and unconsciously tune yourself into the same obsessive forces which ruled the minds of the authors of these books, and they are, dear student, part of the populace of the 'pits of hell'.

We are very appreciative of your avid interest in what is obviously an attempt to verify or vindicate the Unariun Concepts, from this book; however, you will find—if you so try—ample evidence in the world and in your daily life. In fact it would be much better to more thoroughly introspect your daily life and this world, with the Unariun Concept rather than to seek out verification in some musty tome, composed by a highly neurotic mind under intense psychic pressures.

As a matter of fact, being a good Unariun student means not only studying the written Works, but using them in your daily life as a basic platform of reference wherefrom you can correctly analyze and interpret your own life and the world of form and motion about you. And may I add, if you do this honestly and sincerely in selflessness and solely in virtue as the creative Principle of life, you will always find the great Unariun Brotherhood at your side, ready and willing to help and aid, yet with jurisprudence, so that you will never be robbed of your inalienable right of self determination—a right which is given by any person who relegates his future, his moral and spiritual values into the hands of some priesthood or in symbolic form of its false deities. Unarius is the first honest teaching since the time of Jesus and, in the idiom of our twentieth century science, much more valuable, more extensive and comprehensive. Yet this honesty is seldom fully appreciated for millions of people would shun it because it presents the very obvious—personal moral responsibility—a responsibility which constantly perpetuates itself through endless incarnations until progressive evolution is substantiated in this personal moral responsibility.

It is much more convenient to these millions of people to shrug off, so they think, their sins and iniquities, in the false concept of intercession or that 'His blood washed away my sins', etc. It is much more convenient for these millions of people that they personally, through their religion, will be 'saved' for future immortal life, and simply because they 'believe'. It is far more difficult, more demanding and self-sacrificing to assume personal moral responsibility, to realize individually, the proposition of progressive or retrogressive evolution, according to how we think and live. Thus the world has in effect, become one of the 'pits of hell' for these countless millions who revolve in their daily lives, trying to live parasitically, one upon the other in the falsely constructed mirage of their personal material life.

Let us hope the future will show you are not one of these, and like the parable of the one lost lamb, you will eventually be gathered into the arms and onto the bosom of Infinite Wisdom—there to be carried into the endless Immortality of an ever progressive higher evolution.

CHAPTER XXVI

Hallucinations

One of the most important problems confronting the Unariun student is that which can be contained within the defined term of hallucination. To the psychologist, hallucination involves a whole host of traumatic conditions which inflict, to a more or less degree, every member of the human race; and in an attempt to adjust various differences in hallucinations, a doctor or psychologist would use a long list of seventy-five cent words in an attempt to bolster up his pseudo science. He does not, however, at any time understand the true nature of the numerous mental processes which make life possible for every person, that is, unless he has been an electronic engineer and has, somehow, succeeded in transferring the symbology of his psychology into a tangible science.

The understanding of any mental faculty, mental expression or conformity, the different mental functions, etc., always must be immediately resolved into wave forms of energy. No reality or appearance of life is possible unless it manifests as such wave forms. All five senses and paranormal faculties function as oscillating instruments or entities in the inception or propagation of expressionary wave forms called life. In some respects and in certain instances, man has, mechanically and electronically, duplicated the wave form qualities expressed by humans and other forms of life; the television set is one such device. Properly speaking then, life itself, as it is lived from the material plane, is one big, compounded hallucination. The illusion of mass, as it is compounded in the tremendously complex 'civilized' life in which we are presently involved, is illusionary in nature. As hallucination is only improperly defined as illusion, and as life really exists as oscillating wave forms—life being supported by these compound oscillations—we must, therefore, relegate the material life as one vast hallucination.

Not until the student understands, in the pure idiom of science, the transference of consciousness as oscillating wave forms rather than an illusionary reaction appearance, does such a student begin to understand life, either here or hereafter; then only, can he begin to dissociate himself from the constant illusionary hallucination of life itself.

The approach to the Infinite, from this illusionary plane of experience, has begun for many people—a life which becomes increasingly embroiled in various psychisms and which may, or may not, have a relative or connecting factor with the individual's life. With the increasing acknowledgment, desire for, and realization of higher ways of life, the student is increasingly confounded by the complex compositions of his material life under such conditions; stresses become more acute; the demands for adjustment are much greater to his personal ego, and he becomes increasingly sensitive to the interplay of complex wave forms which are pressing in upon him from all sides.

Visualizing for the moment that the human is, in all effect and principle, an electronic instrument as is the TV, this increased sensitivity can and does give rise to a host of intangible realizations which would not otherwise affect a less sensitive person. He will, therefore, realize within consciousness, either in a vague or a more realistic form, a host of picturizations which can be considered hallucinations. Such a mind condition can be further intensified if the person is basically, either introverted or extroverted, that he has long sought for public recognition, or that he has improperly identified himself with society. Also he is under strong, though undetermined, subconscious influences from countless numbers of life experiences, psychic shocks, etc., which were incurred in numerous previous lives. Under such conditions traumatic illusions can easily be incepted whereby he believes he is the reincarnate of some great personality who has lived in the past. This can be considered as sort of a subconscious device used to bolster up a deflated ego. If such a person should come under the jurisdiction of our present-day practicing psychology, he might be confined to a mental institution, given shock treatments, etc.

Such a course of action is just as illusionary as are the hallucinations. If this mentally obsessed person—and a person is obsessed by an hallucination—could have the facts of life explained to him, as are contained in Unarius, and providing this person could accept them and learn of them, then these hallucinations would cease to exist—either here or hereafter. In more advanced instances, hallucination is supported as the only tangible in a host of intangible elements, and as it is the only tangible, it eventually can become the entire center of existence. When this condition has reached such a point, the person is usually judged insane, and almost needless to point out, there are several hundred thousand people in this country who have arrived at this terminating point because our present-day science, psychology, materia medica, and religion do not contain all the basic principles and concepts of life as they are explained in the Unarius lesson courses.

To the student, therefore, the dangers and perils of hallucinations are all-important and especially when he is involved in the 'working out' process of various past lives and past lifetime experiences, psychic shocks, etc. Methods, procedures, results, etc., are all matters of careful personal analysis. Should the student persist in believing he is some great personality from the past, and should this belief not be properly vindicated by unalterable proof, and that such a belief does not, or has not aided him in any beneficial ways, then he can be considered obsessed with an hallucination.

In the near future in a reference work which will be compounded, this and other all-important elements of human life will be entered into much more thoroughly; proper methods of analysis, diagnoses, and corrective therapies will be fully explained. This book, however, will be a text, not largely understood unless the student has first acclimated himself to the concept of life as a constant, never-ending, vastly complex series of successive wave forms of energy.

For the present, therefore, learn to curb any strong hallucinations that may repeatedly occur. Devote your time to the study of the pure science involved, and into daily life comparisons. Depend also upon help from the Advanced Personalities who are working for you and your cause as a Unariun student. It is safe to predict that at any future time when you so conceive the more complete entity of Creation as an oscillating principle, involved with countless interdimensional planes, that at that time you will not be troubled, either with hallucinations or any other attendant psychisms which are a heritage of any earth man who lives the material life.

One more point that should be strongly emphasized: hallucinations can be, and often are, disincarnate entities, or, in other words, dislocated or misplaced astral people, living in one of those nether worlds where, through frequency attunement, they try to live their own hallucinations through some unsuspecting earth person. Mental institutions are filled with such victims who believe they are 'Josephine', 'Napoleon', 'George Washington', etc., etc; they even adopt mannerisms associated with these historical figures. Yes even physical disturbances and diseases can be re-created or vicariously attuned and made manifest in the physical body; even death can be 'relived'. This is indeed a sad ending for what might have otherwise become a very wonderful person—a person progressively instituted to creatively oscillate with the Infinite.

The warning here is obvious; likewise the importance of the knowledge contained in Unarius is even more strongly emphasized. It is a life preserver in a vast sea of probables and improbables, harmonies and inharmonies, vices and vicissitudes; yes, even the complexity of life itself as it is generally lived, becomes defeatist in purpose, useless in any attainment which always terminates in death; for such are the material worlds and which can be truly said to be, in respective comparison to the higher worlds, one of the many pits of hell. You, as a student, here at this time and place, have arrived at the turning point in the most serious crisis of your life. It will turn either downward or upward. It will move, just as do all other cyclic forms in the Infinite Cosmogony.

You, as a human, have that great preconceived difference from all other forms of life—that is; your ability to control your direction and your destiny. You do this either by lack of knowledge which will give you retrogressive motion or with knowledge which gives you the progressive motion; that is the determinant in every human life—the determinant which relegates you either to Heaven or hell.

In a final analysis, however, it should clearly be indicated that when you have reached that time in your life when you begin to work out your past lives, you should not resist the scenes or flashbacks which you may have. It is most necessary that they should reappear at the correct time or with the proper in-phase or out-of-phase motion, whereby the negative content is cancelled out, and they will no longer have a pernicious effect upon you. There will also occur at that moment, a more distinct polarization of that past lifetime experience with the Superconscious or the Higher Self. When such a flashback and workout occurs, it will have unmistakable symptoms and results. It will usually appear more vivid and real than even the present life about you. It will also cause great emotion and a flood of tears. Afterward you will have a wonderful sense of relief, a feeling of buoyancy or lightness; you will be able to look back and remember that past experience, who you were at the time, etc., without emotion and without recrimination, only a firm feeling that you're glad it is over and it won't happen again.

Thus it will have no more effect upon you, even if you should see yourself as some historical personage in the past. The self-importance of that realization will pass with the working out; you will not necessarily feel flattered; neither will you use this knowledge as a crutch to bolster up a constantly deflated ego. Instead, you will have a passive view of those past lifetimes and their experiences when they have been so correctly worked out. More specifically speaking, any person who comes back to work out past lifetimes, does so on the basis that it is a preconceived plan which he has worked out for himself while in the spiritual worlds, before he incarnated. Also, at that time he enlists the aid of the spiritual organization which is working with the earth plane during that period; thus it will be, he will again be born into the material world. He will live his life until the proper time when he meets the necessary catalyzing agencies in his earth plane life, and at the proper moment, the Advanced Personalities, Scientists, Doctors, Teachers, etc., will bring in the necessary instrumentation. They will psychokinetically project the necessary power and picture impulses which will enable the mortal mind to go back through time and space, so to speak, and see himself as he was and what he was doing; yes, even thousands of years ago. Yes, this is indeed different than hallucination; and after you have passed through one or more experiences in 'working out' the past, you will learn to recognize what has taken place—not the inception of some vague energy image, nor the self-constructed thought form body called the 'alter ego' by the psychologist, but rather each workout will be an unmistakable event in your life, most often followed by others in rapid succession, each one different but always with the same soul-cleansing action.

This is the true repentance and redemption, spoken of by the religionist, but never attained by any mortal man until he reaches that certain threshold which has been so often spoken of in the works of Unarius—that place where the individual has, in his spiritual life, caught glimpses of the vast interplay of the Supercosmic worlds. He has walked the streets in the Heavenly cities and has read his own akashic which he has written for himself in his past lifetimes; and often he has used the blood of his fellow man for the ink in his pen of life. So he will come to the threshold, to his time of repentance, not at the behest of some religious evangelist; neither will he grovel on the floor nor on the sawdust before the altar. His is a repentance reached and found when he compares the brilliance of the Infinite future with the sordid darkness of the material past. He will see the necessity for rebuilding himself, to reconstruct an entirely new kind of body in which he can live as he journeys into the Immortal future. He will see the glowing forms and faces of those who have already accomplished some of that purpose. And while he is still viewing these people, while living in his lower astral body, he will see them as radiant Angels, hardly knowing that these radiant Beings are also looking up to even higher worlds.

And so his quest for life begins; yet most properly from his last earth life, and after completing his plans and preparations, he will again seek the moldy fields of earth and from the cradle launch himself afresh into a world well known by himself, yet not recognized by eyes that feed afresh upon a world that's filled with childish lore. And as the days pass he is molded more and more into the likeness of all the things he was and did in those long past days. He apes the forms and motions of his fellow man, but always has he thusly been so conformed; and so he meets the stranger, a friend he may have known upon some 'Hill of Calvary' or have seen him as a Light among the Heavenly hosts; and then from deep within, the hidden purpose of his life springs forth. Again he sees his past, not once but in a thousand times, and in a thousand different ways, the scenes of life come flooding back, the days and acts and deeds of yesteryears and long-forgotten lives, stand stark and clean and bright against the blackness of the doom they prophesy for those who live for them alone.

And as he weeps, the flooding Light of Infinite Life

streams through the fabric of his soul; a Light that cleanses, a Power to purify all deeds, yet leaves in knowledge, the image of their transgression, a silent warning of the earthly life. But with this knowledge there comes a strength, a will and purpose, and the understanding lives; and powered with this knowledge, this soul will reconstruct himself, and from the sordid past, becomes a radiant thing, its garment white against the Infinite Light; it seeks and finds a Heavenly Host.

CHAPTER XXVII

The Mongoloid

One of the more important aspects of life which has, as yet, not been thoroughly explained in the liturgy of Unarius, is a complete presentation of conception; how various different kinds of physically and mentally defective children are born into the world: such children as are classified mongoloid, mentally retarded, hair lip, or other forms of physical and mental defects; barring of course, such defective children who incurred their defects from organic causes such as syphilis, accidental blows, abortion attempted, and instrument deliveries. The process of conception is extremely complex inasmuch as it involves a great interplay and linkage of harmonic attunements, etc., in what might best be described as an extremely complex system of energy wave form integrations.

As medical and genetical scientists do not understand or know about the psychic anatomies, theirs must be a purely physical understanding of conception which grew out of the studies made by the Austrian monk, Mendel. In genetical science as it applies to a human, the process of conception goes something like this: the male germ cell—the spermatozoon—succeeds in making contact with the female ovum and penetrates the outside membrane of the egg. The male and female germ cells contain certain numbers of chromosomes, 22 in each male and 23 in each female cell. Inside the chromosomes, there are large numbers of what are called genes or units of character, such as dark hair, blue eyes, etc. After the male germ cell penetrates the ovum, there begins a pairing-off process,

198

something like an old-fashioned country square dance, at which time there ensues a struggle for supremacy to see which genes are the most dominant and which will control the physical characteristics of the human to be.

Now, this may be all right as far as it goes; genetical science may be partially or wholly right in describing what they believe is conception; right, as far as some of the physical characteristics are concerned, but like all other physical sciences, this is only part of the picture. First, there could not be any of this mating or pairing unless there were psychic anatomies involved. It is the psychic anatomies of the parents who generated the germ cells, who are partly responsible for this mating and pairing process. There is also a third factor involved, or more correctly a third psychic anatomy, a disincarnate spirit person, if you please, who is trying to get back into the material world. At the moment of conception, there may be one or a thousand such entities or persons trying to get control and attach themselves, so to speak, in a psychic manner to the newly-forming germ cells on the basis of frequency relationship. One of the more dominant entities will succeed. In this respect, it is most likely to be a close association or relative or polarity who has been with the parents through many lifetimes.

Now, picture in your mind this extremely complex process; there are literally billions of energy wave forms oscillating in and out of each other, all trying to get something done, or gain control. These billions of wave forms determine all the characteristics of the human to be. Sometimes the wave forms from the mother's psychic anatomy are more dominant and the child will look and act like the mother, or sometimes it may be the father's wave forms which gain control; and then, again, it may be that the mother's and father's wave forms will only partially control and form the physical anatomy and the newly attached entity or person will be the dominant character. In rare instances a more highly developed person, not necessarily a polarity with the parents, will attach itself to the new fetus; such as has been recorded historically, where an infant prodigy, or genius, was born into the world. A classical example is Mozart, and while his family was musical, he did not have any polarity with them; the musical plane of reference made it possible for him to be born into that family.

At this point of our introspection, you should have begun to form a somewhat vague idea of this very complex process, yet according to the law of harmonics, precise and exact in every way. However, under certain conditions, portions or sections of wave form spectrums will be so balanced they will cancel themselves out, and they will become neutral. When this happens the child will be born defective, mentally or physically, or both, according to what portions of this newly-forming psychic anatomy were affected, for a certain portion of a psychic anatomy must form and grow before the physical body can form and grow.

This is better understood when we understand that the parent psychic anatomies are all oscillating their varied intelligences into the newly-forming psychic anatomy; the spirit entity which is the mental portion of another psychic anatomy is receiving, helping, sorting out, so to speak, the various received wave forms and is also reflecting its own influence in the same manner. This must all be done ahead of the time before the infant can grow. As stated before, under such complex conditions certain maladjustments can occur, such as the case of identical twins, when the newly-forming psychic anatomy splits in half, so to say, to maintain control over two evenly divided parent influences.

Ordinary twins are simply the doubled process of a normal single birth: two ova and two spermatozoa, two spirit entities, etc., which grow into two separate placentas or bags; likewise triplets, quadruplets, etc. Now, in any psychic anatomy there are many centers composed of vortexes of energy which control the physical anatomy, its metabolic rate, etc., and all of the many and varied processes which the physical body performs automatically. When the newly-forming psychic anatomy is in the process of adjustment, at the time of conception, there may enter in, as stated before, certain factors which may cause the child to be born defective. As the outline of each physical characteristic is contained in one or a multiple number of wave forms, alteration or cancellation can change the respective portion of the physical anatomy. It can be easily visualized then that the portions of the psychic anatomy which control the shape and size of the head, together with the brain, can be so affected that the child will be born a mongoloid. The same condition applies to any other defect which may appear in the newly born infant. From this objective introspection it is at once apparent that modern sciences which deal with the factors of human genetics are, like all other sciences, very incomplete. That is why most doctors can only shake their heads and say, "we don't know", when asked the cause of these constantly occurring physically malformed births. Almost needless to say, nothing can be done about the situation until they understand the true human which is the psychic anatomy.

Other variables which may enter into this complex process may be the character of the newly-attached psychic anatomy or the disincarnate entity which has taken possession—so to speak. If that spirit person is mentally defective or has formerly lived as a defective person, he may be entering into the world by reason of karma to work out a former lifetime situation with one or both parents. The spirit entity may also be a criminal, a murderer, or some kind of a hellion, such as in the case of Genghis Khan or Adolph Hitler.

During the past several decades there has been a great interplanetary transmigration; that means hordes of spirit entities from other planetary systems from all over the galaxy and the universe are swarming about the earth trying to be born into this material world. That is one of the dominant reasons why we are having such troubled times, and especially with the juvenile portion of our population. At present, according to the Federal Bureau of Investigation, there is a 5 to 1 ratio increase of crime in the United States, 43% of which is committed by juveniles under 18 years of age. It is easy to see that these juvenile malcontents are spawned from the lower astral worlds and who formerly lived on other earth-like planets where their respective civilizations decayed just as ours is now doing.

Just as the prophecy of doom was written on the wall in ancient Babylonia, so as of today the same message is quite apparent to all those who can read it in the daily newspapers, on television and movie portrayals, in different vital statistics which show the inclinations of our civilization. What can be done? Philosophically then, as with the mongoloid, the savants of our time can only shake their heads and mutter, "we don't know". Classical words of doom, yet with all, again graphically portraying the message of Infinite Creation, the rise and fall of civilizations, epochs of time, the forming of new worlds all mutely portray cyclically, Infinite regeneration; Cosmic Creation, carried as it is, from the mind of the Infinite into an infinite number of dimensions, each with its spectrums which function again in the common denominators of harmonic interplay to create new suns, new planets, and new civilizations. The countless billions of planets which float like microscopic bits of dust around countless billions of suns which form countless billions of galaxies and universes, all these planetary systems can be, and are, the spawning grounds of multitudinous forms of life, each form a way the Infinite Creator regenerates Itself.

How small then is a single human personality; yet how important this personality is when he is developed to a point where he reflects, and also regenerates, the Infinite Principle of life. These are the latter days, as prophesied in the Christian Bible, latter days of a civilization, and they are the latter days of many who have approached the threshold. For, as death comes as a thief in the night, so will death steal away the material world from all those who believe in it and leave them the blackness of oblivion.

The most recent scientific discoveries on conception involve the newly discovered DNA molecule, a subject which has been separately covered in another supplement. According to science, genes are now believed to be composed of these DNA molecules, a very complex molecule resembling somewhat a spiral staircase—the various atomic structures composed of different known atomic equivalents. However, irrespective of such subdivisions or even new discoveries which may develop in the future, the principles of harmonic regeneration are still very much in effect; in fact the DNA molecule discovered further substantiates this regenerative principle as has been explained many times in the Unariun Liturgies.

Any atom, regardless of its designation or kind, is a miniature solar system of energy, a complex unit of cyclic wave forms, each with its own particular frequency. The parallaxes of their orbits are presently referred to in atomic science as neutrons, protons, positrons, etc. However, there are no solid particles in an atom. When an atom is split or broken up, tiny bits of this energy formed by these parallaxes retain their respective polarities according to the original cyclic motions within the atom. It is these cyclic wave-form motions together with the radiated electromagnetic field which controls their respective reactionary position on the scale of atomic weights or equivalents.

However, again it must be repeated—there are no solid particles in any material form, neither will they be found in any other dimension; for the Infinite Creator or Intelligence is this oscillating wave-form energy substance which forms all things irrespective of their form or function, or the dimension in which they are found.

Part Two

In the foregoing text, there has been presented a rather broad and generalized view of that all important factor of life—conception. This presentation, quite naturally, leads us up to a question which is always asked by those who have the burden of caring for defective children. It is quite obvious that as various branches of science do not know about psychic anatomies, there are no doctors, clinics or therapeutic centers which could possibly institute some corrective measures.

In all cases, it is first necessary to individually classify and diagnose each defective person. There are many types and kinds of defects which could not be helped from the material side of life. These cases will all have to wait until they have lived the physical cycle and return to the spiritual worlds and under proper conditions before very much can be done for them. In other cases certain therapeutic healing can be projected by advanced personalities from the higher spiritual planes. Classifications and diagnoses are, at the present time, impossible to obtain in this material world, as only a person highly trained in various clairvoyant aptitudes could pierce the material veil and see the past lifetimes of all individuals concerned with each case.

It is also comprehensible that should such an advanced person appear and start practicing this kind of diagnosis and therapy, he would almost immediately be stopped and incarcerated by the all-powerful materia medica. So the advanced intellects wisely do not tamper with the different evolutionary factors present in any civilization at any time; only benign spiritual help is psychokinetically projected. The advanced intellects await a more propitious time as in the spirit worlds. It must be remembered that the all-dominant factor in human relationships is the individual prerogative of self-determination. This self-determination tends, over a long period of evolution, to develop the mental faculties of any human. To alter or affect this human self-determination is, in effect, destroying the human. He would become a zombie-like creature entirely dependent for guidance, quite useless in the Infinite plan.

As you may have discovered in our previous discussion, a physically or mentally defective child may be here at this time trying to work out some burdensome karma. He may be mentally defective from circumstances suffered in other lifetimes; he may also be a migratory entity from another planet or he may be an elemental, like one of the primitive Australian aborigines or an African Pigmy; or he may come from the jungles of another world. So, you see, to personally classify and diagnose every defective human would be a task which could be performed only by thousands of doctors, all suitably trained and developed in paranormal functions; and if these doctors so existed, they would, quite naturally, have at their disposal various electronic devices which would aid diagnosing and whenever so indicated, proper therapy could be entered into.

In many planets throughout the universe, there are civilizations which have such doctors and therapeutic practices. It should also be pointed out that in these civilizations, the rate of inception of defective children is correspondingly low in proportion to the applied knowledge. Only planets like the earth which are abysmally ignorant of the facts of life make themselves subjective to and become victimized by the ignorance of their time; and as a consequence, the development of a physical or material civilization brings a double indemnity of human misery and wreckage.

If you have a defective child in your care or custody, or if he has been born to you, try to understand him on the basis of the introspective facts which have been presented. Understanding the child will be of great assistance in bringing about corrective measures. By understanding, you become a polarity whereby the higher Advanced Intellects can work through you interjecting intelligent energies which will form the foundation for a future complete healing, most likely in the spiritual worlds.

Do not give false emphasis to the importance of life in the defective child; if he is mentally retarded, he will have his own world. His years of earth life will mean little to him. If he is physically deformed, make him as comfortable as possible. And in all cases, look forward with joy to the time when he will leave his deformed body and go back into some spiritual world where he can be more properly cared for, and when this happens, your understanding and participation will be projected energies which can be utilized by the doctors and others involved in his therapy. Much depends upon a constant positive attitude, one which is born of understanding. A negative fearful and doubtful attitude will only deter progress in his therapy.

The physical world is only the reflective plane of understanding for every human who is associated with it and believes that it is the paramount place of life. No person can be said to be truly human until he has passed the necessity of his material life, and can see some small part of the vastness of Infinity. Therefore, to all potential humans involved in earth lives, the importance of the earth life is the prime motivating drive of his existence. He will do anything and everything possible to prolong, even for a moment, the span of his years, not knowing that death gives him a much greater advantage to advance the purpose of his existence. For in the spirit worlds there is much greater opportunity to gain some comprehension of life and prepare for future evolutions. For indeed these spiritual worlds are the Kingdom Within; they are the Many Mansions; and through the psychic anatomy, regardless of whether he knows it or does not, every person actually functions and lives from one or more of these spiritual planes.

Life then, in an actual reality, is all spiritual. In essence all forms are spiritual, or energy forms. They are held in their respective position by your former associations with them, over long periods of evolution; and the reality as mass exists only as a development of consciousness.

In the future it is possible with every human to develop the same consciousness in a higher plane of life where the relative factors of reality are quite different. There are no mass forms composed of atoms; instead energy is held in some form of reality by consciousness developed by understanding it completely. Work then, for that future time in your evolution when —like the caterpillar which develops into the pupa and which in turn, leaves its old form behind and becomes a radiant butterfly—you, even as a radiant spiritual being, will have far more purpose than could now be conceived.

CHAPTER XXVIII

New Theory of Matter Outlined by Physicist

Evidence Presented to Society Indicates 'Jelly' Bundles of Force Make Up Universe

By Robert C. Toth*

NEW YORK—A Harvard physicist presented evidence Wednesday indicating that most of the pieces of matter in the universe are jelly-like bundles of forces throughout with no "hard" cores.

The finding does little to make sense out of the jungle of strange particles in the nuclei of atoms. Whether the proton and neutron have cores, or whether they are homogeneous clusters of force, the physicists are still unable to explain all nuclear events.

However, the scientists preferred for "sentimental" reasons to interpret earlier experimental data as meaning that these nuclear particles had half their charge concentrated in a central core, according to the Harvard physicist, Dr. Richard Wilson.

Partial Explanation

This was because they have a theory which works well for explaining reactions between forces that seem concentrated at one point, such as the way like poles of a magnet repel each other. But they have no theory to explain how a cloud of force reacts with another cloud of force.

Among the ramifications of the finding, Dr. Wilson said, is that "an end may be in sight for the continual search for structures of smaller and smaller size".

Strong Reactions

He suggested that all of the 40-odd particles which engage in strong reactions—roughly all the larger pieces in the nucleus of atoms—have the same spread-out force structure as the protons and neutrons he studied, and moreover, that they are all about the same size.

This means the particles would have a diameter of about one hundred of a trillionth of an inch (or 10 to the minus 14 centimeters).

The work, reported to the opening session of the American Physical Society meeting here, also adds further evidence to the idea that every bit of matter is just a cluster of forces. Nothing is "hard" despite what man's senses tell him.

For example, pushing against a desk does not cause pressure because two "hard" objects meet, but because two force fields impinge on each other.

Dr. Wilson's report was one of the first to come from experiments at the Cambridge (Mass.) electron accelerator, the nation's newest atom smasher, which is run by Harvard and Massachusetts Institute of Technology.

Shoot at Targets

The 6-billion-electron volt machine speeds particles to the highest man-made velocities yet obtained—99.9997th the speed of light. Light travels at 186,000 miles a second.

The scientists shoot electrons at targets, such as the protons and neutrons in Dr Wilson's experiments, and the way the electrons are deflected provides information on the structure of the target particles. In a sense the accelerator can be considered a "super-duper elec-tron microscope", one scientist said.

Center of Particles

Dr. Wilson's tests probed 90% of the distance to the center of the particles. He found that 95% of the electric charge and the magnetic moment of the particles are distributed evenly to that depth.

"There is no sign of a core," he said, but concluded with scientific caution: "We tentatively say there is no core."

In contrast, the electron, with about one-two thousandth the mass of a proton or neutron, behaves as if all of its charge and mass were concentrated at a point.

The annual meeting of the society, held jointly with the American Assn. of Physics Teachers, will run through Saturday. About 6,000 physicists from this country and abroad are expected to attend.

As it has so often happened in the past, the world of science is, in one way or another, constantly vindicating the Unariun Concept. Through newspaper articles and other informative media the different scientific branches reveal their efforts to probe the secret mysteries of life, secrets and mysteries which have been fully and adequately explained in the Unariun Liturgies.

One of the more recent exposés—and by far the most important revelation—came during the opening seminar of the "American Physical Society Convention", which took place in the Los Angeles area in January 1964. It was in one of the meetings of this convention that a certain noted Harvard physicist, Dr. Richard Wilson, unknowingly completely reinstated the basic Unariun Concept which is the proposition that the Infinite Cosmos, interdimensionally speaking, was composed of energy matter, wave forms, the oscillating Principles, etc. So important is the noted doctor's presentation that it has been reproduced in its entirety just as it appeared in the Los Angeles Times, January 23, 1964, in the foregoing pages.

A careful study of the contents will reveal all basic equivalents, reactionary values, etc., as they are presented in the Unariun Concept. These basics, of course, so far as Dr. Wilson is concerned, relate only to the third dimensional perspectus of energy. A complete and comprehensive digestion of this article will not be attempted; indeed, this would be superfluous, as all introspections have been thoroughly covered. It should also be noted, Doctor Wilson presented several imponderables which will remain unsolved to these savants until that day when they can integrate these new findings as an integrated interdimensional science, which is the basic Unariun Concept of Creation.

Just as it is so stated in the article, these new revelations made by Dr. Wilson could completely upset the apple cart of the scientific world and could very well make all existing science, from the time of Newton to Einstein, archaic. Unarius has already reversed this scientific world in regard to many factors which are in basic equivalents of creation. While the modern scientist still holds the third-dimensional earth world as the origin and seat of life, Unarius refutes this by presenting the Infinite interdimensional macrocosm and microcosm wherein even the humblest atom assumes its proper position, a nucleus of cyclic wave forms produced in an interdimensional vortex or centrifuge, just as it is with planetary systems, galaxies and universes.

If the good doctor had your books and lessons and could conceive what is in them without the rhetorical bigotry customarily expressed, he would understand to its fullest depth the creative cosmic science which he has just faintly begun to envision.

This article also carries a happy prediction wherein the future of this planet earth could easily develop into a scientific evolution which could nullify and destroy the pernicious effects of present-day religious, political and scientific systems. And if that evolution is ever achieved then, indeed, would the earth man take a giant step forward toward his visionary Utopia.

As a Unariun student, however, be philosophical on any evolutionary achievements accomplished by the earth man. Infinite Intelligence, in all Its Creative Agencies, has a system of checks and balances which relegates and regulates all forms of life in suitable environments. Evolution is a substation of these checks and balances. No man indigenous to an earth world will ever exceed the perspectus of his environment; when he does so he is no longer an earth man. Perhaps it could safely be said, Dr. Wilson is a migrant emissary coming from one of the scientific centers, such as Eros, timing his visit to the earth world at a most propitious time, and perhaps there are others like him; and if this is so, then it is, indeed, a healthy sign that the earth world is in a progressive state of evolution toward a time when science can cut the Gordian knot of human ignorance.

CHAPTER XXIX

The Cyclic Interplay of Infinite Polarization, or 'Regeneration'

From time to time in various liturgies of Unarius, the student is urged to learn and use the knowledge presented to him. Inasmuch as the term—'learn and use' or 'learning and usage'—could cause some confusion or misinterpretation to the student, it would therefore serve a good purpose to objectively analyze these terminologies. Learning, to the average earth man, means simply becoming acquainted with some particular objectivism. He learns by reading a book; a child learns not to poke his finger in a candle flame, etc. More correctly, so far as the material man is concerned, learning is the combination of two objectivisms which are: the object or noun, and the action or verb. A child learns that by horse, a carriage is drawn, the horse and carriage the objects with the moving action. As he passes through his educational period, all of his studies will therefore be predicated upon this same objective and reactionary system. He may read that two chemicals combined will produce an explosion; he will actually reproduce this reaction in the laboratory, and so through his various studies he is always called upon to synthesize an action from some objectivism.

In order to better facilitate and make more accessible different groupings or classifications in the general synthesis of life, man uses a third element which is symbology. The numerous interplays of life which are ever about every human are forever thusly being classified and reclassified under divisions and subdivisions of symbolic forms. Indeed, so much so that all artifacts and appurtenances of life are therefore more minutely objectified as symbols. The symbol is an auto-suggestive factor; a combination of such symbolic forms constitutes an objectivism which is always followed by the customary reaction. In a sense then, all life patterns in whatever variations they may assume are only auto-suggestive automations, and no human actually goes beyond the dimension of these autosuggestive forms, which are in constant interplay about him. On this basis, therefore, no human can actually think; neither is he intelligent, despite diplomas which he may have obtained in some University. His thinking is still the same reflex automation, pressurized by the necessity and the demands of his existence in his respective society.

True intelligence is the faculty of individual human mental integrations and assimilations of thought forms, concepts, etc., beyond the range of his material existence, involving factors which are beyond normal earth-life transitions. So far as the earth man is concerned, such a mental faculty would be considered paranormal or psychic. However, the term and understanding of paranormal psychology is as badly misunderstood and misused as are any other extra-terrestrial factors. Therefore, a true representation of correct intelligence, and in such so-called paranormal activities, cannot be understood by any person until he understands the psychic anatomy as it is presented in the Unariun Concept. In such understanding the difference in intelligence quotients from the subconscious reactive or memory processes—now called intelligent—as posed against the very highly-developed intellect of the Superconscious Self—functions and lives in an interdimensional atmosphere and which is instantly conversant with all known and unknown factors of life—

irrespective of whether or not they are personal experiences—learned the hard way, as is customarily done by the earth man.

At this point we must now bring in the second objectivism which is usage. Here again is a dissociation with the material concept. In earth life, usage is the reflex action which materializes the objectivism into the reality of his earth life. With the highly-developed Superconscious Self however, usage is not a reactive reflex. In the vast interplay of interdimensional regeneration, the action is already in full swing. The Superconscious containing as it does within itself the exact facsimile of Infinity—and assuming that this Superconscious Self has more completely polarized this Infinite facsimile in countless earth and spiritual lives and their attendant experiences—this Superconscious can therefore be assumed to be completely in tune with the Infinite. And in such an attunement, concept or objectivism is complete. Action is already in effect. Therefore, the complete attunement with objectivism also completes attunement with action which is the creative principle in action.

By now, the differences between the common earth life understanding of thought and action, or learning and usage, are quite different than such mental functions as are in full force and effect in the Superconscious Self—assuming, of course, that it is a very highly-developed Superconscious. This proposition immediately suggests several important considerations: the average earth man has not developed such a Superconscious Self. If he had a highly-developed Superconscious, he would not be an earth man! The same situation is quite true with you, the student, even though you may believe in, and recognize all of the things associated with the higher way of life, you are

still not conversant with them. You have not yet learned enough of life, of the scientific principle of creation
and all other factors involved, to have sufficiently developed your Superconscious Self to the point where
you can live in complete harmony with Infinite Intelligence, and without the seeming necessity of the
material body and earth life. And at whatever time or
place you so begin to develop this facsimile of the
Infinite, which is as yet only beginning to take on your
own polarized life quotients, you will have to reconcile
yourself with certain obvious compromises which must
necessarily be made—until it can be assumed that
after hundreds of thousands of years, and thousands
of earth lives, you will have sufficiently polarized your
Superconscious to the point where it becomes the
dominant or controlling personality of your existence.
And at any given point in that future evolution, you will
return correspondingly less and less to the earth as
spiritual life becomes increasingly feasible.

For the present, therefore, your material earth life
and all its attendant factors are extremely important
to you. You should learn to compromise them, to use
them to objectify and learn Infinite Creation as it is
going on about you. You should determine the different
factors and symbolic forms which are no longer useful
to you. You should become conscious of the fact that
different symbolic forms and usages have passed the
point of your necessity in usage, because you now
understand them and how they were brought into life
and of their function. For instance, you have been
given a rather thorough and complete presentation of
the historical background of Christianity; the psychological implications have been explained to you. Likewise, the presentation of Infinite Creation has been
presented to you—all of which has completely nullified

the validity of religion so far as your personal position is concerned—even though it (religion) may be very valuable to many earth people. Therefore, in the final count-down, to determine a more proper course of action in the immediate future just ahead, desist from all such common practices which are done in the pure intent of symbology. Do not use prayers, affirmations, mantrums, etc. Don't try to concentrate with a conscious mind which can, as yet, only oscillate with that "bucket of fish-worms" you call your subconscious.

Various other symbolic forms should be abandoned, such as Yogi breathing, different postures, diets. Throw into the ash can, along with your Bible, any other symbologies, such as astrological charts and begin to replace them with a more intelligent, constructive and life-giving, life-preserving science. Start looking at the Infinite Creator not as a white-robed Santa Claus ruling through emotional vicissitudes and supposedly creating through hocus-pocus abracadabra—but rather, view the Infinite Creator as the Master Scientist who not only created all things, but which is the substance and form of all things—an unemotional Creator who presents the same opportunity on the same basic plan of evolution to any human who can and will learn of this Creator, its Creative Principle. And in the learning, you will find the Principle in action, for such is Immortal life—a direct and personal continuity with the Infinite Creator which is expressing this same infinite creative thought and action with you, thus supporting and giving you life in your inter-dimensional world.

The Cyclic Interplay
Part Two

In the foregoing discussion, we discovered and re-discovered some very important basic psychological equivalents, a psychology which, in its true form, is relatively simple and just as scientific as is any other true presentation of life. And in no way should it be compared to the pseudo Freudian psychology which is a vast jungle of vague unrealistic pseudoisms, supported by equally vague terminology and nomenclature. To be tangible, life in any form animate or inanimate, third-dimensional or interdimensional—must always be reduced to and understood as energy wave forms and configurations. More specifically, however, our discussion was directed toward a more suitable re-orientation with thought and action or learning and usage. Our hypothesis and analysis presented an obvious conclusion—not theory but provable fact: that man is, individually and collectively, a creature who exists by virtue of the fact that he is an oscillating entity with the world about him. He is supported by wave—form oscillations; he lives and reacts according to the interplay of wave form motions, transposed as consciousness, through the psychic anatomy and the psychic mechanism which relays those impulses and which resynthesize wave form motion as consciousness.

On the basic platform of understanding, it is therefore clearly indicated that no material man as human has developed the paranormal faculty of interdimensional conversation. All third-dimensional humanity was therefore relegated in its life processes as wave form consciousness, supported and sustained from the subconscious which, in turn, partially preserved experience quotients from numerous past physical lifetimes through the subconscious into the conscious mind.

The conscious mind must therefore be considered to be only an extension or an extrusion of the subconscious and other past lifetime affiliations which constructed this subconscious from wave form impregnations, implanted by experience. It is quite evident then, that this conscious mind could not reproduce any wave-forms or facsimile which were not directly connected with the past, save only in very exceptional times when this conscious subconscious oscillating process was momentarily suspended, and which could happen in a moment of extreme stress. For instance, certain people at the point of death or a temporary cessation period have seen their past life in a brief flash. In other words, a different alignment took place with the psychic anatomy which made this flashback possible. However, such instances are rare. Most people are only occasionally motivated or impelled by a psychism which can be considered to be slightly paranormal, such as a hunch or an instinctive feeling, etc. In certain isolated instances, people who are generally classified as spiritualistic mediums have acquired what seems to be a paranormal function, these people having gone through some great emotional crisis in their life or they have become somewhat misaligned from more normal oscillating conditions. This misalignment can be sufficiently great as to temporarily cause a trauma or trance wherein, at such times the alter ego, assuming the form of a spirit guide, takes control and supposedly re-creates in descriptive forms, the spirit world or summerland with vague suggestions as to how life is lived there. It should be noted that no spiritual medium has in any trance state, given a true scientific dissertation on life as it is lived in the spiritual worlds. All information given by spirit guides and their attendant apparitions in the supposed spirit forms and relatives are all cast from the same mold. They are all thought-form bodies given life by a person who does not understand life. He is filled with fear and insecurity and is attempting, through this so-called mediumship, to invert the mental disturbances into a tangible supposition whereby power, personal identification, etc., are superimposed upon a few gullible adherents.

How different is a true paranormal function—or if you wish to call it mediumship—whereby a person can, under any and all conditions, mentally detune consciousness from his material life relationships and retune consciousness to the higher Superconscious Self which, living as it does in the vast interdimensional worlds, and assuming it is a conscious entity polarized through the ages of time and an infinity of experience then becomes the true consciousness making any and all parts and subdivisions, even the entire Infinity of Infinite Mind, immediately available to the conscious mind surface, where it can be suitably utilized, materialized, or re-created into the material world. It should be noted that any Advanced Personality who is, in reality, a highly developed Superconscious Self, maintains the physical body upon the earth plane merely as an outlet for some particular expressionary forms of life. If this Superconscious Self is sufficiently developed, it can and does maintain a number of such outlets: it can, in other words, have any given number of physical bodies simultaneously, and at any given or opportune times, express and demonstrate the more highly developed paranormal spiritual life. This highly developed Superconscious can and does have other expressionary outlets in different spiritual planes or spiritual planetary systems, all such functions being part of that activity generally described by Unarius as oscillating infinitely. How all of this is done will, in due time, be more clearly explained providing, of course, that you have begun to understand the more basic and elemental concepts which have been presented to you in the lessons and books. It would serve no useful purpose to give you these scientific facts of creation if you have not learned to identify creation as oscillating energy—the principle of creation contained in the harmonic interplay called regeneration which makes the sum and total of the Infinite.

In view of this great and vast interplay of Cosmic Intelligence, Superconscious development, etc., how infinitesimally small and puny then are all of mankind's efforts to sublimate this Infinite Creation into his daily life, expressionary forms, and in particular to his religious beliefs. How elemental and ignorant it is to centralize Infinite Creation into an emotional godhead; and after creating this nebulous form, worship it, give it great power over you, blame it for all things which you cannot equalize, attempt to pacify it by vows of felicitation, giving it intelligence enough to create Creation, yet believing it can be duped by false promises; for such is man's religion Christian or otherwise.

As a student, therefore, you should begin to realize that this material world is indeed a primitive place in the scale of evolution. It is an elemental world where even the most learned or advanced segments of society still maintain the same savage primitive instincts as do the jungle beasts. Yes, they do more than that; they capitalize their savagery and barbarism by using their reactive power of reason to construct and reconstruct increasingly horrible atrocities against their fellow man. They will deliberately sacrifice a hundred thousand or a million humans in attempt to prove a difference of opinion; and even now they are prevented, perhaps only temporarily, from imminent mass destruction which would destroy both the destroyed and the destroyer.

For the moment then, and until some future time, do not attempt to reconstruct your present life from out the shambles of the past. A better future must be constructed from better stuff and it must be more intelligently put together. This is the purpose of Unarius—to bring the first constructive elements and the knowledge of construction. No person can live into the future in a higher life until he has so reconstructed his psychic anatomy, or more specifically, polarized himself as a human entity into Infinity by the reconstructive polarizing process whereby his superconscious facsimile becomes his entire being.

The Cyclic Interplay
Part Three

Now we have discovered that learning and usage are synonymous and are actually equalized or balanced motions of energy which do, in effect, re-create the psychic anatomy, and which also help to polarize the Superconscious Self. Polarization, like all other Infinite functions, is extremely important; and in understanding polarization, you will begin to understand the very essence of creation. For it is through polarization that the Infinite Intelligence recreates atoms, planets, solar systems, galaxies and universes. Also through the understanding of polarization any person becomes Immortal.

The Superconscious has been frequently mentioned as an Infinite facsimile of the Infinite. You can picture this situation if you can see, in your mind's eye, a certain whirling vortex of energy. This vortex is actually composed of billions of other vortexes; each one, in turn, contains vast numbers of much smaller vortexes. All of these whirling masses of energy are actually billions of wave forms of energy each one vibrating at tremendous speed. They are, in other words, becoming positive and negative, and in this phase shift, they determine their respective affiliation to any and all other wave forms and vortexes in the Infinite Cosmos. As all of these vortexes revolve within themselves, their cyclic patterns are therefore complete. They do not, in a sense, go anywhere; nor do they come from some place. You can find them only if you can tune into their respective wave lengths; otherwise, they do not exist in consciousness.

Now, any vortex will, within its own circumference,

encompass enough wave forms, which, when harmonically re-linked, will, in all effect, make this one vortex the entire Infinite Cosmos—if we can so temporarily contain it for the moment. Therefore, within any vortex —either as it is self-contained or as it is harmonically attuned to the Cosmos—is contained the net sum and total of Infinity. That means that all life, all humanity, everything which you can think of, and very, very much more, can figuratively, be squeezed into a vortex smaller than an electron. Actually, in this way, time and space have been eliminated, as was somewhat theoretically postulated by Einstein; for even in sub-infinity, or the smallest portion of such a sub-infinity is, in effect, as large as the whole of Super-Infinity. It also means that when you understand this whole concept, you will, by the simple process of attunement, be able to travel through space from planet to planet, from universe to universe—not with the speed of light—but instantaneously, simply because not only any one portion or portions thereof, but the sum and total of Infinity can be tuned in by a person who so understands this concept. It is just as close as the end of your nose.

Getting back to the Superconscious: Its personal beginning for any human begins in that singular or multiple life-form expression. Everything in the earth life, from the most ancient to the present is, therefore, so self-contained in any small or large vortex. They do not exist as the materialized physical form; they are the energy and the intelligence which will manifest in a physical life reaction, either adversely or constructively according to how we are biased in respect to these energy appearances. For example, a woman drowns in a lake. To this woman, this drowning incident is a fearsome experience; it becomes karma to her to be worked out in future lives. However, the Infinite did not conceive this experience as fearsome or evil. In fact, the Infinite conceives all things perfectly. When the woman drowned, the different wave-forms of energy which portrayed and made the drowning possible were oscillating in a vortex in the Infinite. They were oscillating not as a drowning experience but as a certain combination of wave-form expressions all harmonically attuned. In the act of drowning, the woman in effect—unconsciously and beforehand, in her many days upon the earth—had created a certain number of negatively biased wave forms, which, when under certain circumstances became so attuned to the wave forms in the Infinite vortex that this attunement brought about a certain convergence of energy which, when expressed as physical action and motion in the material world, the woman re-created or reformed and remotionalized this energy movement in the act of drowning.

When you have fully digested this concept, you will begin to see it as some sort of a scientific metaphysics —not to be confused, however, with certain metaphysical forms currently in existence but which were similar in their original form as was taught by the Lemurians and others—the processes of energy transmission expressed and re-expressed from the fourth to the third dimension, as they were just described to you. However, since their introduction into the earth plane consciousness, much time has passed. Furthermore, the earth man has at no time even partially comprehended what is being given to you, and so through the passage of time and passing through ignorant superstitious minds, these concepts have degenerated down into numerous decadent forms. These decadent forms have been, and are, the different kinds of witchcraft, sorcery, etc. They are also the basic equivalents in religious systems; for in these religions, man has only attempted to deify the Infinite in a personal form which is more understandable to him.

The mind practices of concentration preached by so-called divine religious sciences, occultisms and theosophies—even astrology—are all parts of this degenerate pseudoism. One, so-called Christian Science, attempts to separate god from the material world or says that god created nothing but good. There is nothing scientific in this supposition, and nowhere in their liturgies are any scientific principles explained; nor can a sine wave be explained or understood by either the ministry or the followers.

They are all hypnotically immersed in a blind supposition wherein they hope to escape reality. Other evangelistic movements attempt to keep the white-robed god in the sky, and to keep him separated from the scientific world of reality. Theirs is a supposed hocus-pocus god who, with a magic wand, promiscuously creates and destroys without rhyme or reason. In fact, he does not even know how he does it! At least none of his self-elected priests can explain his motivations, the reason why he exists, or where he got these hocus-pocus powers! And so the unalterable scientific principles of creation remain, regardless of puny attempts by earth people to decipher them in terms of material happenstances. The earth and all attendant forms of life—mass, etc., represent only small differences in impedances in energy transmissions from the fourth into the third dimension. It is in these impedances that other wave forms are regenerated, expressed or degenerated, giving rise to one or more of the infinite ways Infinity reconstructs Itself.

To the drowning woman, the experience was an evil one. She knew nothing about this cosmic interplay.

Had she so understood, she would not have drowned, in fact, she would not even have been an earth woman. When Jesus walked upon the water, he did so by virtue of His knowledge; He knew all the science involved in that situation. The differences in polarities of certain electromagnetic fields, one of which is called gravity were fully understood by Him. He was able to so change the polarity of His physical body that it was no longer a statically charged particle attracted to and held by the earth which is a larger and more highly charged particle. If you remember, like poles repel each other and unlike poles attract, such as north and south poles. By completely understanding the cosmos, the universe, the earth, etc., this knowledge immediately and automatically compensated whatever action Jesus expressed. This was done intelligently in respect to what was to be achieved. For instance, when you walk across the room, you can't describe how it's done because it's a built-in development acquired over many lifetimes and re-expressed into the present. So while the woman drowned, Jesus could have walked away from the scene without even getting His feet wet. No, not magic; not god-like, but as a human who had studied, learned and was practically using his knowledge.

God is not a deity; He is not to be worshipped. He does not need your prayers and felicitations; neither is He dependent upon your loyalty. Just as He constructed you through the evolutionary process, He did so with His own substance—energy, if you please. And in this construction and evolution, He does hold the Principle of Creative Regeneration one of paramount importance. He is not emotionally concerned with you. There are countless billions of inhabited planets; each person an infinitesimally small particle, all going through the same regenerative process. This regenerative process is a progressive principle; if you do not so evolve progressively, you will degenerate progressively. The choice is yours. You cannot hold on to your earth life forever. You will surely perish if you do. Only by progressively attuning yourself, will you become an immortal person. Right at the present time you are in a very precarious position. Your present and former earth lives are still the dominant force in your life because that is really all there is of you, save just a little bit of polarized Superconscious which you have somehow acquired through numerous life experiences. That little cell of Superconscious is your Christ. It is the only thing between you and total destruction. It is the only guiding Light to help you survive the material worlds. It is your own little personal treasure chest of treasures which you have laid up in Heaven. No, rust and moth will not corrupt them, but well you may, if you renege. Don't depend upon nebulous promises of salvation made by ministers and priests who may be even more fearsome than you are—who may, in their preachments, be attempting to placate the awful gnawing fear within their hearts. Like a drunkard trying to drown his sorrow they, too, are trying to drown their fears, born from ignorance and superstition by a superimposed edifice of divinity, flowing robes, altars and incense.

Polarization of the Superconscious is simply this: we have constructively reformed or reshaped certain energy wave forms which, as they were so expressed in the secondary impulses of physical action, were thus again regenerated and superimposed according to their own basic frequencies in the vortexal forms residing in the fourth dimension.

Conversely, if the same reaction had taken place negatively biased, they could not enter into this vortex and reform or reshape it with any basic frequency. The negatively biased experience would then remain as a karmic form in the lower astral portion of the psychic anatomy where it would accumulate with other negative static forms, and must be worked out as karma at a later time. The problem, then, is to see in any secondary physical actions taking place about you, the more ultimate purposes and reasons for these expressions. If you understand this principle and concept thoroughly you will, in effect, be able to turn all apparently evil things into good. In that way, then, evil does become good and Infinite Intelligence lives as It should live—perfectly.

Remember in the future, all thought and action on your part must be polarized in Infinity with your own particular basic frequency—an action which auto-matically takes place when you understand the principle of regeneration, harmonic attunement, etc. What little you have already polarized has been done more or less by sheer accident, so to speak, or by what you did in the spiritual worlds in the in-between lives, also aided by the Advanced Personalities, as you did not, up until this present time, have even a smattering of understanding of the science involved. You beheld the spiritual worlds as Heaven, the Advanced Personalities as Angels, etc. Our purpose here is to teach you how to achieve the practical reality of this higher life. You should be forewarned, however; it is not a life of indolence and ease which is so generally believed. That ideosophy is spawned and nurtured by the big "escape mechanism".

When you advance into a higher world, you will be very much busier than you could possibly imagine. You could be literally appearing and living in hundreds of places simultaneously, simply because you have learned how to tune into them. No, you will not be using hands or feet, arms or legs; neither will you have wings; in fact, you won't even have a physical body. Instead, you will be one of those Glowing Radiant Balls of White Fire which have occasionally been seen by certain earth people, and when so seen, have been believed to be God.

And do not think for a moment that they are all good angels. Strange as it may seem, there can be beautiful glowing energy people who have nothing in their hearts and minds except their own personal desires. Oh, they developed as good Angels up to a certain point; then somehow they became side-tracked, and while you may still see them as radiant and glowing, their fire is rapidly going out as they plunge deeper into the pits of Hell. And so the same prerogative of self-determination is always apparent either on earth, in Heaven or in Hell. The self-determinant or the determinant of self will eventually make you an Angel or it will destroy you, just as it destroys Angels and makes Angels out of Devils—according to each personal self-determination.

Don't look into a crystal ball for your future—your future is built in; you can select your own future from the vastness of Infinity. You can select what you choose by what you can conceive, and there will never be any Master over you except the masters of ignorance and superstition which you may have created, or at this moment, are re-creating this same master in a different form.

The Cyclic Interplay

Part Four

Another way which might better help you to understand is to picture in your mind's eye the vast Infinite
Cosmos, a sea of Radiant Energy, infinitely filled with
whirling vortexes. Just above the earth is a great sieve
perforated with countless billions of tiny holes, and
through these holes this energy is streaming into all
forms of earth life. Every human receives his own
individual stream of life-giving energy. This is the 'mysterious' energy which is behind all thought and action.
Through the psychic anatomy it gives life to all the
cells; it keeps all constructive life formations constantly reconstructing their own form and purpose.

This Infinite life energy flows into each atom and
exactly equalizes its position to all other atoms through
these electromagnetic fields. Yes, even the stones which
form the hard core surface and the earth itself are held
so equalized by the exact equilibrium expressed in all
these apparent physical forms. Yet, they too—just as
you must—are progressively or psychically being
reformed; even in the beginning of any form whether it
is an atom or an earth or a solar system, or even a
galaxy. The beginning of a cycle also marks its end. For
all these apparent forms are only following in this third
dimension, the cyclic movements which engendered
their existence.

They are portraying on the surface of your consciousness the same normal progressive evolution
which you also are expressing. Life or the existence of
any material form would not be possible unless it had
been in existence as energy in the great Infinite. Yes,

and even this great Infinite is again reinstated and superimposed in the super effigy of Creative Consciousness from an even greater Infinity. And so your life as a human has, in its evolution, begun to take on or use certain values of self-determination where each person arbitrarily selects or rejects the numerous values of life. As an earth man, he does this pressurized by the conformities of his society and only vaguely inspired by the great mysterious cacophony of creativeness which is ever about him. And in his systems of equilibriums which are brought about by these reactive consequences, he attempts to reward himself either with self-eulogy or promises of immortal life as a reward for virtuous conduct.

The Infinite, then, represents and is the Supreme Supply. It is esoterically neither good nor evil; because it is perfect in itself, it presents no emotional contrasts. Man therefore selects and uses from this great supply just as he so desires and in whatever manner and form he so chooses within the limitations of his society and his understanding. In this action he will, through many lifetimes, begin to vaguely learn of the exact equilibriums which are constantly in effect in all forms of action. This is his first beginning in learning the law of cause and effect which he has transposed in such reactionary concepts as an eye for an eye, a tooth for a tooth. If he can progressively sustain his evolution, this carnal jungle law will undergo a metamorphosis. He will begin to lose the necessity of self-reward and see that virtue is its own reward. He will begin to rebuild his life transpositions, not as a reactive reagent against his neighbor as he seeks to equalize his neighbor's reactive expression; instead, he will begin to realize the vast potentials and possibilities, the perfect equilibrium which is presented in cosmic regeneration. He will begin to see that self-security is not a flatulent edifice of monetary or material values which are valuable only in lieu of something more constructive.

Eventually a man may arrive at some point in his evolution where he will see Infinity as an enormous, pulsating entity of Intelligence which has, in the intricate fabric of interdimensional interplay, created and is creating, all forms and substances. When you have personally acquired some sort of a picture wherein you can see all this vast pouring in of the re-creative life substance, you will, by comparison, see how silly and unintelligent it is to pray to some self-constructed god-ideosophy for numerous benefits and actions when, in actual reality, all these things and many more are already in superabundance all about you. It only requires your personal knowledge of their existence and your ability to tune into them and make them a part of your life; or, more correctly, you will then become part of this Infinite Creative Life. You will also realize that as you acquire knowledge of the Infinite and the synonymy of usage, you will become more constructively inclined and, in a direct ratio, the seemingly destructive, nonsensical, inane earth-life dispensations become more obnoxious to you and you will participate in them, either directly or indirectly, less and less; and they will have a correspondingly lessened effect in your life.

This is the true creative evolution—the many multiple lives each person progressively lives into the future Infinity. A progressive evolution is always positively biased; there must always be new hope, new aspiration, new knowledge, etc., which gives a constant impetus to this evolution.

Faith and inspiration walk hand-in-hand with achievement. For all these things, too, are ways in which the Infinite Life Force streams into us. So be it thus— a progressive evolution, not a stagnant life steeped in false idolatries—not a system of symbologies bound tightly in the fetters of conformities but an unbounded realization of the human potential as a Creative effigy in Infinite Consciousness.

CHAPTER XXX

Sex — Man's Strongest Drive

In common psychological equivalents, the average human lives under the impelling forces of a number of drives or libidos. In the pursuance of his everyday life, the average human does not attempt to separate or classify these different drives. In fact, most people seem to be totally unaware of them despite their great efforts to satisfy these drives. Generally speaking, the net total of drives can be called simply the lust for life. Freudian psychology is based on these material drives and in an individual classification, the sex drive heads the list; and of somewhat secondary importance are such drives as hunger and food, personal identification, etc. While it is well and good to recognize symptoms in a disease, the true cause as well as the method of life reproduction, etc., must also be ascertained before the disease can be treated successfully.

Freudian psychology is only a general recognition of symptoms and a reclassification of such symptoms wherein the psychology attempts to establish some form and continuity—something like pointing out the differences in spots between smallpox and measles without recognizing the virus sources and all attendant factors which materialized the spots. Freud did not know about psychic anatomies, except possibly in that vague reference, derived from the Greek word, psyche, or spirit. However, this psyche or spirit was just as vague to Freud as it is to any of his contemporaries past or present.

It is quite apparent that no psychologist has even a small smattering of scientific understanding as it might be classified, electronic, and even if the psychologist had such knowledge he has not identified common psychological processes as electronic in nature, except perhaps in encephalographic patterns. The subconscious still remains a vast and unexplored hinterland, an impenetrable jungle, etc. So as of today, psychology, medicine or any other specific classification of human endeavors and relationships do not contain the factors of interdimensional planes, making the reality of life as a surface appearance in association with static energy forms called atoms.

The world at its present state in the development of scientific electronic technocracy, presents an obvious paradox or enigma. For while science has definitely established the incontestable fact that all mass is energy, all transpositions of life are made possible only as different forms of energy transmissions. Even mathematical science, as first postulated by Einstein, has proven the existence of other dimensions or spiritual worlds. Strange indeed, then, that psychology, materia medica, etc., refuse to bow down before the incontestable apparency of this great abundance of proven evidence. The human still remains a creature biologically generated without cause or purpose, living an extremely complex life, hounded by a thousand insecurities, tightly bound by conformities, ending it all in a senseless death.

The colossal ignorance of such suppositions could be somewhat justified in a very elemental mind, but when we are confronted by the obvious fact that psychology, medicine, science, etc., does literally accept and support this useless biological supposition, this does pose a great enigma. Only in his religious systems has man vaguely recognized the great interdimensional Infinity. Here too, however, his suppositions are equally ignorant and elemental. His religion still resides in the realm of fantasy; he still believes in the magic hocus-pocus of his childhood. He has only identified this fantasy in a somewhat enlarged version and redeveloped the religious artifacts of past civilizations, pagan or barbaric; and only quite recently he has succeeded in deleting human sacrifice, even though the sacrifice of human prerogatives is still made by all those who embrace a false religious symbology.

In a balance of comparative values as they exist in the world today, mankind in general is very sadly and very badly out of balance. In the development of new sciences, systems of communication, hygienic measures fostering population explosions, lack of proper genetical controls, etc., all the while clinging tenaciously to old customs and rituals, man has indeed complicated his life far beyond the point where he has any compensating values or the intelligence to use them. Statistics, newspapers, television, movies, etc., all graphically portray the increasing decadency of our civilization. Even the armed forces of our nation reject 60% of our young men as physically unfit. Despite great self-eulogies, this is a dying nation in a dying world. Yes, even the idealistic aspirations compounded in the Declaration of Independence and the Constitution have inadvertently contributed to this decadency; for, individually speaking, no person possesses either the knowledge or the incentive to live completely from these idealisms. He is still too strongly motivated by the carnal drives which make his life possible in an animal kingdom.

Yes, indeed, man is still basically an animal; and in the endless and timeless reaches of the inner dimensions, he has, under certain harmonic laws and interplays, compounded his present psychic anatomy from the millions of animal and vegetable forms which swarm on the surface of the earth. He does not know that his sex drive first began in the primitive ooze of a long bygone time when a simple cell split in two. Man does not know that all physical appearances, movements, transitions, etc., are sponsored by and reflect from the inner dimensions and as they so appear, so they, in turn, regenerate new cyclic forms back into the inner worlds; and from this vast interplay, the psychic anatomy of every human emerges.

It has been formed and reformed and added to by these countless regenerations of life, all polarized in a personal entity of expression. Despite religious or personal beliefs, no man can reject this overwhelming truth which portrays his evolution; even his personal characteristics which are apparent in his physical form, his manner and way of living are all graphic depictions of this evolution. The bird's nest became a burrow, the burrow a cave, and more finally a house or a skyscraper. The scream of a jungle animal has now become the lilting voice of a soprano singing an operatic aria. The fins of a fish have become man's arms and legs.

Men such as Darwin have recognized these incontestable facts. Only fanatical and ignorant religionists have tried to deny them, and in their denials they have denied their God and proven Him false; for such is the way of Infinite Creation. The most sublime of intelligent attitudes—a never-ending succession of recreated forms compounded from the very substance of Infinity and formed within the very vessel of the Infinite Cosmos—are reflected and regenerated into the material worlds, where life again is proven immortal.

CHAPTER XXXI

Informal Discussion — 1961

Good evening, friends: We are very happy to join you here in what promises to be an informal discussion. There has been much already spoken in the way of Principle and Truth to you who have gathered here, yet there is much more which can be spoken—much more which can be realized; for life is an ever-expanding consciousness, a continuity of self with purpose into the infinite reaches of the great All-Creative Mind. This, in itself, has no limitations, nor can there be such, for even in Infinity do we find no end.

May we say, you are indeed fortunate above all people of the earth for having so joined in spirit with us here in the Centers of Unarius, for truly, as we have marked the way, yet these markings are invisible save to those who have sincerely dedicated their lives to purpose, to fulfillment, to attainment wherein they will join the Infinite Creative Mind; for the substance of the world yields not the things of spirit which can truly sustain you in a journey beyond the dimension of this earth life.

For even as the earth was so created, it became substance and form only in the sense that you could so perceive it, and this was the beginning of your evolution. From out of the various conglomerate formations of form and substance from which the earth and its kindred and allied forms of substance are so constructed, these things, in turn, must be so sustained by constantly being joined in spirit from the higher dimensions. This is done in a manner and form which can be realistically achieved and conceived within the dimension of your own mind, for in its conception do you give birth to the new self—a new self which will sustain you in a continuous and ever-expanding evolution.

The Principles which we have set forth in the various studies and which have been transcribed to you are to some degree scientific in nature—at least we can use the nomenclature, indigenous to your life on earth. And while this is quite true, it may at first seem to arouse adverse or insurmountable obstacles within the dimension of your conception. You may think for a time that you cannot conceive these things, but that is not so, for surely, as effort and purpose is maintained, realization will be achieved; and while only word forms remain in conscious mind, yet a magic alchemy takes place within the psychic self and these things are surcharged and revitalized with an all-pervading, permeating life force which stems constantly from out of the great Infinite Creative Mind.

As you are so surcharged and revitalized, so you begin to grow. Consciousness assumes more than word forms, consonants, vowel structures, or other things which are familiar in the pattern of the educational systems of your world, for concept is not contained in the various structures of material forms which are everywhere about you. These things reside purely within the dimension of the autosuggestive nature of each person, and they in turn by the inflections of certain wave forms of energy, automatically suggest to you compatible experiences which you have maintained throughout your third-dimensional earth life.

And so it goes that as each day adds new forms, new rapports of consciousness with the past, so they must be restimulated, revitalized and again surcharged with the infinite vistas and perspectives of Infinity itself, for this surely should arouse not only your curiosity but a challenge to each one of you—a purposeful attainment of consciousness whereby the long sought-after functioning integrity with the higher way of life can be finally achieved.

This is indeed worthy and commendable and perhaps far above the sphere of normal consciousness which is indulged in by the average earthean, for he is insecure of the things which are not supposedly tangible to his natural or native expression. Those things which he cannot hold, touch or see within the confines of his five external senses indeed become something which is enigmatic or paradoxical—something which must be destroyed, because the very virtue or strength of the unknown presupposes that he, in himself, is inferior mentally to conceiving such objectivism. Animalistic as these instincts are and primitive as they are, born from out of the past reaches of life upon this planet, they too must pass with each person. They must pass so that he can reach up into the more sublime and pure essences of the Creative Spirit.

Yes, indeed, dear ones, there are many things of which we could talk in which visitation is possible to you through the mind and the vocabulary or the speaking apparatus of Him whom you call teacher. Yes, indeed, it is so, for even as He so maintains his vehicle of life upon the earth, this, in turn, has become something in which we too all take a great measure of inspiration and courage in achieving such similar dispensations of life—for this is our ultimate goal and attainment that we too can function in an infinite number of ways simultaneously in many earth worlds, just as He is doing. And as ye so strive, ye shall so achieve. Each measure of dedication will be matched and met with an equal portion of wisdom and of knowledge in that which you are striving to accomplish.

This is indeed the pattern of evolution—a pattern which must be met and matched in the mentality and the consciousness of all humanity, ere he will destroy himself or he will precipitate himself into some under-world where, gradually, he will lose the life force which has sustained him in his evolution until he made the wrong turn. (Yes, we can see the thoughts of a visiting student), and may we say that one, too, should not cast personal recriminations, for like the parable of Lot's wife in the Bible, in looking back and indulging in self-recrimination, so does our world become salt and it turns all of these things into a negative portion. But look at the past as a great and tremendous lesson that you have learned, and resolve that in the future you shall be more discriminating, you shall use more choice, you shall be more analytical in the things which come into your life. And above all else, whatever they may be, see them as gifts from the infinite wellspring of consciousness—gifts which you alone can determine their usefulness and their purpose. In this way, all things which come to you shall again speak with a voice much louder than you can utter, for they shall be turned into goodness even though they have come to you in the blackest of evil circumstance.

To the others here who have also accomplished, may they always remain steadfast; may they always remain dedicated to the pursuit of knowledge which will determine for them their course of evolution. May it also be that they will not transfer the purpose of this attainment into the false avenues of personal deifica-tions, of various form structures which may destroy the pure intent of wisdom, for wisdom is that magic alchemy which will free us from all iniquities—free us from all purgatories and will keep us firmly upon our path of evolution. This wisdom must be proportionate to how well we can achieve the dimension of consciousness of this wisdom within our own minds and so express it in our daily lives.

Never should we attain imbalances. Never should we strive to use this in a way in which personal benefits can be so acquired that will give us purpose or dominion over the material world and circumstance but rather, we should reside within the pure dimension of consciousness that all is well and that we are a functioning participle of consciousness with the great Creative Infinite.

We know that in this Supreme Consciousness all things are perfect and well-ordered; and in proportion to our ability to so align and attune ourselves to them, so do we become perfect. Only with the earth man is strife borne within his mind for purpose and attainment which is sometimes, in fact, most often quite unwholesome for him. He strives mightily against the very forces which could mold his character into something which was much more constructive and useful. He sets up for himself vast and preponderant systems of comparisons and justifications when there is a simple altruistic analysis which will level all insurmountable mountains and make his horizon into the Infinite complete. And this is the way, dear friends, dear brothers and sisters.

As we have gathered together many times in the past in the white chalk caves of Mt. Carmel, and even ancient Atlantis, so we will gather again. And some day in the not too distant future, we will all gather together in the great halls of Unarius.

CHAPTER XXXII

Idolatry, Symbology and Iconolatry

According to Webster's dictionary, iconolatry or idolatry is the worship of images, or the excessive worship of idols, or a reverence for some person or thing. Under this definition then, Christianity as a whole, is idolatry, such idolatry being more strongly expressed with the Catholic church than it is with Protestant elements. In all religions, Christian or otherwise, this same context of idolatry is universally expressed; whether it is the worship of cardinals, bishops, popes, the eulogy of ministers and priests, or the holy men in the Eastern occultisms. In all these many and diverse religions which so universally worship people, images, and gods, they do so without accredited knowledge or proof that any of their gods or god, any of their falsely vested powers which these gods invest are actually existent.

While there is ample proof of a great Super Intelligent Creative Expression, there is no proof of the individual or collective god concept as is so currently expressed in religion despite claims made by advocates and devotees. Such claims cannot be proven scientifically or otherwise, and therefore must remain as hearsay, subjective to individual interpretation.

Therefore, as all religion is idolatry, it is also a great hypocrisy. It relegates creative and destructive powers to individual deifications in direct opposition to a provable and conclusive science of creation which has no central deification. In fact, quite the opposite is true, for this creative intelligence exists by virtue of its Infinity and is equally important in all phases and expressions of Infinity.

In view of these facts then, the great hypocrisy of religion is immediately apparent and far greater in the Christian elements who consider themselves the true believers—all other religions pagan, etc. To paraphrase an old quotation, "the pot calling the kettle black", would be applicable here. Yet, hypocrisy is not confined to religion and idolatrous systems of worship.

Different governmental systems, past as well as present, have exhibited the same bigotry. For, in such governmental systems, whether monarchies, democracies, fascisms, or communisms, these systems all become the central figurehead of worship, a continuously re-manifested patriotism which has all the elements of worship and idolatry.

Different cultures, arts and sciences, too, fall under the shadow of idolatry. The classical art and musical interpretations of past expressionists have, through succeeding generations, been raised and elevated in a common system of idolatry, each expressionist being so eulogized and called a master, etc.

Other and more common aspects of life which are idolatrous include the current fashion modes of women, the general addiction to alcohol and tobacco, the common way in which the average American attempts to keep up with the Jones and bonds himself hopelessly in debt. All these things, too, denote their respective images worshipped as a universal idolatry.

To pause and think for a moment upon these cold, hard, ever-apparent facts could easily give a great sense of depression, a defeatist attitude, unless other perspectives were added to this analysis; and in such perspectives, we must begin at the very starting place in the evolutionary concept. As has been stated, man is universally different than animal in his ability to develop certain proclivities and readapt them in certain re-expressionary forms. It is in this redevelopment and re-expressionary phase that man takes his first great stride into the Infinite. Through the constantly expressive and re-expressive elements in his life, he is beginning to learn to combine and recombine. He is learning also of the infinite nature of Infinity.

He is, in short, preparing himself for the second great stride; a time or place when he can become completely conscious of Infinity and not subjective to different interpretations of values on the emotional plane. Until the second great stride is made, however, the idolatrous worship of graven images, nonexistent gods, nebulous politics, hero worship, self-adulation and all other expressionary accouterments of life can at least be partially justified. They do largely form anchor points in the daily concourse of life whereby the recognized sequences of individual conduct can be perpetuated sufficiently to insure the personal health and well-being—a crutch, to be sure, in view of a more ultimate state of logic and reason, but also a very wise and necessary condition in the general scale of evolution.

Idolatry, Symbology and Iconolatry
Part Two

The proposition of an idolatrous world, worshipping the symbolic form, could conceivably arouse controversy. To avoid accusations of hairsplitting and to further justify such a proposition, more analyses are necessary.

Contrary to the existing Freudian psychology, sex is not the dominant inherent instinct. The fear of death or survival should more properly occupy this position. For indeed, would sex be possible without survival? And sex, as a procreative effort, is the largest single counteractive force against death. However, sex cannot occupy even a secondary position until all adjunctive expressions of the survival drive or libido are explored.

Heading the list of these adjunctives is personal identification, and from the moment of birth to death the individual life is a campaign of personal identification. As every mother knows, every child spends his waking hours in some sort of a system of identifications. Even in the world of childish fantasy, the child is further identifying himself as a counteractive effort against the fear of death. For despite environmental conditions which seem to indicate great safety, the survival instinct is dominant nevertheless, and like all other instincts, is merely human attributes and proclivities perpetuated from other lifetimes.

Personal identification then, can be considered to be, in psychological parlance, inflation of the ego. The personal ego must always have as a counteractive balance, a supersedence in the reactive values of life. Thus, the selfish or ulterior motivation is the dominant human characteristic which sponsors all human efforts; and no human can express any effort which can be considered to be altruistic without some stigma of personal gain, and which again becomes, subconsciously or consciously, a placating value against death.

While human emotions have been classified as fear, hate, lust, avarice, love, etc., by far the strongest emotionalism is fear, and is the dominant reactive force in every human life; and it can be said that fear is basically the instigative motivation in living life underlying all other emotional values.

The emotion of love is perhaps the most misunderstood human emotion, and again it is humanly impossible to express love without ulterior motivation; for love does indeed involve all configurations and attributes of the material world as a means of sustaining different emotional values.

In living life, all people must and do live this life in a form of sequence values. The objects and artifacts of life become familiarized and reactive values subtracted from them. This rote system—even the so-called rat race—is very necessary for human existence and, should it be broken, the individual can become frustrated, neurotic and mentally ill. Therefore, the average human loves life; he loves all familiar artifacts and expressions. He loves them because he fears death, for without these familiarities these objectivisms, these reactions, he would die. In fact, they have sustained him through his evolution. Thus it is, the two most different and widely diverse human emotions, fear and love, cannot be separated; nor can they be considered to be actively expressed without ulterior motivation.

However, man's reactive life is not confined to the material worlds. There are extraterrestrial forces in great evidence and abundance with which he has no material association values, and which are not clearly defined or explained in any existing expressionary arts and sciences. These extraterrestrial forces and agencies become the basis for all religious systems. Although man does not understand such deistic forces, he therefore has an even greater fear of them and recognizes in them a greater potential for either his good or his destruction.

He will therefore set up some sort of an appeasement system, hoping to placate emotionalisms which are supposed to be expressed by these deistic elements and forces. Again the ulterior motivation. Again the same reflex action of fear and love, quantitatively expressed as it is in the material values. As these deistic forces are unseen and quite largely unknown (except for emotional values) man therefore erects symbols to personify them; or he may endow the deistic symbol on some earth man whom he considers to justify such deisms.

Again the same reactive sequence of emotional expressionary form is found as in any other material phase of life. It can therefore be concluded that as man worships deistic forces, he does so by the symbolic form; he also worships his material life because all material forms are also symbolic, inasmuch as he has extracted the life-sustaining emotional values from them.

The proposition of personal identification is also carried into the dimensions of deistic expressions. In worshipping in a church, the churchgoer hopes to identify himself with his deistic forces. He is also again re-identifying himself in his community society. The African gorilla identifies himself by beating on his chest and howling; other animals, birds, plant life, all have their own way and means of personal identification, and which is just as important to them as it is in mankind. For upon personal identity resides the responsibility of superiority which, in turn reflects into a progressive evolution of a species.

In mankind, however, the progressive propensities of such evolutionary factors are quite often subverted, and through false emphasis given a place of supremacy in the concourse of human life.

The motion picture and television arts have given host to thousands of individuals of neurotic or psychotic disposition, and even though largely without talent, they have, through common channels of exploitation, been erected in high positions of public adulation, again the symbolic form wherein the common individual sublimates his own values of life against the fear of death.

Curiously enough, such expressionary forms currently idolized and eulogized do inversely represent a decadent form of living; in fact, it seems the less talent, the more such an expressionary is eulogized. This is an inversionary reaction wherein the common citizen again sublimates his own life and sees in it some fancied superiority, nebulous and tenuous, to be sure, and one which is also indicative of our present 'civilized' decadency.

The struggle between good and evil therefore still goes on just as it has for thousands of years; so will it continue for every earth man or material human who must, by necessity, symbolize his life in form and worship it accordingly. He will continue to do this until he can develop his consciousness to a point whereby he can live life without the symbolic form, without the reactionary values instigated through the five material senses—until the time he develops a paranormal function of life lived in more complete harmony with the Infinite Creator.

CHAPTER XXXIII

Lose Face — Ego Deflation

The many contributors, great and small, to our modern version of psychology, of whom Sigmund Freud was perhaps the greatest, added much to our basic understanding in the realm of human emotionalism, and yet this present-day psychology is singularly devoid of spiritual values, quite diametrically opposite to various ecclesiastical concepts, orthodox in nature, where the greatest values in life are placed in spiritual tenure.

Freudism does, however, contribute several basic concepts which are valuable to everyone regardless of other philosophies. An age-old revival of an eastern psychological concept is one in which Freud explains "justification". The sum and total of personality quotients called ego which are most valuable to the person are sometimes seriously subjected to external emotional shocks or setbacks. Unable to immediately compensate such shocks, a person suffers a deflation of the ego consciousness. In the Orient, this is called losing face. Regardless of race, creed, or color, such deflation always has an almost immediate reaction. The person subjected tries to destroy the source of this emotional deflation. This may be done in a number of ways—by criticisms, more usually by stout denials and will even many times, cause violent anger.

Moreover, these repercussive reactions are always aided and strengthened by external forces, such as astral entities from the lower astral planes, who hover like unseen shadows, on the fringes of the auras of unsuspecting persons awaiting the opportunity when the negative vibrations of emotionalisms permit them to connect themselves, through frequency relationship, to the subconscious of their victim, and thereby interject their pernicious and often vicious rebuttals, which in turn will be objectified by the utterances of that reactionary individual.

It is obvious that any sane person would try to prevent such subastral telepathy. Likewise, any individual who believes in some ultimate spiritual destiny for himself and mankind would refrain from such emotional justification. He would realize also that failing in his attempts at either a mild or violent justification, he would be forced to erect another type of defense mechanism against that situation. This and other such emotional experiences will form a rubbish pile which the individual attempts to cover up and gloss over with a smooth exterior of self-satisfaction, or even wave the flag of arrogance, defying the whole world to take his citadel of smug complacency which he has erected on the dung heap of his emotionalisms.

An old adage says that it is always wise to try the edge of one's sword before entering battle. If we are to become true spiritual personalities, we must become cognizant of certain basic facts—that destructive emotionalism does not exist in the minds of highly developed spiritual people. Moreover, we must also be aware of the insidious evil forces from the lower planes who use every device, trick, and opportunity to extinguish any luminous light of spiritual truth which may begin to permeate the darkened reaches of their underworlds and, by the same token, like moths to a flame, the brighter shines our light, the more of them will try to beat out our light with the thrashing of their blackened wings.

It has been written to try the spirits, yet—even more important—to weigh our thoughts and words which become their children; for such things, as they are, thoughts and their progeny, are the fruits of spirit and endure forever.

Like stones, which can be used to build either prisons or temples, or silken fibers for either a shimmering gown or a strong noose about our neck—so our thoughts and their utterance become the fabric of our lives, our prison or our temple. Make sure that the doorway into your mind is well guarded, lest it become a highway used by thieves and robbers, or herdsmen with goats and swine, and the stench from their coming and going passes all endurance.

And so Freud, like others large and small, passes into the limbo of time and takes with him, swung across his back in a tattered pouch, a bag full of wailings, groans, and ailments, wrung from the lips of those who were damned to hell by the godless philosophies, for there too, Freud, like others, will see the spirit of the anti-Christ ferry these lost souls across the river Styx and the dogs of Hebrides will mark each one who passes through the gates.

It can be said that in the realms of personal psychology, the basic derivatives of life are obtained from some system of justifications—a weighing and sorting process in which every person attempts to compromise previously incepted emotional experiences. Such a system of justifications is valuable only to the individual who tempers the emotional content of each experience in its full reactionary nature with the leavening agent of wisdom which is contained in the vessel of tolerance which, like oil poured upon the stormy waters of ruffled complacency, immediately calms these surfaces where newer and greater tranquility can be mirrored thereon. For wisdom too, calms the winds of confusion, dissipates the fog of passionate hatreds, and broadens the horizons of the infinite seas of truth to the questing mariner.

It must not be misconstrued that in using the term "shocks", that these are necessarily various depictions or portrayals which are violent in nature. Quite the contrary—these shocks are usually new truths and concepts which, when first presented to the individual, present new problems of reorientation which not only show the individual he is vastly incomplete in his philosophical aspects, but also make immediate self-evident demands that he tear down the false super-structures of thought patterns which he has erected for himself.

There is usually enough of the sadistic and maso-chistic and sexual elements in the average person's subconscious which make it possible for an immediate appeal through these base structures to any of the more perverted portrayals of life, while such things as murder, bloodshed, etc., may seem to superficially shy from him, yet these reactions, like birds of a feather, always find suitable bedfellows in the lower reaches of the subconscious.

If we are to become recipients of new truths, then these things must be combined measure for measure with wisdom which gives us the power of reception, so we shall not be as stony ground when the sower passes our way. Nor shall we harbor the seeds of tares which, when like the teeth of the dragon were planted, grew to warriors, for our tares too, are watered with the venom of hatred and leave corrosive acid of reactionaryism, and will rise, clothed in the armor of narrow-mind-edness—a garden full of dragons and sporting place of devils.

Contrary to general belief, neither money, war, atom bombs, nor women, are the root of evil, for the parent of all evil is reactionaryism. In this, each person becomes his own Judas and sells himself, not for silver but for some emotional outburst which makes him captive and nails him to his own cross—a cross upon which he has hung his own epitaph, which reads, "It Isn't So".

Among other things called Freudian psychology, which are much less valuable and in fact quite destructive, were certain fabrications of materialistic concepts which reduced man to a mere automation of reflexes, refusing to recognize the spiritual creation of man, and making him a creature of genetical happenstance. It would indeed be fortunate if we could mix Einstein with Freud and introduce into the mind of this material psychology a matrix of pigmentation which would at least give life and luster to an otherwise sordid mechanization.

With the wisdom extracted from the mind of Einstein would come a magic elixir which would lift the dull gray dross of protoplasm and brain cells, infusing into it a sparkling radiance derived from countless hundreds of billions of jewel-like atoms scintillating in pure radiant luster of spiritual ecstasies, for in such materialistic dross is found the essence of creation, and lifts all things up to become participating elements in the divine constructivisms of the Infinite God. What man has ever had the power to delineate the mind of God away from any substance, form, or creation found in the Universe? For man is but the imagery of all creation, not powered by a beating heart or even motivated by elemental reactions, but actually a pulsating entity uniting in the vessel of life all of the infinity of God. He who would deny the birthright of God condemns his own soul. Since each soul is but another fiber in the infinite fabric of life, and since all fibers must combine as threads to make the warp and woof, let no man tear another man asunder, but cleave to all virtue, lest he find weakness in his isolation.

CHAPTER XXXIV

The Plane of Life

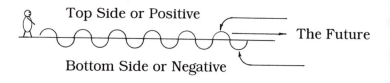

Top Side or Positive

Bottom Side or Negative

The Future

The top side way + — a concept of life that holds all things perfect and as a function of the Infinite; a complete vision of perfection which is obtained when proper knowledge is acquired whereby Principle is the action behind all things and makes all things possible.

Symptoms that you are working with this concept: A positive way to see all things as Principle in action—no anxiety, no fear, no doubt or worry. Perfection in all daily expressions.

Formula: No concentrations, no prayer, no incantations, no supposed directions given consciously, but rather, a complete knowing.

Bottom side or negative —,—a negative concept of life composed of age-old beliefs, superstitions, present anxieties, fears, frustrations—all things which are reactionary, etc., etc., etc.

Symptoms: A fearful reaction to any new happenings or manifestations; a constant strife to attain anything; a repetitive endeavor to constantly equate inequalities by fatalism, prayer, reliance on charms, incantations, directives, etc.

Result: Confusion, despair, sickness, reversion of the

progressive evolution, backsliding, etc.

(This was a letter written to a student who was having difficulty in recognizing positive from negative, and as she and others have benefited so from it, we felt it should be included here.)

How to acquire the top side way: First, study Unarius. Learn something about energy. Begin to see energy in action in all daily expressions. Combine this with the conscious knowledge that this energy functions according to an inviolate Principle—that this energy is the Infinite in action.

The perfect concept will therefore resolve into consciousness whereby you will be able to attune yourself to a more perfect way. This is not done with a directive conscious effort but by making the conscious mind subservient to Principle, and which is done by direct jurisdiction of the personal Higher Self (which everyone has).

This Higher Self is an abstraction of the Infinite and functions infinitely according to Principle. Result: Perfection in daily life according to how well conscious mind, functions in a subservient way to the Higher Self and Infinity.

In the future and in the many lives and countless years you will yet live, the conscious mind will gradually become atrophied and the Higher Self will begin to supplant the function of the conscious mind. As this transition is taking place, you will begin to lose your physical world and the material life. Instead, there will come an ever-increasing scope of intelligence and function which is brought about by a more direct function with the Higher Self.

As your Higher Self is 'living' in higher or spiritual dimensions, it is doing so by its ability to function (or oscillate) with Infinity. Therefore, when you have completed this transition, you will be one of the very Advanced Personalities which the Christian religion calls archangel or godlike beings.

For the present, realize your present position in your daily life. How you react (or think) is only the net development of your past lives. Principle is dynamic; it is always progressive; therefore, you must also be progressive or perish.

Up until this point in your evolution, your physical life supplied a certain quotient of progression, sometimes called libido or drive, to attain a better life. Now, however, you have passed that point where this material world can supply your drive; you have been spiritually quickened to a higher spiritual life.

This higher life cannot be lived in the old material way; you must learn to re-adapt yourself to this higher life. This is done gradually, through many lifetimes and countless experiences, trial and retrial, until your old self or psychic anatomy is completely replaced by your newer spiritual psychic anatomy. Then, you will no longer return to earth lives.

Therefore, learn to carry in your conscious mind the perfect concept of Infinity that your mind, your daily life is a clean slate whereby this Infinite can superimpose its perfection. Then you will begin to witness small and great miracles happening to you. All things necessary in your daily life will appear at the proper time and without conscious or physical strife on your part; you will get the answers to all problems; you will become ever-increasingly intelligent in all dispensations and relationships.

This is the finding of the Kingdom Within and the Father—or Infinity, and your Higher Self—or Christ-Self, as an abstract facsimile of the Infinite which you have developed through polarization as your personal entity through ages of material earth lives, spiritual lives, etc., and their countless experiences, all polarized in Principle.

For the present then, be realistic. Do not attempt to live a perfect way overnight. Begin by first carrying the complete perfect picture in your mind, the vast complete Infinite which is everywhere. It is all things visible and unseen. It is constantly regenerating into new forms. Realize and learn in your consciousness to tune yourself to the correct wave lengths which will materialize into your daily life.

No, you do not say to the Infinite, "I want so and so to happen or appear". You must realize this Infinite knows far better than you do what you need; that it is much more important to learn about the Infinite than to try and use it for personal self or gain. For in learning about the Infinite you accomplish your best purposes, including eternal life—bearing in mind, of course, that learning is synonymous to use as an absolute in daily life and supersedes all other forms of consciousness, and that you are completely dedicated.

This is the reason why prayer, affirmations, directives, etc., are all useless and always detrimental because not only do these conscious mind efforts obstruct, but they retard development in an intelligent approach to understanding the Infinite.

In other words, your conscious mind 'thinks' from memory of the past. As your past is composed of the same materialistic derelictions, it is impossible to construct an intelligent hypothesis from this past; likewise, reaction is predicated by former reactions, all based or biased in fear—the age-old fear of survival—the jungle law.

Consequently, all happenings appear as reactions

instead of more correctly seeing that Principle is expressing action; and individually each person should equate all things in this manner.

In such introspection a more complete abstraction can be made. Sin, evil, etc., will have lost their former positions, and now you will see it is a matter of positive personal resolution as to what takes place in your life as well as its nature.

Cease letting your old past lives, your old self rule you. Realize that every time you feel insecure, fearful, frustrated, guilt, anger, etc., these emotional reflexes are your old self rearing its ugly head. There is a much better way to live—by seeing Principle in action and Principle the will of the Infinite Intelligence.

Just in case you have arrived at some erroneous conclusions, and you may say to yourself, "If I am not supposed to use my conscious mind, then how do I go about in my daily life; or how do I obtain correct usage with my conscious mind?" First, no attempt should be made to try and abstain from using your conscious mind. You could not stop using it even if you tried; nor has any inference been made that you should do so; but strong emphasis has been placed on how to use it, or how it is used.

Picture in your mind a small worm and how it wriggles in pain when it is pressed by a stick. When some new adverse expression appears before you, it becomes a stick 'pressing' your mind; in a sense, you react. There are many wriggling worms of energy coursing through your brain cells. These generate certain harmonics which are detrimental to health and well-being.

Instead when this adverse condition appears, you would stop it short in its effect by first properly placing it as one of the many infinite expressions which is part of the evolutionary scale. Then, so far as your own personal relationship was concerned, it would begin to fit into your understanding of the Infinite.

CHAPTER XXXV

Angels, Devils and Demons

In the liturgies and expressionary elements of Unarius, there has been on several occasions mention of devils, or of how devils became angels. It is conceivable that some person or student may, to some extent, misunderstand these statements; therefore, it would serve a good purpose if we might fully explore this dimension of introspection, and which would also serve a double purpose, inasmuch as it would acquaint any person or student with these particular dimensions of expression which are everywhere about him, or in which he could conceivably become so enmeshed at some future time.

Our first classification of devils should be made clear and distinct. They should not be confused with one other classification which could more properly be called demons. Everyone who has seen pictures of devil masks used by natives of Africa or in the religious ceremonies in Tibet has seen these weirdly carved and contorted figure faces used on these occasions. They were called devils but most properly should be called demon forms; for the witch doctors or priests who contrived these forms did so somewhat in replica or facsimile from the demon forms which they had envisioned perhaps in a trance state, or even brought back the memory of these visionary forms from one of the underworlds. Briefly then, a demon is simply one or more astral bodies which have undergone a complete deformation of all forms and continuities in the wave form structures of these astral psychic anatomies. They are oscillating without cause or purpose; they are wildly gyrating in numerous expressionary elements without thought or cause. Therefore, these expressionary elements, if they could be considered as a personal form, would indeed have a very insane attitude toward all things involved, so much more so that they would become extremely violent and destructive in all intents and purposes.

On the other hand, a devil is still a rather intelligent person in earth-world evaluations—intelligent, that is, in the reactionary factors of the material world. In fact, the first mention of the devil in the Bible refers to a son of God who was cast out from Heaven unto the earth; therefore, the implication clearly states that the earth is a hell; for God really cast his son into hell for insubordination. Briefly then, a devil can be classified as any individual who does, in all intent and purpose in his daily life, use such forms and expressions for his own personal gain or his own selfish interests, without thought, without consideration for the purposes and the life of other people. Therefore, in a general classification we might say that almost all human beings (non-Unariuns) would come under this heading as we see them going about their daily tasks. They are under the carnal law of the jungle or the earth world, first and primarily interested in and motivated by the interests of self; they survive by the different reactionary complexes which have been fostered and engendered in these earth-world existences.

However, these people do have a saving grace. That is, they are for the most part intuitively aware of a certain balance system in these transpositions: they are also aware of great and unknown powers of creation which are quite evident all about them. And so their motivations are, to some degree, tempered by the thought of some repercussive reaction which might take place if they became wholly engrossed in the selfish attitudes of the material world. They will, therefore, on occasion express some of these more unselfish attitudes; they may even become heroic, or use other different forms of expressions wherein they portray some of the more ultimate and better qualities of human expression. However, for the most part, humans as a whole are completely ignorant of the vast interplay of cosmic intelligence which is going on about them. Even in their earth life and in their numerous selfish motivations of life which make life possible for them, they have no way or means of discriminating against others who may be using them for more selfish purposes.

In the world today, we can see many more highly developed forms of devils who are expressing some leadership in some form or another wherein they are attempting, so they think, to better the cause of man; at least so far as the exterior surface of their consciousness is concerned, they believe that they are doing good. Actually, however, there is an ulterior motivation behind these movements. Therefore, we can look into such fields as politics, religion, and other different social structures and we shall see leaders in these fields who are, in their attempts to better the cause of mankind, actually only furthering their own interests and their own intents. They are also furthering the interests of the material world. They are attempting in these efforts to solidify all people in the earth world and material world dispensations; for all of their thoughts and actions are circumscribed by the usual third-dimensional-world attitudes and knowledge. It is only when we find an expressionary element or leadership which presents the whole of Infinity and the morality of this Infinity, so far as the personal position is concerned, do we find leadership and expression which can be said to be truly motivated by the highest interests.

Therefore, it can be said that of this time and day, with the exception of Unarius, there are no other expressionary elements in the world today which do not circumscribe their efforts within the dimension of this material world and they can therefore all be considered to be devilish forms. Their leaders are, in a sense, devils, for devils still maintain a certain intelligent perspective or attitude toward the material world. They are quite aware of all of the reactive factors involved in this third-dimensional transition.

The same analysis is applied to your own personal evolution. If you are at this time working out karma— and most students are—you therefore can consider your past life and your past lifetimes to have been devilish expressions. You lived in the material world and incurred its karmic intent and therefore, all things which you work out were, in their own time and place, merely purposes served as a devilish form of development. When you realize the implications of this analysis, you will easily see how it is that unless we are very careful in our daily actions, in our daily thoughts and in all things that we do, we can easily be led down the garden path. We can very easily deviate at any time from the true course of constructive evolution. The graphic illustration of the "Temptation on the Mount" in the New Testament, illustrates the problem which is ever with us; we, at all times, are being tempted. We are tempted by lax attitudes, by intemperances and by compromises; and if we give way to these temptations, if we succumb in any one particular expressionary form, then it becomes increasingly difficult to reinstate ourselves on that path of evolution.

Therefore, if we have become devils, we are in actual

reality, paying for these things by the tremendous amount of effort, will and determination that it takes to get back on the constructive pathway of evolution. The term, 'seven times seven' or 'seventy times seventy' is easily applied in every case. For the deviations into these expressionary forms which are self-motivated will, as a consequence, require a greatly increased effort for any person to turn the sum and total of these expressionary elements in a reversed manner so that they become constructive. Therefore, in the future, do not be tempted by any of these earth-life vicissitudes. You will learn that the earth life is a temporal existence; one which is fashioned and contrived, in the process of evolution, as a way and a means in which you can learn, you can evolve into a higher state of consciousness. You cannot expect to occupy a high state of consciousness without learning, in all dimensions, the reason for life, the application of life principles, the evolution of consciousness. These are of the utmost importance and you could not, at any time, occupy any position in any spiritual world advanced from the earth until you have undergone this metamorphosis which is always a part of the earth world function.

For the earth world and all other attendant worlds, such as are similar to the earth world, are, in themselves, similar expressionary or evolutionary elements in your transition or in the transition of any earth human. I could relate to you certain classical examples or stories of individuals who have aspired to a higher way of life and then were tempted and fell to the temptation; and from that time for thousands of years, came back into the earth world and fought this personal battle of self-emancipation. Always, they seemed to be apparently motivated by the most humane interests, by different expressionary forms which, in themselves, could be considered idealistic in nature or very constructive to those people who were concerned with them. However, as it always turned out, it became a battle between the old past life and having fallen under the temptation, and the Superconscious Self which had been developed, to some degree, by this individual before he had fallen under temptation.

In certain instances, this battle was always, to some degree, lost to the more negative forces with which this person had been so engrossed in expressing. As each life was so manifest in an evolutionary pattern, so did the Superconscious Self gradually dwindle in its net effect upon the equilibrium or the balance which had been set up in this individual's life. And so through the passing of many thousands of years and hundreds of earth lives, the person finally emerged only as a very weak earthling, only vaguely inspired to do the right thing. Yet, in attempting to do right and to work out these karmic impregnations, the person was always ultimately faced with this decision to accept them and, in facing this decision, always reneged on the purpose of the evolution or reincarnation, always rejected the most ultimate purpose which could be served at that moment.

This is the problem which you, too, may encounter in your future evolutions should you be tempted and should you fall and become one of these more strongly expressed devilish forms which you see about you in your world today. Then most surely will you come back to the earth world time and time again to try and try, to work out your temptation, to try and reinstate yourself in the evolutionary pathway. The chances of being successful in this endeavor are extremely remote and, while it has been accomplished, it should not be advocated. It should not be inferred that I so advocate such an action; and it should not be misconstrued by any person that such an inference gives him any form of laxity in his daily expression; no more so than the Catholic confessional gives the person a right to commit murder on the premise that he can be forgiven for his sins. For forgiveness is not, in a sense of the word, the action or thought of some deistic god. Forgiveness, in a true sense, means that we have taken the sin and intent of some action and we have reversed its cyclic motion so that it is again reformed in a reconstructive element of expression. Forgiveness is not a prerogative of determination expressed by a priesthood; it is not an expression which can be voiced by any person to another person. It is a personal proposition where we take the negative content of this action and thought and reverse it into something constructive.

The effort required to reverse this destructive energy conformation is, as it can be correctly assumed to be, quite difficult and requires an immense amount more of personal effort than it would have, had we taken the same energy wave form and used it constructively in the beginning. This is the problem all people, at this present time, are confronted with whether they are on this earth plane at this moment, on some other earth, or in one of the more immediate spiritual planes. The problem of self-determination, that arbitrary value which we see in every life transposition, is that we can use it either constructively for the benefit of Infinite Intelligence, for the benefit of mankind, or for the benefit of self. These motivations must always be carried on unselfishly, without thought of personal gain. The reward system is dangerous, yet it is a system indulged in by all humanity on the earth planes; everyone seems to feel the necessity for a reward for any effort which he extends.

This is not a constructive motivation; it is destructive because the temptation of self-reward is, in itself, very great. It is one in which every person must constantly equalize within the dimension of his own perspectives. The selfish motivations always determine the success of living in some of these earth worlds; however, in the spiritual worlds, the determinants are quite different. Self can only be expressed in a completely reverse fashion; that is, self is only enlarged, only strengthened and fortified. It becomes intelligent only in direct ratio and proportion as to how well we express it outwardly, without selfish motivations, into the Infinite Cosmos about us.

In these earth worlds, the situation is quite the reverse—at least so some people think. They believe that they can go from one hour to the next, from day to day, from year to year, with nothing but the most selfish motivations within their hearts and minds. Everything concerns them personally—what their value is in these different transitions of life about them. In fact, the world, in itself, revolves around the little citadel of selfhood. All things must come to them and this, in a sense, is a devilish form of expression. It is indulged in only by devils, and it will make devils out of anyone who indulges himself in this idle fantasy of life.

The evolution of mankind is bi-directional; that is, if we could look into time and space, into Infinity, we would see streams of human souls evolving into two directions. They would be evolving upward into the Infinite Cosmos, becoming more and more intelligent with the passing of millenniums, or conversely, we could see streams of humanity traveling that downward trail into oblivion—people who have fallen victims to the numerous selfish devices of their earth lives. They had succumbed to the numerous temptations; they had made certain compromises. They had lived life without knowledge and without the necessity of evaluating their own existence as the more ultimate achievement of personal expression in combination with Infinite Intelligence. And so these poor souls do travel this downward trail. They may become more highly developed devilish expressions or devils; and they may eventually evolve into the lower sub-astral worlds where they become demons; and demons, in turn, eventually destroy themselves in the wild convolutions of unintelligent expressions within their own psychic anatomies.

Now the question may arise in your minds, "How can we best protect ourselves from these devilish forms and expressions?" Fortunately, Infinite Intelligence has a built-in protection system for everyone. It is simply your attitude of life because, on the basis of frequency relationships, you can completely insulate yourself from the apparitions of physical temptations. You can, in the development of intelligence within the dimension of your own mind, rise to a certain position in your scale of evolution where the devilish forms, the demon apparitions and other astral underworld characterizations cannot possess you; they cannot influence you and they cannot intimidate your thought and action.

For the present, however, your greatest protection will be found in how well you apply yourself in all constructive purposes and intents, how well you evaluate your daily life experiences, and how well you can evaluate your position toward Infinity. If you do this constructively, if you are not tempted by either the obvious or unobserved temptations which constantly oscillate about you, then you can further your progress. You can be insulated against the apparitions of these devilish forms; you will not be led or influenced by them. In this way then, you can be reasonably assured that you will have protection. Moreover, there is always the added benefit in your constructive efforts. There are always higher spiritual worlds populated with many millions of more advanced personalities who will, and do on all occasions, further your cause. They will use all means possible to help you in your efforts; they will project energies to you; they will inspire you. They will even use certain scientific instrumentation which they have at their disposal to rectify certain conditions which have been brought into your lifetime.

In this present world you should always realize, however, that you are, to some extent, subjective to the way of life which is generally expressed by mankind. As such, you are harmonically attuned to these earth-life dispensations. This, then, will require redoubled effort on your part to keep these things from becoming psychic impregnations or, in other words, that they will become dominant factors in your personality which will be so expressed in your future evolutions. You can accept these earth-world dispensations on a philosophical basis; if you have knowledge of why they exist and how they so transpire, then this will, in itself, automatically insure you against psychic impregnation. It will automatically insure against future incarnations where you will come back with the double burden of karma in these earth-life dispensations.

This is the purpose of Unarius: to present to you the complete morality of Infinity, your own position to Infinity, either as a creative and a regenerative entity of expression or whether you revolve down into one of those lower sub-astral regions to eventually be absorbed back into the Infinite supply. That is why Unarius is unique among all other earth dispensations. In fact, it may appear to be completely opposite from all other earth-life dispensations for, in truth, it is. It immediately emancipates any person in the presentation of Infinite Science and in your relationship to Infinite expression. You are not bound or fettered by the conformities, the restrictions of your earth world. You have the atmosphere wherein you can develop in perfect freedom and in perfect harmony, into the more ultimate realizations of human metamorphosis. You can become a spiritual being. You can become practically anything which can be envisioned within your mind; yes, and even far beyond that. You can become a demon. And, as I have forewarned you, you can eventually be absorbed back into the Infinite supply. This is the Infinite prerogative; it is something which is immediately presented on the face of Infinity to every person. The Infinite Intelligence makes no demand on any person because the Infinite is inviolate; it cannot be changed by any human. It is a problem of self-determination; a choice which you and you alone must make. You make this choice in every thought and action. Regardless of whether you understand it as such or whether it slips by you unobserved, you have still made a choice. Therefore, let all your future choices in your transitions be constructive in nature. Let them be intelligently expressed. Let them re-create the morality of Infinity.

Angels, Devils and Demons

Part Two

Now that we have discovered certain differences between angels, devils and demons, and we have found that the earth is one of the astral worlds—an underworld, peopled and populated by such expressionary forms as can be considered to be devilish in intent and purpose—this introspection leads us more directly to the comparisons between good and evil. Actually, the biblical depiction of God casting Satan into hell because he was insubordinate has a much more complete and abstract evaluation. It is a typical depiction of how a more advanced personality who had developed to that point, where he was godlike in nature, could therefore be considered to be a son of God. At that highest point of his evolution, somehow he became tempted and, in the temptation, plunged himself, mentally and spiritually speaking, back into some earth-world environment, involved again in the intricate mazes of comparisons which are found in these earth-life dispensations.

At this point then, the differences between evil and good are all-important. In numerous places (in Unarius Liturgies) it has been mentioned that God has become merged, from an old deistic configuration into the sum and total of Infinity; and, as Infinity is, in itself, an expressionary element constantly regenerating all forms with the substance of itself, as energy from these interdimensional planes; therefore this Infinite, or God, is also the net sum and total of all good and, is also the net sum and total of all evil. God thus becomes good and evil. Now this concept is not acceptable to the common, ordinary earth man who lacks the knowledge of the Infinite or who lacks other different, fundamental and basic concepts which would more rationally integrate the factors and the apparent truths in these statements. It is in the comparisons between good and evil and, in the determinants which are so superimposed that evil, in turn as a destructive element or a destructive intent does, by direct comparison, point out the goodness in good; and, as such, this evil therefore, whatever it is, does become good in this comparative system of evaluations.

The common, ordinary lot of the life of the earth man, therefore, is a highly evolved, reactionary process of comparisons between good and evil. In whatever his system of life, his society, his political government or his religious affiliations, in whatever dimension of life he so cares to evaluate the different factors with which he is involved, he will find these direct comparisons between good and evil. And if he is successful, he will see, not only the good, but he will see the necessity of inseminating or using the good in a constructive form and purpose to perpetuate his future. If he does this, and if he is successful in it, then we can say that evil has become good.

Now another fact becomes important. Should we, at any time, sufficiently evolve in our evolution to that point where we can immediately discern the comparisons between evil and good, and we can intelligently motivate our lives, we can predicate action with this goodness which is apparent in contrast to the evil; we can therefore naturally assume to have escaped the perditions of the evil itself. This is a highly-developed reactionary form in which evil does again become good; it is again the common evolutionary reaction contained within Infinite Consciousness which reconstructs itself in all thought, form, purposes, etc. Logically then, any person would be wise and intelligent if he could immediately discern the differences between good and evil. If he could render his own judgments, his own personal actions, etc., according to these comparisons, he could then be said to be a more advanced personality. He would, in all effect, be much more intelligently inclined in his expressive actions with the Infinite Creator. He could also be said to have evolved into that state of consciousness wherein there were no more of these karmic impregnations of good and evil consequences which he had formerly incurred in his earth life. Logically then, every person should try to aspire to such a dimension of consciousness. This cannot be done in some such vague or esoterical fashion as is supposed to exist in religious systems. We must all have certain constructive knowledge, scientific in nature, which will determine for us how well we can evaluate these differences in our daily lives.

Moreover, these evaluations must always be carried on very objectively. This is a demand which, in itself, is of such nature that it requires intelligence beyond the common ordinary denominators so expressed by earth people. For people are only reactionary elements which function to the five senses and oscillate with these different wave forms which come into their consciousness from these different expressionary elements. The average earth man is not sufficiently advanced in any of his philosophies or sciences of life whereby he can immediately recognize all of the factors which are of immediate concern to him. He is completely blind to the more ultimate objectives and purposes which can be said to be in store for him should he succeed in intelligently inseminating in his consciousness, all of these numerous interdimensional factors which are so constructively inclined and, which would so give him the progressive impetus in his evolution.

Good and evil, therefore, must become some sort of a science. It must become a wave-form expression which expresses, within itself, both the positive and negative terminals of evolution. It automatically relinks itself in cyclic motions either to the more highly-developed expressionary forms or the more highly-conceived idealisms of life or their ways and manners in which they work themselves out; or, conversely, the same forms can relink themselves, harmonically speaking, and in cyclic motions to the lower and more retrogressive factors of life. These retrogressive factors always completely isolate the individual from Infinite expression. To the earth man such isolation is only partially complete. He is still in some sort of a nether world where he is trying to evaluate the constructive principles of creation without the necessary knowledge.

At this present stage of development, the earth man is attempting to kick down his circumscribed third-dimensional world. He has a great urge to explore the outer regions of space. While such explorations are neither philosophically justified, nor are they religiously justified, nevertheless, man does feel the urge to explore space. He manages to contrive rocketry, satellites, etc., which have penetrated to the immediate fringes of space. He has attempted with other scientific devices, to penetrate into some of the more remote regions through such apparatus called radio telescopes and other attendant scientific instrumentation. He has determined that the universe is, as a whole, a pulsating entity and that it gives off signals. It is also now, reasonably assumed by these savants of science, that there are literally hundreds of millions of other planets in our galaxy, in our solar system and, in our universe.

These planets could therefore be inhabited by human life which would, in some respects, be quite similar to our own; however, the earth man has not yet ascended to that plateau of understanding where he can conceive the Infinite as an interdimensional proposition, that life can and does exist without the necessity of the physical form, or the apparent necessity of such form.

He does not realize that life can exist in a spiritual or energy body without temperature or without blood; or without any of the other adjutants which are found in our physical bodies. This is so despite the obvious facts that he has radio and television transmissions. He knows that sight and sound can be carried as a wave form. He has not, however, carried his science to a point where he can see the inner dimensions, which function without time or without space as harmonically linked units or entities of intelligence, into such expressionary forms as the psychic anatomy, which has been repeatedly described to you in the Unariun Concepts. Almost needless to say, that until such time that he can and does conceive the Interdimensional Creation, the psychic anatomy, and other attendant factors in this interdimensional science, he will not aspire either to any of his long-dreamed-of emancipations, his freedoms from the material worlds which actually sponsor all of these efforts into space, his longing and his desire for some sort of an utopia where he is freed from the vicissitudes of earth life and its intemperances. These, too, are only vague inclinations and desires which he inherently possesses as a system of comparisons between good and evil. There are also glimpses into the spiritual worlds which he may have had in his spiritual lives in between lives.

As a student of Unarius, you are immediately confronted with the necessity for survival—survival beyond the physical world into other dimensions which constitute the Infinite. The survival beyond the earth world cannot be accomplished by ordinary means. The purpose of survival cannot be realized within any of the philosophies or sciences now contained in earth-life dispensations. The Christian religion, itself, only hints vaguely at survival. It is an unrealistic survival. It is predicated upon earth-life dispensations. It is therefore unintelligent and has no place in the infinite scheme of Infinite Creation. Therefore, suitable knowledge must be inseminated into your consciousness beginning at this time whereby a more constructive and purposeful evolution can be instituted by yourself. This must be constructed by scientific principles which are at your disposal and this science is further extended into Infinite proportions. The science is a descriptive terminology of the lives to come and of how these lives are lived.

In a more purely philosophical stance, this science also automatically absolves you from the evil intent of the world about you, because in this science, you can make the necessary objective comparisons in your daily-life transitions. You will be immediately concerned and alerted to the possibilities of evil. You will see the comparisons between these negative or evil forms and the positive and the constructive effigy of consciousness which is also apparent at that time. In this way then, you will, in this philosophical and scientific understanding, have actually reconstructed evil into a good purpose. It will have made the necessary comparisons for you or, rather, you have made these comparisons with these attendant good and evil factors. But whatever way in which you attain them in the immediate objectivisms in your consciousness, so evil then serves a good purpose. It, therefore, like all other things which stem from Infinite Consciousness is, in actual reality, good. God does then, in this more abstract evaluation, represent nothing but perfection. He is all good, all encompassing. He is the sum, the total, of everything. He is the supply and His substance enters into the construction of all things.

The Infinite Wisdom of this evolutionary plan then becomes apparent. For it is in this evolutionary process that any individual can become supremely intelligent or at least supremely so, in comparison to the different earth life values which you now find about you. You can say that in this Infinite Wisdom, you have actually been absolved from the evil of these material worlds. You have been saved by them. In a sense then, evil has become, indirectly, your intercessor; it has become your savior because it has enabled you to use the comparative values of scientific comparisons in these life-to-life evaluations. You have subtracted from evil, the condiment of good. It has given you the impetus of comparison and the stimulus to reconstruct your own life according to the values which you have found as those of paramount importance.

However, the evil ways of the material world are almost as infinite in nature as are the comparisons which you can make. These different evil ways and the temptations involve, not only the common ordinary denominators which every human finds and which he selfishly inclines for his own personal good, but they can also be evils which we find in such psychological equivalents which might be called escape mechanisms.

An escape mechanism is that safety valve which every human possesses whereby he can normally discharge certain static pressures built up within his psychic anatomy, which would otherwise recapitulate and enlarge to such proportions that he would, in a sense, become one of those demons in the underworld. His psychic anatomy would become so supercharged with these static forces that there would be no coherent relationship between the different dimensional factors so involved in this oscillating process. He would, literally, be torn apart or psychically dismembered by these tremendous static forces which prevented normal alignments and transpositions of energy. The escape mechanism, while it may be considered to be an evil thing, in reality also serves a very good purpose. However, an escape mechanism can develop to abnormal proportions.

A person may be only mildly disposed in such an escape mechanism in such expressionary forms as religion, or he may seek to escape the reality of his physical world by chasing flying saucers. He may be obsessed with music, with art, or with politics or medicine. But whatever he finds himself involved in as this expressionary element, he should seek and find the more ulterior motivations of his expressionary element. He should question himself, "Am I truly motivated by a constructive purpose freed from the intimidations of an escape mechanism? Am I really involved in whatever I am doing because it is truly understood by me, as an expressionary element, intelligently linked to Infinite Expression as an evolutionary element, but which can constructively progress not only myself, but all humanity?"

When such questions are asked by you as a student, or by any other individual and the correct answers to these questions can be found and objectively analyzed, then you, the student, or the person who so arrives at these conclusions and answers can be said to be constructively inclined; you can be said to be constructively instituted in the evolutionary sequences which will eventually lead you into a higher spiritual world. However, here again, you must not use the reward system. You must not attempt to aspire to a higher way of life for some hidden or ulterior motivations of which you may not, at the present moment, be conscious. You may even think or say to yourself, "Well, I am doing it because I love Infinite Creation or, that I love God or, I love my fellowman." But in actual reality, you should penetrate much more deeply into the maze and intricate thought patterns of which your subconscious mind is constructed.

In order to ferret out these ulterior motivations, you may find that these desires, these idealisms which are valuable to you at this time, are actually instigated; they are propagated by those same carnal lusts and desires which formerly made your different earth-life evolutions possible—just as they are making them possible for others around you. Here again, you may assume that if these lustful earth-life purposes have, in themselves, contrived to motivate you into more inspirational and idealistic transitions of life, then in your philosophical attitude, in your knowledge toward them, you can reasonably assume you have converted the evil of the past into the good of the future.

Life therefore becomes an infinite proposition. We cannot contain life into any singular expressionary form. We cannot say that it is purely religion or, that it is purely philosophical or, it is purely science. All of these factors become one and the same if they are properly and intelligently used in our expressionary attitude of life; if they are fully realized within our own mental introspections. In this respect, we cannot bisect or sectionalize our particular expressionary motion or intelligence in any particular form or dispensation. We cannot say we are scientific or that we are philosophical or, that we are religious. Only man, in his own earth-life dispensations, has found that this sectionalizing has been important to him because he is primarily motivated by escape mechanisms engendered from these earth-world dispensations, the contrasts between the creativity which is ever apparent about him and the destructive intent of his own carnal life.

These factors all engender these escape mechanisms and so, he is constantly pressurized into some system whereby he relieves himself from the reality of this escape mechanism. Religion serves an obvious purpose in this respect; so do any of the other social systems in which the earthman may so undertake. He may even find some consolation, some escape, in other escape mechanisms which can be called persecution complexes. The whole complexity of human emotion, as it is portrayed from the psychic anatomy, is one complete fabrication of all the factors and transitions which the human has ever lived. He cannot at any time, escape them until he does so cancel them out with the necessary constructive energies which will so neutralize the pernicious, negative effect of these experiences. And even if he so cancels them out, he still retains them as sort of an edifice or storehouse of knowledge which makes him intelligently factual with all of the different transpositions and factors involved in infinite evolution.

No highly-developed spiritual Being could have arrived at his place had he not gone through these different planes of transition. Evolving to that position, he has become intelligent by virtue of the fact that he has made these comparisons between good and evil and he has turned evil into a good purpose. This, then, should be your philosophy of life.

CHAPTER XXXVI

Mass, The Illusion

In referring to the structure of mass, there are some very important and avowed secrets in regard to the gravitational field, the effect of changing the vibrating rates of atoms and molecules and other different combinations of various elements which the scientist calls mass. We will take any given group of molecules which concerns mass, such as iron and we introduce heat. We must first picture in our mind the molecules as they are concerned with iron. Although they appear very dense to us, they are not really dense at all. If we were able to look into the iron say, with an ant's-eye view, we would find that there are wide spaces between these molecules of iron and that they really were not solid in any respect to how we imagine them, as being solid.

That which makes them adhere together is this mere fact that every atom is a transducer. In other words, by taking certain energies of the various atoms with which it is combined and, in turn, due to the fact that the molecule is spinning on an orbit or within itself with this group of atoms and has taken certain energies and combined them or transduced them with the gravitational force so that they, in turn, radiate an aura or a field of force which is very strong and which combines, in direct frequency relationship with other molecules of the iron. It is this field of force around each molecule which gives the iron its apparent illusion of solidity.

Now, if we introduce heat into the iron to the point where, we will say, that the iron becomes molten and runs like water, it merely means that we have accelerated the orbital rate of the molecules to such an extent that their entire frequency relationship has been changed with each other and thus they have become fluid instead of maintaining a solid aspect. If we follow the same transference pattern back, down into the atoms themselves and picture atoms, like the molecules, spinning in their orbits and generating a very strong field of force and which, in turn, is connected to other atoms, we find that this forms the molecules. By introducing an external field of force into the atom to such an extent that we can accelerate or decrease the natural aperiodic rate of the atom to the point where the field of force which it externalizes is changed, we have the principle which actuates the flying saucers or which changes or transmutes metal from one element to another, depending upon how far we carry this particular principle into existence. What it means, of course, is that in the future when the scientist learns how to speed up under a controlled rate or decrease under the same controlled rate, the actual aperiodic rate or the natural vibrating frequency of the atom, he will be able to change its characteristics to the gravitational field of the earth and therefore, he can nullify gravity on any given element, by acceleration or decreasing its natural vibrating rate.

In combination with other metals to form some sort of a vessel or a vehicle, by nullifying the gravitational rate, he can also alter the relationship of any group of atomic structures or their relating vehicle, to its own particular point in the material space. In other words, he will have passed from the third dimension, which is the material space, into another dimension and by the same changing of frequency rate, the vehicle, whatever it is, will automatically be transferred from any one or a given number of points in free space; and therefore

286

he can very easily see how the flying saucers travel in that very same, similar fashion simply because he sees them only in a way which we might see a mirage, a reflection. He does not see the true flying saucer; he is seeing only a picture or a form of this saucer in this dimension and this same picture projection, as we shall call it, as we would see the image in a mirror, is still sufficiently strong to activate a radar impulse; but it is not the true picture of the flying saucer because the flying saucer is, in that position, already traveling through, what Einstein called, free inner space.

And when we are changing atoms, their inner vibrating rate either accelerating or decreasing their speed in relationship to our own gravitational force field of the earth which is the primary mass field as it is concerned with the solar system in which the earth is rotating, we can also change its relative position in free space, at a rate which could be considered almost instantaneous, from one point to another.

The foregoing is one big step in the right direction toward understanding what flying saucers are and how they are operated and, how the scientists in the future will be able to simulate conditions, and the science, which is already existing in other planetary systems and other universes. They have learned to that point, because of their knowledge of atomic structures where they can take and alter the frequency rate of the atom, without changing its basic structure, to the point where it is no longer affected by the gravitational field on any one particular planet or any solar system but, that it becomes a transferable element, in a different dimension. And as a group of atoms, becomes a vehicle which is transferable in terms of almost instantaneous relationship, to any given point in the universe—the unseen, the invisible universe—which is not seen by science and which cannot be seen with the physical eye.

The appearances of stars and various other heavenly bodies are, in themselves, only external appearances of atomic forms which have been changed, in their relationship or their frequency, through common denominators of astrophysical science, if we like to call it that, which is, of course, the working out of the Infinite Mind, into various different objects which we call stars, suns, moons, or planets. In fact, mass, as a whole, is merely an external manifestation of much which takes place on the interior surface and which is not apparent to any of the five physical senses. The old theory that a planet or a sun is a sort of compressed mass of celestial gas or very finely divided particles which come from out of space is, of course, a very fallacious concept and one which will pass, in time. Actually, what it means is that in the formation of huge spiraling forms of vortexes in the unseen world or unseen universe, we find, through the linkages of various cycles which are the formative part of this great celestial vortex that in the interplay of positive and negative energy transferences which form the relationship of what can be similarized as centripetal or centrifugal forces, the apex or the center of this spiral becomes a sun or a planet. It is actually, in a sense of the word, materializing a form of atomic energy into this world as tiny, minutely divided, particles of so-called mass and which the so-called scientist of today calls atoms which, in themselves, are only the external appearances in their proper relationship of internal vortexes which, in turn, relink them to some cycular patterns to the Infinite Vortex which originally formed them.

CHAPTER XXXVII

Life No Happenstance

Certain wise Avatars who have visited this planet have always stressed man's perversities in distorting spiritual virtues into some subversive malfunction to obtain power and glory over his fellow man.

History reveals kings and emperors have thus been born and, as of today, they are still reappearing in different clothing and with different names. Not the least of those who set themselves up in some position of power over mankind is the priest and just as are other forms so represented, the priest and his ecclesiastical dispensation is still an all-powerful influence in almost any land on the planet earth.

It is a fact which is almost beyond analysis that the masses of people who have so lived in their time have accepted without quibble any and all claims of those who proclaim a visitation from the prevailing ruling god of the times.

And so, whether it was Moses and the burning bush, Mohammed, Joseph Smith, or any other historical configurations, these claims have caused these believers into forming a religion or cultistic pantheology which always becomes extremely rhetorical; in fact, it lives and thrives by a fanatical demand that all mankind must so believe. Nor is this fanaticism always confined to religious beliefs. Today's cold war with Russia is a point in toto as a political example of man's proclivities to either individually or collectively bend all other men to his or their will, that they must obey and live by his credo.

Unfortunately for those who believe and follow

some self-styled prophet or holy man or politico, the claim to 'divine' leadership is, and always has been, completely false. The claim of divine visitation and command and leadership has always been born out of the warped and distorted subconscious of this self-called prophet.

He has created this god in the dungeon of his own mind, given it all of the various vicissitudes of his own character, then gives it a false doctrine which in application creates a convenient escape hatch to all those weaklings who are gullible enough to swallow his story and have neither brains nor willpower to solve their own differences and problems in a realistic manner.

It was in this way that Paul destroyed the mission and purpose of Jesus. There are others, too, who followed after; other teachers who created their own all-powerful effigy. The motivating power and purpose was to relieve the psychic pressures in their subconscious, which were born out of want and insecurity and their failure to adjust themselves to life.

Then, too, the strength of this false leadership is seldom the product of their own particular life; it has developed in the course of their evolution which involved past lives and somewhat similar characterizations; also other life associations born and relived, always tend to collect and add strength to this self-styled expressionist. And he is further aided and abetted by under-astral world entities, some who have lived there 'even unto the time of Moses', as was quoted by Jesus.

And so as of today, we find the world in a chaotic state of existence, one which could and will destroy mankind unless new constructive leadership is found and which can solve all these extremely complex problems. Such leadership would indeed be hard to find;

much less would men be prone to accept it, for it would be predicated upon the individual responsibility of each person to assume a constructive pattern of life, to accept his own moral responsibilities for every thought and action without the convenient escape hatch furnished by some fancied savior or intercessors; that each person would collectively express with all the masses of humanity a life of purpose and moral development, tailored by a long-range comprehensive plan of future evolution into higher planes of life where various expressionary forms of living were constantly expanding the mental horizons of these people.

A moment's thought reveals the tremendous change which would have to occur in the thoughts and habit patterns of mankind as he so lives. It would mean a complete abandonment of all previous reactionary elements motivated by the carnal and animalistic instincts which are still being expressed by humans. The lusts of hunger, sex, power, wealth, etc., are all inherent to mankind either as of yesterday, today or tomorrow as necessary adjutants in his struggle for survival upon a material planet which sponsored his very beginnings.

It would also mean destruction of his religious effigy; he could not further depend upon the moral opiate of religious salvation; he would have to destroy other ideologies and systems and to re-create in his own mind an entirely new concept of life based upon the great creative principle which Jesus called the 'Kingdom of Heaven within'.

Each man would also have to destroy the illusion of mass which compounds his material world and replace it with a functional science of interdimensional re-creation. These and many more elements of earthly life would have to go 'down the drain' before man could follow leadership which could lead him out of this present-day chaos.

Obviously, no person could make these tremendous changes, at least not in one lifetime. Nor would such a course of action be wise even if feasible or possible; neither would any Avatar capable of such leadership be unwise enough to attempt it. To any Advanced Personality who has so attained a higher way of life, there is always a wise jurisprudence which gives this individual a correct knowledge of the function of various dimensions and their attendant modes of expression which are characteristically lived in various planetary systems and their attendant forms of life.

This Advanced Personality knows that man, as an evolutionary creature, is expressing a direct creative continuity into his earth life and thus begins to build the Supreme Creative Effigy within the dimension of his own mind and his attendant life expression. This is the ultimate way in which this Infinite Creative Intelligence becomes a personalized expression of Infinity, again re-expressing the creative function in all things, for it is conceivable that any man can attain this growth and expression. Therefore, the Avatar would not be so unwise as to try to change all men. He knows that any change which occurs within any person must be born from his own individual desire. He knows also this desire for a change and a better life is the result of personal quickening or preconditioning which occurs in the life lived in between lives, or in earth-life realizations. Then and only then can any person be helped.

Even so, again a wise jurisprudence must be maintained; a delicate equilibrium must be established whereby this person can always progressively maintain his development. At times he must be helped; he must also have suitable demonstrations to help keep his desire alive.

But always must such help be given in such a manner and quantity that he does not learn to depend upon it. The past has held for him religious beliefs which taught dependency upon the self-styled purveyors of salvation. So a double problem must be overcome; absolution from the past, rebuilding a future from a host of unknown elements. And always must he be aware to be ever alert, to constantly analyze thought and action completely impersonally and objectively.

By now it is quite evident that collectively man cannot be saved; neither will he be destroyed on his planet earth, for this planet is indeed a creation of Infinite Intelligence, conceived as a place whereby man could start a progressive evolution. To destroy either or both man or planet would destroy the plan and purpose of at least this small segment of Infinite Expression. Yet small as it is compared to the vastness of Infinity and its infinite forms, even such small destruction is inconceivable. Beyond and behind this seeming chaos and destructive trends, this Infinite Creative Intelligence is at work. It is functioning in an immutable way far beyond the dimensions of human knowledge.

And in this function man will survive; this age will pass into another, and a great cycle will have been expressed in countless past ages, each with its systems, its religions, its creeds and dogmas. Yes, this too is the future, for as man lives his evolution so he comes and goes upon this and other planets, each time seeking an environment he can understand and in which he can live; and each time he adds to his knowledge of the Infinite.

And we who are wise in the ways of evolution, we who know of the plan and purpose can only add some

293

small part to your understanding—a part which is compatible to the way in which you interpret your present life; nor can we exceed the limited dimension of your earth life, for to do so would only add more confusion to that which is already rampant in the world about you. But do not despair, for even as the earth has so fostered its many ideologies and expressions, so there are countless other worlds, each with its own expressionary forms of life; and as a human, you possess the power of selection and discrimination which is above and beyond the circumstances of your environment. And if these worlds can be so conceived and are held fast within the vision of your inner eye, so will these worlds be achieved, each achievement a product of your dedication, your desire and your ability of conception.

CHAPTER XXXVIII

Man's Greatest Fear

Without question or doubt, the greatest single fear so far as the general races of humanity are concerned is the fear of death and taking a secondary place of importance, though not one of fear, is the concept of birth. How strange then it is that mankind lives in fear of death, anticipates with joy the events of birth, yet knows nothing of the basic facts which relate these two events so closely together. Only when we understand the scientific application of knowledge as it is applied in the factors of evolution called reincarnation, do we substantially increase the knowledge and ascertain for ourselves the direct relationship between these two important events.

Almost needless to point out that when such knowledge is available to every human, and humanity as a whole has inseminated this knowledge, man will be by contrast, just as much in joyous anticipation of the event of death as he is presently in the event of birth. For they are, in fact, the doorway in and out of the spiritual worlds. While some knowledge and evaluations have already been given in the numerous liturgies of Unarius, we shall, however, at this time attempt to more fully portray the scientific concept and circumstances which enter into both death and birth. It will also serve and facilitate your understanding in the whole problem of progressive evolution and show why it is that people are born into the world in their present state of circumstance.

Let us take, for example, one of the ordinary citizens of our time. We will call him John Q. Citizen, or just plain John; he has just passed into that nether-land or spirit world through the doorway of death. Now John as an average citizen had no particular or dominating characteristics; he drove an average car, had the average number of children, was married to an average woman and had the usual church affiliations. He voted and paid his taxes and held down a steady job. All of these various material factors were, of course, the necessity and the supporting edifice of his material drive or life. Now John, like everyone, has a psychic anatomy, so when he found himself separated from the physical body he was quite concerned about the event; perhaps not so much at first, but he became more involved in the situation after a little while. Consciousness of the surface of his conscious mind was absent, and as his psychic anatomy did have a very strong subconscious portion, his mental part of his psychic anatomy began oscillating back and forth with the subconscious; and in a sense, the mental psychic anatomy lived through the different wave-form picturizations which were presently in oscillation. The condition was a form of consciousness, and so far as the psychic anatomy was concerned was something which was very much like a rather vivid dream—one which you may yourself have had at one time or another. However, the solid substantial reality of his former earth life was gone. He did not have the full reactive physical connotation of different factors involved in this nightmare, dream-like state of consciousness.

Also as he did not possess any knowledge of the spiritual worlds, he was therefore quite unconscious of the great Infinite Cosmogony around him, just as he was in his earth life, so none of the more highly Advanced Intellects could come to him and help him because he refused to acknowledge them; he could not be conscious of them, etc. Therefore, in this dream state of consciousness, he relived through his subconscious into the mental part of the psychic anatomy, the different transpositions and events that took place in his material life. As he progressed further in time in this spiritual state of consciousness—this nebulous hinterland—he became more and more involved in the problem of trying to reinstate himself back into the material world.

If you have thoroughly studied the second lesson course and the lesson on the psychic anatomy, you will more fully understand the problem which John had. It was also complicated by the fact that he did not have a conscious mind, therefore, the present reality, or as I have said, the dominant solidity of his former existence was missing. Therefore such efforts or functions which he made had to be carried on strictly on the basis of frequency relationships; in this respect he was or was not attuned to different energy transpositions which were taking place about him. That is why he could not maintain consciousness with the Infinite Cosmogony, and it is also the reason why, when some time later, certain different wave forms of energy began streaming into his psychic anatomy, these wave forms of energy, he recognized, or in other words, he oscillated with them. They were the wave forms of energy given off by two people who were very much in love, and as it so happened, they were his grandchildren. These two young people had been married and were about to put in their order for a baby.

Now, these love vibrations came to John very strongly; he, too, had a sexual drive and had lived in a world filled with sexual impulses. So it was quite natural, then, that John should go like a homing pigeon to the scene wherein the future mother-to-be was being impregnated. We must still bear in mind that John had little or no knowledge of what was going on, he was merely attracted to the scene because it was the only thing he understood, and so he 'tuned into' it. At the moment when the spermatozoon, or germ cell of the father entered into the ovum or female germ cell, there was automatically set in motion through the chromosomes and genes a very complex oscillating condition. It involved the psychic anatomies of both parents, for it is so, that through the electromagnetic fields in the atomic constituents of the atoms, sort of a telepathic condition exists continuously between these two parents, and the ovum and the spermatozoon are in the act of beginning to pair off and of starting fission or the generation of a number of physical cells and which will, in time, constitute the entire physical anatomy of the fetus or the child-to-be. Therefore it was that John became very thoroughly involved in the oscillations which were going on through these genes on the basis of compatible frequency relationships.

Now his subconscious here was of little or no value whatsoever; his relationship to this process was carried on more from the mental portion of his psychic anatomy. Also, as he had not developed a Superconscious Self, or facsimile of the Infinite, this cell of Superconscious was a dormant factor and remained passive more or less to a certain extent throughout the whole procedure. As time progressed, and the cells began to multiply and the first rudimentary form of the infant began to develop, John became more and more intermeshed or intertwined with the process going on. The parent psychic anatomies were still in full force; they were still objectifying the different continuities of physical form which they, themselves, were so currently expressing. There were also other connotations of wave forms which went on, back through the different lifetimes of these two parents. John also was, to some extent in this oscillating process, exerting some influence in his own way and manner, although it was in his particular case, rather dormant.

He was not as strong a personality, in a sense, as were the two parents' psychic anatomies. That would simply mean he would be born into the world in a physical body which looked very much like either one or both of the parents, and he would not exert a very strong or dominating influence one way or the other. Also, John would not remember his former life; that is, he would not remember it as you would remember the incidents which happened in your life from yesterday. That is because the different consonant frequencies in his subconscious psychic anatomy were 'out of phase' with the present forming psychic anatomy of the infant, for as the psychic anatomy formed, it was also related to the exact and proportionate development of the physical anatomy.

This psychic anatomy development was, as I have just explained, the combination of the three different psychic anatomies involved. The subconscious, however, had not developed; for if you remember in your lesson course, the subconscious is that portion of the psychic anatomy which reflects, or oscillates, or reacts directly with the surface of the conscious mind. Now, as the fetus or infant had but only a very small beginning of his conscious mind or brain beginning to grow, he did not have any oscillating surface to speak of. Moreover, the brain in itself is a two-way conductor. That is, the five senses of the infant, such as sight, sound, touch, etc., had not begun to function. He had only barely begun to feel, in a sense of the word, and so the whole situation was still a telepathic communication and a regeneration in different wave forms which were constantly building the framework of his psychic anatomy. And as this building process went on, John was very busy interweaving himself, so to speak, with the different intricacies of the wave-form patterns which were going into his psychic anatomy. That would mean, of course, that when the infant was born he would carry over all of the different intents and purposes, all of the development, and all of the psychic shocks which he had impounded in his psychic anatomy from previous lifetimes. If you remember, these are wave-form impregnations and vortexal patterns which have been developed and polarized in the mental part of the psychic anatomy. It is this part of the psychic anatomy which remains insoluble throughout time, and can be carried over a period of many thousands of years before there are any basic changes taking place in it. It is a rather slow process of development as it is concerned with the average citizen such as John.

Soon, however, John was to be born into the world. Up until this time he really had not had very much to say about the whole thing; in fact, he had not even properly determined his sex, and so he could very easily have been born into the world as a female. However, this was of very small concern to John because he had been born a female in a number of past lifetimes, just as he had lived a number of other lifetimes as a male. In that way he had, in his evolution developed the whole consensus of evolution in the male and female polarities. He could properly live in the present because all of the factors of these different evaluations and relationships with the different perspectus were oscillating in the various vortexes of his psychic anatomy, and he could relate them through the subconscious in a normal fashion and integrate his surface life accordingly.

And so it was of rather small significance whether John would be born male or female. The point which is most important to remember is that he was carrying all of his former lifetime impregnations in that mental part of his psychic anatomy, and so far as his subconscious was concerned, it was, to some extent, out-of-phase or out-of-tune with the present, and it could therefore only exist, or partially exist, in some respects, as an influential factor. Now, after John was born as a new infant, the process of breathing oxygen was immediately resumed; this is one of the factors which he had lived through in being born many other times, and so it was quite natural that his mental psychic anatomy could, at the proper moment—and instigated by such reactive factors as were then presently dominating him—oscillate with these factors and complete the whole mental and physical reaction which started the breathing process.

This was quite true with all other different functions, voluntary, or involuntary throughout his entire physical and mental anatomies. Now his mental anatomy or brain was still comparatively underdeveloped. The brain cells were, however, fully impowered to do their respective jobs. In the different cortexal layers, there were certain brain cells which would conduct wave forms in one direction, but they would not conduct them in the reverse fashion. When these different layers of brain cells were so interjected and reconnected through the oscillating process with the subconscious and mental conscious, John could therefore, go through all of the complex reactionary and reflex automations and the voluntary reactions which are normally associated with life. This was his first new process of reorientation into his new environment, and at the moment of birth the subconscious began to rapidly develop so that during the next five years, he would very actively form some of the more basic patterns of his relationship to the world which would last him throughout this present physical life.

This fact is known to present-day psychology and it is in this analysis that certain elements of psychosomatic medicine are entered into; however, the psychologist always stops short of the threshold of birth. He is not clairvoyantly developed and therefore does not look back into the different past lifetimes which are, in all cases with all humans, much more dominant than are the present lifetime forms.

Now, for contrast, let us take a person whom we shall call Mary. Mary is a more highly developed person than is John; that is, she is a person who has gone through many more lifetimes than has John; she has passed more time in the spiritual worlds, and she has approached that often mentioned threshold of perception wherein she has begun to recognize the vast infinite and the numerous mansions or dimensions of which it is so constructed.

In this precognition and preconditioned state, let us trace the course of Mary through practically the same period as we did with John. When Mary lost her physical body and found herself in the spiritual worlds, the conditions were quite different in many respects; she did not have that very highly-developed portion of the subconscious psychic anatomy as did John. She had, in her former associations, begun to lose that portion of the psychic anatomy called the subconscious because she had begun to attach less and less importance to the different factors of her material world; she had begun substituting and rebuilding her psychic anatomy from the different factors and other knowledge which she had gleaned in her spiritual lives.

And so when Mary found herself in the spiritual world and devoid of the flesh, she could look about her through the shell of this astral body which we have called the subconscious, and she could see something of the Infinite Cosmogony going on about her. She could see her friends and her relatives who had advanced and gone beyond the point that John had gone. She could see also other Advanced Intelligences or Beings who were coming to her aid and assistance, and who would help her in whatever endeavor she so wished to further plan for herself in future evolutions and reincarnations into the earth plane. And so Mary would spend some time among these spiritual people; she would study her own Akashic record, which is, in all essence and effect through certain devices, known to the scientists in the spiritual worlds. She would be able, in a mirror-like fashion, to actually look into her psychic anatomy and see the different malformations or the different vortexes which were necessary for her to cancel out when she returned to the earth.

And so she would again be born into the world in much the same manner and form as was John, with some exceptions here again, of course. In that process which began with the impregnation, she would exert much more effect on the rebuilding of the psychic anatomy than John could possibly have hoped to achieve. She would be able to do this somewhat voluntarily or consciously to the degree that when she was born into the world, she would quite naturally be different from her parents in certain basic respects. She would be an advanced personality or an old soul which would be discernible to even a common ordinary layman. She would be different in many ways; she would have talents or developments, or expressions which were beyond the normal range of human expression. She would also be able to exert much more influence with her own particular personality on her fellow man than would John.

And so the pattern goes. We can personally find some of these people going about in their different daily tasks, and yet we know them to be people who have gone beyond the ordinary boundaries which hold the average earth man.

They are people who have approached that mysterious threshold of life which separates them from the great unknown or the Infinite; and in this approaching process, they are, in actual reality, entering into their own personal millennium—that phase of development which may take thousands of years, or it may take millions. The time is not important. That which is important is this: that each person should most ultimately achieve some destiny in these higher worlds of expression, that this person should suitably develop mentally to the point where he or she—and here again sex is entirely absent in the higher worlds—can become a constructive oscillating polarity with the Infinite Consciousness. It is in this way that the Infinite Consciousness achieves Its most ultimate development. For in the highly-developed spiritual personality, Infinite Consciousness, which has formerly been called God or gods by some of the heathen aspects of earth-world dispensations, has, in essence, re-created the exact functioning facsimile of It.

Thus the pattern continues. We can analyze and introspect these different factors in our daily life. Introspection is of the utmost importance and it is equally important that we learn to analyze and to introspect objectively without being influenced by those subversive elements which are constantly oscillating in our subconscious selves. For the subconscious is our old self. It is the thing which we must ultimately destroy. We must replace it with a body which will enable us to live in the higher spiritual worlds. But as for now it is your astral body; it is the body which will, to some extent, either impede you or aid you when you make your transition into the spiritual worlds. It will aid you if you have refined it to the point where it becomes some sort of a window which will enable you to peer through the maze of material dispensations and see the Infinite, to see those who are stretching out their hands to help you.

Man's Greatest Fear

Part Two

Now that we have objectively analyzed two people who were in very apparent differences in their spiritual evolution, certain of these differences are immediately apparent. In the case of John, he would return to the earth and more or less lead the same vegetative life that he formerly lived in previous lifetimes. He would not, during that lifetime, express any particular psychic equivalents except perhaps an occasional hunch or premonition. The situation with Mary, however, would be quite different. Her life would be primarily guided and motivated in a spiritual way, and through what I have described quite frequently as the influence of the Superconscious Self.

This leads us up to the most important point in this discussion—the development of this Superconscious Self. As has been postulated numerous times, the polarization process is all-important in the development of the Superconscious just as it is with any other aspect of life. In the case of John, he was able to make certain psychic affiliations, I shall say, with the newly-forming fetus within the womb of its mother on the basis of very strong affiliations which could be termed polarizations. That is, the different relatives or other people with whom he was closely associated in previous lifetimes would be the dominant vibrations or wave forms which would guide him into the situation whereby he could be reborn into the world.

On the other hand, Mary was not so strongly motivated. She was able in a more advanced state of spiritual consciousness to more or less prepare herself, in a way, to her advent into the new world whereby she would be able to accomplish one or more very direct purposes, principally, the cancellation of different psychic shocks which she had incurred in other lifetimes, as well as to work out strong polarity affiliations which had been developed over a long period of time with different earth-life personalities and earth-life forms. Therefore, in her spiritual world, after being disembodied from the flesh she would have a certain degree of intelligence something akin to her earth-life consciousness, which was not possessed by John when he found himself in the spiritual world. The reason for the differences in these two conditions is found in the Superconscious Self for it is the Superconscious Self which lives in the spiritual worlds and is an oscillating entity with the spiritual worlds. Therefore, any person who has a more strongly-developed Superconscious Self will correspondingly live more and more in the spiritual worlds, and especially in times of transition when they find themselves minus the physical body.

The development of the Superconscious as it concerns all people in the more elemental stages of evolution is a happenstance situation; that is, they are not consciously motivated to direct any kind of polarizations with the Infinite to form this nucleus or life cell. The situation of polarization is based entirely upon the linkages in harmonic interplays which occur when any material earth person has such moments of temporary transcendency or inspiration, or when he can consciously turn his attention to the creative forces around him, or where he apparently resolves these mysterious forces and interplays of nature into deistic configurations. In this sense then, his religion does serve a useful purpose in the first formative stages of his evolution.

307

The point to remember always is that in religions, as in the case with all other things, it passes a point of diminished returns, I shall say, wherein it becomes merely a strongly associated symbology, and as such, it can actually retard the progress and evolution of any human who constantly seeks to reinstate it in his consciousness beyond the dominion of his useful purpose. Now the moment any person does, in the spiritual world, begin to ascertain or determine to visualize or in some way to become conscious of the spiritual worlds, there is an immediate increase, a rapid rise in the proportions of inception which takes place within the Superconscious Self. And in this inception, in its combination with the mental portion of the psychic anatomy, the Superconscious then, will in its respective inceptions and introspections, be so polarized in these inceptions in an individual way. That is, by the combination of such elements as are interposed as time, etc., from the physical worlds, these polarizations remain the inviolate property of the person to whom they so occurred or to who was responsible for their propagation. This is the beginning of the more ultimate destiny of personality as it is achieved in that abstract evaluation of an oscillating entity of a highly-developed person who has passed into the higher reaches of the spiritual worlds.

As Mary had begun to function in a more normal or mental manner in the spiritual worlds in her lives in between lives, she was therefore able to introspectively plan an earth life and to make it sort of a campaign. Now when she was born into the world, she would or she would not necessarily remember the spiritual worlds, for here again frequency would determine whether memory consciousness would be so superimposed into the conscious surface of the brain cells.

Actually, no person can remember the spiritual worlds except perhaps in a moment of transcendency wherein they can temporarily relink this former passage or again reform himself in a spiritual rapport with the present.

So all in all, these different factors are incorporated in that part of the psychic anatomy known as the Superconscious which, as it does, living in the higher Spiritual dimensions and oscillating with the Spiritual worlds, can proportionately exert influence in a very influential way into the life of a person like Mary. She will thusly be guided or motivated in a manner which may be quite strange or even miraculous to those who are not acquainted with such things. She will, from time to time, have certain psychisms which can be classified as flashbacks into her past, wherein, in the most propitious moments which are linked with cyclic movements in her psychic anatomy, the pernicious and negative influence of these past psychic shocks or events can be suitably discharged. They will, of course, remain as image reflections or polarized elements in the Superconscious as well as in the mental conscious portions of the psychic anatomy. However, from that time they will not have their influential effect or their subversion in the life of the individual.

And so with Mary, while she could more constructively plan an earth-life incarnation, she could, in fact, to some extent actually choose her parents on the basis that such planes or elements in the earth-life dispensations of these two parents would be of some advantage to her, such as has been pointed out in the case of Mozart, the musician and composer, who reincarnated deliberately into a musical atmosphere to further his reincarnation. This is quite typical of some of the patterns followed by people who plan these particular campaigns to work out different karmic conditions which they have incurred in the past, and to further such progress which they have made in teaching centers such as are pictured in the works of Unarius.

Now we have obtained something of a constructive picturization in the development of the Superconscious, and how this continuous development enables a person to progressively reinstate himself into a higher and higher dominion of spiritual life; how it does, in a sense, intercede into numerous earth-life dispensations to the extent that we can say we have personal intercession. We have guidance and motivation which is beyond the normal range of human understanding, and we have a correspondingly greater degree of perfection in our daily lives. If we can look further into the future to a person who has so developed, we can more ultimately envision such a person as having mental capacities which are quite beyond anything which could be properly understood by the human race. This was exemplified by the Nazarene almost two thousand years ago.

Conversely, such a development can also take place with the subconscious and this in itself is the basic understanding for the development of the lower astral regions, which are described by Dante in his immortal poetry called "The Inferno". Actually, such places are in a pure sense or a material sense nonexistent. They exist as oscillating entities of consciousness within the confines of the subconscious or the astral self. If a person like John, for instance, had developed the material life to that degree where it became the dominant and the subversive elements in his existence so that when he went into the spiritual worlds, these same subversive materialistic elements would have been reinforced by certain additives which were possible under certain conditions, we can then envision John as being progressively inclined downward into an ever-increasingly larger dimension of negative interpolations of consciousness. These are the true pits of hell, for in the conscious realizations which form between the mental consciousness of the psychic anatomy and the subconscious, and providing that the subconscious had developed to that enormous proportion, that it is the dominating factor in that relative oscillating process, then we can quite easily see that all of the hellish nightmares pictured in such prose as was given by Dante, or preached by the religionist can be a factual reality to such a person who has so counter-developed his evolution.

At this point we must again resort back to one of the basic elements of our introspection with the Infinite—that the Infinite does present the possibility of all things which can be conceived by human configurations and transpositions and environmental factors. The proposition of selectivity then becomes increasingly apparent and more demanding as the burden of our own material world or its impregnations of karma become more apparent to us; the demand increases that we must select something either environmental or spiritual in nature, or any other relevant factors which can begin to discharge these different negative karmic intents which are oscillating into our conscious. The proposition of selectivity, therefore, is of paramount importance. It is the keystone in the arch of progression or retrogression. Any person here or hereafter is immediately confronted with this same proposition of selectivity.

In a sense then, because God is the Infinite Intelligence, God is not emotionally inclined toward any person. God is therefore assumed correctly to be all-forgiving; that is, God can and will reinstate us in a healthy evolution, in a sense of the word, provided we have enough intelligence to realize where we are on the scale of evolution, providing we have enough will and determination to about-face and start a progressive climb back in the right direction. In this sense, God as the Infinite makes no demands from us. It is inviolate in Its supreme and most ultimate introspection. It is also the substance of all things. It cannot be destroyed even though we personally may attempt to destroy our own facsimile of the Infinite.

So it is thus: even if a person does in his mental capacity and in his astral developments literally and figuratively descend to the pits of hell, he can at any time, if he so realizes, if he so makes the necessary determinants, if he exercises the will and determination, he can begin his climb back out of these illusionary materialistic configurations which have created his hell, and he can again reinstate himself in a healthy and progressive evolution.

Likewise anyone who has ascended the scale of an evolution to some of the more advanced points in these Higher Spiritual Worlds, conversely, can descend. The moment that he becomes lax in his equilibriums, in his evaluations and, in his personal introspections, his oscillations with, or his constructiveness with the Infinite, when he begins to personalize these, when he begins to lose the entire abstraction of Infinity which enabled him to so progress, if in the slightest degree he becomes more personally rhetorical in his spiritual life, then he will begin his plunge downward. And there are fallen angels, just as there are reincarnated devils who now live great and wonderful spiritual lives.

Here again is one of the more abstract evaluations of spiritual consciousness and apparently even more infinite than is Infinity itself, for the numbers, the degrees and the differences, the personalities involved would be so vast and so infinite as to defy a constructive analysis, except that we constantly resort to basic principles of evolution; we classify and reclassify, we diagnose and we analyze. The motivation of life must be thoroughly and completely understood, otherwise we are waylaid by the material apparition, the necessity of our own personality, the demand of our ego. These factors are all apparent; they are ever ready to destroy us. If they are not properly compensated for, if they are not equalized, and if they are not so introspected as elements in evolution, then they become things which are personally attached to us in a way in which we do not recognize them; we cannot become objective to them.

And so the lesson of John is quite apparent. It is again the portrayal in two personalities wherein certain determinants are made most apparent, the determinant of evolution as it is posed in the constructive scheme of evolution; how it is that man can and does ascend in such a series of progressive evolutions from out of the more primitive elements of the earth worlds. He can, in a sense, be said to have started his evolution in the formation of a simple hydrogen atom, for, in turn, this atom becomes helium; and so these cycles are constantly and everlastingly perpetuated in our consciousness if we so wish to seek them out, if we so wish to analyze them and gain from them the constructive message of creation.

How different then is this life from the life of John, the rhetorical material life that is lived within the conformities of his community or his nation. He lives primarily in a constant and never-ending succession of fears. It is fear that his neighbor devaluates; it is fear that he will lose his job; it is fear of death; it is fear of various other interpolations of his physical life for which he has no apparent compensations. He has no equilibriums to establish against these overwhelming vicissitudes of material life. Small wonder indeed it is that people become increasingly mentally disturbed as their civilization advances, as the complexities of the material life increase beyond the normal proportions of such evolutionary development which people have incurred in their past lifetimes.

Yes, and all people today are suffering from the same derelictions, the consequences of an over developed scientific technocracy which has not equalized the proportionate development in metaphysical fields, in religious fields, and in other factors which would relate man more scientifically to the interdimensional creation.

If such development had taken place, then indeed at this time man would not be fearful of the consequences of atomic disintegration or nuclear warfare. He would not be concerned with other consequences which are so stringently emphasized in our daily lives. Yet a more constructive analysis must be entered into; we must realize that in evolution there must be a correspondingly large number of planes of development. The earth is such a one of these planes, elemental to be sure but quite necessary in the scale of infinite evolution. For here the earth man begins the first stages of development which will determine his spiritual evolution, his emancipation into the spiritual worlds where he increases his mental perspectives; he increases his abilities, and he lays aside all of the old earth fears. Yet even again in the Spiritual Worlds new factors, new dimensions, new horizons open up—things which might be considered improbables or absolute fantasies

so far as the material man is concerned, but are existent nevertheless.

These concepts, in turn, will be most properly dealt
with in such suitable circumstances, and should the
purposes be vindicated for the exploration of life in
these Higher Spiritual Planes. The purpose of life, however, is best served to the material man as a proposition of his own personal development in his immediate
environment. It would not be wise to superimpose
other objectives which are beyond the dimension of his
understanding. Even so, what we are presenting is
indeed a herculean task for any human to assimilate
even partially in one life. The Unariun concept is, in
itself, the most absolute of all concepts because it
encompasses Infinity in all proportions and all dimensions. It is for the moment sectionalized and divided
into material perspectives which evaluate material life
in contrasts to spiritual environment. It makes the
demands, the prerogatives of personal will, determination and other efforts for the average individual to
supersede or to go beyond the dimension of this physical environment.

While you may start your studies into the Unariun
Concept, you will indeed never finish them should you
so dedicate yourself into their pursuance into the Spiritual Worlds, for indeed, the Unariun Concept is the
presentation of Infinity. And so whether you remain as
John, whether you become John, or whether you develop as Mary did, or beyond the time of Mary even
into the spiritual worlds where you become one of
those luminous Orbs which have been in certain circumstances described by certain earth individuals, the
problem here is always one of self-determination, self-
will. This is of the utmost importance. For while Infinity, in itself, presents a most staggering proposition,

one which could not possibly be encompassed by any human, yet a constructive start must be made. The more immediately it is made, the less there is in the way of consequences, for each moment you live the material life you are adding to the consequences of the material life. You are adding to the net and total of your karmic burden. You are, in effect, reinforcing all of these past lifetime subversive elements. They must all be worked out, torn down, discarded; they must be replaced by other constructive elements which will enable you to live in the higher worlds of consciousness.

We, the Unariuns, do wish you success in this undertaking and we further pledge ourselves to aid and abet you in every constructive effort which you make and in ways and manners of which we best know. Until such time as we meet in the spiritual planes, we will ever be with you. We will always be faithful to your cause and purpose, but only proportionately as you devote yourself in your personal dedication and your self-determination.

CHAPTER XXXIX

Hope Springs Eternal

(The following teaching was given in a reply-letter to a student requesting healing for another.)

Dear Unariun: As of your communication received December 20th, I note that you have enclosed a clipping of a four-year old boy dying of leukemia, and your remarks of deep concern regarding this and other examples of what seems to be a terrible and sad state of affairs, also the lack of knowledge and ability for medical science to relieve these incurable illnesses and a direct plea to myself to do something about these paradoxes.

Now, my dear friend, your concern is quite humanitarian; it is well that we are so concerned with our fellow man, but should be in a more compassionate and understanding way. Here at the Center, we are daily confronted with newspaper accounts, personal pleas, etc., from various people to relieve their conditions. However, in a true compassionate understanding, we must be concerned with many factors which are involved with each case and which are not apparent to those concerned with them.

Let us review these various factors which will enable us to, more properly, understand these inexplicable dilemmas and paradoxes which seemingly refuse to yield to what the average person thinks is a reasonable equation.

The first factor involved is reincarnation; lack of knowledge on this subject gives the earth man his greatest fear of death. However, this is rightly so, in his present position in the scale of evolution. He is still comparatively speaking, an animal-like creature which is just beginning to become spiritually minded of the great Creative Infinite Intelligence and which is called God or gods by various religious factions.

This Infinite Creative Intelligence is Infinite and Creative only by being finite in an infinite number of forms of consciousness and in constantly re-creating these forms, sustains and regenerates Infinity. A planet, such as the earth, becomes a third-dimensional place where this abstract consciousness assumes countless millions of forms of expression in some external configuration which we see as the plant and animal life of the earth. This re-creative and regenerative process is so sustained by certain principles: one of these was called by Darwin, "survival of the fittest", which means simply that inferior plants or animals will not survive to breed their inferiority into a succeeding generation.

This is most necessary, not only to strengthen any or all such species, but to ultimately resolve these species into new and different forms (which is done on the inner plane). If the inferior misfit did breed his inferiority, a retrogressive cycle would be started which would destroy the form and purpose of the species and eventually render the planet earth sterile.

Human beings still live and function under this principle despite attempts, scientifically and otherwise, to circumvent this action. This meddling with the principles of function of the Infinite has caused grave conditions to come about in this world of today. For instance, the population explosion in India and in other countries is the result of science using various insecticides and sanitation methods which have upset the balance between birth and death in these countries.

Now, this may sound heartless and cruel, but this is not so. People who die before their natural time, and under diseased, accidental, or other similar conditions, are almost always trying to work out certain psychic conditions from which they previously suffered or died in a former lifetime. With such strong psychic impingements, such a person inevitably attracts himself to a similar condition in the present life, subconsciously hoping to conquer it. This is done repetitiously from life to life, until such a person learns how to live through it.

Here again the Infinite Intelligence is, in this human expression, re-creating itself in an infinite number of experiences. Thus, after many lifetimes and living an infinite number of these experiences such a human can be presumed to be infinitely wise and god-like. Under the principles which the earth man lives, the carnal law of survival of the fittest also gives the earth man a great sense of importance to his present physical life. This is most necessary for any individual to live from birth to death without becoming a victim of the innumerable forms of death which await him every moment of his life. So each person has thus, through this evolutionary process of life to life, become predominantly minded of the importance of his earth life, i.e., that it is all, etc. This is not so, however.

As of this time and day, no earth man properly understands that he is actually a spiritual creature and lives his earth life from the spiritual or fourth dimension. His body and the earth itself, with its many forms of consciousness, are only apparent and relative to him because he has developed an association with them, through countless experiences in numerous lifetimes. He does not know that, should this earth-life consciousness cease to be a reality in his physical body, that he will go right on living it in his mental body or psychic anatomy until some such moment comes when he can again, in a sense, re-create his physical body by attaching himself to the germ cells of a newly conceived fetus. Thus, he will again come into the world and psychically relive all his former lifetimes. The baby with the leukemia no doubt died in infancy in a previous lifetime from some violent condition. He is now attempting to relive through that former moment of death which is so strongly impinged in his psychic consciousness. If he did not do so, this previous death could become a dominating malformation in his psychic anatomy and eventually destroy him.

To miraculously heal this child of his condition would be cheating him of the experience he will gain in this lifetime and under somewhat different conditions. Through succeeding lifetimes and similar experiences, he will gradually amass enough know-how to enable him to live through the former psychic shock of abortive death and thus he will become that much wiser and stronger.

So you see dear friend, we are not primarily concerned with healing people, even though great miracles happen when people join Unarius. Our primary purpose is to teach people all the unknown factors of life which will tremendously aid them in overcoming their conditions, saving them many lifetimes and countless hours of torture and suffering which they would have to go through under ordinary conditions.

If the child in question was miraculously healed (of leukemia), he would not possess the knowledge which he would otherwise attain which would enable him to prevent such similar happenings in succeeding lifetimes or should they accidentally occur, he could quickly rectify the condition with the proper knowledge which he had so attained.

So far as we are concerned, the earth must largely remain what it is; people will live and die under an infinite number of conditions as a part of their educational curriculum and wisdom which they attain when they master these experiences. We would only be defeating the purpose and intent of the Infinite Creator if we miraculously healed anyone from any condition without imparting to him all the necessary knowledge which he must have to master succeeding experiences.

In reference to an example of healing mentioned in the lessons, it should be noted that even if a disease is correctly diagnosed according to "classified" symptoms, the condition under which the disease was incurred in some previous life is always different. Likewise present conditions surrounding the ill person have a direct bearing on what would constitute a correct healing procedure; the case described in the lesson (#5), where the infant was healed of encephalitis, the mother and grandmother were evolved, and provided strong, active polarities for the projection of the power. Moreover, all conditions were previously set up in the Spiritual World; it remained only to start the force in motion at the proper time.

May I suggest to you, a more thorough study of the lessons, especially the second, or advanced course, which will explain more extensively the scientific principles involved. There is, as of today, a singular lack of knowledge on the subject of healing, whether it is a simple reaction produced by an aspirin tablet or a "miracle". This is so despite some scientific knowledge of atoms, electronics, etc. The advanced lesson course will give you a preface of the active principles involved. In the near future, Unarius will, if sufficient interest is shown, present to the world, very accurate diagnostic techniques and procedures which will enable the new-age doctor to start healing therapies in all the so-called incurable diseases.

A spiritual healing, or miracle, is not a simple finger-pointing, "Be thou healed" situation like those described in the New Testament. The Bible was written by men ignorant of all the factors involved, in each case. They were also mindful of creating a religious atmosphere which would attract and hold multitudes of people all bent on an easy escape from disease and death.

The Bible does not tell of the many who turned away and were not helped, despite their strong pleas. The Bible does not describe the great amount of preparation and preconditioning that took place, sometimes hundreds of years in advance and in such times as the life in between earth lives; living repetitious earth-life conditions until the person in question could attain a transformation in his psychic anatomy.

It is nice to think that there is some great Master ready to heal us of any and all disease and sin; religions of the world survive on this preface and have thus created an escape mechanism in all people who follow this false teaching.

No Master who is a real Master would heal a person of any condition until that person has attained the necessary knowledge and conviction that he can be healed; this does in a sense heal him in that timeless, spaceless fourth dimension called the Spirit World. It then only remains for this person to re-enter the earth world and after his psychic anatomy has re-created his former condition, he will start to seek out some catalytic agent which will start that certain lightning chain-like reaction in his psychic anatomy which cancels out the condition. Yes, sometimes the action is so strong the catalyst (healer) can polarize enough additional energy to help change physical cell structures which makes this person "whole" again.

At present the world is inhabited by millions of sick people; their conditions are named and nameless, but as a whole most of these cannot be helped or cured because they have not yet attained sufficient preparation and conditioning to make their healing possible. And so doctors will go right on cutting out their cancers and diseased organs, and these poor souls will come right back again with the same thing, or worse. This will continue until they realize such crude and barbaric practices will not permanently heal, that they must find the answer and the cure from the "inside" and from the Creative Intelligence which can give them the necessary know-how and power to get the job done.

This is all part of that finding the "Kingdom Within", and becoming acquainted with the "Father" which dwelleth within, and which is that great Creative Intelligence which has created the Kingdom and all subsidiaries, atomical forms, the macrocosm and microcosm.

And when there is a sufficient knowledge obtained and put into use, then this person changes; his disease disappears; more than that, he begins his climb from out the pits of clay of his barbaric earth world and begins to live in a new Spiritual World. Yes, he has found his Kingdom and has an eternal lease on occupying it. As stated before, the Creative Intelligence is Infinite, the sum and total of all things. To be Infinite, this Creative Intelligence must re-create through all forms and in all dimensions; man is the one form in which this Creative Intelligence lives as a personal entity of consciousness.

The development of a man is predicated upon evolution, or reincarnation, through countless thousands of lives and innumerable experiences. Such a man can be presumed to be infinitely wise by having gone through his early experiences, including death, and mastering them; this brings him through his early stages of development which are his many earth lives.

Understanding this very important concept clearly indicates the value of experience and nothing can supplant the value of actual experience. No person can master a sinful life, or resist sin, until he has had the conscious knowledge of this sin and can, not only recognize it when it appears, but has practical knowledge of how to conquer it.

Any person suffering from any disease or condition, mental or physical, is in the grip of sin, for in this broad frame of reference, such conditions are contrary to what might be assumed a healthy, happy life. Therefore, such an ill person is in the formative stage of learning; to take away his condition leaves him without cause or purpose; worse, he will, in the future, depend upon similar healing to be done for him in the event he "comes a cropper" so to speak. Thus, he gradually becomes atrophied, he loses his desire to strive for a better life, and finally he will lose any and all semblance to what can be called a human being.

The astral underworlds are full of these forms. Dante tried to describe these poor souls living in their dissolute and atrophied conditions. So they will remain until the substance energy of these malformed psychic anatomies are reabsorbed back into some great dimension of universal supply.

Do not be too concerned about the physical life; what you are today, and the world about you is really only a mirage. It is all part of that consciousness you have developed in your evolution. When you develop a higher form of consciousness, this world and what you now are, physically, will pass from you and you will live in a new world in your higher consciousness in a more spiritually developed body, so with the child. To teach every human who is, or who has lived on this planet earth should be the proper course of evolution followed and the subsequent mastery of the earth world.

E. L. Norman, Unarius Moderator.

The foregoing letter was composed in an attempt to explain to all and sundry individuals concerned, what might be called an extremely broad and abstract scientific understanding of life, realizing however, the foibles of human understanding of human frailties and the predisposition of everyone to subconsciously select or re-conform such known or unknown factors so postulated according to the dictum of his own understanding.

It is therefore conceivable that the author of this letter could be seriously maligned in thought, at least by any person so reading it; defense for the author is however, not needed. Present and future science does and will corroborate these presentations. It remains, therefore, for the reader to rationally integrate these concepts into a formative approach to an infinite understanding of life—a case, in a sense, where "Mohammed goes to the mountain".

Truth is infinite and remains absolute to all people, yet is understood in the progressive evolution in an infinite number of ways by each person—a formative process which builds and rebuilds the psychic anatomy thus enabling a person to progressively evolve.

In understanding the broadest and most abstract tenets of life, the author therefore does not view the physical life as does mankind in general. Neither does he stress its importance in the physical sense that is held by the average individual.

Also, in a scientific understanding, a personal ego is not held or evaluated in the manner of most humans. A person, in pure science can be seen to be, not a strong personality or ego, but as a conglomerate collection of energy wave forms, derived from past experiences, oscillating endlessly in a timeless dimension and remanifesting themselves in a third dimension as physical remanifestations and counterparts of these past experiences and, under the law of frequency relationship, oscillate or become active with subsequent contacts with various earth-life dispensations with which they come in contact.

Understanding this concept will do much to correct any imbalances which may occur to an individual who becomes emotionally involved in various earth-life happenings. The importance of the physical life recedes from the emotional plane to a more proper position, wherein an individual can rationalize and find suitable and true answers to what would otherwise remain an emotional enigma.

The position of the author can be somewhat allegorically summarized in viewing a motion picture or television screen depicting some story or happening. The person so viewing attains a psychic rapport with what is being pictured and is transcended into the actual happenings. This is done on the net reactive content of the subconscious as it presents similar basic happenings to the present depiction; and through frequency relationship, transcendency and emotional participation occurs.

The person so involved is not analytically summarizing this depiction as a series of light and dark patches traced across a fluorescent screen by an electronic gun or some similar apparatus. The whole process is purely autosuggestive and relives in the viewer by that attunement process with past experience facsimiles. This is the way in which the author views the earth life of mankind. He sees people not as physical flesh and bone creatures, but as amalgamated formations known as atoms harmonically attracted together under the scientific laws of frequency attunement. The expression of consciousness between polarities, either as it is contained in the singular atom or the complex structure of the human anatomy controlling the formation, the constant rebuilding and regenerating this physical anatomy is the true human—the psychic anatomy is, as has been previously stated, the amassed conglomeration of an infinite number of wave forms, oscillating vortexically, each expressing its own consciousness with innumerable, positive and negative polarities sustained throughout the entire structure.

Disease can, therefore, be seen not as an important life-destroying occurrence, but rather a remanifestation of one or a number of previous life-time indispositions, or psychic shocks, which must be corrected before evolution can be progressively sustained. Mankind however, as he lives on such a planet as earth, is not conscious in his physical life, of all the factors which have been discussed. Therefore, he must eradicate such malformations, more or less, by the hit and miss, trial and error method, until he succeeds, and will in his long-drawn-out conquest, gradually begin to learn about the Spiritual Worlds. And a man's more ultimate destiny is not the development of a strong personal ego, which lives by the carnal laws of the jungle, but rather the development of a human being who is both intellect and function. A first-stage cell development of a mind or entity of consciousness functions infinitely in all directions simultaneously, an entity which is capable of not only receiving in a cohesive intelligent relationship, all the known and unknown factors and concepts of Infinity, but which is also capable of recreating them infinitely and which is done by regenerating them in various dimensions and through different dimensions of consciousness.

However, it is realized by the author that such abstractions are beyond the comprehension of the third-dimensional mind which can only function in a singular fashion with one objectivism at a time and which is harmonically attuned to his past. This third-dimensional mind can therefore create only from these past formations or institute new conformatives for them. It is also realized by the author the importance which the third-dimensional earth life holds forth for the earth man—a consciousness mandated by necessity if he is to survive through the progressive cycle of earth lives.

This, then, is another way to present to any and all so concerned, a more infinite understanding of life. Assimilation and understanding must also be progressively inclined, and any person who reaches a certain threshold becomes more conscious of the great Infinite; and with this consciousness, there is born an ever-increasing desire for that person to live consciousness where it actually begins, in the spiritual worlds, or higher dimensions, for such is the nature of consciousness.

Consciousness can always be resolved into energy formations oscillating between various polarities, each a functioning concept of the great Infinite. This is true whether we view mass as energy atoms or in the transmission of any other factor of consciousness. Being so minded, the author does not believe in death, but rather in the cyclic change of consciousness from one dimension into another. Nor does he believe in disease, for in pure altruism and altruistic ideals, we again find the concept of Infinity living as a Creative Principle, even in death and disease as it is conceived by the earth man.

The author also holds no belief in the various emotional gods or fates which are supposedly controlling the destinies of men. Like all concept, belief becomes the creator and he who has so created, often becomes the victim of his creation. If any person can conceive and hold in his mind that the Infinite Intelligence is a creative function sustained infinitely, he can, by this understanding place himself in a correct receptive position to this Creative Intelligence and induct into his own life and consciousness, the constant never-ending regenerative and reconstructive Infinite, which will, in his future evolution, constantly rebuild him in a progressive manner into his more ultimate destiny, an entity which is far more god-like than any god entity heretofore conceived in the mind of man.

CHAPTER XL

On Astral Flight

The following discourse has been dealt with to some degree in the lesson series and various other transmissions; however, there has recently been called to our attention a certain concept or terminology referred to as astral flight. Since the mechanics and concepts involved in this spiritual transposition are generally misunderstood, we will explain it as a short cut to various students who may wish to understand more about the subject.

Astral flight is generally understood and is taught by various self-styled spiritual teachers to be some sort of a transitory flight of the psychic self to some far distant portions of planet earth or various other points of interstellar interest. The process involved is usually supposed to be one in which an individual will sit or lie in some sort of meditative attitude, and by some strong or concerted effort of will, project his psychic self from the physical body and thus travel to the desired place. It is generally supposed that this psychic body maintains contact with the physical self through a silver cord of some sort of energy.

This concept is quite fallacious and can easily explain why so many persons who try this formula do not achieve success. Even many of those who claim to have the faculty of astral flight are only partially successful, using this false concept.

Resorting again to the basic elements of our teachings that all things are resolved with energy wave forms, in various dimensional transpositions—man is actually a spiritual being, functioning from a closely allied spiritual dimension sometimes called the fourth, from his psychic self into his physical body. The countless billions of atoms in the physical body are supported through the inflow of energy from the psychic body as well as their I.Q. which determines their final combinations into useful cell structures, organs and other parts of the physical body. The physical or mental mind is also activated and controlled from this inner self through the various thought patterns, experience quotients, etc., which are a part of the mentality quotient of the millions of tiny wave forms of energy in the psychic self. This psychic body, when compared to the physical, becomes a conglomerate mass of these billions of energy wave forms combined in various and numerous vortexes, allegorically similar to the physical. The activating part of this spiritual or psychic self is the superconsciousness. It can be called a life cycle or a spiritual brain, or even the Christ self. It is made up of an infinite number of energy quotients, all of which not only portray the Cosmos, in the infinite sense, but are actually part of that Infinite Mind.

A human being functions either one of two ways—externally or internally—speaking in the mental metaphor, of course. The vast majority of humans can be said to be functioning externally, that is, energy quotients of previous experiences from the psychic self are being used in the daily physical life as part of their reactionary process of life. All action in the present tense is motivated from such previous experience quotients. Now if the individual can think for a moment, he can picture his daily life as something like pushing his arm through a hole in the wall and searching for some hidden object. His arm and hand become his physical body but, the energizing intelligence is the psychic self. If he ceases to externalize thought and action from the physical self and the world and reverse the process turning his superconsciousness like a searchlight beam shining about into the spiritual world in which it lives, he will have achieved true astral flight. It is as simple as that. There are no mantrums, no positions, no effort of will, in fact, nothing which can be defined as extraordinary.

When once achieved, it becomes a consciousness of the spiritual worlds, just as we have the consciousness of the material world. There is no traveling from the body, no silver cord. Let us enlarge this concept and view it something like the process involved in television transmission and receiving. The transmitter radiates a carrier wave or vibration; superimposed in this wave are other numerous little waves which are the picture and sound when picked up or received by the television receiver. They are amplified, integrated, and projected on a phosphorous screen as a very rapid succession of light and dark spots of energy impulses which make up the matrix of the picture. The same process used in reverse by any individual is astral flight.

In other words, as all objects or substance being energy and supported and re-supported from higher dimensions, this energy is re-created and portrayal combinations of form and substance are therefore vibratory, as they originate and live in dimensions which do not have time and space factors as we know of them. They can therefore be tuned in or seen by the psychic self just as easily as our physical eye sees the world about us. In fact, much more so, for this mental psychic eye is actually, through frequency relationship, in tune with everything both in the cosmic and celestial universes or to any place, planet, object, world, dimensions, or anything which is not only possible to imagine but an infinite number of such objectivisms beyond the realm of the present individual's understanding.

Therefore, if any person wishes astral flight, as it is commonly called—and should more correctly be termed conscious participation—then he must first learn to identify himself as a spiritual being, living in an Infinite Cosmogony with all proper faculties for living and functioning in various interdimensional relationships. He must learn the faculty of turning away from the exterior reactionary materialistic expressions and focus his attention inwardly through the spiritual eye back into the great Spiritual Cosmos from whence he sprang. A process of acquiring this ability may vary with different individuals. To the more materialistic-minded person, it means thousands of years of learning all forms and facets of wisdom which will relate him to a basic understanding of Infinity. To a comparatively few who have started up the path, a much shorter period of induction is required before such faculty of universal consciousness is acquired.

If you are spiritually progressive and wish to acquire infinite wisdom, then infinite persistence is necessary, and with understanding there comes to this person not only such acquirements as astral flight or consciousness but all other spiritual faculties which have been portrayed by the Masters who have visited the earth.

A much more simple and easily understood concept of "astral flight", or spiritual consciousness, is to realize that as all forms or substances are energy, they are transmitting or "giving off" certain vibratory wave forms just as the television transmitter. By the simple process of "tuning in", we see this object or place as the process is taking place in a dimension where there is no actual time or space as we understand time and space. In the tuning-in process, your psychic self does not need to travel, nor does it do so, no more than your television set travels to the transmitter. The radiating wave forms take the place of time and space or the need to travel.

CHAPTER XLI

The Lemurian Continuity

It is generally conceded by one and all that we are indeed living in an age of miracles and it may well be that the fulfillment of the last prophecies of the Bible are about to be fulfilled. Since the close of World War II and the explosion of the first atom bomb, there have been many great and wonderful transitions which have happened and are still happening in the course of history of mankind as he now dwells on the planet Earth.

From the factories there have come streams of wonderful new inventions, plastics, textiles, electronic devices; our streets and highways are crowded with gleaming, wonderful, mechanical contrivances which are marvels of precision known as automobiles. Our homes contain numbers of electronic devices which would have been miraculous in any other day and time had they suddenly appeared. The television set which is an accepted part of everyone's daily life is, in itself, one of the miracles of this day and age. In the skies above us, planes race from one continent to another with regular precision and there have even been some craft which have flown at several times the speed of sound.

From the laboratories there too have come many more wonderful things besides the various synthetic products such as plastics and textiles, and some wonder drugs which have given the modern doctor power over many of the killers of the past. Synthetic vitamins, cosmetics and even many other substances, with which we are becoming familiar, have all been synthesized by modern chemistry.

There are other straws too, blowing in the wind, which indicate that many, and the world as a whole, are going through a great change or transition; yet apparently few, if any, seem to know actually what is happening or the direction in which the general trend of development is heading. To explain not only your position but to countless thousands who may be in similar circumstances and are somewhat confounded by many of the extreme complexities of life as it now exists, the following pages and paragraphs may help to clear away some of the fog and miasma with which you are now presently surrounded.

Our modern civilization at the present time is filled almost to overflowing with various purveyors of different spiritual truths, ideologies and beliefs. This, too, indicates a great transition is taking place in the thinking of mankind and there is everything which tends to substantiate the symptoms which are all pointing to great things, not only in the general living processes of life for mankind but that his mental and spiritual processes and positions are likewise being rapidly changed.

The reasons behind any great changes in the general behavior of mankind are usually very spiritual in nature, or can be classed as astrophysically spiritual and are not readily understood by the present-day teachers of truth or by the scientists. Because of the lack of clairvoyant faculties and in the ability of mankind, as a whole, who has up to the present time neglected the higher spheres of consciousness, man is still trying to artifact his daily life from the lower physical and material planes of existence, not realizing that there are great dominant and controlling forces which are constantly extending into his everyday life, internally and externally, which not only govern behavior, but actually every living thing upon the face of the earth, as well as the very elements of the planet itself. These sustaining and motivating life forces come from different spheres of relationship and while some are spiritual in nature and stem from the psychic self of each individual through the superconsciousness, yet there are others which too are very dominant which come through from other sources.

Everyone, I believe, has seen a picture of a universe which has been portrayed in photographs in magazines and textbooks as well as in planetariums throughout the country. This is a whirling pinwheel-shaped mass of cloudy star clusters which faintly resembles the old familiar pinwheel seen at the Fourth of July fireworks. From a central vortex there stems out in a concentric radial pattern throughout the vast cosmic distances of space certain radial lines of magnetic energy. Along these lines there seem to be thick star clusters of great suns and planetary systems. A better understanding of the universe can be had if one takes a pinch of iron filings and drops it on a piece of paper and by holding this over a magnet and tapping the edge of the paper lightly, the iron filings will form themselves into the same pattern over the poles of the magnet as seen in our universe. Exactly the same conditions of adhesive relationship take place with the various suns and planets which have lined themselves up along these concentric radial lines. This is one way in which the Infinite from another dimension pours in an infinite supply of energy and governing forces. Each one of these great radial lines has secondary or lesser lines which fill in the spaces in between and, like the carrier wave which extends from the television transmitter, these various magnetic lines also carry other frequencies of vibrations which are actually the content part of the intelligent life force which comes through into every atomic substance of the planet Earth as in the infinite number of suns and planets throughout the universe. These are actually the controlling and motivating forces which energize the various atomic structures which we know of as mass. These forces give rise to the various fluctuations of magnetic energy around the earth which are known as the aurora borealis, and are actually responsible for such phenomena as sunspots and other types of heretofore unknown celestial phenomena.

Now you may be asking how does this really control the destinies of man? Anyone who has studied the Bible and the various textbooks and histories of the world will find that there is some sort of a peculiar cycular pattern or similarity in the occurrence and disappearance of any of the great civilizations and empires of the past and the rise and fall of these various epochs of time were quite similar to the rise and fall of the tides upon the seashore. Science today has already begun to explore a whole new dimension of cycular phenomena in which there is found, to a large extent the key to the behavior of many different kinds of life cycles. Every individual has major and minor life cycles just as does every other animate and inanimate thing upon the face of the earth, and even the earth and the solar system; yes, even the universe in which we are presently occupied has these major and minor cycles. The old Avatars and Savants of the past possessed a high degree of knowledge and learning in these astrophysical concepts and were thus not only able to govern their own lives much more realistically than we presently do but were also able to predict with amazing accuracy what the future would bring forth, such as was depicted in the great corridor of time in the pyramid of Gizeh in Egypt. The Bible contains numerous mentions of these transitions of various cycles such as are contained in the opening chapter of Genesis and in Revelations in reference to the millennium.

To better trace your own position from the past to the present, it will be necessary for the average student to understand thoroughly just where he started and how it was, through reincarnation, he contacted in various cycles the different civilizations of the past and also he will know something of his future position in the world to come. There has been in the course of the last million years upon the surface of the earth the rise and fall of many great civilizations; however, for practical purposes and to best suit our needs as it is indicated that the prophecy of the Bible which states that in the last days the Ten Tribes will be gathered together again, this refers to the present and future tense wherein the inhabitants of the ancient civilizations have now reincarnated for purposes of working out karma and to re-establish a more spiritual position in their personal evolution. In the opening chapter of Genesis, the Bible states that God made the earth in six days and on the seventh He rested. To most Christians and Bible students, this is still to a large extent an unsolved parable, and there are many versions of translating and accepting this parable into the individual's own personal state of consciousness. Actually, it is a reference to a great astrophysical concept which is known as the cycle of the recessional.

The sun, with its little flock of planets like a mother hen with chicks, is presently leading these little chicks at the rate of about three thousand miles per hour out into the outer rim of this great cosmic universe along one of the magnetic lines which were previously discussed. The earth in rotating about the sun and the sun so moving in its position through the universe make it possible for not only the earth but the other planets, as well, to regularly intercept and bisect these various major and minor lines of magnetic force with all of their various intelligence quotients contained therein. In the orbit of the ellipse around the sun, the earth again emerges into contact with certain cycles at about the rate of two degrees minus, each 365 days. In this gradual slipping back process through the various cycles, at the end of about 25,862 years Gregorian time, the earth has made a complete 360 degree rotation through all the major and minor cycles with which it is so presently occupied. This means that it has manifested and remanifested the various motivating influences which are contained in these magnetic lines of force, just as would be similarized to turning the station selector on your television set, in a counter-clockwise fashion from channel two to thirteen.

The old yogi concept of the East had a similar understanding of this cycle as 24,000 years and the ancient Lemurians knew it as 33,000 years. These differences in time, however, mean nothing except in the way man has so divided these things up in order to better understand them in his own way, and as far as the time is concerned in the astrophysical sense of the relationship of the cycles, there are no changes. This great cycle of 25,000 years can be cut up roughly like the sections of a pie into lesser cycles of a little over 2,000 years duration each. As a cycle can be pictured either as a circle or a half-circle wherein there is a rise and fall, it will very easily explain to you why it is that there are certain differences in the changes and epochs of time and why some civilizations have risen and fallen during the duration of these two thousand year cycles. By adding up the six cycles of 25,000 years, we arrive at a figure of about 156,000 years. This is actually the starting of Biblical history, and the written history of mankind on the earth today so far as we are concerned at the present. It also means that this was the starting of the great Lemurian civilization at that time. To some students, and as is found in the works of such men as Churchward, there is the historical story of a great space ship which crash-landed somewhere close to the northern Himalayan Mountains close to the Gobi Desert. This space ship contained eleven Lemurian Masters or great scientists from another planet which was far removed and closer to the central vortex of the universe than is now our present position. These eleven men survived the crash and later used portions of the ship to build an amphibious vessel.

These men were very tall in stature ranging over eleven feet high and weighed eighty or ninety pounds as the atoms in their bodies were much more expanded than the atoms in our own bodies and thus they were less affected by the gravitational field. These men also had copper-hued skin and auburn hair. The modern American Indian can trace his ancestry directly back to these Lemurian men who landed on this planet in that dim past age. The Book of Mormon which is the foundation for the Church of Latter Day Saints contains an exact parallel to a large degree of this story as was translated by the prophet, Joseph Smith, from the plate of gold buried in the hill of Comora in New York. There are also existing present-day records which substantiate and give us information on this great past age and its beginning. Churchward and two other Europeans actually visited the cave in Tibet and saw the remains of this space ship. It was constructed of noncorrosive metal.

Now after these Lemurians had constructed this ship, they traveled over land and sea until they came to the great continent in the Pacific (which sank many thousands of years later due to subterranean volcanic action) and after they landed, they began building the great civilization which is called Lemuria. There was, in that day, a wonderful way of life as these great Masters taught man to live from inner consciousness. With their various vessels and Emissaries they plied the seas and highways of the world and gathered the Ten Races of people who were scattered about the globe at that time and brought them to Lemuria to teach them this better way of life. There were none of the terrific pressures and the numerous compromises with which we are constantly surrounded in our present time. Instead, there was a peaceful and pleasant continuation of each day wherein everyone had sufficient to eat and wear and to occupy his time in pleasant tasks of producing necessities of life. After many thousands of years, Lemuria sank beneath the waves and carried to the end of their lives about seventy-two million people. This great cataclysm left behind only small remnants of that once great and wonderful civilization.

Incidentally, many of the stories in the Old Testament such as Noah's Ark, the Tower of Babel, and others actually have their origin as legends from this great civilization. It was in gathering about the Ten Tribes of the earth that the Lemurian Masters were confronted with the task of training them all in one universal language after having them build the great city of Mu which was on the southern tip of the continent. You can well imagine the trouble these great men had in educating the barbaric half-savages which they had gathered here, there, and yon over the face of the earth, and how they fought and battled among themselves in their efforts of adjustment. Thus the story of the Tower of Babel came into being.

Noah's Ark actually depicts not only the barges built by the later race of Atlanteans to escape the impending doom, but also refers to some of the ships which were built by the Lemurians to escape that oncoming catastrophe which had been prophesied. Many people escaped from Lemuria into various portions of the globe before the cataclysm occurred and began re-establishing their lives in the various colonies which had sprung up under the dominion of Lemuria.

Atlantis was one of these and Atlantis was known at that time as a great continent which existed off the coast of Spain whose last remaining vestiges are the Canary Islands, and this Atlantean civilization grew up and was almost as great and wonderful as the former Lemuria. Here again, history began to repeat itself in one of the great cyclar patterns. On the plains of Atlantis grew great wonderful cities which became the cultural centers of the world. People came and went in great space ships powered with strange devices which actually gathered their energies from the magnetic lines of force from the great universe around the earth —flying saucers. The cities themselves were also powered by great and mysterious engines which used these magnetic powers and which had been brought down and left to them from the Lemurian scientists of that bygone civilization. However, in the course of time, Atlantis began to deteriorate. A migrant race of dark-skinned people began filtering in from the east. These people had been displaced by an Aryan race which had migrated from out of the plains of Mongolia.

These dark-skinned people worshipped serpents and through the many years, began to lay plans to take over and control the great cities of Atlantis. After the passing of thousands of years, they succeeded in stealing the secrets of these wonderful cosmic powers and the control of various types of spacecraft used by the Atlanteans. Using their stolen secrets, they actually blew Atlantis into nothingness and just as in the case of Lemuria, here, too, millions of people perished in a few hours time. Before this happened, however, the impending doom of this civilization had been forecast and a great migration had already taken place. Great barges and other types of transportation were used to carry thousands of people into Egypt and into Central and South America. These people later became the forefathers of the civilizations which were known in history as Egypt and the Mayan civilization as well as forefathers of the North American Indians.

The Lemurian Continuity
Part Two

To the best accounts and records and to the knowledge that has been given, the destruction to Atlantis occurred about 25,000 years ago. Since that time, other civilizations have risen and fallen. From the time of Osiris more than 12,000 years ago, Egypt was, at that time, in the height of its ascendency and was a brilliant and luminous star in the historical firmament of the planet Earth. Gradually, too, Egypt deteriorated. The dark-skinned snake cultists again succeeded in robbing the power from the Egyptian priesthood and instilled in its place a warped distorted concept of black magic wherein animals were worshipped instead of Amen-Ra or the sun, the one god monotheistic religion which had existed in Atlantis and in the time of Osiris.

To those who know something of these histories and that in the time of Osiris, Egypt too had the story of the Immaculate Conception and that Horus, the son of Osiris, was borne by mother earth, or Isis, through immaculate conception. In those ancient days, immaculate conception happened quite frequently and to almost all of the men who came as Avatars or Savants to teach a better way of life and that with the passing of these men, they became linked in a historical way with the immaculate conception. Zoroaster, who laid down a great religion in ancient Persia and Arabia, also was believed to have had an immaculate conception which was witnessed by shepherds as he was born in a hillside but under almost identical conditions which were given in our present-day Biblical version of the birth of Jesus in the New Testament. Actually, a Catholic Pope borrowed this story.

With the passing of the Osirian Age in Egypt and the inception of the black magic mystic cultisms of the serpent people who had destroyed Atlantis, there came the time of Moses wherein he was confronted with one of these priests who also cast down his rod and it too became a serpent just as did Moses' rod. This was an actual demonstration of the powers of the priests who lived in that day and time and, as Moses had lived many years in the Temple of Dendera, he knew of these various black magic arts and sciences and was able to practice them quite liberally in his position as governor of the tribes of Israel and these powers have, in our day and time, been attributed to having been given to him by the Lord. This, to a large extent, accounts for the differences in the old vindictive monotheism of the Old Testament wherein God was a temperamental ruler of people, who very frequently gave vent to His wrath and judgment, not only to nations but individuals as well, and this concept was contradicted by the appearance of Jesus who taught the God of love and understanding which came from within every person.

Thus it was that Egypt passed and, with the passing, left behind many traces of a once glorious and beautiful civilization. India, too, is sometimes credited with being the birthplace of mankind and well this could be so, for more than half a million years ago upon the southern plains of Mongolia, close to the Himalaya Mountains, there was a great and wonderful city which is still today called Shamballa or the spiritual city wherein the very angels and hosts of heaven were said to have lived. It is known that from other planets there were people brought into this great city who were later known as the Aryan race. They were people of light-complexion, blonde of hair and blue of eyes, tall in stature, well-formed, and highly intelligent.

346

In Kashmir, in India, today there are many remnants of this last race of people who are still blonde and blue-eyed. The migrants of this Aryan race traveled north-ward with the passing of the great civilization of Yu, as it was called, and went up through Siberia and Russia and migrated into the northern latitudes of Norway, Sweden and England and later became known as the various Nordic races which inhabit the world at this time. As these Aryans, later on after the passing of the city of Shamballa, migrated and took with them the Vedic translations which later became the basis of Hinduism and all its pantheology as it exists today. Brahma, Vishnu, and Shiva, the Holy Triad, as it is called in Modern Christianity, is still known and practiced in India and comes from the Vedic or ancient transcripts which were brought by the Aryans who displaced the dark people whom they found living on the plains and valleys of India. These Aryan people later became known as the Brahmans or the high-caste people and, in order to preserve their race, established the caste system which existed for many thousands of years in India.

Some of the migrants of the dark-skinned people who went westward settled in ancient Arabia and Persia and, here too, with the mingling of migrants from Egypt and some of the leaders of the Aryan races who reincarnated through the pages of history, built up the great civilization known as Babylonia. It was here that Father Abraham led the tribes of Israel into Egypt about 2,000 years before the time of Solomon and it was here also that five hundred years after the birth of Jesus the prophet, Mohammed, again re-establish-ed the first five books of Moses which are presently known as the Koran.

Some thousand years before the birth of Jesus in

the Holy Land, another great civilization began to form in the mountains and plains of Greece from the various tribes which roamed the plains and hills of that country at the time of Homer, the blind bard, who sang the Odyssey and many other classics of history. This civilization gradually drew unto itself and from the many tribes, the Corinthian and Hellenic culture from which the seed of a great and wonderful philosophic age was fostered. From these various tribes of people who were drawn together in this union and became known as the Athenians or the Corinthians or the Greeks, there came such men as Plato, Socrates, Archimedes, Pythagoras and many more who established great cultures known as academies and whose philosophers largely taught the old Hermetic science which came from Egypt, India and other places of the globe. It was Plato who described, in numerous works, the history of Atlantis and this too was known among other Avatars and sons of that time.

Then came the time of Jesus and with it was incepted the age of spiritual miracles which laid down the foundation for a great church which later became the dominant and ruling force of the whole European continent. From Paul, who started this church, and through a schism which became the Greek Orthodoxy, and Peter who labored in Rome, there sprang into existence the great Catholic Church and although it did not really function until the reign of the Emperor Constantine, more than two hundred years after the death of Jesus, yet from that time it began to flourish and grow. By the year 1,000 A.D., it controlled the life destinies and owned most of the property of every individual on the continent of Europe and was known as the Holy Roman Empire.

There was also at this time a great invasion of the

Turkish and Moslem religions from the various ruling sultans referred to in history as the Ottoman Empire which at one time actually conquered the lower half of the European continent. Then, along toward the twelfth or thirteenth century A.D., there began upsurgings and beginnings of a great spiritual renaissance through the beginnings of such men as John Locke, William Shakespeare, Harvey, Martin Luther and others who emblazoned brilliant pages in the book of history in the liberation of man from the tyrannical despotism which was practiced by the Holy Roman Empire at that time. There began a great movement of spiritual as well as political freedom throughout the various nations of Europe. Many men and women were burned at the stake and suffered martyrdom in numerous ways by believing and following the teachings of the leaders in their time. From out of this maelstrom and chaos sprang great churches, such as led by John Wesley which became known as the Methodist Church, the Brothers or the Quakers led by John Fox, the Puritans who established the first northern colonies in America and numerous others, all of whom became ostracized in their own land by this Holy Roman Empire and were forced to migrate into the new frontiers and wildernesses of America.

So it was that from the far distant dim reaches of the unwritten and written history of the world and through the most crucial pressures which were exerted upon the various races of mankind were regenerated a new and motivating wellspring of force which seemed to regenerate the races of mankind and bring him forth to a new time and a new place, to again re-establish himself in a new manner and form of living.

This is the principle and the concept behind reincarnation and through these long written and unwritten pages of history and through the uncounted millions of persons who have come and gone through these numerous pages of history, they have, in thus so appearing, not only established within themselves the principles in the continuity of life, but have bettered and furthered the purposes of their own evolution.

To you and to every student who is so laboring and struggling at this present age to bring into focus some new concepts or understanding of spiritual truth and to work out the various karmic or psychic happenings of the past wherein great negations were imposed on the psychic consciousness—to all of these individuals in their own time and day and in their many struggles and working-out—they are indeed preparing themselves for that Seventh Day of the Lord and for that future civilization which has been prophesied as the new City of Jerusalem. This preparation can be called the Millennium or the thousand years of preparation wherein, during this thousand-year period, the Ten Tribes and the hundreds and millions of untold numbers of people who have so inhabited this planet earth and have known of Avatars and Savants of the past and their teachings, and of the spiritual way of life, that here too they are again trying to re-establish and to incept these age-old principles of living into their daily life.

The longing of the inner consciousness to again establish a rightful continuity with the emanating God force or the very creative life force has become an essential ingredient in the everyday living of these hundreds of thousands of people who are thus seeking in this age and time and to the many hundreds of thousands who are being born and are yet to be born in the coming thousand years, who, too, will pass through these great psychic transitions wherein the old karmic blocks of the past are removed. They are prepared by the rebuilding of the psychic self so that they may be re-established as leaders and citizens of that future day and age wherein God will actually rule the world through the inner consciousness of man and man will realize and incept into his daily living habits the very essences of spiritual truth, brotherly love and spiritual emancipation which will give him freedom from all earthly pressures, desires and compromises which now exist. It will remove his warlike attitudes, his jails and penitentiaries. It will cause navies and armies of the world to become only dim memories of the past. It will also mean the surcease of the now intangible and incurable diseases which plague and kill millions of people each year. Thus man will come to know his Utopia, his Aquarian Age, and live unto another great cycle in his new spiritual City of Jerusalem.

And so, dear fellow student, or fellow traveler on the pathway of life, thus you may trace your own course of evolution through these many histories—you may have a longing or a liking for ancient Egypt, India or China, or it may be that you have even had flash-backs of former lives—but however you interpret your longings or dispositions toward any of these ancient cultures and civilizations, you may rest assured that you are reflecting outwardly into your conscious memory, the existence of one or more lifetimes lived in these civilizations and pages of the past. You will likewise see about you in the various expressions of fadisms adopted by the feminine sex that they too are expressing a form of inversion or a recurring conscious memory of some previous life cycle wherein they may adapt to their feminine form certain fashions which were worn by the ladies of the past. You may thus see yourself as one of the numerous citizens at the time of Cleopatra or Moses, or as one of the artisans who helped fashion King Solomon's temple. You may remember something vaguely in your liking of the teachings of Plato or other Avatars of that time, that you were one of the cultists in the great philosophical academy. You may also know, too, those who are clairvoyantly trained and can factually portray different scenes from your past lives and the therapeutic value contained in such portrayals, actually reliving sequences of these past episodes. However, do not use such knowledge for the purposes of strengthening some existing conflict which you now have. You may see about you numerous instances where you can wrongly use the knowledge of some previous existence in your present day or time. You may completely change your thought patterns in your way of life by believing you were some king or emancipator when you were actually only a follower and that in so following, you longed to be like him and have, through the ages, actually changed yourself into him by so believing you were as far as your own concept is concerned.

The actual value contained in all knowledge of reincarnation and in the various evolutions and cycles of life in which you have thus progressed is contained in the strengthening qualities it gives you by assuming mastery over such negative experiences by the working out of such karmic episodes in your past lives, by strengthening your belief and knowledge that you are not a frail earthly form subject to birth and death and, that as you come from nothing, you will pass into nothing. Such a concept is a violation of every established precinct of knowledge as it exists upon the earth today. It is a direct contradiction of all life forces which you see constantly recurring and stemming around you. You must constantly visualize within your mind that you are the beginnings of the ultimate personification in the spiritual form of the Infinite Intelligence that has been compounded within your life cycle and in the spiritual way, the exact portrayal and counterpart of all of this infinite nature, that you are completely reliving this Infinity throughout the eons of time not only on this planet and its pages of history, but that you will relive and constantly relive on other planets, other solar systems, and in other spiritual or material transitions before you have even started to realize the meaning of the term, "Infinity". Through such recurrences and through such relivings and the constant evolutions and cycles, you will rebuild the psychic structures of your innermost self so that they can gradually adapt themselves and be reinstated into higher and higher spiritual planes of consciousness. Thus you will gradually pass from the old karmic material world and you evolve slowly in your evolutions as Buddha calls this, Nirvana, and Jesus, one of the many mansions which he mentioned.

So be not concerned that you were such an identity in a past life, neither give strength to some negative experience by constantly reliving it and portraying it in your present life; do not be sad or nostalgic of the past and bygone days of some lifetimes spent in the company of a great Avatar. But instead, look forward to even greater pathways of spiritual emancipation; look forward to brighter days in greater worlds, where you will portray a much greater quotient of Infinite nature. Resolve within yourself that you will work out the last vestiges of the materialistic karmic experiences which have retarded and impeded your progress through the many thousands of years of time. Know that they mean nothing to you except in the value of experience quotient so contained and in the mastery over these things, you have furthered and bettered your spiritual progress.

To the student of Truth, just as in your own case he may rest assured that he has spent a hundred or more lifetimes in seeking and searching since Atlantis and he may spend another hundred lifetimes unless he takes a more directed course wherein he can shorten this lengthy period of useless reincarnating into the lower material worlds. This is only done through self-mastery, the learning and incepting of the principles of life, and the overcoming of self as it is projected into the lower realms of negative consciousness, to lift it above these earthly mundane experiences into the realm of superconsciousness where it dwells in contact with the infinite self through the future eons of time.

CHAPTER XLII

Man, A Musician In The Great Symphony Of Life

All quests and unsolved indispositions which are manifested in anyone's daily life are simply the result of lack of a definite spiritual psychology in that person's life. Such quests, searchings and seekings can and will only be dissolved when such adequate spiritual psychology replaces the reactionary material psychology which has given rise to not only each individual's own personal unsolved quests and searchings but that such reactionary philosophy or psychology is either directly or indirectly responsible for all of the large numbers of classified and unclassified ills of humanity.

When the light of true inward introspection from the inward consciousness is brought down and focused into our daily life as our guiding light, then all quests, searchings and seekings are dissipated as shadows before the rising sun.

Remember, too, a common metaphysical term, "like attracts like", so one unhealthy situation would only attract another, or "two wrongs do not make a right", and two unhappy people do not make one happy person.

True happiness is not found in the belief that any one person can bring us happiness, nor can we, by the same token expect to find true happiness by trying to make someone else happy. True happiness is found only when we have properly placed ourselves as a positive reciprocating polarity for the Infinite Mind, and in becoming such a polarity, we incept into our daily lives a certain proportion of Infinite Wisdom which supplies all our needs and answers all our problems—remembering, however, that this is not done selfishly but rather, in a broad overall sense of interpretation which deals directly with the universal man, his infinitely numerous interpretations of life, not only on materialistic earth-plane existences but in the countless numbers of astral and spiritual worlds as well.

The idea behind the libido or sex drive is quite well-founded and very necessary on the materialistic planes of life and one which, through procreation, not only sustains man through the evolutionary process of reincarnation through the first and informative experience periods of this evolution but these various unions between man and woman, which are primarily motivated by sex in the procreative process, actually become starting points from whence he begins to build up from within himself, his mate, and members of the family, a pattern of oscillating polarities. When constantly built up, rejuvenated, and added to through the numerous life cycles and contacts in these family relationships, they begin to link him in a broad and universal pattern of introspection whereby through the law of harmonic or frequency relationships, he is not only a part of all the universal brotherhood of man but also becomes one of the positive sustaining polarities for this universal brotherhood.

Unfortunately, however, such a universal spiritual brotherhood has not yet been lived or expressed in any true proportion upon the earth or in any of our more ancient or recent epochs of time, and is a utopian goal which has long been envisioned within the hearts and minds of countless millions who have lived and are living at our present time. Such utopian visions may indeed spring from within the spiritual consciousness of each individual and which may be a vague memory consciousness of lives in between lives in higher spiritual dimensions; or the very form and nature of the perfect existence may spring from the spiritual embryo or life cycle of each person. In man's struggle for survival, any one individual finds himself—just as any other one of the countless billions of humanity who have lived or are living—confronted by a seemingly endless succession of daily problems, experiences, dispensations, reactions and other numerous elements which go to make up this daily life. And he may well ask himself, "What is the use of all this seemingly endless succession and procession of various experience quotients of life?" And such a person will indeed become lost should he lose sight of the perspective and purpose of life. Neither can it be said that any one person has within his consciousness this true continuity of purpose nor could he give voice or utterance to the most abstract of all equations which is life.

Within the psychic structures of self, the inner man gives forth constantly in the unheard voice, the unsung song of creation. The various procession of forms of life can thus, in the melody of this unsung song, become part of the infinite abstraction of not only the universal man, existing in his countless dispensations, but all of these things in themselves and in their infinities become the ways and means in which Infinity lives and relives, multiplies and replenishes, re-creates and expresses.

Thus it is in such infinite introspection that man is no more or less than the leaf on the tree or the blade of grass at the feet, or of the beasts of the field or the fowls of the air, for each one in himself is expressing the infinite continuity—a direct proportion of this great Intelligence. Each and everything so created has become a musician in the great symphony of life which sings and plays its unheard song of creation, springing from whence no man knows and ever returning to the unknown limbo of Infinite Consciousness.

CHAPTER XLIII

"Know Thyself"
(An Informal Talk)

I wish to speak to you this morning; we will call it about the "big stick", as Teddy Roosevelt said. Well, of course, we do not wish to walk about with a big stick in a sense of the word that we have a big stick. What we mean here is knowledge. Knowledge becomes our big stick, not only in the sense of the word that it defends us but it can also be used as a constructive implementation in our lives.

Now, there are many ways to approach an understanding of life—Infinity. We can say evolution as a whole is prefaced upon that situation. There are three or four billion people upon the earth today and they all have their own individual approach in evolution to what is truth or of what the higher way of life really consists. Up until the time that they become knowledgeable, of course, they are going to have to use many obvious devices and many different kinds of placebos or pacifisms or whatever it is that you like to call these things, because those things always have to be used in lieu of something constructive.

Now if we think for a moment of all these people around us and they are all using these things; they use their religion, their politics and they use whatever else it is that seems to be the most important thing in their lives. What it means is that people are, in a small way or in a large way, grouping themselves together under these different definitives of expression. You could say that in a nation as a whole here are a lot of people who are grouped together—one hundred eighty odd million people—and they all believe that they are a nation, living under a flag. So here are a great many fearful people; they are huddled together and the more fearful people that they find who are in an equally as fearful state as are they themselves, they seem to gather strength in their fear, because the more that their own fears are justified, the stronger they become.

That presents a rather peculiar situation but it is exactly the way that it is. These are all what we call inversions and they all relate to the transpositions of cyclic forms or manifestations. So we must be intelligent about this and in order to get a good view of what this consists and how it works, we must get into the actual science; otherwise we are lost. We are only going to take from life as we come along, because everyone has this libido or the drive to live. They do not really know why they are living and they do not know where they are going when they leave here; in fact, they know not where they came from. But still they have a drive to live even though apparently if they really tried to analyze it, there would not be any of them who could really tell you why. Isn't that right? No one knows why he is living, why he expresses in this particular expression. So these things are all abstract evaluations and we have to carry them into a dimension of science before we understand them.

One of the very obvious devices which is used by many people today, we will say, in the expressions of truth is that they have sort of hypnotized themselves, autosuggestively immersed themselves. They go around and say, "well, we have to love everyone". Well, that is all right to love everyone certainly but first, we must understand what love is. Love is not what the average earth man thinks it is; it is not a natural reflex; it is not an emotionalism where we hope to pacify the inherent or the basic fears of our existence. As Jesus put it, we must love each other as we love ourselves and love our Father with all our heart and soul. So love then becomes knowledge; we have to completely understand every individual as well as ourselves. As one ancient Greek put it, the wisest man in the world would be the man who knew himself. If we understand ourselves we understand all human beings and by the same principles we can understand Infinity; we can understand creation, for the same basic principles apply to one set of conditions as they do to everything else. So then, love is not a reflex emotion where we say we blindly hypnotize ourselves against the common recognition of all factors involved in these transpositions of life and instead, love becomes an understanding, a complete understanding, a basic knowledge—knowledge of not only what our fellow man is but what we ourselves are and what everything is that surrounds us in our scale of evolution—and so on, ad infinitum.

And there is only one way in which we can understand love. That is to begin at the fundamentals of creative science as they are expressed in the nomenclature of the modern science of today, which are basic derivatives. So that is what we are here to do this morning. We are trying more or less in a rather informal fashion to draw out something here for you so we do not go around saying, "We love each other, I love my fellow man and no evil can come to me as such", and all of these other things which really amount to naught because they do not give us the "big stick" that we are trying to carry around with us in the sense of the word that we cannot only have an understanding or a defense but that we can also have a constructive evaluation to our world.

Now I am going to draw a sine wave here—you have

seen sine waves in your lesson courses—which are simply an up and down motion and which means that the Infinite Creator is dual in nature, that is, everything is expressed simultaneously in two directions at the same time; everything assumes a dual polarity, a positive and a negative. Even though we have cyclic motions in the fourth dimension which are complete entities in themselves, that is, they have no beginning or end, yet the structure of every cycle is the same in the sine wave proposition. It is very important, too, to remember that information is carried on a sine wave. There really isn't anything else except sine waves; everything in life that comes to you is a sine wave motion. Your entire life is a sine wave and on that sine wave are carried hundreds of thousands or millions of other little sine waves piggy-back, so to speak, or that they are part of that wave.

We put a positive or plus mark up top and a negative or minus sign on the lower portion of the sine wave. Now we have two different points of introspection. We will say there are two different ways that we can view everything—a positive way or a negative way, that is, according to where we are or how we are biased on our path of evolution, as the earth man as a whole, as a materialist, is always biased with the past. Now in these sine wave motions there always has to be equilibrium, so there is a constant attempt to equalize any sine wave as positive and negative. Now if an earth man smokes a cigarette, his cigarette is a negative bias, so that bias is in rearward unto all other negative cycles that he has ever lived in the sum and total of all other negative cycles, so that he has precipitated himself in a backward motion. He has really detracted from the general equilibrium of positive and negative in his own life by adding that negative bias.

Now let us take an automobile, for instance. You'd be surprised to know that every automobile is a sine wave; at least we are going to look at one as a sine wave because the automobile is going through time and space, we will say, so the entity or the consciousness or the thing that the automobile is and all that it is, is a basic sine wave. On that sine wave are millions of other little sine waves and up on the positive side of the wave of what that car is, we will say first it can be a rather beautiful piece of machinery. That is positive and we put a little check down here on the positive side of the sine wave. It is utilitarian, another little positive check. All of the other factors which go to make up that car, what it is, what it performs positively, we put on the plus side. Then we will go down to the other end and we will say, well, it is an engine of destruction; it can kill. We put that down on the negative side. It deteriorates; in a few years it will be scrap on the junk heap. We put that down and we will do the same thing with the bomb that dropped over Hiroshima. On the positive side, here was a great attribute to the consciousness of science in their expression but primarily, of course, we are concerned with the fact that through the negative part of the cycle which was the killing of a hundred thousand people and injuring several hundred thousand more was the consciousness that man now had to live without atomic warfare. So that then became a positive part of that cycle, didn't it? Yes.

And that is the way we equate all of these things as we go along in our daily life. We must understand very realistically that this third-dimensional sine wave in whatever it is that we are looking at, is actually a sine wave as it comes to us. That is true whether it's a stone we stumble over or whether it is a star in the sky. We can always equate and we can always establish some sort of an equilibrium with the transposition of this, whatever it may be, our perspectus and our introspection and we can also see the biases plus or minus, which either precipitated to keep it going forward in our evolution, which is the constructive or forward motion, or that it is biased and is retrogressing.

Now let us take another problem or proposition. I will draw another sine wave and we will say that this is Infinity up here—or that is a very highly developed person. He, too, to a degree, if he looks down here into the third dimensional world—and these same principles hold good up there too—he is going to see the third-dimensional world negatively. Why? Because if he views this, as we say in the little sine waves which come to him, and it is the law because negative goes to positive and positive to negative, and so, then we have the cyclic motion again which is the fourth-dimensional concept—the whole of the whole infinite concept which is cyclic motion. So now if he views the third dimension, he can view this in respect to the fact that there are certain harmonic oscillations in force. He is in tune with them. He can see these things but from where he stands or from where he is up there, the earth world would be from that position negative, as he is on a much more positive plane. But at the same time in order to realize that, the positive from the earth world would have to come to him because here we have the flow of the negative to the positive and the positive to the negative.

Now how is this being going to maintain a relationship with the earth? Well, he does not do this by hurling a thunderbolt like Zeus might have, or anything else like that. He lives in this world through an earth body so that in this earth body he can look out in the

364

world, so to speak. He has a little radio or a facility such as they are planning to put up on the moon and through this earth body he can look out into the world and he can tune himself into everything that is going on in direct relationship with the world. Now he cannot have that body in any other form except that it is with every other earth body. It has to be subjective to all the conditions of the earth world. He has to eat, sleep, has to drink water and it is subject to disease and accidents and all the other things, because the moment anything is taken away from that earth-world body, it loses a certain part of its relationship to the earth world. So, therefore, the man or being up here in the Higher Worlds could not possibly lose his relationship with this earth body, as he is working through that earth body, we say, in a manner in which the man on the moon in his space station might be working with the scientists on the earth through radio or through radar or through the laser beam, whatever method of communication it may be. We call it clairvoyance or coming from within. So through the earth body, he maintains the proper relationship with the earth world and all the values which embody him with it. He does not really try to perform a miracle in this world with his own body for the main and simple reason that he is way up here (in the Higher Worlds). The moon station down on the earth is more or less dispensable. If it is destroyed he can raise another one. In other words, it is not the dominating factor of his life as it would be with the earth man or as it would be with the man who lived on the moon, for the moon would be all his world.

It is the same way here. We must have the realistic approach, so now we are establishing certain values with how these things are incepted to us or how we realize these things as they come to us in this world.

We have to see where it is that there are positive biases or where things are positive and where they become negative and where the biases are which precipitate us back into the negative dimension of the past or whether they precipitate us in a forward dimension.

And loving people is the consistency of all this and a lot more because we have to know of this knowledge. We cannot possibly love another person until we can see in him everything that we are and we cannot possibly see all that we are so long as we go along blinded to our own particular self in the relationship of the emotionalisms which are within ourselves, because emotionalism in itself is a negative bias which is always superimposed from the past, because you lived on the emotional plane of the past. The primary purpose was to survive, to eat, because that was necessary in the first part of your evolution. But as you progressed, there was a certain ambivalence of consciousness which was constantly integrated or we shall say, developed into the psychic anatomy to the point where the mental consciousness began to polarize a certain facsimile of self on a positive plane, so then you began having a part of yourself becoming the man upstairs, of the Higher Worlds.

Now at the present time, the man upstairs is not the important part in your life; he is not the dominant polarity of your life; you are still biased by the past. And until this being upstairs is completely polarized so that you, in turn can live again through the earth, to help other people help polarize their higher self, then you really have not learned the important thing of life and how all of these things come to you in a scientific manner and a scientific form, the consciousness that these things are biased from the past, so they are biased from the future, whether they are positive and that we can put them on the positive end of that cycle or whether we can put them on the negative. And if there is an imbalance there, like a man smoking a cigarette, well, we must know or we must not emotionalize it and say, "Oh, what a horrible thing it is", or become emotionally conscious of that, for if we do, we automatically attune ourselves to that negative bias that he has superimposed in his consciousness by tuning in and smoking the cigarette and we become part of his retrogressive motion. However, if we visualize, this is a balance in his evolution—that through the cigarette and through many other things which come to him, he is going to finally persecute himself into such a state of consciousness that he is going to have to seek out the right. And here again is the purpose of the Infinite—to re-establish the balance in the polarity, because the lower a person becomes, the greater becomes the desire to become more positive. And so then, sin or evil becomes good, does it not? But we have to see this evil and this good in the positive way in which the cyclic motion is transferred into a sine wave motion.

So, as we go through life and as we go out into the world, we must not have any set or fixed opinions about everything, because an opinionated person is a very stupid and ignorant person. A wise person is one who maintains in his consciousness that he is fluid or he is ductile to the extent or the purpose of the true principle that he can become a much better person, a much more intelligent person. He can have a forward bias, a progressing bias into the future because the future always presents to him the proposition that so far as he is concerned—or mankind in general—that there is always much more positive and constructive evaluation, knowledge, etc., which can be obtained from the future. This is different than the earth man living today. His supposition is that he lives only once and that he will get all that he can out of it while he is here, so he becomes some sort of a hellion as he runs around. He drinks and he smokes and does many other things which are not morally right, so what does he do? He increases his negative bias to the past and that becomes karma. In other words, all these things live in his cycle of life. Every one of those little experiences live. There are little oscillating wave forms of motion on that cycle of his life and sooner or later he is going to have to establish the equilibrium; he is going to have to get back to where he can have the small positive bias which comes to him from the future, because the difference is that the further you go backwards, the less and less chance there is of your having the positive bias which comes to you from the Creator or the positive source of all things. The further you dip away from it then, the more backwards you go into the past, the more you are going to have to live on your memory consciousness or you are going to have to live on other people and become parasitic, as the dark forces from the underworlds do. And eventually that source of supply ceases; they get to a point in their retrogression where they actually disintegrate themselves to an extent.

So here we have science so very firmly established. We cannot use a placebo or an opinion or a pacifier when we go out among people of the world. If we turn over a stone, let's turn it over so that we shall not be bitten by the scorpion that may be lurking underneath. We have to approach this thing realistically and realize that here is evolution; and the proposition in evolution in itself is to always keep ourselves positively biased in respect to the Infinite so that the Infinite can always flow into us and, in turn, by our positive attitude, our positive inception, we return to the Infinite and we keep this positive bias flowing into us. There is the cyclic motion which is paramount and dominant throughout the fourth dimension or the Higher World, if we wish to call it such, because everything there is without time and it is without space, in a sense too—in a sense of the word that anything, whatever it is, an entity of consciousness is complete within itself. It does not stop and it does not start. You can tune into it at any point of that cycle. If you draw a circle, it is merely the proposition of putting your mentality down at any particular given point. That is the reason I can tune into any place in your lives, here or in the past, because your cycle of life, whether it is in this immediate cycle which is a minor cycle or whether we say the entire cycle, which is the complete cycle of your evolution, you can say in a million years, it makes no difference. If you have the properly trained mind, you can put that mind at any particular point on that cycle and you can, within your consciousness, determine what these little wave forms which are oscillating on that cycle or the entire cycle contain, for the information is there. And if people knew that every act or deed, yes, even every thought they expressed was indelibly engraved within them, they would begin to act differently, would they not? Yes, indeed.

When you have developed your consciousness to the point where this information is an electrical motion, it conveys a picture; it is being done every day in your life now. As you sit here, you look around the walls of the room, so what is consciousness? You see all these things as sine waves which come into your eyes or come into your ears or through other faculties of perception as the sense of touch or smell, etc., but they are really sine wave motions. In a higher world it merely means that you have dispensed with the physical body to the degree that you no longer have five senses. The entire being, your body, everything is a big radio sending and receiving set or television set. The proposition of life comes to you that way. Here are billions and billions of sine waves which are coming to you in their cyclic motions from out of time and space or from out of the Infinite simultaneously. There is the proposition that you tune in to them. You determine what this consciousness is within yourself on the basis that here are harmonic relationships.

Now, as the professor in Harvard, Wilson, said, when you press your finger on the table you are not actually pressing your finger on the table, just as I put it in the books years ago. What you are doing is that you are bringing two electromagnetic fields or electro-static fields in direct opposition with each other. If we turn the poles of two horseshoe magnets together and the two north poles are together and the two south poles are together, we cannot push them together. We turn them around the other or opposite way, then they draw to each other. Here is the same proposition, the positive and negative, the conveyance of whatever it is that is being brought into effect at that moment because it is a cyclic motion. It has to be. There is nothing else. So that is what we mean by calling, or saying we are carrying a big stick. We go out into the world or wherever we are at any particular moment—or even sitting in the house for that matter, the proposition here, or it should be with all of you if you are going to develop into a spiritual being, if you are going to continue on in your evolution or the future positively in a forward manner, then it's mandatory that you have to form some concise evaluation of the principles that are involved, otherwise you won't get anywhere. You will be biased by the past. You will set up these placebos or pacifiers in your own mind and you'll take out of what I have written certain sentences or certain statements which are relative to your lack of knowledge and you'll use them to bolster up a sort of false citadel of conformities within your own mind.

You say you love people and yet you do not understand yourself. How can you love people? You cannot. You can't possibly love people until you understand yourself, because love is the complete understanding. If you completely love the other person, you completely understand him; you see in him the exact counterpart of the Infinite Creation as it is within you. The proposition here is where you incepted all that you are in a different relationship with time and space. As far as the Infinite is concerned, it is different than any other person but basically the principle is the same. So that gives you the difference in integration of consciousness; it gives you the difference in form—what you consider form—or portions of your evolution. For instance, you look different than the person next to you —we all look different. And what is this difference? It merely means that somewhere along this cycle of life so far as our conscious and subconscious integrations are concerned, we have incepted wave forms and integrated harmonic structures which made us look different than the other person. That is your personality but that's the way and part in which the Infinite re-creates itself infinitely. You see how that is now?

I might bring this point out here that we had quite a difficult time clearing up this little difference with one certain individual, for it has been quite a challenge to every student—for there was a great lesson here that should be objectified and could be very valuable to him. Instead, there was some doubt, perhaps a little distrust and some criticism, whereas there should not have been. Had each one taken the positive end of the cycle and found the corrective evaluations and balances, there would have been no suspicion and no doubt and there could have existed no criticism. The lesson was very objective in itself and there was strategy involved on both sides because here we had two diametrically opposed worlds of consciousness, we might say, the old retrogressive world which was going back into the past and which is opposed to the forward world.

This is the struggle since man began, the struggle throughout infinity, if we wish to call it struggle, because it really isn't. What it means is that we always have the cyclic motion involved in which the Infinite expresses itself in all forms and all manners and in all things, and is actually a part of that because everything is really energy anyway.

"Know Thyself" (An Informal Talk)
Part Two

So how are you going to hope to convey a higher way of life to any person or to any group of people if they refuse because they constantly want to be biased by the past? They have set up a block within themselves; they want to hold on to the past because there they have or find their security. It's familiar to them. Even though it's a snake in their bed at night, it's familiar to them and they like that kind of a snake and they'd not trade it for any other kind of a snake in the world because it is their past; it is their betrayer. It is their apple on the tree of life, the security of the past. And what is the past and how to give up the past is the biggest problem with any Unariun student or for anyone, for that matter, because that is the proposition with every human being that goes through this pattern of evolution on any earth world. He is either going to go backwards and be destroyed or he is going to have to give up the past and go forward. That is the sum of it, the long and the short of the whole business and it doesn't make any difference to me whether he gets to that point in a thousand years from now or a million years from now because I am absolutely unemotional about it, because I understand him thoroughly and I understand where he will go if he does not make the right decision and go on the forward motion; so I am not concerned whether he lives or dies anyway because he is part of the Infinite. The Infinite is not emotionally concerned with him either. Because I understand him thoroughly, I could not get emotional with him even if I wanted to. You cannot get emotional with anything if you understand it. It is only when you do not understand anything that you become emotional.

Now I realize even as I sit here and I make certain statements and when they may come out of that tape there a little later—and someone will come along and he is going to take something out of these words and will make a pacifier out of them. He is not going to use the entirety, the concept as I have presented it to you here today.

Two hundred and fifty years after Buddha died a prince named Asoka, in one of the provinces of India, took what Buddha had taught and preached and made a big system of it—the baskets of bread, the three Pitakas, etc. You can read it all in the encyclopedia. It's a big system and it was not that way at all. All Buddha taught was just what I am teaching today—and this is a junction of consciousness with the Infinite. He called it Nirvana; I call it Unarius. Jesus called it finding the Kingdom and the Father Within. It's a Principle in which we express consciousness, in which we are joined with Spirit or that we are joined into the Higher Consciousness—joined with the Infinite in a timeless and spaceless world where we can actually see life—not as an emotionalism that is lived from one moment to the next and biased from the past but which is something constructive and is biased from the future and is very scientific.

When Dr. P. Quimby taught Mary Baker Eddy back in Boston a hundred or so years ago, he taught her all of this but she did not understand it and so she made a system out of it; and today there are many thousands of Christian Scientists that have made a big pacifier out of it. They have blinded themselves to the reality of life. They go around and they say, "God didn't make the door because the door is material; God didn't do this and he didn't do that. It is a different world. The material world is separate from God because it is an evil world." Well, how ridiculous can one get? If they were wise, they could see that it is the very nature of the diametrically opposed opposites as it is put on the sine wave in which man becomes intelligent. He cannot become intelligent any other way. He has to have the two complete opposites for comparisons before he can develop the mentality within himself. And that will distinguish him from the other animals, the birds, the beasts, the plants and flowers on the face of the earth, because theirs is strictly an instinctive or a reactionary way in which they live their little life.

The little bird eats worms or seeds or of whatever his diet consists and he goes through the mating season and builds the nests or whatever it is the birds do, but he is not concerned a bit with anything else in his life. But human beings are a little different; their mentality is a little more prehensile. They can reach out and can bring a few things together which are not actually relative to their own immediate environment, yet if we look at the thing scientifically, here is a great connection through harmonic principles. We say the multiples of two plus two or the subtractions of two plus one, the harmonic structures of the cello string that vibrates at 100 cycles and generates harmonics up to 10 or 12 thousand cycles or down the other way. And it is the same with everything that we do; it is a system of harmonics involved.

When you go out into the world and you see people, you go to the market. And why do you go to the market? Well, because here is a direct continuity when you went out into the jungle with your bow and arrow and you shot something to eat; but the direct continuity exists. It only means that in evolution you have developed, we will say—and using the word "developed" rather loosely—to the point where now you go to the supermarket and pay forty prices for something which you used to go out and shoot down with your bow and arrow or used to pick from the tree. Now we question what evolution is, whether it is intelligent or whether it isn't intelligent. It is only intelligent to the degree that we can realize that there is an infinite number of ways by which we can manifest and out of that consciousness comes a development of conscious knowledge to the degree the possibility of life in a higher world, lived under principles that are very different than they are on this earth; and if they are different principles, then we are not subjective to the things which make life on this earth possible or impossible.

Everyone who is born on this world is immediately sentenced to death. He has the unalterable proposition that in a few years plus or minus, anywhere up to 70 or 80 plus or minus, he has to die; he is sentenced to die. He cannot escape that death. But if you are in a higher world, you do not have that sentence of death hanging over your head all the time because your intellect enables you to live constantly and continuously without time and space because you're integrating at least a part of the consciousness of the Infinite. I hope you can understand now what the proposition is for a Higher Being, at least to manifest himself as a polarity into this world. If I were to add or subtract one bit from this physical body in what I say would be miracles, then I have subtracted from the purpose of my being here. That may take a bit of going around with in your own minds but we have Principle involved here. The moment I have subtracted from Principle, I have subtracted from the effectiveness of whatever it is that I have set up here for myself and the same is true for you people too, in a way. And the further you go into your evolution and the higher worlds into which you

376

go, the more dominant these Principles are going to become, the more you are going to have to rely on the polarization of the Higher Consciousness, because the Higher Consciousness is, in itself, a facsimile of Infinity in which you have polarized with self as a part of your consciousness. How have you done this? Well, it's moments of inspiration, it's recognition of deistic forces, it's recognition of creative forces or creative forces within your own life, whatever it is that is constructive or positive on your cycle of life that has helped to polarize your higher self. But as yet, it has not become the dominant polarity.

That dominant polarity will come about and you will know that it is there when you have reached that state in your evolution when you can live without the body and do it very intelligently and comprehensively. Then you will know you have arrived at least, we will say, to the second point in your evolution. That will be your second point in your evolution. Now what your third point will be, I shall not try to tell you anything about because it is even difficult for you to understand the second step. This is your first step—the evolution of your physical consciousness. Your second step is the evolution of the mental consciousness and so on, etc.

Now are there questions? There are always questions! S - Well, I guess I had great misunderstandings. T - That again is why I have stressed so very emphatically that you have to somehow or other tear yourself away from the physical consciousness. This is your own problem, how you do this; but if you do not do it, you are going to be like all the other materialists—you will keep going backwards in your evolution. As I said before, I am not going to be emotional with you about the situation. I will not cry if you do not make it nor will I laugh if you do; because I have a complete sense of fulfillment which is not possible to speak in words when I see that you have gone forwards in your evolution, because I can see creation in an unemotional way; and we have to be that way before we can see. Now, do not pick me up and say that I am some kind of a heartless beast, that I am not capable of compassionate understanding, because that is far from the truth. The realization of life or death for a physical person or whether he is filled with suffering, to me means something very different than it does to you. It means something much greater and in a sense of the word, I suffer with it much more than you would. Now, that may sound strange, doesn't it? But the proof is already there that I have come back on several occasions and have died for people just to prove to them that there is possibility of life lived on higher planes without these emotional repercussions. But I do not want to go down on the record as saying or being some sort of a beast that is incapable of appreciating these things in a compassionate form of understanding, because that is far from the truth. But I would not attune myself into them negatively—not for all the world, because I could not help people by doing that. If I would become emotional with them to the degree that other people become emotional with them, I would be of no benefit to them.

I would not go to a funeral on a bet because I do not believe in funerals. It is only a way in which emotionalism is expressed to the past; it is Principle in action here. If they want to celebrate for the person who has gone on into the future, well, that is a little different because that is a graduation for him and the further he goes along the pathway of life, the more he should be celebrated for making these emancipations.

Yes, we must all face these propositions of life but if

I saw any of you suffering from a very severe accident or some such, I would not become emotional about it at all to the degree that the average person might to someone they loved very dearly, because here with everything that I know there is only one proposition that is important to me and that is the good that will come out of it. I am going to see everything that is positive on that cycle. I am going to see how you are connected with that accident or whatever it is in your past. I am going to see all of the other positive things, how I can help, etc., but I won't become emotional with that particular thing so I won't suffer the pain in the sense of the word that some persons may stand there and wring their hands and actually add to the misery of that person. I am going to realize that even if that person dies right there on the street in that accident that he is not really dying; he is only going into another phase of his evolution. I am going to see all of these positive things in which they are part of that particular experience and which eventually if that person proceeds on his pathway of evolution he can get the same evaluations out of it that I have. In that way we have turned the evil into good. We have put it back onto the positive plane. Although it may have been or seemed evil down here on the lower side of the sine wave, I am going to remain right up here on the top side of the sine wave and see everything good that will come from it.

How is that done? Because I can look back into that person's life and I can see similarities in his past that have brought about this act; it is part of his learning. He has to learn them as I learned them and the same as you people are learning them. It is the only way we can develop. Instead of creating man from mud and making him into a material or emotional creature, why didn't God do a real good job of it and make him a perfect being from the beginning, if we can look at it in the Garden of Eden way? It would be very unintelligent. If He did, there would be no purpose. It would not serve His purpose at all, would it? To make a race of Super Beings, He'd only be making an image of Himself—and He did, in a sense of the word, but this is a fourth-dimensional equation because in every person there goes everything that there is in infinity. It is the proposition of every person to discover that for himself and he cannot do that if he is just a materialist or a zombie in a materialistic world where he is going through all the forms of motions as material people express themselves.

So when you go out in the world if you like to for the time being to more or less protect yourself from these things, as I say, walk positively and passively. In that way you are carrying the big stick in the sense of the word that in your mind you can look at these things passively or introspectively and you can look at them more or less separated from them in an objective way. There is a dimension between you and them; as Rod Serling says on the television, it's the Twilight Zone for them but you are not in this dimension. That is the dream world out there and you keep yourself insulated or isolated from them because you don't tune yourself into them directly. You have a certain harmonic relationship with them just like all of the things of the Higher Self which come through me have a harmonic relationship with my mind and through that they can speak the words or project the energies or whatever else is necessary to make this possible, this evolution of consciousness.

So we will not make a system out of it because people are prone to making systems out of everything.

They get into a little groove or a rut; they go round, back and forth with it because that's an opinion or a system or whatever it is with them. But if they are intelligent people, there is always apparent the whole proposition of the Infinite, how all of these things are added to Infinite Consciousness as they expand on these plus positive and minus consonants as beat frequencies in all of these energy motions which are around us and which they all are.

The clerk that waits on you in the supermarket is just merely expressing a lot of beat frequencies; the man that pumps the gas in your car, that's only beat frequencies, or the man that built the automobile that you drive down the street and here are the sum and total of a lot of other beat frequencies that make it possible for you to express a certain motion in a time-space world. Yes, I know there are a lot of people in this world that might call me an anarchist or a lot of other things or very bad names but that does not bother me one bit. It does not disturb me in the slightest because I have been called all kinds of things in the past and it has not disturbed me. And there is no reason to believe that it would here or in the future because I know why they are calling me these names. I have a proper mental perspective. Even if they come to me and they burn me at the stake or crucify me like they did in the past, I still have a proper perspective. He said when He hung on the cross, "I forgive them, they know not what they do." Well, what else was there to do? He maintained consciousness through the physical body and any time He added to or subtracted from that as they mocked Him saying, "Where are your angels to rescue you?" but if He had called upon those angels to come to His aid, He would have deviated from the true purpose and principle—principle in His own mind and His own development and His own evolution —and I am speaking of the Higher Self. He knew it was up to the individual, of every one who was there in the crowd and taunted Him. He knew, just as I know now today, that is a part of their future. They are going to have to learn the very same thing or else retrogress because evolution is that way and we can't be emotional with it. We have to view it as a constructive principle.

Emotionalism is only a substitute for intelligence and a very poor substitute at that. It is only something that helps to sustain man in a primitive world—it is his emotional reflexes. It is very unintelligent because through the emotionalism he instigates wars and he kills himself and he fornicates and rants and rages up and down the lands 24 hours a day on all fronts, just as he is doing today. He has made a great cesspool out of this world and the further he goes along in these things, the worse it becomes because it is all out of balance.

Well, I think the bell has rung to bring this little session to a close but what we have gone into has been more or less of an informal discussion. I have not attempted to put things down into a format where we would compete with the elocutionists of the world but we have tried to present certain facts to you. Now, I do not advocate immediately any of you trying to abandon the emotionalisms of your life. Do not do that. Don't abandon anything in your life that you have now. It is very important to you as it is. Do not abandon it until you have this energy concept and when you do get it, you can go out there in the world and you can see the world as I see it, through the Higher Self, then you can abandon it or rather, the dissolution of the world consciousness comes about naturally and automatically.

You do not have to do anything about it. It becomes a higher way of life. You evolve from one state of consciousness to the other but it is a lot less painful than is childbirth or something like that. It takes a long period of time; it would take you a million years but do not be concerned about the passing of time because here again we have cycles.

The cycles mean nothing in the eye of the Infinite. It's what goes on here and how we tune ourselves into it. The Infinite is not emotionally concerned with that because either in one form or another you are still part of It. But if you want to develop to a personal position in your own evolution where you can become a part of the Infinite, as you begin to express Infinity in a positive way, that is evolution; that is something you have to determine for yourself. Like the advertisement they put out for the Ford Company. There was a dog standing there beside it and someone asked the dog if he thought everyone should be a dog and the dog said, "Well, that is something that everyone has to decide for himself". Well, this is the same proposition.

Really, people are not what they think they are at all. You can say scientifically that people are a conglomeration of wave forms of beat frequencies, oscillations in the psychic anatomy and to the people of the world they are very precious to themselves. They have tremendous egos. They are all inflated with all of their own little circumferences, their little citadel of life. But it is nothing; it is but a twinkle in the eye of time. We say as they used to quote, "It's but a wart on the posterior anatomy of time". But it is even less than that! So now again, what is all the sum and total of all of these things? Where are we going to evolve to? What kind of a consciousness do we come into? We know one thing, that when we come into any kind of a consciousness we won't have an ego the way that you do now because there will be no necessity for it.

The principle of life in a higher world is merely like I tune into the past with some of you students or like the radio or television tunes into the station. How does the station function and manifest itself on the screen? Exactly the same way. There is a big sine wave which they call the base tone radio frequency, a million cycles per second or whatever the need may be—or a million megacycles per second. Here lies two synchronization pulses, one at 60 cycles per second to synchronize the horizontal and the other beat frequency of 17,000 per second which synchronizes the vertical. Then there is sound and there is picture. Now your life is the same principle. You have the same frequency or all the positive values of your past and all the negative; you are in tune with them instantaneously at all times. It is a part of you. It is what you are, the sine waves, just the same as the sine waves in the television. In time and space you are projecting through Infinity just that way, in frequencies which are your base plane rate. It is your position on the earth world at the time.

Down here on the lower or negative side, we will say, that is all the sicknesses, the accidents, the mean things you were in the past. They are the little beat frequencies which are oscillating down here. Up on the positive side here are all of the good things you have expressed, your inspirations, your resolutions to do better, your good deeds and all these other things which were inspired to you, we will say, from Infinity or from the higher sources or from the people upstairs. That is a great deal better than going around here blind saying, "Gee whiz, I love everybody and everybody loves me and I express nothing but love", etc., etc. That is being blind. We must be realistic. Surely; you love one another but you have to realize what love is; love is an understanding of people; it is not an emotionalism. It is a complete understanding, for when you understand yourself you understand other people. If you understand yourself, you have to begin to put it in ways and manners in which it actually exists, because there is nothing else in Infinity except energy. If you are going to understand Infinity, then you are going to have to understand it for what it is—energy. The walls of this room, what is that? It is only energy being held in a time and space element. Time has been separated from it and yet, as far as the radio waves are concerned, they can pass right through the wall like it wasn't there because they are a different frequency than are the walls or the atoms in the building.

And these are the things which we must conceive if we are to maintain a progressive evolution. Until a later time, so be it.

CHAPTER XLIV

Mechanics And Dynamics Of Life

You ask something about the basic principle of life. I shall explain: now we are going to draw the cycle (of life) here and in our hypotheses we have established in our minds that anywhere else except as far as the third dimension is concerned that everything is a cycle; that is, we can draw a circle and see everything complete in itself as far as any idea or form of consciousness is concerned, because in any other dimension we don't have this thing they call time and space because time then becomes an additive part of that particular thing. In other words, we can make an "x" anywhere on a cycle as a point of reference and from there we can say that that is negative and our "x" up above the line will be positive and from anywhere that we have an oscillating condition with this cycle as it goes around, it completes itself in a cycular form either from negative to positive or from positive to negative. Any point on that cycle, it is complete in its own consciousness. That is the dynamic principle it always has to oscillate, because in the oscillation or carrying the idea or the form of consciousness, it is completing what it is. Now if we draw a line through that cycle as far as the fourth dimension is concerned and we bring that top or upper part down below the line, then we have the same cycle but we have subtracted time from it. In other words, we have time as expressing itself into another dimension in two ways; here we have time and space. The idea or form of consciousness is always carried from positive to negative or vice versa, which we call oscillation. Oscillation is what some people confuse as the word vibration. Now if we remember that dynamic principle either in the third dimension but primarily in the fourth dimension, because this third dimension is merely a place which reflects, so to speak; it is merely a way in which something else or the true cause is expressing itself in countless other dimensions from somewhere else. So the third dimension is always secondary. Now we will draw another big circle and we will call this you or me, or any individual you wish. This is the life cycle and we will put the "x" here from birth. That is negative because he starts from there. We could say at 30 or 33, if we are going for the time of years as three score and ten, we can say that 33 is his positive—or his greatest part of his life is in his early thirties. And from there on, he starts to deteriorate because as far as his physical expression is concerned, all of the things in which this cycle is, carries only the idiom of his past experiences with which he has related himself to this dimension through time and space. In other words, thousands of past lifetimes are always oscillating with this life cycle as far as his own concepts are concerned, so far as he is indoctrinated with, and this is linked up with them. We could say there are any number of these cycles large, small and greater sized—and these cycles go on down, and down and down. These are all past lives. As far as the future is concerned, we have the same situation here, because it is Infinite up top. These cycles are all touching; they are all linked in a certain way through what we call frequency relationship—the same principle we use for tuning a television set or a radio, because when they oscillate they do so on a certain basic frequency. The basic frequency is their own particular consciousness or what they are expressing. So the individual is linked either into the future or into the past continuously at all times.

Now the process of evolution or reincarnation merely means that the individual is traveling through his cycular pattern or path which is, in itself, a huge cycle which goes round and round—and he is traveling around until he begins to express and contact other cycles which are larger and larger in nature. But for the time being, we are saying that he is traveling into the future very, very slowly, simply because the preponderance of associations is reflected from the subconscious or the negative side of life down into the pattern in which he has previously lived before because those frequencies are closer to him. But at the same time, he has a leveling agent or a stabilizing agent or a progressive agent, which means that he has also partially, so far as the superconsciousness, the positive side of his nature is concerned, he is oscillating into the future—or into the Infinite. So therefore he is linked on up, shall we say for convenience, into the infinite cosmogony where Infinity lives in a much greater affluence or abundance than It does in this third dimension.

Now, if a person understands these mechanics that are involved in this particular process, so what happens? If he is oscillating in a predominant sense with the subconscious that means that going back through his lives we can hypothesize that he has at any time been a murderer or he has been a thief or committed acts of extreme aggression or violence, etc., etc., because he has lived a thousand or so lifetimes. He may have been a warrior, he may have done this or he may have done that and the other—and it is quite likely that he has. But in one form or another, those past violent expressions of life are all very actively oscillating in cycular fashion as far as the subconscious is concerned.

Now we go over here at another place and we see an individual and he is committing an act of murder. Well, if you look at that man and conceive him negatively and you say he is doing evil and you are overwhelmed by the sense that this man is doing a very violent act, you are oscillating from the subconscious and you are automatically, through frequency relationship, going back through the past into your own situations where you have either done these same things before or that you have witnessed them or they have been in some way or another very active in your own past lifetimes. In this way, they are again just as destructive as they ever were before. It means that all of this past has again been carried into the consciousness at the present time and therefore you have become just as destructive as the other individual.

Now if you were conscious and you possessed the knowledge of these dynamics of life, then you begin oscillating in a preponderant sense or in a positive sense much more to the upper planes of relationship into the future than you do into the lower. The lower are now becoming subjective or subversive to the extent that you are conscious of the mechanics that are automatically going to link you up to the higher oscillations into the future in a way in which you say you are oscillating or vibrating with the Infinite, indirectly through these various cycular movements and in which we find these things subdivided as far as frequency relationships are concerned, and which as frequency carries its own idiom, its own idea because the Infinite is Infinite and it expresses Itself infinitely in all directions and in all things; and that is why It is Infinite.

Now, supposedly, we are witnessing this act of murder but if we were consciously linked up with our mechanical knowledge, with our hypotheses, with our wisdom which we know of by evaluating these things constructively, then we are oscillating from this sense. We can say now we see that energy is either stemming upwardly from the past or it is stemming downward from the future. If it is constructive energy it stems downward from the future because we are assuming that your pathway, your evolution is, in a general sense, constructive or going up into a spiritual world. But if it is down below or from the past, then it is destructive so it depends upon wherever you are drawing your water from your well of life. It is either from the subconscious or the past life, or whether you are drawing it from the future or what we call the inspirational side of your nature which is linked directly to the Infinite— which some people call God. So if we witness this act of murder, if we are in a state where we are oscillating from the subconscious, we have done two things. We have automatically attuned ourselves unto him and this act of murder so far as this man is concerned, and we also are oscillating with him and not only tuning into our own past subversive elements, we have also linked ourselves to him and all his past by looking at that thing negatively and judging it evilly. But if we look at it positively and are connected with our knowledge of this concept, we have insulated ourselves because we have erected a barrier, we have changed our own frequency to the point where nothing that he does can reflect into our consciousness in a negative way.

And the second great thing that we must remember —that instead of absorbing energy like we would say that earth absorbs rain or a sponge absorbs water, we are reflecting energy to him of a positive nature which he will be able to use and which will help to reconstruct him in the future. That is the difference, because coming up through past ages when man was a very elemental creature, well he still is for that matter—but we are looking backwards into the very primitive forms of life as we see them expressed by man on the earth today, and that man always learns from the beginning of time to start to rationalize the unseen or mystical forces that moved around him. He could not understand the cycular movements or cycular forms because he was not advanced in his evolution to that point, so he did the only thing that he could do—he compared them with his own nature with the only thing that he could visualize as happening with him within his own mind or consciousness. Therefore, he began to subdivide all of these things into personalities which he called evil spirits or ogres and he gave them two classifications—either one was good or the other evil. He did not stop to think for one moment that in order to become a God or a force which was invisible in the physical sense, that he was beginning to divide this Absolute which is the infinite sum and total of all things that the Christian calls God but that he also did another very bad thing and that is he became very conscious, predominantly more so, with the subversive negative than he did with the conscious or the higher. So there were many bad things that he did when he began to divide the absolute into subtractions of evil forces or spirits and gods or demons, etc.

Well, the Christian is no better off than the pagan because he has subdivided the absolute, the Infinite into several categories, such as Satan and Christ and so on and so forth. He has made the same mistake as the pagan has; he hasn't really progressed very far in his evolution—no more so than any of the rest of them have because he still does not have the mechanics and the dynamics of life. These things are all, in themselves, the transpositions of energy forms, energy wave forms, because the Infinite is the sum and total of that energy substance which even the scientist knows nothing about. The scientist is limited in this way. He is limited by the space-time factor. He has established within his own mind 186,210 miles per second as the absolute and so long as he adheres to the concept of time, he could never visualize anything in the future where time does not exist even though we had men like Einstein come along and point out that in the absolute or abstract there was no such thing as time. Time became an integral element of form and substance within itself—or within everything else. The only way one can understand that is to establish the cycular concept within our minds as part of the Absolute.

Now by drawing consciousness here from upstairs we are oscillating to this man positive energy. If we are connected in consciousness and get our energies from the past, or the subconscious, then he is oscillating to us negatively. When he oscillates to us negatively, we are going on down into the lower reaches of our subconscious nature and linking ourselves up with all the subversive elements that have happened to us in the past. Also, we have linked ourselves through frequency relationship and attunement to all the subversive things which have been in his past. So therefore evil has a double nature or double meaning as far as a condition of that kind is concerned. When we have attuned ourselves with the Infinite and the positive nature of ourselves then, as I say, we are oscillating to him positively and in that sense of the word he has also, shall we say, at that particular moment started to oscillate by these oscillations with his higher self. So that ringing situation (we call it ringing in electronics) means that all these cycles that are connected to his higher nature will now be stimulated to this point where certain alignments begin to take place. So far as time is concerned he has been immediately constructively started on his pathway into higher dimensions of consciousness to the point where he can no longer commit murder or do anything of this particular nature because we have given him something that he did not have before by reflecting that consciousness or positiveness to him.

And that is the principle that Jesus called turning the other cheek and something that has never been understood by the Christian or by the layman—or anyone else as far as that goes—for until you understand these dynamics, you'll never understand how these things can be concluded or arrived at.

When our sister there who just wrote gets this, she will cease to struggle in this turmoil and this pit of clay in which she has enmeshed herself for so many thousands of years; and the same thing is very true with all other people. You and I are no exception either because our struggle here to some degree has been of the same nature and the same self, because even coming into these worlds or even knowing of these things means that to some degree we have compromised ourselves, for being able to live in a physical world means that you have to assume some form of compromise with these things, otherwise, you could not live in your body. You would get to the point where, well for instance, Yogananda, when he left his body, his body lived for over three weeks without decomposition. That meant that his body, as far as the atomic structures are concerned, had begun to vibrate in such a high plane of relationship with his own Superconscious that they were not subjective to the bacterial action or decomposition as are commonly accepted forms of atomic structures. We say common flesh would deteriorate in a few hours time when left at room temperature simply because the atoms were vibrating with incompatible frequency to germ life which had established itself in that definite relationship and continuity.

Whenever we have a reaction, we don't have a reaction chemically or otherwise unless it can take place within the very auric nature of the atomic substances themselves. In other words, it is an infusion or a connection as far as the relationships with the very vibrating frequencies of the atoms themselves. Either atomically and subdivided molecularly, it is the same thing. We have to have frequency relationship before we have any kind of a reaction or a reactive process taking place. It cannot exist otherwise. And it is all done through frequency relationship or attunement, which is the same principle of oscillating which is used in television or radio transmission or any other particular type of communication systems which are based primarily on frequency relationship.

So that should, in a very short digest, explain the complete dynamics of life.

CHAPTER XLV

Science Of The Atom

Regarding the atoms themselves and the field of force in which they revolve as it is internally concerned with the structure of the atom, we shall say that the atom itself can be considered similar in principle to looking down from the large end of the telescope. We find that objectivism is compressible as a factor of ratio in proportion to the idea that as we extend on downwardly all proportions can be assumed to be negative in respect to the one with which we are immediately concerned, in the present, as to looking into the future, as we will say, looking downward through the large end of the telescope. Therefore, proportions are negative as we extend on downwardly and they recede or that they grow smaller in direct proportion.

The same is true when we look through the small end of the scope and we expand outwardly because there we are going outwardly in time and space and therefore our position is negative, always in proportion to that which is immediately in front of us as we are expanding outwardly. The same condition is true when we carry a hypothesis into vortexal construction as we picture a spiral in which there are a large number of related cycles which are revolving or moving or expressing themselves in this vortex.

Now we have to picture these cycular patterns in this vortex as something like the cogs on two gears which are meshed together and whether we are concerned with the fourth dimension or whether we are concerned directly with the atomic structure itself, cycular patterns as they are expressed in the infinite construction of the atom are exactly similar to that as they are expressed in the vortexes. In other words, we find the various positive and negative particles as they are moving around the nucleus is supposedly the positive particles. These cycular patterns are always linked together much in the manner and form in which gears are meshed in a watch or a piece of machinery; that is, we can always assume that the magnetic field or the negatively or positively charged particle of the atom is always extending its field of force—or a radial extension of force. This can be called magnetic in nature but which is an expressive wave form and as such, it can only link with another wave form on the basis of frequency relationships, which means that it locks or interlocks according to the negative and positive cycles of the wave itself. That is the reason we get this supposedly theoretical grouping of various atoms which the scientist has set up to represent each one of the various elements in the scale of his atomic weights.

While that may or may not be a close approach as to what an atom actually looks like, it serves the scientist up to a certain purpose because it fits a certain technical aspect of his work and he is able to group or regroup atoms in respect to molecular patterns in such a way as to form various different plastics, synthetic materials, etc., which he has done, as well as to synthesize drugs and dyes, etc. To a certain extent that works out rather reasonably well, however, the atom, as I have said before, has been underrated from the standpoint that all of these elements are transforming in nature, as far as the atom is concerned, whether it is in chemical synthesis or whether it is a reagent as concerned with some reactive component when it is expressed in relationship to tissue in the human body, as a medicine or as a drug. And these things always follow definite patterns of electrical transferences or they can be considered as magnetic linkages between the atomic structures themselves in relation and proportion to whatever resistive element which they meet in their path.

That is one reason, too, why the atom is very difficult to split so far as the scientist is concerned; he must construct a betatron or something which can accelerate a certain stream of negatively charged electrons in such a way that he bombards a certain atom until sooner or later he believes that the atom flies apart. It merely means that we have there an aggravated condition where the magnetic fields of the atomic particles themselves are disrupted to the point where they have no interlocking value with each other and which also proves our hypotheses here in this particular case. But it must always be remembered that the atom is, in itself, always expressing an exact counterpart in an infinitesimally small space or form, as we might call it sub-infinity, with all the component cycular patterns of the vortex which are actually responsible for its creation; in other words, as it has been pointed out, the atom is the cone or the apex of the center part of the vortex. However, it has only been brought down into that form because now it represents an exact negative counterpart of the entire vortex which brought it into existence; that is, negative in its relationship and that all component parts of that atom are being expressed in some negative relationship with the vortex, even though they themselves are expressing cycular patterns as energy components within themselves in either positive or negative relationships simply because of the pulses which are contained in the aura or the magnetic field which each particle is radiating. They lock and interlock just as do the gears in a piece of machinery or a watch but that the locking is even a much firmer or stronger process than that because they are also concerned with pressures, we might call them, of magnetic emanations from the vortex which has actually created that atom.

In other words, the vortex is constantly pushing in upon the atom with a very terrifically strong magnetic force. If, for instance, we will draw two cycles as interlocking and we see that they are expressing from the negative to the positive in a cycular pattern their exact frequency as a wave form, they can be said to be traveling around the periphery or the rim of a cycle. Now if we bring the other cycle up to it, and in order for the second cycle to lock or to mesh its particular wave which is expressed in the periphery or the rim of the cycle, it must mesh or interlock with the other one, otherwise it would have no affinity whatsoever. That can be termed, in a sense of the word, as frequency relationship within the various negative and positive charges of the atom itself. That is actually what holds the atom together—that and combined with the fact, as I say, we have a pressure—pressure which is from within the vortex itself, because it can be assumed that any atom is the center of the vortex and therefore the pressure around it as far as magnetic structures are concerned are, in themselves, very strong and very pronounced to the degree that it would actually mean a transference or a breakup of energy from one dimension to another to transfer that atom or to break up that atom and actually means the breaking up of an interdimensional pattern.

In other words, we can assume or picture that an atom, in a crude sense of the word, is something like a man who goes down into the ocean at a very great depth in a diving bell and when he gets down several hundred feet in this circular sphere of steel, the pressure of the water around him is terrific. The atom, in a sense, is in very much the same position except that now instead of the diving bell, the atom becomes the diving bell and the water around it is the vortex which has created it. The more charges which are contained in the atom means that the greater the pressure which is manifest upon it from the vortex around it because the vortex then will have, in relationship, a much larger pattern or a different amount of cycular patterns which are contained within it, because each of these cycular patterns in themselves are expressing an I.Q. or an intelligence which makes the atom that which it is when it is expressed into this dimension.

To put it in a different way, we can assume that an atom is, in a crude sense of the word, just a bit of energy which is extruded through the center of the vortex into this third dimension, much the same as we would say that the sausage is being pushed through a grinder, through the tiny holes at the front of it. That is a very crude allegory, but it is very much that way. We must realize the intense pressures, as far as magnetic structures are concerned, which cause the various frequency relationships to properly mesh and to actually hold the atom together. For in frequency relationships we find not only a very strong affinity so far as positive and negative are concerned with magnetic structures but they themselves have that intelligence for cohesive relationship due to the fact that there is a much higher degree of intelligence which is expressed in the vortexal patterns which have created them.

Now, it might be more easily understood for the scientist if we bring these things into another perspective, for as it was written the gem of truth must be turned in many different ways so that the various facets will shine so we may appreciate its full beauty. So we shall turn this gem of truth around and we are going to put it on the basis of interdimensional relationships. We will say that we bring it in terms of the EMF which is, of course, the source. In any condition where there is an EMF, there is an expressive quantity of energy in any given direction. That is a crude definition of an EMF. In other words, an electrical motivating force is the EMF. If we go up into some higher dimension, we will say, calling this force the Infinite, that it has a libido or a drive; and if it is going to be expressive from infinity into everything finite it must possess a certain libido or a certain drive, and that drive is expressed in regular sequences of harmonic relationships which we call dimensions, as these dimensions are constantly being regenerated from above much the same as we would be looking down through the large end of the telescope. The libido or drive, the EMF, whatever you prefer to call it, comes down from, we will say, forces which are staggering in proportions which could not possibly be even faintly envisioned by the human mind and that they are expressing into infinity because in infinity we find all things finite, so that even the atom becomes an expression of that EMF or that libido.

The pressure there—that which we have termed as pressure—can be said to be the will to manifest into another finite form or substance. That is, the atom itself and each atom portrays its own particular atomic weight, yet the scientist knows that every atom on his scale has isotopes or atoms which have the same negatively and positively charged particles within their structure but which possess a different atomic weight. This will, of course, explain to him exactly why that situation exists because there we have in the vortexal pattern a different relationship to the Infinite, which makes the atom of a different weight in proportion to its own particular specified gravitational field or in any other way in which the scientist cares to measure the weight or the density of the atom.

We have to use the Infinite as a common denominator; we have to establish the Infinite as the absolute and it must become the denominator, such as the zero in our scale of mathematics or any other particular configuration. We must establish the absolute and learn to pivot our introspection from the absolute wherever we are concerned in respect to the atoms themselves. They are merely expressive quotients of intelligence as compared to the absolute when we are dividing them into finite forms down into sub-infinity. Any atom possesses an equivalent of so-called atomic weight on the scale according to its linkage through the vortexal patterns of structures on into the Infinite in direct ratio or proportion as to how they express their certain quantity of EMF.

It is common fallacy with these functions in understanding; for instance, many people believe that a battery contains an electrical charge but it does not. Even the scientist perhaps does not know exactly how the sudden and instantaneous charge of electricity can come from out the poles of the battery when circuit is established. It simply means this: when we get down into the molecular and atomic structures, as far as the electrolytic of the battery is concerned—which is a caustic acid—it means that we are interrupting with the molecules or the atoms of the electrolytic, a certain sequence or flow from positive to negative, as they are concerned with the atomic structures of two different types of lead oxide which are pasted in the grid of the positive-negative plates of the battery.

It is simply an electrical process, not a chemical

process as most scientists believe but oddly enough, the charge is not in the battery. When we charge the battery, it merely means that we are substituting in a crude sense of the word, a DC current or a polarity to the battery which tends to separate the three active components as they have been reactive against each other and so reconstitutes the magnetic auras or the fields of force around the various atoms. When we establish continuity between the two poles, it means that we give electrolytic, as far as their atomic structures are concerned, free play to engage in the act of discharging the magnetic auras of the atoms themselves as they are concerned with the two different types of lead paste. That is a rather crude thumbnail description of what actually takes place in the battery but so far as the battery is concerned, either in the charge or the discharging of the battery, we have added nothing nor have we taken anything away. It is something which the scientist is fouled up with and he does not know where the power comes from which is within the atom. He thinks it is contained within the atom but it is not. It always comes from the EMF which is contained within the vortex which has created the original atom and which is linked and relinked to harmonic or frequency relationships with an infinite number of vortexal patterns throughout the invisible infinite universe.

Fortunately for the scientist and for the others concerned with these various processes, whether it is exploding an atom bomb or a thermonuclear bomb, there are certain natural barriers which, we shall say, stops a chain reaction which could extend on and destroy the Infinite Intelligence. These barriers are contained in the vortexal patterns themselves. It is simply an inverse equivalent of the law of inverse proportions, that is, where we are expressing a downward flow—as that which takes place in an atom bomb—of energy into a lower dimension. It can be expressed only so far, as far as the relationship upstairs, so to speak, is concerned simply because it has no place to go. It is ever-increasing in its negative intensity and until it can assume a cycular pattern and return into a positive condition, it has to quit.

In other words, when we keep this concept in our mind of looking from the big end of the telescope down or that of looking from the small end up, we have so far as the third dimension is concerned with all atomic structures, two very natural barriers as far as any interplay of energy is concerned from any given point within the telescope tube which is—as we shall theoretically assume—an atomic bomb. So, if the power which explodes in the atomic bomb travels upward, it meets the natural barrier which is the resistive element of its own self, because sooner or later it is going to balance itself out so that the equilibrium between the vortexal EMF which is coming into the atom naturally cancels out any EMF which comes from the lower dimensions.

Or, putting it differently, the force of the power as it is generated from some changed atoms contained in the bomb is going to meet a certain restriction of power which comes from above—the EMF which comes from another dimension. It is going to find a balance in that we will call it the netherlands and the dimensions immediately above it, which are sometimes referred to as the astral worlds. One force tends to counteract the other. The same is true when we go into the other direction in our telescope tube and we are looking downward into sub-infinity. There we find that it will cancel itself out simply because it is traveling in a negative dimension and unless an EMF is always supported by a positive force which is in frequency relationship to the negative force below it, it again meets contradiction and cancellation takes place.

The scientists were very fearful for a long time before they exploded the first atom bomb that there might be a great chain reaction. There were two schools of thought. Some thought for it and others thought against this possibility; they thought that by exploding atoms it would start a chain reaction which would explode every atom as far as the earth was concerned, including all of the oxygen and it would cause the earth to disintegrate into nothing. And so you can see, as we have explained so far as the atom bomb is concerned, that it represented a positive proportion of EMF or expressive energy as far as the earth or the atomic substances of the earth are concerned. That was the same thing as the power of the atom bomb was, looking from the large end of the telescope down. The earth represented an increasingly negative proportion or relationship which was not supported by the proper frequency relationship as far as the power or EMF of the atom bomb was concerned simply because it was an explosive force.

The same is true with the hydrogen bomb. Naturally, the atoms of the earth could not come into a chain reactive condition with that atomic or thermonuclear explosion simply because of that very obvious fact. And the same was true in reverse when going into the astral worlds because there we find that we had to have the same condition in reverse—the same as looking up from the small end of the tube into the large end of the tube—that we had to have the similar relationships so far as frequency relationships were concerned, on up into infinity through the vortexal

404

patterns. That condition was nonexistent and so the atom bomb could not run wild into the upward dimensional relationships; only into the netherlands between the physical world, the material worlds and the so-called astral planes which are immediately linked to it and which actually contain the whole of the vortex or the EMF of the vortexal pattern itself, so that the atom, as far as it was concerned in the explosion, was merely liberating its quantity of energy from the vortex which had created it or of which it was the center part of that particular vortex. The pressure which held the atom together was liberated in the third dimension.

CHAPTER XLVI

New Age Psychiatry

Talk to Monrovia Group 1956—I am almost always overwhelmed at the feeling of coming before a group of people and separating any one of the different topics or facets to talk about. From the standpoint of a clairvoyant, and I believe there are some here who are clairvoyant and can appreciate what I am saying, that the enormity, the vastness of the Infinite Universe is beyond the concept and the realm of conception in our own third-dimensional minds.

So tonight for practical purpose, I am going to use more or less a topic which I believe will be one of universal interest with every one of you here this evening and is called the "New Age Psychiatry". In order to best present this topic to you, it might be also necessary to give you a little background. Now we all know and can trace the course of our own history since 1945—suddenly Western minds and Western nations were precipitated headlong into a new age.

Man himself is comparatively inflexible in his thinking. This new age came suddenly and we were unprepared. To what is sometimes referred to as the profane world or to those who are traditionally steeped in the reactionary processes of thinking, the new age meant tremendous repercussions in the mental processes of our everyday lives. Man suddenly found himself confronted with problems, with questions, with fears for which he did not have the answers. Medicine, psychiatry, various other agencies which are devoted to the upliftment and to the development of mental and physical health and well-being of humanity and especially to our great nation of America, tried to step in and tried to fill the breach.

Since that time there has been great acceleration into the realm of physical science. We have today something like over forty different isotopes which have been brought into use in the science of radionics as they are used in the laboratories and hospitals of the present day. We have had many other new and wonderful developments along the lines of antibiotic drugs and which have helped to relieve some of the physical pressures or diseases which are, incidentally, byproducts of this new age. And yet with all of this, statistics forced us into a conclusion that we are in a very grave situation. There is no use of backing around this and playing Pollyanna or saying, "Let John do it", but we must face these issues squarely.

To we who are dedicated in the realms of what is called the expression and the freeing, the service and the liberation of mankind, whether this is done spiritually, psychokinetically or whether it is done in any other way, we as individuals represent the collective masses of humanity. Each human is in himself at least one strand of the moral fiber of the nation so that we bear some small measure of responsibility for the health and well-being of our fellow man. Medicine and psychiatry today do not possess the answers to the ills which are besetting mankind at the present time. The old fundamentalisms of the past orthodoxy in whatever form or shape or expression in which it is expressed upon the earth today does not have the answers.

These fundamentalisms were largely composed and dedicated to the service of mankind for some era or some epoch and while the truth contained in the precepts and the confines of these various orthodoxies or fundamentalisms are in themselves inviolate and not subject to change, yet it is always that mankind must change in his attitudes of discernment. Today it is very evident that there are certain missing elements in the translation of science, of medicine and into our various aspects of religious interpretations, and statistics will prove this fact. To we who are acquainted with the types of propaganda which daily come through our various means of communication, we are reminded that: one out of four die of cancer; to contribute to the heart fund; multiple sclerosis, dystrophy, cerebral palsy, all of these so-called incurable diseases; children with diabetes of only a few weeks old; ten percent of the school children suffering with either duodenal or peptic ulcers; many of these other conditions which fifty or seventy-five years ago were unknown and unheard of. Oh, it is true they had smallpox, they had bubonic plagues they had scarlet fever, they had many other killers and which have been stamped out by different methods of science and sanitation and other ways and means which have been devised to eradicate these killers but civilization in itself has given rise to new problems.

And yet with all of these different incurable or so-called incurable conditions for which medicine and psychiatry has no answer, we can also say that the number one health problem of this nation today is not in the realm of physical physiognomy or the translation of man's ills into his physical nature but it is a mental problem, a mental health condition. Doctors, scientists, educators, all who have their pulse on the beating heart throb of this nation are concerned with this mental health problem. It is generally also conceded by foremost thinkers and exponents in the studies of these various statistics that by and large at least ninety percent of people who find themselves in either physical or mental conditions or aberrations have contracted these conditions strictly in the way and in the intensities of these highly civilized and refined times.

We could quote statistics on the mental problem until sunrise but a brief statement of a few facts might acquaint you or that you already know, at least five or six hundred thousand people tonight are occupying beds in hospitals and the asylums in the country with incurable mental aberrations. They are incarcerated with what might be properly called conditions of ignorance; nothing more or less than pure and simple ignorance simply because the psychiatrist and the modern man of medicine has not yet devised ways and means of interjecting the simple philosophy of Jesus into his practices. In spite of the great amount of work which has been done, the huge piles of streamlined stone which they call hospitals and clinics are masterpieces of art and architecture, the vast array of instrumentation which goes on in the physical dimension and realm staggers the imagination. And yet, not one of them knows or can deal with the human being as he should be dealt with—as a spiritual being and the atoms of his body are spiritual in nature and are supported from a spiritual dimension.

So as this struggle goes on, the scientists and the doctors seeking the answer to these incurable conditions within the physical body are obviously not going to find them there because they are not there. What he calls an incurable condition and whatever it is, is simply the result which started somewhere further up the line beyond the physical body. There will be in the future considerable and a much larger amount of these factors entering into our present-day psychiatry or the psychiatry of the future. If nowhere else in this world that these missing elements could be taken from, we could get them from the New Testament; we could get them other ways and places and through the channels of clairvoyance. Fundamentalism or orthodoxy do not include in their modern interpretations any of these facts or facets which deal primarily with the actual constructive evaluation of man's spiritual physiognomy.

A psychiatrist can attach electrodes to a person's head, give him shock treatments, either insulin or through the electric needle, but he does not know that he is shocking out an obsessing entity. The entity may or may not leave permanently because the entity suffers the pain because he has obsessed the mind of the patient. The witch doctor in the jungle puts on a mask and rattles around his legs and jumps around the patient hoping to do the same thing—scare out the obsessing entity. The difference is, of course, that the witch doctor knows that he is trying to scare out the entity and the psychiatrist doesn't.

We have recently in psychiatry developed, and it has come into being since the death of Freud and other exponents of the pure physical psychiatry, a branch of this interpretation which is known as psychosomatics. It has been found and we have had several other modern interpretations, scientology or dianetics; the basis of this context or this philosophy is based primarily on the integration of certain factors which deal with mind energies as they reside in the so-called subconscious mind of the individual which were incurred during childhood. The fact of the matter is that the psychiatrist is taking it for granted that the child is strictly a creature of spontaneous regeneration. He considers the child newly entered into the world without any spiritual background or without anything else at all, apparently.

We are simply, according to psychiatry, products of sex or products of whatever other reactionary phase

410

of our everyday life that man has seen fit to interpret into that. And so science is going to have to revise its position; it is going to have to consider first (and I am speaking for fundamentalism and orthodoxy too) that we have lived not only this life but many other lives before. We may have lived hundreds or we may have lived thousands of lives and that basically, and wisely, most of these psychosomatic illnesses which beset man today in whatever position of life he now occupies, quite possibly and likely were incurred within the past two or three thousand years and he has come here to work them out under similar conditions in which they were incurred. You have often heard it said that the murderer returns to the scene of the crime—and so we do. We return to the scenes of the crimes many times. Inadvertently, experience has a way in which it has created a vibration which is the sum and total of energy in transition so that we link ourselves in the various factors of interpretation as movements or monuments of energy so that we are linked and counter-linked with the harmonic structures of all these past lives.

So how is this done? Psychiatry must know that man possesses what is called a psychic body or a psychic structure, a spiritual counterpart. You and I know and have heard through various channels of occultism, whether it is Leadbeater, Blavatsky or whoever writes on these things about the chakras, centers of energy, whether they relate to the hypothalmus, whether they are the kundalini at the base of the spine. Where did these energies come from and how are they transposed into the physical body?

We must first begin in our minds with something which might be called an abstract hypothesis whereby we can see the Infinite in motion; and we will start off in an abstract way with a huge vortex of energy. This

411

great whirling universe of energy which is pictured in your minds something like a whirlpool is whirling and counter-whirling. There are great tremendous forces in this whirlpool because it represents a large portion or segment or degree the intellect of what is called the Infinite Intelligence, for the Infinite is not personal. The Infinite Intelligence is the sum and total of all the integrated concepts, abstract, material or otherwise which are in the universe and in the world about us today. And so we look into this great vortex and we see energies multiplying, regenerating, changing form, weaving back and forth into different wave forms, into different intelligences. The light which lights these lights around the house and which turns the motor in your vacuum sweeper is a 60-cycle alternating current which we call a sine wave. It is simply an up and down elongated 'S' motion, ⌁ positive to negative or negative to positive. Positive is merely the supposition of polarity.

If we visualize energy traveling in any other dimensional concept in whatever dimension they are so interpreting their various intelligences that they, too, must assume wave forms or wave shapes because energy has that unchangeable and indomitable characteristic that it must always exist as energy and so that it portrays in itself, because of the wave forms and the wave shapes, its own particular intelligence. In this great vortex which we might call the Central Vortex, we will see forces which we might call centripetal and centrifugal forces. Actually, they are the generic action of frequencies beating upon each other and heterodyning on down into the central core of this great vortex and forming a hard core nucleus, and this is comparatively dense to what all the outside energies are so that it counter-radiates into the dimensions below it in similar divisions of vortexes—and so on and so forth, ad infinitum.

Getting down into the material or the terrestrial dimensions in the world and in which we are so far removed from this great high Central Vortex, we see about us energies residing in what might be called two forms, two polarities—static and dynamic or kinetic. The walls of this room, just as the atoms in your body, are all energy—no difference. It is merely energy in what we might say a static form; it is energy suspended in time and space. But it is energy; it obeys the same immutable laws which are inviolate and which were conceived of and which are part of the Infinite Intelligence. Infinite Intelligence (called God by some) actually in a pure abstract way, does not have laws because It is in Itself multiplying and showing these various laws unto mankind. So when we begin to understand what energy is and the transposition of energy or into whatever form or relationship with mankind, we can get the solution, we can get the answer to all of our questions because that is where our answers are.

The psychic body is like a huge central vortex composed of innumerable tiny vortexes. You can call them psychic atoms if you wish. Within each of those tiny vortexes of energy reside an innumerable and a multitude of tiny little wave forms of energy which are pulsating and throbbing at the speed of light, 186,000 miles per second, if you would like to picture it that way—but they are pulsating and radiating. All of those little wave forms or wave shapes have in themselves, certain little distortions, certain tiny steps, little gyrations and these, in turn, portray in their own code their own way and manner or mathematics a certain experience which happened to the person because that little vortex was created out of that experience and reflected back into your psychic self. And it makes no difference what that experience is.

If you think a thought and you discard that thought and continue the train of thought as it progresses through the reactionary mind, it is merely a linkage and a relinkage and an extraction of all the sum and total of your past experiences. You do not think at all. To think constructively on a higher dimension in which is said to be purely creative is utterly impossible with this objective mind. You are merely linking and relinking yourself back into that subconscious or that psychic self daily, hourly and by the minute, with all the sum and total of all the experiences which you are, whether of this lifetime or any one of the hundreds or of the multitudes of lives that you have lived before.

If you suffer cancer or that you were stabbed by a spearman riding on a horse, if you were destroyed by fire at the stake or whatever experience you had in a previous life, they live in your psychic body today until you have ways and means of canceling them out by recognizing that condition. In the television and the radio we have a rectifier coupled with condensers and a choke which gives us instead of the pulsating or the alternating current, a rectified DC current which can attract electrons to it when it is superimposed upon the plate elements of the vacuum tube. This process of rectification merely means an inverted condition of the alternating current wave forms.

So rectification must take place within these vortexes in the psychic body, otherwise we relive and we relive this same experience time and again until we learn the way and the means of cancelling it out. If you died of cancer way back there when, you are quite likely to die of something very similar and undetermined in the present life. If your husband did so and so to you way back there, he is quite likely to do so and so to you here in this lifetime and so whatever it is or whatever the condition, you will find the answer in your psychic self. Now there is a definite therapy, a psychotherapy which happens and which takes place when certain Conscious forces are set in motion. I say 'Conscious' forces because the personal Savior as was interpreted and taught by Jesus, which was the sum and total of most of his preachings, was the conclusion of the Christ 'Consciousness'.

Jesus did not separate man (or Christ—and I like to call Him that because He did express a higher closeness to his Christ Self than the eartheans are even close to approaching) but that was the basis of His whole theology. His whole philosophy was based upon that one cardinal virtue, that we in ourselves were linked to this great Infinite Force, this all-permeating God Force, this Central Vortex or the innumerable vortexes, the sum and total of all the astral worlds and the causal worlds and the Celestial Kingdoms of Swedenborg. So whatever it is, they are linked up to those things through our Superconsciousness which is our Christ.

We could portray it a little more factually to you this way. We will create for you a great cycle or vortex which you can call your own life cycle, as God created it for you, because God is Infinite, so to become Infinite He must become finite in all things. His ultimate achievement in creating a finite element is mankind. In all other things God has become Infinite by the mere virtue of being finite into whatever you can conceive. In the abstract, we will say that Infinite Intelligence created for each and every one of us as individuals (and long before we ever knew that tenure of the earth life as physical beings) our life cycle wherein It placed within that cycle in an electronic wave form of tiny convolutions and vortexes of energy the exact portrayal of It's own nature. And so it became, after the creation of this life cycle, the thing of man himself as he resided in the supreme intelligence of that life cycle to come down and to evolve through the countless dimensions of the terrestrial and astral worlds to gain the value of the infinite experience.

It is a pity today that through the channels of orthodoxy, man has so confused this great realm of interpretation into one great big fat guilt complex. He teaches in the church, the little children in Sunday School that the children are born in sin and that God created only Christ, which was His Divine Self. So what does that make the rest of us? We must be illegitimate products from some other kind of a thing of which we know nothing about. Getting right down to it—and as Jesus explained it—that He and His Father were one and the same, so that each and every one of us are also and none of us are any more or less important in the sight of God than He Himself was. And that was His message. If it works for one, it works for all of us, otherwise we are completely defeated before we start. There would be no beginning nor an ending to our philosophy. We would have no grounds to stand upon.

The reading of the Akashic is an Egyptian word meaning secret and merely means that whoever it is that is doing the reading has that unlimited concept in his mind that these things exist and that he can look back and actually see just exactly what it was that occurred in the person's life that caused that indisposition. Whatever the condition was, when it is brought into the conscious realization of the subject at hand, does certain things. It links him immediately because it lifts temporarily the focus of self into some other dimension and unto some other time where these things took place, rather than the immediate or the objective present. And so that in the actual disintegration of the continuity of his present lifetime, the Superconsciousness reacts and so the vortex is cancelled and made neutral. The patient then goes out into the world; he has been freed; he has been liberated. He suffers no more. And not only that but lots of other things happen to him. He will find that in that moment of voluntary or involuntary connection with the Superconscious Mind that the whole world has been changed around him. He has literally been precipitated into a projectory through space and time into another dimension of relativity. Values around him change, the people change, his interpretations of life change. He will never be the same. He has done more for himself in those few brief moments of interpretation and integration with the Superconsciousness than could have been gained by his own will and volition through his incarnations for thousands of years.

Now it is obvious, as the old saying goes, that an ounce of prevention is worth a pound of cure. If we have five or six hundred thousand people incarcerated in mental institutions suffering from advanced conditions, whether they are paranoid, schizophrenia or dementia praecox or whatever else you might want to call them, the obvious thing would have been to give them a little corrective therapy before that thing started. As it resides with them at the present time, they are so inflicted with demons or obsessions, or whatever you want to call them, malefactors from the astral world, the problem is one which is very difficult to solve and requires a great deal of concentration and a great deal of application of the higher principles of psychotherapy.

If you remember the revelation of the story Jesus gave when he cast the devils from the man at the cemetery and they entered into the swine and cast themselves into the sea, yet psychiatry has neglected that little important translation of the Scriptures.

And orthodoxy overlooks those things, too, although we do have in Catholicism a sort of an advanced or secretive form of exorcism where the priest can go someplace and cast out earthly thought-form bodies which have been pestering people for maybe hundreds of years in some old haunted house. But the whole thing isn't carried into a practical realm or a dimension where it can be used to relieve hundreds of thousands of people who are suffering from the most abject obsessions. And it can be prevented so easily if the person or a child, for instance, was schooled in the ways and the means of knowing the continuity and the purpose of life and how he or she was so constructed into these various spiritual realms in which they do actually reside most of their time. It is quite probable too that there we might have a greater integration of these higher forces of man's nature to prevent a large amount of this physical degradation that he goes through, this malformation.

And so to sum this all up to focus something of an objective relationship with our own particular problems as to whatever the basis or the means of evaluation whereby we could use these factors in our everyday life in the integration of our own selves, it doesn't mean just in the coming days or the hours in which you will pass the remainder of your life in some terrestrial planet as you now find yourself.

There may be some among you here tonight who are the leaders, the teachers, the well-doers of mankind in that future Aquarian Age. Who are you people? Have you asked yourselves? Have you looked into the mirror of the spiritual nature of yourself and asked that question, "Will I be able to reach out my hand in a thousand years from now and do something of what Jesus did two thousand years ago? And where am I going to start?" So, friends, I rest my case.

CHAPTER XLVII

Progressive Thinking

To any student who begins the study of Unarius, the keystone in the arch of understanding this way of life will be the new or positive way to think. This new way of thinking is quite different from the old way which has been used through the thousands of years and many lifetimes, and therefore, it is extremely difficult to describe such a process unless the student becomes somewhat familiar with energy and the structure and function of the psychic anatomy as described in the second lesson course.

If you will think for a moment, you will easily see that it would be most difficult for you to describe this mental process to your neighbor, especially without the knowledge which is contained in the lesson course. The difficulty is increased a hundredfold if you were to attempt to describe thinking in an entirely new and different way. That is my problem. Actually, there is no short cut. It requires constant study and familiarization with the mental processes which are described in the lessons. It also requires a constant alertness in every thought and action, always being aware or trying to analyze if this thought or action comes from the subconscious or from the higher portions of the psychic anatomy.

If you had suffered some psychic shock in this lifetime, the shock would have created some malformation in the subconscious. There would also be a memory facsimile in the mental conscious. Now the Superconscious represents Infinity. In other words, it is in tune with an infinite number of dimensions; therefore

420

this shock facsimile in the mental conscious would be, through the Superconscious, in tune with a large number of different forms of this same experience and as many different ways it could re-happen to you. And if you continued on into your many future lifetimes thinking from your subconscious, you could actually encounter this old experience in many different ways, always as a negative happening because of the fact that the various biases or controlling influences would be harmonically reshaped to form basic material used in reconstructing the new subconscious, which is done at the beginning of each new earth life.

Briefly then, to prevent this constant repetitious karmic happening, the mental conscious, through its attunement to the Superconscious, must always be held in a positive bias. That is, behind all thought and action there must be a positive knowing, a positive awareness, a realization that through the Superconsciousness good will flow into your life and manifest itself. In this manner, you are keeping your mental conscious positively attuned to that polarized portion of the Superconscious which represents and is your spiritual selfhood living in the higher dimensions. In keeping this positive attunement with it, you automatially give it the power of guidance, selection, etc.

Therefore, you can see that knowledge of this function is most important and that there is still a great deal of work, practice and usage which must be done through the coming years and lifetimes before it becomes your dominant personality. When it is more completely developed as the real you, then you will no longer incarnate into the earth.

One word of caution: do not substitute new lamps for old. Remember that this Superconscious represents Infinity. Any attempt which you will make subconsciously, from time to time, to control by some rote, ritual, system or configuration will only slow down and defeat the acquisition of this new way of thinking and your new life.

Of course, while you are on the earth, you will, to some extent, have to render unto Caesar the things which are his, simply because your earth life will demand a certain amount of interplay. However, as memory elements in your daily life, these must always be given a secondary position. Also, it must be constantly borne in mind that they are subject to higher guidance from the Superconscious.

In this way then the subconscious earth life's experiences or events will gradually become more well-ordered. They will seem like they have already happened, which they actually have so far as the higher self is concerned. You will also note that they seem much less important and with less emotion. The feeling of detachment from the earth life will also grow and be replaced with a warm feeling of kinship with the higher worlds and the way in which these Advanced People are helping you on a practical basis to overcome the old lower earth life.

Therefore, continue to study the function of the psychic anatomy, the principles of energy which make all things possible, for energy in any form or dimension and shaped in any kind of a wave form is the actual thought process of the Infinite Intelligence. They carry the messages; they do the actual constructing and the tearing down through the process of harmonic regeneration and even most important is the obvious fact—your future life in the higher realms will be lived entirely in this new way of thought which is described in Unarius.

One more way which might be helpful to you: visualize yourself traveling rapidly into Infinity. You are always facing an infinite number of experiences. You automatically select certain experiences as you travel on the basis that they are harmonically attuned to past experiences. When this is done, as in the case of most earth people, there is the usual karmic sequence because the new experience, combined with the old, only reshapes it into a somewhat different form as it appears in the surface earth life.

The psychic anatomy is in various ways, as I have described, always oscillating or is seeing this Infinite. Every experience so contained in it (the Infinite) can be pictured as a sine wave, that is, the up and down positive and negative. If this sine wave experience comes into the psychic anatomy and reaches the subconscious, then it will be negatively attuned to you and your past and again reappear as a negative experience.

However, if it is stopped, so to speak, and which is done when you attune yourself to the positive side, the effect of this new experience will be entirely different. It will now be friend instead of foe. So you see, it is most important for us to keep positively attuned through our Superconscious to the Infinite and which in turn, becomes automatically selective on the basis of this positive bias and all future experiences cannot be harmonically attuned and reshaped in a negative fashion to your old (former) past.

Remember, the negative end of every experience wave form is harmonically attuned to every other negative wave ending in the Infinite. This means that it is, in a sense, directly linked to the lowest pits of hell and on this basis of frequency relationship, portions of these hellish forms can come directly into your life over this connecting linkage of negative wave forms. Conversely, the positive pole or plus side of every new experience in Infinity is attuned to every other positive polarity in the Infinite.

In this manner then, the highest and most god-like influences can also flow into your life over this harmonically attuned network. That is the "Big Picture" and one which you should carry about with you in your right hand mental pocket and use it in every thought and action to determine whether you are harmonically attuned to the negative pole or side, or to the positive side.

In effect, every wave form carries two complete and opposite pictures of the same thing. One travels around toward the negative or bottom side, as is pictured in the circle of life (second lesson course). The positive picture or pole is harmonically attuned to the ascending portion or cycle of life and constantly regenerates or reappears into higher and more perfect forms. This is the gist of the new way of thinking.

CHAPTER XLVIII

Atomic Science

It has always been the big problem for man to visualize that the atom is connected up from the inside —to say that the whole dimension which comes from the atom comes from the inside of the atom. This might be more easily understood if we can picture the whole Infinite Universe as a globe, and on the surface of this globe we find the appearance of all composite elements which we know as atomic substance that goes to make up the surface of this huge globe of either planets or solar systems—and that they, in turn, are composed of the electrons which are very similar in many instances to the planetary systems. Now, would this not make a more figurative picture in your mind? All of the interior of this great globe would actually be all of the other dimensions which would be stemming outwardly onto the surface.

The scientist or the astrophysicist says the interior of the earth is molten and composed of molten iron and nickel which is a very fallacious interpretation, because the scientist cannot visualize in his mind how energy can come from the interior and make its appearance on the surface any more than a crude savage, listening to a radio, can picture the music coming out of that square box is really coming from a broadcasting station thousands of miles away. What we are endeavoring to bring out is the fact that if the earth were molten in the interior and had a hard crust as he likes to picture it, then it would be completely reversed from the same structure as the sun. That does not bear out in reasoning because there is always the same pattern of exterior constructions and fabrications so far as atomic subdivision is concerned with any particular visible object in the Infinite Cosmos or the galaxy.

Actually, the astronomer has not seen the surface of the sun! Now that may seem odd to say, but it is true. All that he has ever seen is the chromosphere which is the field of energy radiating outwardly into space which is several thousand miles from the surface of the sun. And that is borne out factually, because what he calls sun spots appearing on the surface of the sun are only whirlwind or vortexal patterns in the turbulence of the chromosphere wherein momentarily he can vision some sort of dark spots in the interior of this vortex. This merely means that, for instance, if you were flying over a big bank of clouds in a plane and all of a sudden you came to a little spot where there were no clouds, you looked down and could see the dark surface of the earth. When the astronomer or the space man gets out into space and visualizes the earth, he will see in a thousand or so miles out or even ten thousand miles above the crust of the earth the surface of the earth will disappear, and he will see the chromosphere which will be the magnetic field of force which surrounds the earth, much the same as it is about the sun. Of course, it will be of a much less intensity but still he won't be able to see the surface of the earth any more than he can see the surface of Venus.

The situation is just a little different with Mars, for instance, although to some extent it is quite similar, except there the force fields are not residing in ionized layers to the intensity or the density as they would be around the earth or around the sun. And still he has not seen the surface of Mars any more than he has seen the surface of Venus or the surface of the sun. What he thinks are the various bands around the surface of Mars, and the various light and dark patches (green and brown, etc.) he sees are only relative. He has looked through only a partially transparent ionized field of force. When he can penetrate through that, he will see that the surface of Mars is much different. What it all means so far as the sun, it is the same as with the earth. When we get into the interior of the earth and to that great and terrific mass of molten metal (which they suppose) and that we have at least twenty-two thousand miles of that molten metal, it would give off a tremendous amount of heat. That heat would have to have a point of radiation, otherwise it would build up tremendous pressures and explode. The volcanoes that come to the surface of the earth and shoot off a small amount of lava could not possibly take care of even a small fraction of the caloric output of that big ball of molten mass.

What I am getting at is that the interior of the earth can be pictured thus: in going down into the surface as an increasing density of magnetic fluxes atomic structures begin to diminish so far as their relative position to each other; they expand and become less and less or more gaseous in content as they go on down into the interior of the earth. In other words, it is entirely reversed to what they think it is. It will be found that in the interior of the earth, there are intensely dense magnetic fields of force which are the actual core or the radiating center of the great vortex.

An atom represents a comparatively simple or a complex structure of intense magnetic fields of force; that is, lines of force which meet certain parallaxes. These parallaxes the scientist has called electrons and protons, the relationship to each other in the atom. At that particular parallax where a number of lines of force cross each other and make a junction, we have a seemingly solid particle of energy which isn't solid at all but merely means that we have compressed in a sense of time a much larger amount of energy in a given space at a given moment which, in turn, because it is dynamically balanced, the whole atom revolves in its orbit and which is the pulse of the whole atom itself as it gyrates with the whole vortex which is the radiating part of the exterior of the atom. We find these same conditions whether with the atom, the earth or with the sun; they are basically the same, because the earth, as the atom, is the negative polarity according to the number of parallaxes, the wave forms which the scientists have called electrons, and various other negative equivalents. The surface of the earth is the same way. We find that the atoms on the surface are posed as solid in a dense field of force as negative polarity from the interior which is the positive field of force in its equation and which again assumes the relationship of the negative in respect to the great vortex in the interior.

So this molten interior will have to go down the drain with a great many of the other fairy stories in which they presently believe before they can get very far or before they can understand some of the intangible mysteries of the universe. We will find when we get out thousands of miles from the exterior of the earth that there will be much the same conditions as are true with the sun so far as the force field is concerned. This has already been borne out by the fact of the aurora borealis, where we can actually see the flames which leap up into the heavens from the earth and which are statically charged energy fields of force which are waving back and forth like great sheets of flames above the poles. So far as the human eye is concerned, when we see these things whether from a telescope or whether from any other particular type that we care to view it from, it only means that we are relating the senses to an equation which is only familiar to us in the sense and the terms that it has impounded these various infractions or interdimensional relationships from past lives in various primitive aspects. Therefore, the astronomer or astrophysicist is largely at fault when he tries to equate certain appearances of anything by the impingement of wave forms in the retina of his eye, because as an immediate repercussive effect, this must be correlated in all the past interior, retrograde or erroneous concepts of life that have been incepted since the beginning of his evolution. In other words, in order to gain a true perspective of what he is trying to view, it must be expressed from an entirely different direction before we get polarities, etc. He cannot get it from the past and all that he is seeing today is from the past. In true relationship, it has to be integrated with new concepts. Therefore, he is only looking into his past; he is not looking into the future in any sense of the word, which he must do to overcome his present limited concepts.

CHAPTER XLIX

Leukemia

During the past several years in what is known as the "space age" and "space age exploration", science has learned many wonderful and amazing things about our earth and the so-called space which surrounds it and, with this new knowledge has also come the usual puzzling and unanswered enigmas which are revealed by these new discoveries. One of these new discoveries is in relationship to the astronaut who travels either in space or in his many orbits around the earth where he breathes almost pure oxygen in his capsule, the reason being that a fewer number of bottles and equipment is needed for his supply.

This pure oxygen diet has been found to cause anemia or a depletion of the red blood corpuscles which are believed to have been consumed or eaten by the scavengers of the body—the white blood cells or leucocytes. In this direction then, there is strong evidence which may well confirm the belief by science and medicine that leukemia, or cancer of the blood, may be caused either from a small change in environmental atmosphere or in the case of prematurely born or incubator babies where the infants breathe pure oxygen for a week or so, these babies could develop leukemia even several years later and die. The same conditions would be true with pneumonia patients or any other illness wherein a person breathes pure oxygen over a period of time, and in this respect, many hospitals are now remodeling oxygen equipment.

Leukemia, as you know, is a sudden overproduction of leucocytes which, instead of remaining scavengers and living only on germs and virus, become cannibalistic and begin to devour the red blood corpuscles. In the beginning of this disease, doctors can relieve the symptoms to some extent through blood transfusions, even forestalling for a considerable time the moments of death. However, eventually the victim succumbs, as there is at the present time no known means of stopping the over-abundant production of leucocytes or in changing their nature.

In order to better understand any such situation which involves anemia or the more advanced form of blood disease, leukemia, let us explore the chemistry involved, remembering that chemistry must always be reducible to atoms and their electromagnetic fields. The air you breathe is more than 75 percent nitrogen and 22 percent oxygen, the balance made up from inert gases such as argon. Now with the exception of oxygen, none of these gases are utilized by the body but remain in suspension. Disturbing the normal suspension of nitrogen gives a diver the bends or a cramping paralysis which is fatal if not properly treated in a decompression chamber.

In a human body, and electronically speaking from an atomic standpoint, the nitrogen and other inert gases act either as catalysts or stabilizing elements which aid and abet the normal transmissions of information energy between all other atoms and their respective psychic anatomies which are a part of the whole human psychic anatomy. Now let us take a single leucocyte; he is a shapeless blob of protoplasm, something like Charlie, the amoeba. He can travel swimmingly through the blood or slip easily between different cells. He has no brain but he can receive a telepathic message from any portion of the person's body which has been invaded by germs; and like a homing pigeon, he

431

goes straight to the spot.

There are several different kinds of these leucocytes, all quite similar in most respects but each species has its own particular group of germs which it recognizes and devours on sight. By simply wrapping itself around the bacteria, it pours enzymes upon its victim dissolving it. Leucocytes have a comparatively short life. A child who has had measles will grow up and go through life immune to this disease. Even though there have been thousands of generations of leucocytes, they still pounce upon measle viruses when they see them—a remarkable memory considering they have no brains. All of these known facts about leukemia, leucocytes, etc., are at present a great mystery to science and medicine. They do not know how or where a leucocyte's intelligence comes from or how it passes on its memory factor through countless succeeding generations. They do not know why an imbalanced oxygen factor can cause leukemia; no more would they understand how leukemia could very easily be a karmic condition incurred through some circumstance in a previous lifetime.

The answers to all these facts and the questions they suggest will not be known or the problems solved until science and medicine know about the human psychic anatomy, and for that matter the psychic anatomies of all other things of the material world, including bacteria and viruses. Then and then only will science be able to trace reactions and consequences in these and all other human indispositions by seeing the electronic reactions involved in various atomic combinations and which are, in turn, controlled or biased from their own respective psychic anatomies, all of which go to make up a considerable portion of the human psychic anatomy. And when this truth or concept is firmly established in the future medicine, then conceivably science may find a way to develop certain electronic instrumentation which can change or alter these transmission factors between the psychic anatomy and the physical body. These changes or biases will alter the inharmonious or disease factor or re-establish normal transmission, thereby eliminating the disease. This type of therapy would be effective not only with leukemia but any and all other diseases, mental conditions, etc., to which humanity is now subjected, as well as any and all future diseases or conditions which might arise in the concourse of human evolution.

It should be mentioned that this type of therapy is in daily use in almost countless numbers of other planets throughout the galaxies and universes, a fact which again glaringly depicts the rather elemental position of the planet earth and its inhabitants. Leukemia and all other diseases and conditions can therefore be re-solved in a simple concept which is: an inharmonious transmission between the psychic anatomy and the physical body, and this inharmonious condition is always the result of some small or large portion of the psychic anatomy being either diseased or malformed in some previous life through shocks or that said psychic anatomy is inharmonious with external physical conditions or a combination of both. In all cases, however, an analysis must be made which includes the psychic anatomy and until this is properly done, science and medicine will never arrive at the true source of any disease, or for that matter, will never understand life and the why and wherefore of all things and even creation itself.

In itself, knowledge is inseparable and indivisible; it cannot be dimensionally divided, for to conclude any hypothesis or analysis based on singular dimensional characteristics will defeat the acquisition of knowledge, for knowledge must be understood as Infinity which includes all things undivided and interdimensionally related; for this is indeed Infinite Intelligence.

CHAPTER L

The Jungle Law, Survival Of The Fittest, Still The Driving Force In Man

There is, as of today, a generally acknowledged legal concept that ignorance of the law is not a legitimate excuse which can be used by any person who has committed some transgression against moral and legal codes of his community; and to those who have and are being daily tried for various crimes which they claim were innocently perpetrated, there is a feeling of frustration and injustice when sentence is passed upon them.

In more general spiritual classifications, it must also be borne in mind that here again ignorance of various moral and spiritual values, codes or ethics does not necessarily relieve any person from the commission of an overt act, and can generally be presumed to have certain deleterious consequences in the progressive evolution of the person who so commits overt acts, or in the general commission of such daily expressions as can be considered negative or destructive in nature. For here this person is being tried and judged in a different court, one which is completely impersonal in its relationship to him and which functions solely in a manner of delicate equilibriums and balances which can be considered esoterical in nature and not immediately apparent to any person at any given time.

A crime, therefore, as it is posed negatively or destructively must be assumed as a motion or intent which is contradictory to a pure forward dynamic motion in which the normal impedances of daily life reactions can be realized and that this contradictory motion therefore, so far as this individual is concerned, upsets his own equated position in the various balances and equilibriums which sustain him through his evolutionary progress.

There is also no justifiable excuse that this person may be so inclinated at the time of commission that he assumes a constructive position even if his position is political, religious or any other customary channels of human relationship; and should he assume some self-styled evangelical position, he is much more dangerous than the foulest murderer who slinks about in the jungles of our great cities. For in his extruded sense of proportions so reflecting contrary motions in normal evolutionary values, this person can become a Genghis Khan or a Hitler; or he can assume a host of various other different dispensations including priesthood in a temple.

No attempt is being made at this time to go into various differences which may be considered psychic or psychological in nature. It can be assumed briefly for purposes of introspection that such extrusions, small or large, can and always do have as their creative and motivating power the various insecurities inherited in various earth lives and in which every individual lives largely by the primitive law, survival of the fittest.

Yes, even in our highest echelons of our modern civilizations, we find this same jungle law functioning as the subversive dominant driving force in everyone's life and which is only being partially temporized by various codes of ethics. To any person who has reached a certain threshold of consciousness whereby he begins to realize that certain factors and elements in his life must be more properly evaluated and understood, he must view his past not as a compelling influence in shaping his future but rather, a platform of

introspection whereby he is viewing a more constructive future evolution.

In his analysis, this person may also be confronted
by other obvious facts; he may be suffering from one or
many of the various illnesses and derelictions in his
daily life. He may even be overwhelmingly impressed
with the extreme urgency for some corrective action
and which he has not found in various therapeutic
institutions.

This will be a point of great psychic stress and in
the moment of these various stresses, his past may be
superabundantly imposed in consciousness as com-
bining all known and unknown elements of evil. This,
too, is a point of great and delicate equilibrium and
one in which almost everyone makes the same inevitable mistake. They attempt to justify themselves in
various ways; they didn't know any better or that living
conditions mandated certain evils, etc; and always
these excuses seemed to relieve the seriousness of his
various offenses, so he has accomplished nothing in
this moment of psychic stress but rather, hardened
and crystallized criminal propensities which make it
possible for even greater violation.

He may even further temporize himself in various
religious beliefs, confessionals, etc., not realizing the
destructive maliciousness of these practices intended
only to enslave any believers. Yet somehow or another,
inevitably every person will reach a more ultimate
threshold where no personal excuses or vindication,
religious panaceas or other moral dodges can be used
by the individual to circumvent an inevitable conclusion that he, and he alone, is responsible for his past
and present.

This particular point is also a position of great
psychic stress, even greater than many of the other

almost countless times he has approached this threshold. This is biblically depicted as the point of repentance, and in ecclesiastical dispensations, he has been falsely taught that he will be saved; and in the weakness of this moment, he succumbs to the apparent escape. Again he has entered into that dimension of personal perspectus which must always be inevitably included: that the present and past are a personal responsibility; it cannot be justified on various grounds of ignorance, pressurizations, etc. Neither can it be relieved or expiated by some supposed deity when this person has entered into this final stage of repentance and analysis and he may ask, "How then can the psychic pressures of the past, as sin, be relieved? How can I remove the moral stigma of their commission and how can I insure for myself a better and more progressive future?"

The answers here are comparatively simple. First, a sustained consciousness that all personal acts—either physical or mental—all forms of consciousness reside as participating elements and values in the great Infinity which is all-inclusive and all-encompassing. When this fact is discovered, it can be immediately correctly assumed that each individual should be selective in these various values, that such selections should always be constructive. They should be made without pressurization from various physical or material values. This selective process is not necessarily a function of the conscious mind, but this conscious mind becomes only an adjutant to selection; nor can the selective process be likened to the housewife who is buying groceries in a supermarket. Correct selection comes about when a proper and true evaluation of function is attained, a true science, not as a metaphorical value as posed in some religion or philosophy.

Learning of the Infinite becomes a process of spiritual insemination, a millennium of gestation lived in the untold lives within the womb of time. Neither can any spiritual birthday be presupposed by the individual when he becomes completely emancipated from the process of selection, learning proper usage as oscillating repercussive and reproductive elements in Infinite expression.

The moment of repentance is always at hand. Simple in principle, it resolves upon one mental element: admission of personal responsibility in the scale of human evolution. Yet, as each man knows he can live the moment of the present, procrastination becomes an odious thief which steals away his future life. So with the blessing of repentance comes the light of dedication, and following this bright beacon of purpose, we achieve the upward way. We have become selective and always do we turn a fresh and hopeful face to the future, our eyes and cheeks always brightened by the rising sun of countless new days born from out the experiences we have selected from the Infinite. This we have done knowing of the Infinite, knowing its function and of all ultimate purposes which are best served in our personal evolution.

CHAPTER LI

A Talk To Group Of Santa Barbara Students On Philosophy And Science — 1960

Greetings, Friends: As you look about you in your everyday world, there is much that seems to cause you great concern. There are rumors of wars and strife and there is great unrest among the peoples of the world. There is hunger and destitution, and disease seems to be the heritage common to all men; and you may have wondered much of these things and of others, too, spoken by men presumably wiser than you, yourself. Yet where is the message of their words? These things and many others they have promised: the peace, the tranquility, the ability to live as we see within the dominion of our own expressed thoughts and actions; what is the answer when we of the material worlds must leave the flesh and journey into spirit? Yes, although much has been written, there has been much more promised; but where can you or any other go with assuredness with all these things which have been spoken and promised? Will they ultimately be fulfill-ed? Indeed, there is not such proof, for if such proof was existent, then surely much of the turmoil and the strife in men's minds would cease to exist.

Much of this restlessness, this seeking for some panacea for man's ills has been bred, brought about and fostered by the insecurities of the material world, by the lack of strength of purpose and proof in the promises of those we have set up as leaders of our destiny. Nor does history presuppose in our search among the archives of the past that any man has found the fulfillment or the attainment of this promise save those who have come with a special purpose and message and have left with the assuredness of that which they possessed. But for the masses, the many who find their way of life among the many material things of this world, from the fields, the factories and from all walks of life, assuredly theirs is neither the knowledge nor the wisdom which would enable them to completely put aside the differences, the insecurities and the many other things which are tantamount to their existence.

Suggestive indeed is other destruction in the ways of men, for have they not even harnessed the power of the Infinite Heaven itself as a destructive means to attain supremacy over another nation? And perhaps in this they have defiled their existence. They have flung a challenge into the very teeth of the Infinite Creative Force and what hope and purpose will they achieve by all this? What is there to be gained to prove physical or material supremacy over one's neighbor? Indeed, there is none; there is no supremacy to be gained in the Heavens beyond the earth, for all things are equal in the sight of the Infinite Creator and no man is superior to another save by the way in which he expresses unison with the Infinite.

If you were to begin at this moment to seriously ask yourself this question: "Can I depend upon spiritual leadership which I have had in the past; can I depend upon their promises, their elucidations as to what my future destiny may be; are these things presuppositions, am I to be assured by positive proof because there is supposedly documentary evidence that exists in such ecclesiastical works as the Bible and many other historical or anthropological writings which are currently available?" Indeed, these things exist solely by virtue of the faith which is exercised in

441

them. Save that which can be extracted as historical content philosophically speaking, there is much to be gained in a system of comparative values which can be gleaned not only from these existing archives but from other different dimensions and areas of introspection which are not currently known to existing man.

The planet earth has swung more or less unchallenged in its orbit for hundreds of millions of years as one tiny mote of dust in a great vast and intangible space called the galaxy which, in turn, becomes only one more mote of dust in a much greater and even more vast universe. Yet even that, too, is but one more mote in the eye of the Infinite Creator. Among the countless hundreds of billions of suns and planetary systems, many of which are inhabited by different forms of life, some of these planets too support an existence quite similar to that which man finds on this planet. Science has already begun to recognize the existence of planetary systems which could well support life in the dimension in which he currently finds himself so situated. In fact, he is at the present maintaining vast scientific equipment and scientists for the express purpose of listening to remote signals from the far-off solar systems. Through means of giant radio telescopes, these electronic ears are constantly alerted for the least sign of something which would betoken an intelligent signal cast off by some electronic apparatus manipulated by the fingers of another man in a far-off solar system.

Yet, what does the man of today hope to achieve? What is the constant, never-ending, restless search which he finds in his heart and mind to expand his consciousness into these nether reaches of space? Is this something which has been born out of the imaginary images in his idle moments? Indeed not, for all men of this time and race, save but small minorities, have lived many lives before the one which they are presently occupying. They have lived many lives in between these lives, lived them in spiritual worlds and in spiritual planets which are more highly developed than the planet earth. All of these things and many more too have been added to the memory consciousness of these people, people who have begun in some mysterious subconscious or esoterical way to sense a great cyclic movement or change. Perhaps it is the whispering of Infinity within their own hearts; perhaps it is other things which have come from these past lives and from the spiritual worlds in which they lived.

These and many other things are motivating thought and action in your present day, for man is seeking not only the riddle of space which is about him but seeking the very riddle of life itself and his existence as a living object. While man has solved many things, yet he has not solved the riddle of his life, at least not by those who are so presently occupied among you at this time.

There are those who have come from these other worlds and who have walked among you and in their own way, they have left you with a subtle message. Very few indeed are those who have had the effrontery to brave the reaction of the material worlds to bring something which was beyond the realm or the dimension of your understanding. And even as they have so lived and given their message, they have died for their cause, yet in dying they have gone on and they have again vindicated that principle which they have expounded among the less fortunate inhabitants of the terrestrial planets.

The scheme and destiny of life itself is vast and of almost incomprehensible dimensions. It is not fitting at any time or with any human to try to encompass within the present tense or moment the full and staggering import of all this life itself. Even those who are still traveling in the throes of materialism and who are not so confronted or confounded with the perpetual and immortal enigma have much yet to learn and understand. To you and others like you who are seeking the answer to this riddle beyond the dimension of your own material world, there is much more indeed that you can learn, much more than you can understand. But before all this can happen, before one single iota of wisdom can be added to you, before one single life-changing action can happen within that which you call yourself, you must indeed gain a comprehensive perspective of this vast and infinite proportion of creation.

And how is this done, may you ask? By constant search and application, by realizing the full and unlimited potentials of knowledge and wisdom which are at your disposal, by refusing to accept those dogmatic lines of demarcation which have been laid down for you by those who were supposedly superior to you in their delineation of knowledge, for only the earnest seeker—one who is willing to put aside the dogma, the creed and the restrictions of the material world—can hope to achieve the destiny of immortality. Should he not do so, then indeed he will revolve in a cyclic pattern, returning time and again to this or a similar planet until he begins to feel the infiltration of sublime wisdom which will somehow trickle into the subconscious reaches of his psychic anatomy. Then he will begin his quest; he will begin his search. He will become anxious that there is this and much more to be gained; and as he asks, so he will receive and each thing will add unto another seven times seven, even unto seventy times seven. Thus he begins to grow and he realizes within the precincts of his own consciousness the unlimited and vast storehouse of wisdom. He begins to find the Kingdom of Heaven within. He realizes that in consciousness within himself in attaining the rapport with this Infinite that there are no insoluble enigmas, no incurable disease, there are no unattainable positions provided a true functioning purpose with the Infinite is constantly striven for.

Yes, there is indeed much that can be added and as we add, so does our consciousness expand; and in expanding, we begin to function much more infinitely. Our dimension of introspection is much wider; our horizons are not clouded with the misty fog of materialism. We begin to feel somewhere within ourselves that we, too, have some imagery or some effigy of this divine substance, this great creative image which is the stars, the moon, the suns, the planets, yes, the very atoms in our body. And how have all these things come about? How are they so maintained? Why are there seemingly inflexible cyclic patterns of the planets, stars, solar systems, galaxies and universes? What is the impenetrable mystery of time itself? These are the answers we seek and in finding them, we will have found the riddle of life, not of this world but of the great invisible worlds which make this world possible.

*   *   *   *   *

Now, we will turn the meeting over to the scientists. My worthy colleague, Manu, has given you some philosophical content as to the purpose of achievement, what achievement is, what we must strive for in our realizations, what we will attain when we begin to fathom this riddle of life. This message, this solution begins here on this earth. It begins on this or some other similar terrestrial planet just as it has done for countless millions of years for races of men, for species of plant and animal life which have inhabited these various worlds. But you cannot hope to understand these things until you first obtain basic elemental functioning principles of creation, for this is a scientific dimension.

We will first begin to destroy the illusion of mass. The world as you see it about you at this moment is 'seemingly' solid. Not so! You can read, and this can be proven to you in a thousand different ways that mass is an illusion. Every schoolboy before he graduates knows about the atoms; he knows they are tiny solar systems of energy. He knows that the spaces in an atom are comparatively as vast as those which you find in your solar system. The walls of this room, your bodies, all which you call mass is not really solid at all. You have only grown accustomed to this illusion through the countless ages of time and from the very beginnings of your embryonic life cell. You have become in direct proportion to your concept, your development in your particular environment, a creature so specifically ordained to live in a reactive environment. We will say reactive because animals, as they so present themselves to you in your surface world, are composite reactionary systems of energy.

In other words, by simply posing a direct equilibrium of positive and negative fields of force which surround each atom and which are a part of each atom, atoms can so react or superficially combine within themselves. That, in short, is a composite evaluation of your material world. You react to the things around you simply because reaction, as it is so com-

446

posed and differentiated by the five senses, constitutes a certain balance formation of equilibrium. Sight, sound, taste, smell or touch can all be quickly reduced to simple formulas of reactive constituents. You are intercepting energy waves which are reflected or which are directly manifest in some reactionary form into one or more of the chain-like reactive continuities which comprise your physical anatomy and which, in turn, comprise a specific integrated element with another body which you have and of which you possibly did not know or of which you are not aware.

At this moment, while we are trying to destroy the illusion of mass, we must replace this concept with the functional and integrated concept of creation as it stems and manifests itself from the true source of all things. This is not of your third-dimensional terrestrial world; this is the Creative or the Infinite Intelligence. You ask, what is this Infinite? You may picture it as a vast and infinitely vast composite resurgent sea of living, breathing, pulsating energy. If you look more closely, you will see that there are many subdivisions. It assumes many forms. Characteristically in these forms you will see there are vast centrifugal motions. These are like the familiar whirlwind which you have seen occasionally in the desert regions of the earth except that they are very complex in their structure. Within the interior of these vast centrifugal motions, we find great forces at work. In regular well-ordered pulsating movements, they are expressing in lines of force; we shall call them, certain clear and well-defined exchanges of polarities. And in the exchange of these polarities, there is a definite idiom of intelligence so carried. Some of these energies are impelled into the centrifugal force or by the centrifugal motion which we shall call centripetal. Centrifugal, as you know, is the outward manipulation of force which throws objects from off the periphery of the revolving object.

Now, as we proceed down further into this great vortex, we will see that there is a constant and more continuous concentration of energies which also increases in direct proportion to a certain ratio of negative polarity to those which are supercharged in other dimensional relationships above them. Ultimately these will end, so to speak, in a concentrated ball of energy. This could be a giant sun such as seen by your astronomers through your present-day telescopes, in which case it will of course find itself, so far as its polarity is concerned, within a different dimension wherein time has a different meaning. In other words, by the act of separating the time element from this ball —and it travels outwardly in this different dimension —time becomes separated from it and these energies which are so traveling now travel, as your scientists call it, in a sine wave. This is simply an up and down motion something like a little green snake which crawls through the grass. There is a positive and a negative. There is a beginning and an end.

This is different from the energy of the parent source from which it sprang, for within the dimension of its own movement, it had no beginning or end. Its polarities existed purely within the circumference of its own movement; it also was harmonically linked to other similar or other energy formations which were vastly different in this original energy formation. Harmonically, or the term harmonic merely suggests a certain attunement according to mathematical formulae; or you may obtain a similarity by picturing the various chord structures on your piano keyboard. All things, all energy movements have these harmonic configurations or attunements. There is nothing happenstance or coincidental in the cyclic movements of the great Infinite Intelligence. All things within themselves, vortexes large or small, other dimensions of expressive energy all have factual continuities within themselves on the basis of harmonic attunements and express thus to one another their own quotient of intelligence, their own idiom, their own expression. Here, however, in the third-dimensional world which you call your earth world, time is separate. As I explained, we have the plus and the minus signs. We have a beginning and an ending because the time separation here is what the scientists call the speed of light, 186,210 miles per second.

Now what does this mean to you personally? It means that you are first and primarily, just as you have always been, an outside configuration of this great vast Infinite Cosmos of which I have just spoken. You have begun in such cell nuclei of intelligent formations which expressed certain condiments of intelligence, certain particular idioms of life and from these things certain amassments took place where, harmonically attuned, other idioms of consciousness could gather together, so to speak, and form other particular expressions of life. This all happens, of course, in that unknown invisible dimension of which you have up until this moment not been completely conscious.

Always as these configurations of energy so gather together, and when certain cyclic motions were so joined, they had a birth, we will say. They were born into the material world as an expressive quotient of their own particular idiom. This is how new species of plant and animal life are developed on any planet. That is how you, yourself, came into existence. No, you did not necessarily descend from an ape or an anthropoid, for these are but physical forms of configurations of the way in which the Infinite expresses Itself through all forms and substances. And in this respect we cannot belittle one species, one plant or one animal from another. We must be more vitally concerned with what evolution has for us individually so far as our futures are concerned. If you do not wish to return to the earth world where you now find yourself, there is no need to do so. You have been doing this many times in your past because you wished it so, because all of the intelligence which you possessed was materially biased. It carried within itself energy wave forms which mandated your return to the earth to make life possible for you; and as you adopted a new body, a new form, or a new substance, so you lived another earth life and when the cycle was complete, this physical appearance of the body which you so occupied returned again to the substances of the air and the earth and you, as the idiom of spirit which had so expressed itself, returned again into that infinite supply.

And yet there came a day when you became a personal being, that is to say, that from life to life you carried with you certain harmonically joined unions of consciousness. There was developed a sort of an imperishable psychic anatomy, a body form which was made purely of spiritual wave forms and of the vortexes which I have described to you, in such a manner and form that it also had a union or joining with a much higher portion of the Infinite Consciousness. You must begin to understand that the Infinite—as I have mentioned this name a number of times—is infinite because God (if you like to call it such) is infinite. This is true because He manifests in all forms and substances far beyond the perspective of your present-day knowledge. The macrocosm and the microcosm is the Infinite. Now one of the ways in which this Infinite so manifests Himself is in the creation of an exact fac-simile of all that He is in a comparatively very small dimension, we shall say. Remember though that space in these interdimensional relationships is only of a very relative nature.

However, now that the Infinite is revolving, we shall say, within an infinite number of dimensions which contain facsimiles of all that the Infinite is—except in one respect—that this Infinite must again relive itself as so compounded within this small dimension from all other different dimensions; and this again sur-charges and re-creates the image of Infinity within Infinity. You have grasped that? No? So, to enable the Infinite to re-create Himself from out of this vast infinity, this united facsimile of Himself in a very small dimension must relive itself, so to speak, through all of the other dimensions. This it does by starting at the bottom. The bottom is an earth world. There it begins to relive itself in very simple forms, the amoeba or any other particular form of bacterial or protozoan life which you may find about you. These forms are the beginnings of remanifestation of the Infinite in recreat-ing itself.

I have approached this particular point in a differ-ent direction from the one I just formerly gave to you. Now when we begin to understand that this Infinite is so re-creating itself and remanifesting itself upon such surface dimensions as the earth, there is the time, which I have suggested, when the Infinite again relives itself as a direct continuity with this higher self which originally started this chain reaction. This then be-comes a man, that is, we can say this is the beginning of a man so individually so created. There is no direct borderline; that is, we will say there is no jumping-off place. This evolution takes place gradually and as the development of this particular form of consciousness so re-creates itself back into the material world, it increases to carry within itself its own particular personality, its own ego, if I can use the word of your present-day psychiatry. It supports from life to life its own succession of life experiences, such things which may be psychic shocks, malformations, aberrations in the wave form structures which so compose this psychic anatomy which have been created over the long evolution of time and earth world experiences.

And in direct proportion, as this ego consciousness comes and goes through these terrestrial worlds, he begins to realize a certain content of these past lifetimes. He may begin to have the fears, indispositions, vicissitudes or idiosyncrasies. These do not yield to present-day psychoanalyses in the term that we can relate them psychosomatically to his infancy. They will yield only when this person has penetrated beyond the veil of birth into the previous lifetimes when he was so incarnated in a physical form in which he found himself subjugated to certain malforming elements in his daily life. When this so happens, the individual has now begun to realize what the old yogi used to call karma and which is merely a psychosomatic science extended beyond his present birth (and death).

The correct analysis and understanding of the psychoanalysis would give mankind a true solution to all enigmas of life, to all diseases. Your doctors will find that cancer, for instance, could be a sword thrust or a gunshot wound suffered by this person in a previous lifetime. The psychic shock so incurred was a direct malformation or an aberration in his psychic anatomy which, when he so re-created himself in his present physical form through his cycle of life, he would manifest this same sword thrust or gunshot wound as a malformation in the physical body. He would have a cancer and he would relive his death from that wound of his previous lifetime. He would become one of the casualties of ignorance.

And so all of the diseases with which your present-day doctors are so confounded have their true seat or origin in the beginnings of any person's life since he first began to sustain the ego consciousness from one life to another, not consciousness in the sense that you would remember as you remember your yesterdays as you have lived them in your present time but as you remember them subconsciously, for the body which you wear as a physical form is only an outside appearance; it is only a cloak, a dress, or whatever you wish to call this body, of all the things which you have lived or developed in these previous lifetimes.

When this is thoroughly understood, you will be ready for your next step into Infinity. Your next step will be, as has been previously suggested by Manu, that you should learn to discard these dogmas as they are set up for you and about you in your earth world. You will begin to encompass within the dimension of your mind certain forms of consciousness which will include this vast and infinite creative world which I have described to you. You will begin to comprehend within yourself how it is possible to live within these worlds, to evolve into higher planetary systems which are not of the atomic form from which your terrestrial world is so compounded. They will be like the lovely jewels which you ladies wear about your necks, far more lustrous, indeed, than any which you have found in your mountains or valleys.

The very substance of your world about you will be a pulsating, radiant energy creation. You will learn how to use this energy constructively from out of the dimension of your own mind. As the bricklayer of your present world wields his trowel to lay up bricks with mortar, so you will be able to partake of this infinite substance as it so pulsates and radiates in the rainbow-hued atmosphere in which you will find yourself and build for yourself a suitable home. And yet the beginnings of this new world, this new mansion which you will construct for yourself must begin now if you are to achieve that. It must begin when you begin to understand how the substance of your material world is so compounded, its source and where you go when its cyclic motion has so been concluded, for you cannot live in these higher worlds until you have gained this knowledge. They would be foreign to you just as the elements of the water would be foreign to you were you to attempt to live in water, although they support life for many creatures which live beneath the surface of the seas.

You possess a pair of lungs; you live in a gaseous atmosphere which is death to the creatures of the sea; and so the scale of evolution progresses. In the higher spiritual worlds, you do not breathe; you live not by eating but by absorbing we shall say, the radiant energies around you. Because you know of their form and of their substance, you know of their re-creative ability. You are in tune with them just as you tune your radio or your television as you "select the particular frequency", and so as you are in tune with them, they permeate through this energy body in which you live. They revitalize you and rebuild you in proportion to how you wish to use them. You do not wear clothes for there is no need for clothes. Your dimension of mind has long passed that sphere of consciousness which has been born from a sexual guilt complex. In fact, procreation itself is far different than the animal-like form which you find associated with you in your present world.

A person who is born into such a world is created in a manner and form which is the direct function and conjunction of a number of minds which create the first energy shell in which effigy consciousness impounds itself. This is the reverse into spirit. It is not the fancied rehabilitation of some long dissipated body from out the earthly atoms which has been posed by your religious systems. It is a rebirth of consciousness which makes these things possible for that person to live in these higher spiritual worlds. And, my brothers and sisters, there is no other way, much as you would believe or you would try to believe. Ultimately you must resolve within yourself that your salvation depends entirely on how well you understand the Infinite which created you. It cannot be dealt to you or purveyed to you for a price. Faith or the belief in such dispensations will only lead to decadency, for the very virtue of your existence at this present moment depends to some degree upon infiltration or absorption of this divine substance—if you wish to call it so; we term it "Infinite Creative Substance".

All things, as I have stated, depend upon life not with the seeming consumption of oxygen or various other foodstuffs, the proteid molecules of food. These are only catalyzing agents which render certain reactionary processes possible with your physical anatomy; but the substance itself from which you live is the Infinite Creative Substance. Your life is only an autosuggestive, reactionary pattern which finds its source and its supply from this Infinite which is ever and always about you and which, up until the present time, you perhaps have not realized what it is or how it functions. Now you have reached a threshold. Your spirits have been quickened, we shall say. You have begun to recognize within yourself certain potentials, certain dimensions of understanding which you heretofore have not recognized.

I could point out to you many other things which are necessary for you to learn; for as truth seekers who would cross the threshold, there is much in the way of orienting yourself into the new life, into the new dimension of understanding which is very pertinent for you to know. You should know of certain things, for as you progress, you will find that in direct ratio and proportion your physical world will begin to diminish in its importance. You will find that as these values change so will your relationship to them change. Your friends will somehow seem to vanish in the distance behind you. The importance of your houses, the protocol of your governmental systems will all vanish as mirages. Yes, and your religions will become only the hollow mockery of pagans who have danced their way through the jungles of antiquity. You will see that the earth world about you has indeed become a place of heathen worship where man seems to be offering the very virtues of himself upon the altar of his materialistic life—and these things will become nauseating to you. You will wish to be freed from them. And if you possess the necessary wisdom and the dedicated will and purpose to achieve a better life, that you will do. Good evening.

Part Two

Questions And Answers

Through consciousness or attunement we can gain certain dimensions and certain areas of wisdom, knowledge which we formerly did not possess. It is not necessary to have a college education, in fact, it's a disadvantage because to be educated in the academic school means that you are, among other things, thoroughly indoctrinated in a curriculum of that school; it mandates that you mold yourself within the strict circumference of what they have taught you. What you have been given tonight is not part of a curriculum of any university which exists in the world today. This is knowledge which has been brought to you by people who live in other planetary systems of other worlds. And as was said, we must begin to understand these things before we can improve our relationship in general, physically, mentally or spiritually. And this we must do by understanding what creation is.

T* - Teacher
S* - Student

T* - Irma, did you find your buttons—three yellow buttons you were looking for? I see you searching for three yellow or gold buttons.

S* - Oh, yes! (She was quite surprised for she was alone at the time.)

T – Betty, has your nasal condition cleared up now; does it not feel more free of late?

S - Yes, it is better.

T - Because I took it on about a week before you came here and until I recognized from whence it came I did not get rid of it. Then after the recognition that it was your condition, it immediately left and I know that this could not happen without your having healing as a result of my temporarily taking it on.

T - Carl, how have you been feeling?

S - I am tired this evening.

T - Are your feet hot underneath on the soles; do you feel a warmth there?

S - Yes, they are.

T - This is the healing power. Your feet are a polarity for your physical anatomy and you are being recharged so to speak. There are two people who have caused you rather an insoluble enigma, and especially one in particular; is this not so?

S - Yes, that's right.

T - Is he not a tall person and has a narrow face?

S - Yes, sir.

T - He has a nice set of china in his mouth, a big smile?

S - Yes.

T - There are so many ways we can obtain these various interesting things. For instance, spiritual healing means that we obtain a conjunction of knowledge of just how we interchange consciousness. We can recognize, too, that each one represents a certain polarity in which these physical things can be discharged. I represent a polarity because of my understanding of these principles. The same holds true of any other field of human relationships—the creation or inventions of various types of therapeutic devices which help relieve people who cannot understand these higher workable principles. There must be a certain amount of material impedimentia that always has to be used and always will be used because we find life upon this world in various different levels and we cannot expect anyone to understand what we understand. They have yet to go through thousands of years and many lifetimes. And speaking of past lifetimes, perhaps you folks do not realize this, but you now have (at this moment) opportunity to find out who and what you were in these past lives; because as far as I am concerned, you are all or each one a radio station, a broadcasting station and you are constantly broadcasting these things to me. Frankly, a television station is more accurate for I see these pictures out of your past very clearly and very accurately.

For instance, regarding the crucifix that you still carry today, this is a carry over from a life in Italy when you were a nun in the 1500's. I could point out many things with which you have certain affinities, certain likes. You did not get these affiliations and attachments in this one lifetime but they come from way back in other lifetimes. We could say, too, that Carl here could analyze himself and would find that he has a fear of climbing high mountains, going up rocky passes. Is this not true, Carl? S - Yes.

T - Do you know why? Because you were one of a group of soldiers, the last remnants of the legions of Rome when Attila, the Hun, came down the Alps; you were killed going up a mountain pass in your effort to help defend Italy. So you see, climbing a mountain pass to you now means a way of attaining a subconscious psychic rapport with that particular way in which you died, by being hurled off a cliff.

Bess, how about you while we are attuned? You should be popping with questions; you were watching a dog the other day, a sort of shaggy black dog which was lying around in the park across the street from your house and you were wondering to whom that dog belonged; you were afraid he was going to get run over by a car; were you not?

S - Sure I was!

T - You see how that is; as I say, you are all television sets. By merely sitting here I can tune myself into any particular happening of not only in the present lifetime but of any of the lifetimes in which you have previously lived. There is no difference; if there is a need, I can tune into it. And how am I able to do that? By knowing that I can and by having the training along scientific lines to learn to realize what the principle is behind these functions, as the foregoing speakers were telling you what creation is.

S - Did you develop this by meditation or did you have a certain innate tendency?

T - I have broken all the rules and regulations; I do not meditate; I do not pray. In fact, to me prayer is pagan. I maintain a Consciousness. I have done it for so many thousands of years I could not even tell you when I began. I have a conscious memory of over 450,000 years of civilizations and planets that I have lived in before. Sounds incredible? Yes, I am sure it does, but some day you will understand and I can scientifically prove that it is possible. Of course, there is one thing that we cannot do; we cannot really prove to anyone unless he has a certain dimension of understanding. If you have not had the training or the knowledge, you cannot possibly understand. You more or less have to accept it superficially until that day when you can. But only the person is lost who says, "It ain't so". That is my mission here on earth at this present time and I can think of a great many better places to live in than this world; but I forfeited what I could otherwise be doing simply because I know that there are thousands, yes, millions of people like yourselves who are on the threshold of understanding. You want something; I am an old scientist from way back when.

460

I came to this planet 155,000 years ago and helped set up the first civilization; and I have been back a few times since then. What is more—I know where I am going when I leave here. I am very sure of it. I do not leave it up to anyone else to presuppose where I am going if you know what the difference is.

S - Are you going to another planet?

T - You could put it that way, yes. In our work here I represent an organization we call Unarius—Universal Articulate Interdimensional Understanding of Science, so far as our present dispensation is concerned and its connection with earth planets like this terrestrial dimension; and we have perhaps 100,000 other different planets similar to this planet under more or less our jurisprudence, to try and teach people who live on these planets. The largest of these seven spiritual planets is a planet called Eros. We will call it Eros inasmuch as we wish to bring a certain association with the earth language. These seven planets represent various different social levels, different fields of human enterprise or relationships, adequate facilities where people can go from these worlds in sort of a jumping-off place, either in some future reincarnation on earth worlds or into the higher worlds.

There are places where people begin to separate themselves, we shall say, in a spiritual sense from the last vestiges of materialism. Several Unarius books are now in print which describe these planets and the descriptions in them are in the words of people who live there, some of whom are the former earth people, some of the scientists, poets, philosophers or other exponents of historical data and knowledge of the past who have delivered some of these descriptions of the way in which they live. There are guided tours in these planets. The purpose there, of course, is to spring the

461

lock on your earthly prison and I believe that science has at this time taken a very definite step in this direction in a material way of trying to help spring people's material prisons. As was described, there are ways and means in which scientists today are attempting to trace the signals from various stars and planetary systems in space and they are listening in particular to any signals which might be construed as originating from another planet or intelligent being.

We have a little booklet in circulation called, "The Truth About Mars" and on my previous astral flights to Mars—which is a way of attuning myself to these places and things—I described the people who lived in Mars, who had gone underground and that they had a very scientific technocracy; they had constructed for themselves these huge underground cities and lived under plastic domes. They have tunnels connecting these great cities. Of course, the astronomer has seen these tunnels from the surface of Mars but he calls them canals.

About two or three years after this book was published, Walt Disney came out with a short picture which was in Technicolor and gave exactly the same description of the life on Mars. It was presented merely as a science fiction picture. Also about one year after the Mars book was out, it was found there was a noted German mystic named Lorber who gave exactly the same descriptions of life on Mars that I did and independently from my knowledge. Now to cap the climax, Walt Disney has constructed in his Disneyland, a prefabricated house as I described that they have on Mars and which is almost identical. Lorber described these prefabricated sheets which formed the house and how plastic foam was sprayed between the two sheets. Lorber did this twenty-five years before plastic was known on earth. This is the same description I have in my Martian book and at which time I had not heard of Lorber nor of his writings on Mars. You may call it coincidence or accident if you wish.

Back in the classical archives of Chinese history, the Chinese know that they are descendents of the people who lived on Mars. Any educated Chinese knows that, if he is educated in Chinese literature. The Martians came to this world about 250,000 years ago and set up a civilization on the northern part of the Himalayan range; of course, there was no range of mountains there at that time. During the course of time they became isolated from their mother planet and suffered various conflicts with the different aboriginal tribes of people who lived around them at that time and they became decadent until they finally arrived at our present twentieth century understanding of what the Chinaman is. Of course, they have off-shoots which are Japanese or Koreans and various others who are termed Mongolians. The Eskimo, for instance, is of Mongolian extraction.

That is a very interesting note in our various root races. For instance, Adolph Hitler was formerly Genghis Khan who came into the northern provinces of India in the 12th Century or thereabouts and found a small race of people there who were entirely different than any whom he had previously seen. They had fair skin and blue eyes and light hair; they were Aryans. They had been living there for hundreds of thousands of years. Genghis Khan—because he did not like what he saw no doubt, or he could not understand it— almost destroyed them all in the hostilities in which they engaged. And when Genghis Khan came back in a subsequent life as Hitler, he had one great psychic urge to re-establish the Aryan people as the master race of

463

the world to justify his guilt complex.

S - Do you see these things as you realize them, which you convey from our past or present?

T - It is a clear picture, a very distinct picture. It is so accurate and vivid that I can describe the very minute details; it is in technicolor. It is similar to remembering what you did a few hours ago except that it comes from you. We will explain it this way: you have a field of force around you. The Yogi calls it your aura and he described it as being of seven different vibrations: the three karmic which related to the physical, three prana which was the mental and one spiritual.

Actually, there is much more to the aura than that. There are many other invisible frequencies which only a very highly-developed clairvoyant mind can see, because it is in these invisible spectrums the picture is carried. That is the reason when I see an aura, I will not actually see the aura, but will see the picture which the aura carries.

S - Is the aura an accumulation of memory patterns of the entire person?

T - Well, to a certain extent, but we must realize that in the understanding of the dynamic function of all substances in whatever they reside in these other dimensions, they are always a radiating pulsating entity. This is their particular frequency. Now whatever time cycle in which they are radiating whether they carry it within their own dimensions as a cyclic pattern or whether they manifest it as a third-dimensional quanta, it is a radiation nevertheless.

You can see the radiations which come from the filament of that superheated tungsten lamp there, but they have many other different radiations. I can see the light with my eyes closed but I can also see other radiations carried by that lamp which show me the construction of the dynamo; it shows me who is attending the dynamo, where it was built and the various other different processes of its transmission. You are unable to see those radiations; you simply have not become conscious of them as yet; one must know of their existence. You must know of the existence of anything before you can become conscious of it. No one has told you and you have never bothered to learn about them; you haven't investigated. But if you had been persistent about your investigations, then you would have become conscious of these radiations.

Let us discuss an atom, for instance. What makes an atom an atom? It is not simply because a certain quanta of energy is contained within the atom as the scientist presupposes it to be; an atom is an atom first because it is an interdimensional vortex. What the scientist sees on the outside of this material world is only the center of that vortex. Now, surrounding the outside of the atom in the third-dimensional world is another field of force—its own aura. It is the aura of the atom which makes it possible for it to link up with other atoms and form an element a bar of iron, a gold coin; that is because the fields of force surrounding the atoms in that bit of gold are linked up; they are holding hands, so to speak.

What happens when we take a bar of steel? We can magnetize iron but it will not hold the magnetism until we do something else to it. What happens when we magnetize something? That means that these atoms all have a north pole and a south pole; they have a positive and a negative, to be more scientific. When we magnetize this element, the iron—which is the only ferric metal which can be magnetized—we thereby align all of the positive polarities to the end of the piece of iron and all of the negative polarities to the other end. This refers to every atom in that piece of iron. But they will not stay that way until we put some policemen in there. What are the policemen? We can melt that iron down until it is liquid and add a bit of carbon. Those carbon atoms have a different rate of vibration or frequency than do the iron atoms. When we subject the iron—which is now steel because it has carbon in it—to a very strong outside magnetic force, a powerful electric current, we can shock these atoms of iron (which are now steel and we call them such because of the carbon) and align their north poles to the north and the south poles to the south, but when we remove that force which made them so, they remain that way permanently. Why? Because the carbon atoms which are all around them will not let them go back into their original way in which they were formerly linked together.

Now you see this iron bar which we have made into steel by adding the carbon is expressing in a certain dimension in exact relationship exactly the way that the world expresses itself to the universe by having a positive and a negative polarity. Why? That is the only way this is made possible and it cannot be because of any earth influence, but is just as I spoke before; it is made possible because all of the atoms within that bar of steel derive their force from another dimension which is entirely independent of the earth. It is the same magnetic field; that great dimension which supports the earth in its magnetic poles, but they are independent; they are manifest because one is in one group of atomic substances which revolve as a north and south polarity; then we have the other and they can function independently from the same source through the fact that they are all atoms supported from the other dimension.

Follow the analogy? Now you begin to see how extremely important it is if you are going to get anywhere with what you call truth or God or any other generic force that you must understand not only what it is but how it functions.

S - How does one sever the bonds of materialism and start to become clairvoyant?

T - I can express it this way; this is your life—by learning about these concepts you gradually learn to do that; you cannot learn it over night. My understanding may have taken me several hundred thousand years and it may have taken me several million, but we are not working in a dimension in which we are conscious of time; we are only conscious of the achievement of purpose. When we have attained this rapport of consciousness where we can visualize ourselves as creative substances, as was formerly described to you in the beginning, we draw this Infinite supply from the Infinite Source that makes us immortal. From there on we begin to become what should be a great independent creative force. We have personalized the Infinite, not because we go about beating our chests and pronouncing who we are, because that would not be an infinite understanding. It is vastly different; it carries no personal ego at all; it cannot.

When I am talking to you, what am I conscious of? I am only conscious of one thing—the complete integration of consciousness into Infinity with all of us here in the room. I am not conscious of how much I am going to get out of it. I am not even conscious of whether or not I am going to impress you with what I know. I am only conscious of the functioning purpose behind all of this, how much it is going to benefit everyone, and how much it is going to benefit the Infinite Creative Substance or Form, because we are expressing a certain quanta of individualism to that Infinite which is again re-creating Itself in another dimension by this action.

S - Then is everything I do or say contained into the subconscious even though I do not retain it in conscious mind?

T - Let us put it a little more strongly than that. There is nothing that you do which is not strictly an automation. In other words, you are following certain occurring sequences or trains of energy formations; you are only manifesting on this outside world what is going on in that interior, that psychic anatomy at the rate of millions of times faster than the speed of light. First you learn about these things, the very elementals of the situation. We learn to picture these things as energy; for instance, if you will look at the eye on the recorder, you will see my voice moving the light in the eye on it. How is that done? That is through a system of electronics. You function just exactly the same as the recorder does; instead of the eye you have your five senses which manifest the same thing on the exterior as that light is to itself.

When you look at some object, what do you see? You do not actually see anything. All that you do in this process is that you are intercepting a set of wave forms of energy which comes to you. These energies hit the lens of the eye and they are focused on the retina which is a little grouping of rods and cones and which contain phosphorous compound. That, in turn, changes the frequency of these incoming waves of energy so that they go back into various centers of the brain. There are about 12 million cells in the human brain. These little cells are like transistors or tubes in a radio; they have the power to let energy go one-way but not the other way or direction. They also have the power to change its frequency; that in turn, when it is so properly ordered and oriented through the hypothalamus which is the old mystical third eye of the human being, is again routed into your psychic anatomy. There it travels over a certain particular way which is called the subconscious. The subconscious is part of the psychic anatomy. We will divide this psychic anatomy into three different portions: the subconscious, the mental conscious and the superconscious. Your subconscious is concerned with what is going on here in the present in this lifetime. It is formed from all the little experiences which you have had since your birth or even more correctly—since your conception.

Your mental conscious retains all the energy wave forms of all your previous lifetimes. Your superconscious contains polarized forms of consciousness of all that you have ever lived and all that you are ever going to live, only that some of them have not yet been polarized. You do that by living them throughout your life, by reactivating them, by learning something from them which can go through the mental consciousness and re-stimulate the superconscious.

However, when you are looking at an object as you see the oscillation as it travels through the brain into the subconscious, the psychic part of your anatomy, it meets a great many other different wave forms there which are similar to the same thing which you are looking at in the present time. For instance, the chair, so you immediately have a reaction that takes place through a harmonic frequency of attunement; there is a regeneration that takes place. It is like when you touch the keys of the piano that creates another set of harmonic wave forms which again oscillate out into your conscious mind and through other sets of brain cells, it reactivates the same feeling of consciousness that you formerly had with other previous associations of chairs; and that is how you see. There is another set of harmonics which travel from your subconscious into your mental conscious; there it meets all of the other old friends of former chairs that you have seen in past lifetimes. Now when these harmonics regenerate another set of harmonics, they, in turn, will go out into the conscious mind and create what we call a bias condition. That means an intelligence quotient, so that when you are seeing the chair as the subconscious reaction, the bias from the mental conscious reaction will give you whatever it is that you need—that which you call thought and action—to go over and sit down in the chair, because you have sat down on a similar chair in past lifetimes, haven't you? And all the time that you are doing that, there is another set of harmonics which are generated which go into the superconscious. There they meet the facsimile of all the chairs that you have seen in past lifetimes. And when they do that, they regenerate another set of harmonics which create a set of polarized forms of consciousness —and they will exist forever. This means that when you attain a certain dimension of your evolution, you pass far beyond the material worlds where you have ever sat down on chairs; perhaps hundreds of thousands of years you will still remember those chairs; you will have a full conscious memory of them, a working knowledge of them, but they will not have any power over you. They will not be a necessary adjutant to your daily life.

S - You must have had many lifetimes of experience to remember all these things?

T - During World War II, I attended five different dance halls—places that I could do (we will call them) readings while I was dancing with the wives, the moth-ers and the sweethearts of the service men. I mentally went overseas wherever their loved ones were, described them by name and what was going to happen to them; and not only that, but we gave them guidance so that none of them were killed or seriously injured. This took place for many thousands of the boys who came back. That was not done in some few isolated cases; it was done many thousands of times. This was repeated week after week, and they got to know me and expected me to come. In order for them to conceive these things, first they would have to have a little demonstration or eye opener, so I would (mentally) go into their homes while they were dancing with me; I would go into details about their homes and, when they were sufficiently oriented, then I could tell them where their boys were and what they were doing.

Some of the descriptions of what they were going to experience went as far as three years into the future and they all came true accurately. Now how is that done? I am merely relating these things to you because someday I want you to be able to do it too, and someday I shall know that you will—I will put it that way. If you are persistent, any one of you can do the same thing. The only thing, we must remove any time element as to when. In fact, Ruth has already begun; Bess, you have already had little peeks, too; haven't you, and the lady sitting next to you also?

S - Yes, sir.

T - While we are on that subject, I want to describe what has happened to Ruth here in the last few days. She has been reborn of the Spirit; she has had a very wonderful thing happen to her. When she was outdoors at the annex, she was relaxed and suddenly the great Spiritual Worlds opened up unto her and she saw all of these great wonderful souls with whom we

471

are working: Krishna, Jesus, Manu and so many of them; all of them we call friends—Brothers and Sisters in the Higher Worlds. And since that moment, Ruth has not been of this world; she has been floating; she is on cloud 9. And it is very wonderful because it will never rub off; she will never go back to the old world again; she is now what Jesus described to Nicodemus. She has been born of the Spirit and I am so happy for her. That is the only way to salvation, the only way we can attain salvation.

I carry papers from several ministries, several churches in Los Angeles. I did that because it gave me an opportunity to bring science to those poor people in the churches; not that I gained anything from this but it gave me a chance to teach those people who were ready to accept something that was not the same old balderdash that had been handed down to them for age after age. Those are pagan beliefs which were born out of the primitive jungles of yesterday, the bowing down and worshipping, all of these indulgences and hypocrisies that people not only experience but what they let others tell them.

You might say that I am opposed to orthodoxy, and in a sense of the word I would take any opportunity that was within my power to show anyone a better way who is ready for it. But I also know the value of orthodoxy to those who are not ready for this better way. I respect their position on their path of evolution very much as a sensitive whereby certain people can begin the first stages of their evolution in the recognition of greater forces, mystical forces or whatever you wish to call them. My position is not radical; it is not fanatical; it is realistic and it works. I would not be that big a hypocrite to get up on any platform and teach anyone a better way of life if I have not demonstrated it myself. And I have not seen a minister yet who could demonstrate what he taught or even half of what he taught. I used to see a certain and quite popular minister of a large Unity Church in Los Angeles step down from the platform and he could not get into the back room quickly enough before he had a cigarette lit and would stomp up the aisle to check out his people. Not that I am any better than he but I would not smoke a cigarette; I think too much of myself and I'd not have the unmitigated gall to ascend any platform and try to tell people a better way of life that I did not understand and practice myself, or that I could not demonstrate what I taught. There is nothing worse in this world to me than a hypocrite; and it speaks of them in the New Testament: "Beware ye in the latter days of false prophets and teachers and of wolves in sheeps clothing."

By the time I was five years old, I had read the Bible through three times. I had a father who was about as well versed on the religions of the world as anyone was and we had many a good argument about them, also many an agreement. It is fine for those who need a crutch, who need some sort of a moral opiate—and that is all religion is. It is only an escape mechanism; it is only a way in which they can relieve their psychic pressures. They can hand all their burdens, their guilt's onto some fancied savior and it is very unrealistic. There is not anyone in this world who is going to be any more than what he develops within his own self. Take the words of Jesus; "Seek ye the Kingdom of Heaven which is within and all things shall be added unto you," and that is exactly what it meant. He did not mean that any priest in any temple was going to hand it out to you with or without fees. He meant that you and you alone are going to have to live life and learn about it; and in living life you will find that Kingdom of Heaven. As you live that life, you assume your own moral responsibility for every act, for every thought, everything that you manifest, because that becomes part of your psychic anatomy; that is what you construct for yourself in that great invisible world which supplies everything. Your thought and your action constructs or destroys any suitable or unsuitable body to live in any other world.

There are many other dimensions or concepts that you can get into. For instance, here is one good point: you see me here tonight a singular person, yet I am not singular. In my understanding—and it was mentioned to you that while there are a certain number here tonight that you can see—there are at least 500,000 that you cannot see and who are listening and 500,000 beyond those and so on. Because with all these thoughts and actions as I put them into consciousness, whether or not you have understood them, I have created and re-created a very definite part of a certain infinite effigy which you call truth. We have taken but we have added; that is the way the Infinite lives. I stand ready to prove all these things very scientifically through the personal demonstration. There is not anything—and I repeat, not anything—I care not what it is, that a trained mind cannot conceive or do, a mind that is conscious of these principles. I have been proving them for twenty years actively (this talk was given in 1960) out in the public.

I could tell you so many stories about those times, some of which are quite amusing; others are quite tragic. I can tell you of one tragic story which happened on a particular Sunday night. I happened to be dancing with a young lady shortly before Christmas; this lady's name was June; her last name I never knew but she was rather a mystical sort of person, always wandering or day dreaming. So I told June, "Within the next week I see something that can possibly happen to you; in fact, if you do not listen and heed the warning, it will happen to you. I see you and your sister getting into a car; you are in front of the Broadway Department Store in Los Angeles. You are getting into this car and there is a man driving; he is dark-complexioned and you drive south. (These people, incidentally, lived in Inglewood.) As you are going around a turn toward Inglewood, you meet another car coming head-on and there is a terrible accident. I see you and your sister thrown from the car and every bone in your body is broken. If you get into that man's car, that is what is going to happen to you." And I said, "For heaven's sake, don't get into that car!" This was on Sunday and on the very next morning, Monday, at 11 o'clock she and her sister were picked up by a man who was going to Inglewood; he was half drunk. As he went to make a turn near Inglewood, he met another car head-on; both cars were demolished. June and her sister were thrown from the car and every bone in their bodies was broken. It was only a miracle of medical science and spiritual help that they recovered. June never fully re-covered; the psychic shock was too great for her. She committed suicide four years later. But the scene was described in detail to her before she got into the car.

Here is another one, a bit humorous. This hap-pened to be a tall red-haired young lady. I told her, "I see you coming home from the market last Thursday and you were carrying a bag of cookies. These cookies have a star on one side with six points." She said, "No, they don't have; I am sure they have five-pointed stars on them." We got into a little discussion about it and I said to her, "You come back next week and you will tell me that I am right." Sure enough, she came up to me hanging her head, saying, "Do you know, you were right; the stars on the little cookies did have six points!" Then I saw her psychically in her kitchen and related to her, "You were down upon the kitchen floor with a lid off a can and you were trying to nail this lid down over a hole in the floor and there is a little mouse that comes up this hole." Of course, she said I was right that she did that.

For instance, my relating to you, Betty, about your buttons the other night or of scratching your foot; these mental activities are just as natural to me as breathing. You ask how do I see these things; it is just like that which goes on in your mind except that I see all the things about other people. This little lady here in the first seat can recite dozens of these tests she has been given; is this not so, little sister?

S - Indeed.

T - Last night her mother who is in spirit came into my consciousness; she was carrying a casserole of macaroni. I described it in detail, even the way she used to take her fork and raise the crust when it was browning.

S - One mind?

T - Well, let's put it this way; this is going on all around you all the time; it does not belong to anybody in particular, just to whoever can use it. It is the Infinite Mind. I tune into It just the way that the television tunes into the transmitter. We have to train by understanding what these things are, what the creative substance is, what or why there are atoms and how and why there is this and that and the other thing. We cannot accept these things superficially or as they appear to be. We cannot accept them as other people tell us they are; we must find out these things for ourselves because only in the dimension of your own experience can you learn to understand these principles, and you must push the dimension of your personal expression beyond the horizon or the confines of what other people tell you are the limits, because there are no limits. You have to get that into your mind right now.

You people can go just as far out or just as high or as low as you wish. If you wish to go all the way and you stick with the study and put forth effort, you can. This is a challenge of your existence because in learning this (and you will have to learn every little bit that you understand), you'll have to learn it through the doorway of experience and then you'll achieve an understanding of the Infinite Creator and what He is. He will not be any white-robed Santa Claus who sits up there on a big throne with a book of life. That belief belongs to the people who wish to escape, who do not wish to understand.

S - And what is beyond that?

T - We should take one step at a time. For the next million years, you work on this and you will learn to understand. It may take a million years and it may take a hundred million; no, it will not seem that long. Time is a very intangible element as far as experience is concerned. You can, in a psychism or in a flash, live your entire lifetime in two seconds; and you can also live far beyond that in a few seconds time or back into the past as well!

S - What do you see as the destiny of the human race?

T - You mean collectively as they exist on the face of the earth? I do not believe in destiny in the common accepted plane of reference. To me the world is much like the first or second grade in school. If we stand off on the school grounds somewhere and we sit there quietly for about ten years, we will see students coming and going. They are not the same students each year that we see because they all graduate and go into higher grades; and that is the way that it is to me because I see people who live a hundred or two hundred thousand years on this earth; they come and go in maybe a thousand or more lifetimes and then they pass on because this world is only a certain dimension of experience in their life. Their destiny is just as infinite; you cannot lay down any set of configurations so far as you say, "What is your destiny?" You, myself or anyone else have never visualized an ultimate destiny for anyone, because the Infinite is just that way.

To learn the infinite means that we are going to take an infinite length of time to learn about the Infinite. That means that we will never arrive at the terminating point. That is true heaven. It is not going up there and floating around on a pink cloud playing a harp or living in some fancied state.

S - How about the state of the world?

T - In the expression of the Infinite, as we were saying of the world, our third dimension or the terrestrial planet, there must always be a definite equilibrium maintained. This equilibrium is maintained in a cyclic fashion; we have big cycles and smaller cycles. One of the dominating cycles with which we are concerned in the world at this time is the cycle of the recessional which is 25,862 years. That means in the elliptical orbit the earth traveling around the sun comes out minus so many degrees each year, so that by the end of that period or length of time, it intersects and bisects in a complete cycle a great number of lines of magnetic force which are universal in nature. That means that the earth has become expressionary or felt the influence of these dominating lines of force. And civilizations will rise and fall according to these dominating influences because you have to realize that man is still an environmental creature. He is still very largely dependent upon not only terrestrial influence in his everyday environment, but he is also very dependent on astral influences which come through these great cyclic movements through the magnetic lines of force. Therefore, if you look into the future and you see this great build-up which is a machination of third-dimensional scientific technocracy, it is creating a great preponderance, a great over-balance. Now there is going to have to be achieved a balance for that. Unfortunately, that balance is not going to take a straight-line turn of reference; it is going to go in a complete opposite or negative fashion. That could mean any one or a number of things. People in the near future because of the fear of war can entirely abandon their present third-dimensional science and go into complete reversion where they become entirely spiritually engrossed. Now when they do that, it sets up other repercussions. Genetical statistics are influenced to a large degree on how people believe because you are also retaining certain rapports with other lifetimes when other different magnetic lines of force influenced your life and caused certain generical or genetical, expressionary forms.

I am not a doom-monger. I do not prophesy the end of the world as in the Bible in the second epistle of Peter, "And the Lord shall come as a thief in the night and the very elements shall burn as with a fervent heat." There will be a balanced sheet. And it also speaks in Revelations; Nostradamus spoke of it very forcibly about the Battle of Armageddon, and the great beasts that came from the sea, and how the beasts were destroyed, and the seven seals. What are the seven seals? The seven seals in the New Testament have a direct reference to the seven days in which the Lord created the earth. What are these seven days? One of them we have not yet had; we are only entering into it; that is the 25,862 year cyclic pattern I just mentioned. We have lived six of those days, which dates back to the Lemurian civilization 155,000 years ago and which is the starting place of the Old Testament, not the beginning of man's spiritual growth on the earth in a scientific technocracy. When we recombine a dimension of this terrestrial world with the spiritual, we are being cast from the Garden of Eden, a pure esoterical state of consciousness, the undulant form which is supposed to exist in a pure esoterical sense, or the primary stages of evolution which I referred to previously as species of plant and animal life that became the amalgamated forms of psychic anatomies which developed homosapiens (man). So the old Garden of Eden was merely the spiritual reliving and reincarnation of all plant and animal species on the face of the earth. And so for this time, goodnight, dear ones.

CHAPTER LII

On The Infinite Magnetic Spectrum
Of The Macrocosm And The Microcosm

Several hundred years ago, mankind began dis-
covering magnetism, the peculiar property of the fer-
rous metal known as iron, and its counterpart, steel.
The exact origin or time for this discovery is not accurately known. There are many stories and legends
coming out of the past which may tend to give the
belief that magnetism has been known for thousands
of years.

However, so far as our present-day science is concerned, it is believed that early-day explorers such as
Magellan and others may have used a crude compass
formed from a piece of loadstone, a fragment of hardened steel-like pyrite which probably came from a fall-
en meteorite.

Ancient Viking lore tells that Eric the Red and Leif
the Lucky and others knew the properties of the loadstone. It has remained, however, for our present-day
science to more fully develop the rather mysterious
force known as magnetism. At the present time, many
mechanical devices such as motors, solenoids, loud
speakers, etc., function by virtue of magnetic force.
Science has also discovered that the earth is a huge
magnet with a north and south magnetic pole, having
certain curved magnetic lines of force extending out
into space from one pole to the other. Until quite recently, this magnetic field was believed to be less than
five hundred miles deep. Recent information relayed
by satellites tell that the magnetic field extends at least
two thousand miles into space, and perhaps much

further, and which will be found so only when space probes can be made to extend further away from the earth.

While the man of science now knows considerably more about magnetism than he did one hundred or so years ago, he is still almost in total darkness. While he knows the properties and reactions of magnetic force, he does not actually know what it is and the method of the more ultimate expression. The curved radial lines which extend around the poles of every magnet are well-known, but the scientist has yet to discover and measure how these lines are so produced, as well as more minute constructive details, such as wave forms of energy and their oscillating frequencies.

Also, the man of science has not yet linked up the obvious fact that gravity and the magnetic flux, which is a controlling and dominating factor of earth life, are one and the same. That is, to more accurately say, gravity octaves and the now known magnetism are only two secondary octaves or divisions of the magnetic spectrum. It is not now known by science that all of the known elements found on or in the earth, derive their particular specific gravity and various other reactionary factors as part of their own particular octave in this magnetic spectrum.

In other words, each known element functions in its own particular fourth-dimensional field and does so by virtue of the same controlling principles which exist in all energy transmissions. Iron or its counterpart, steel, can be magnetic by virtue of the fact that its own particular magnetic octave has a determinant frequency of transmission which makes any iron body reactive, either within itself, or this reaction can affect other similar bodies.

In this respect, iron is perhaps unique among the

other ninety-odd elements, for none of these are able to so manifest magnetic force as an exterior configuration in the well-known magnetic lines of force. However, it must not be supposed that these other elements do not possess magnetic properties. All of them do; and that these magnetic properties are manifest in many other different ways, some known and some unknown. The ability of one element to mingle with or react against another element is a magnetic property and one which can be resolved into frequency relationship within the electromagnetic force fields of the atoms themselves.

There are many other magnetic expressions, such as light, which are more purely the reactive property as these electromagnetic force fields of the atoms to absorb or reflect certain wave lengths of energy known as light. The same holds true with what is more properly known as the sense of smell. The ability to smell an odor is now known to actually be a process wherein the various electromagnetic fields link themselves up through harmonic resonance, finally producing reaction in the surface atoms which compose various olfactory nerve endings.

In general, it can now be clearly understood that the electromagnetic properties of all atoms combined in their respective molecules which augment their force fields make possible all known physical reactions and with all known elements. However, this concept can be extended into a much more abstract dimension. The originating source of electromagnetic energy, in whatever form or manner it is found, is never a physical property and it cannot be generated or reproduced from the third-dimensional plane. It must always originate and come from the adjacent fourth dimension.

Any third-dimensional processes which involve production of electromagnetic energy are merely ways and means of aligning already existing electromagnetic forces into specific channels whereby the magnetic reaction can be produced. Allegorically speaking, this can be compared to drawing water from a faucet. Everyone knows the faucet is connected with a central reservoir, even though it is hundreds of miles away. The same holds true in electromagnetic energy. As of today, the scientist believes the water (or energy) comes purely from the faucet. He is not aware of the reservoir or its connecting linkage, which can be pictured as various dimensions and the actual electromagnetic energy which appears from the central reservoir when he reproduces this energy in one of the well-known present-day forms.

The same allegory holds true with all other elements which are the composition of his earth world and extended on into his planetary system. The known galaxy as a speck of light in the great known universe in turn, becomes another speck of light floating in what seems to be an infinite space, populated with an infinite number of these specks of light called universes— all strangely similar in a vast and expanded way to the tiny molecule of mass which, in turn, is divided and subdivided into infinitely smaller specks of light, all moving or floating in the same proportionately great infinity.

This is the microcosm and the macrocosm, yet only a single expressionary element in an even greater infinity which infinitesimally dwarfs all known cosmic vistas. Yes, even the atom itself, or its electrons, becomes as ponderous as a great universe in comparison to the sub-infinite which extends far beyond this micro-galaxy, all marvelously held together, functioning, regenerating in cyclic periods and motions, reproducing, regenerating and recreating an endless and uncounted number of forms and reactions, all sustain-ed within themselves from the central reservoir, which manifests its intelligence and power through an equal-ly infinite magnetic spectrum, and which relive as one small counterpart in the common horseshoe magnet.

THE "JOINING"

Two thousand years ago, as men mark time,
There walked a Man among men, but
different than all others
For He was "joined" in spirit and kneweth
of all things - of what spirit is.

And He spoke of many strange things and
with His hands, doeth many wondrous
miracles.
So much so, there were those who feared
Him and that the hypocrisies of their lives
would be uncovered.
And so they contrived to destroy Him.

And there were others who believed this
Man, each in his own way but of the world
and of the way in which the world thinketh.
And so it came to pass, in the many
centuries which followed, there were
countless men,
Each, in his own way, contrived to say
what this Man had said. And they sayeth
His words in their own words so that they
add or that they taketh away.
Even so, each of these speaketh of this
Man as one of them, as an earth man, who
is not "joined" in spirit, understanding not
of His "joining".

And so, of this day and of this hour, countless numbers live in a great hypocrisy, a great idolatry in which they have hung the effigy of this Man in mute mockery and testimonial of the savage barbarism which is in their hearts against things which they do not understand.

They have contrived, among themselves, to eulogize His words and they sayeth as He said, "If thou believest in Me, thou will have eternal life".
So they worship Him, even in the bloody effigy of their own making, knowing not that as He spoke, that as
He said, "in Me", knowing as He did that he was "joined" in spirit and was, in spirit, all things.
That if any man should know of Him and His "joining" and what He was, what He believed, and all the other essences of spirit,
Then, truly this man would indeed have immortal life.
For surely, if he understood all that this strange Man was, Of the spirit and the "joining",
Each believer and each man who knows thusly of all this, would be likewise joined as was this Man.

And, by the essences of all this knowing and joining, Surely, then, immortality and life forever was the heritage.

Yet, as of this day, men bow their heads in a great idolatry.
Worshipping words contrived in their own minds which have been divested of spiritual virtues.

They have created a monstrosity of their own divulgences to the exclusion of sanity and reason or logic in the ever expanding, creative universe, which is about them.
They have abandoned sanity in the pressure of this symbolized madness.

For surely, how can this great hypocrisy exist and become as of spirit?
For in this hypocrisy, man has created, unto himself, his own citadel.

And, if he persists in its constant erection, That he makes it his domicile, his habitation in this and other lives, Then he will in time, become entombed.
If a man be "joined" in spirit, he must, in all things, be creatively minded.
He cannot think thusly, that it is of his world, or that he and others like him have interpreted these things within

their worlds and correctly, each according to himself.

Rather, they should feel that, within themselves,
And they should know that, within themselves,
Is the divine spark of intelligent reason which can be fanned into an immortal flame by the desire, within every heart to be creative, To be intelligent,
To be ever conscious of this, "The Kingdom of Heaven Which is Within".

So, each man cometh unto his time and place where he must choose between the world of his own making.
The denominators of his own experiences can become as millstones around his neck if he does not turn them into the Essenic substances of spiritual manifestation.

If he cannot see creative logic and reason, the infinite resources which expand his consciousness, then he is indeed lost.

For, even as I am joined, so that you, too, must also be joined,
That we may live in the House of the Lord, forever.